WE WANTED TO BE WRITERS

LIFE, LOVE, AND LITERATURE AT THE IOWA WRITERS' WORKSHOP

Eric Olsen
and
Glenn Schaeffer

Skyhorse Publishing
A Herman Graf Book

Skyhorse Publishing books may be purchased in bulk at special discounts for sales promotion, corporate gifts, fund-raising, or educational purposes. Special editions can also be created to specifications. For details, contact the Special Sales Department, Skyhorse Publishing, 307 West 36th Street, 11th Floor, New York, NY 10018 or info@skyhorsepublishing.com.

Skyhorse® and Skyhorse Publishing® are registered trademarks of Skyhorse Publishing, Inc.®, a Delaware corporation.

www.skyhorsepublishing.com

10 9 8 7 6 5 4 3 2 1

Library of Congress Cataloging-in-Publication Data available on file.
ISBN: 978-1-60239-735-4

"The Book of the Dead Man (The Writers)" appeared originally in *Fiddlehead* and is collected in *Vertigo: The Living Dead Man Poems*, Copper Canyon Press, copyright 2011 by Marvin Bell.

Printed in Canada

CONTENTS

EDITOR'S NOTE

by Eric Olsen

Vance Bourjaily, one of our teachers when Glenn and I were in the Workshop, once informed our class that if you were a nice person, you should never write in the first person, unless you were prepared to be an unreliable first-person narrator. But Schaeffer's a pretty decent guy and what he has to say in Chapter 1 is pretty reliable, I think, so there must be exceptions to Vance's rule.

Chapters 2 through 7 are made up of the conversations in which those we interviewed speak for themselves, but in the introduction to each chapter, and then here and there throughout each chapter, we interrupt with brief narratives, by way of setting the stage, as it were. In these comments, we lapse into a sort of editorial "we," referring to ourselves by name, in the third person, when warranted. Sometimes, that "we" encompasses the entire group of classmates and faculty we interviewed. We realize that we probably ought not to speak for the others, some of whom have rather emphatically pointed this out, so we hope we'll be forgiven for this presumption. And now and then the "we" broadens further to encompass writers and artists in general, still more creative license for which we hope we'll be forgiven. I won't go near the question of our niceness or reliability in these chapters.

ACKNOWLEDGMENTS

This book wouldn't have been possible without the generous involvement of everyone we interviewed, all of whom tolerated an excess of pesky questions and impositions on their time with good humor, and for that, we thank them wholeheartedly. We'd also like to thank Dave Hickey for his good suggestions about structure and organization; Connie Brothers for her patience and continuing support of this project; Kathy Girsch, a blessedly enthusiastic reader during the book's vulnerable early stages; Michael Buell, who had the inflated confidence in Olsen's writing to save his correspondence from Olsen's Iowa days, a valuable aid to Olsen's somewhat porous memory; Dennis Mathis, whose close reading of the final manuscript has saved us from multiple embarrassments; and finally, Cheryl who helped with the interviews and then read, and reread, and then re-reread and indexed the manuscript, giving it cohesion and some semblance of order. Thank you all, thank you, thank you.

Against the disease of writing, one must take special precautions, since it is a dangerous and contagious disease.

—Peter Abelard, 1079–1142

—ᴍ—

Many suffer from the incurable disease of writing, and it becomes chronic in their sick minds.

—Juvenal, first century CE

INTRODUCTION: AIDING AND ABETTING

Bill Manhire

International Institute of Modern Letters
Victoria University of Wellington, New Zealand

The creative writing workshop can be a troubled and contentious place. Flannery O'Connor graduated from Iowa back in 1947, some years before Messrs Olsen and Schaeffer were born—and she is name-checked several times in this book. Yet it was she who said, "I am often asked if universities stifle writers. My view is that they don't stifle enough of them." I'm told that if you say the words *Nelson Algren* aloud in certain forums, any Iowa graduates present will shift uncomfortably. That's to say, there are people who despise creative writing workshops, and they will hate this book on principle.

But what creative writing workshops offer is not an Iowa invention. If it's the practice of offering advice to aspiring writers that's at issue, you can track back through the Western tradition to rhetoricians like Geoffrey de Vinsauf and Aelius Theon. Or you can go somewhere else altogether. Kiribati, for instance.

Kiribati is a Pacific archipelago—one of those tiny island states that global warming may soon consign to the depths. It was once a British colony: the Gilbert and Ellice Islands. (Kiribati, pronounced *Kiribass*, is a transliteration of Gilberts.) If you had gone there some ninety years ago, you might have bumped into the British colonial servant Arthur Grimble, and he might have introduced you to the poets of the place. The Kiribati poets lived ordinary, real-world lives, though in everything they did, they aimed to be exceptional. According to Grimble's good friend Taata, a poet ought to excel friends and family in the everyday labors of fishing, farming, and building: "Only by becoming a recognized master of the island crafts can he win reverence for his art."

But from time to time on Kiribati, as elsewhere, the need to create a poem is felt. It is then, as Taata told Grimble, that a poet abandons farming and fishing. He takes himself off to the loneliest of places, somewhere he can fast and avoid contact with others. He then marks out a large square on the ground, with a good view to the east, and sits for a whole night there in his "house of song," awaiting the dawn. After addressing the rising sun in a ritual incantation, he returns to his village, where he chooses five friends and brings them back to the composing place.

Now listen to what happens:

> Without further preamble, he begins to recite the "rough draft" of his poem, which he has ruminated overnight. It is the business of his friends to interrupt, criticise, interject suggestions, applaud, or howl down, according to their taste. Very often they do howl him down, too, for they are themselves poets. On the other hand, if the poem, in their opinion, shows beauty they are indefatigable in abetting its perfection. They will remain without food or drink under the pitiless sun until night falls, searching for the right word, the balance, the music that will convert it into a finished work of art.

> When all their wit and wisdom has been poured out upon him, they depart. He remains alone again—probably for several days—to reflect upon their advice, accept, reject, accommodate, improve, as his genius dictates. The responsibility for the completed song will be entirely his.

Probably this practice was centuries old when Grimble encountered it. It sounds to me like the ideal creative writing workshop. Inspiration is acknowledged: a writer begins to work on a text that truly matters to him— that has come to him perhaps because he has put himself in the way of it. Yet eventually, and in a formal situation, he offers it to sympathetic fellow writers for close reading and advice. They respond, offering their points of view while trying to wed their comments to the intentions they sense in the piece of writing. The writer chooses the advice he finds helpful, doing so on behalf of the completed composition, for which he takes personal responsibility. Grimble's wording, "abetting perfection," holds, too—though maybe "aiding and abetting" would be even better. In a workshop, everyone's an accomplice.

There are some differences between university workshops and those of Kiribati. For one thing, we eat and drink better than the Kiribati poets. We sit more comfortably. And the afterlife of completed work is vastly different. We look toward books or the Internet or occasional public readings. In Kiribati, as in many other cultures, poems find their way to choral performance, become songs and acquire accompanying dance actions. The poems' authors are acknowledged and honored, but the poems themselves belong to the community and are performed by them.

The writers in this book were all at Iowa during the 1970s. It was, as they say, a time of transition. The Workshop was already famous but still a work in progress. Teachers and students were improvising, finding things out. "Creative writing" itself had not yet been theorized or professionalized. In some ways, Iowa was building a safe house where the imagination could survive while the academy marched on toward the fields of high theory. Even so, broader social changes were manifest inside the Workshop, reflecting the changing human makeup of university classes.

There's plenty of talk here about the Workshop community and its various formations. We meet some famous names but aren't subjected to a relentless aggregation of the famous. I like the fact that we follow a very particular mixed group of writers through broad stretches of time. *We Wanted to Be Writers* is not just about the joys and agitations of a two- or three-year period—the rivalries over funding packages, the anxieties about status, the deep friendships and the shifting ones, the various writings that came into being—it's also about the before and after. A successful program like Iowa's is an intense moment in a longer and richer writing life, a roadside stop in a very busy road movie. In the beginning, a small child reads a lot, and something quite mysterious occurs. A few years later, parents wave good-bye. Then, ah, there's Iowa, the workshop with the capital *W*. And much farther down the road, folks are doing unusual things: training as Zen priests, working as real estate attorneys, running business empires. Some of them are famous writers. Some of them have stopped writing. There are connections and disruptions and interruptions. No one, though, has left the writing community.

We Wanted to Be Writers has no single set of craft rules to press upon the reader; it isn't some reductive instruction manual. There's a simple sense of narrative here: our old friend What Happens Next turns the pages. But communities thrive on talk, and this book is also full of deftly choreographed conversations. The advice within, and there is plenty of it, comes in the form of experience and anecdote—and we can choose, like the poets of Kiribati, just who we listen to most attentively. If you want to gather a range of views on how to handle rejection—or its sudden neighbor, overnight success—you've come to the right place. Likewise, if you want to debate the value of genre fiction; the particular merits of laptop, typewriter, or pen; the appeal of different kinds of paper; and the importance of revision and self-editing, well, please read on. Learn how to survive writer's block. Learn about talent, tenacity, and different kinds of luck.

There are bigger conversations and disagreements about life inside the Workshop. One virtue of the best creative writing workshops is that novice writers develop a genuine sense of audience, and the audience at Iowa must be just about the most attentive in the world—sympathetic, demanding, sometimes envious, and keener on speaking up for the work that is coming into being than on being nice to its author. Some writers here found the critiquing process aggressive and unsettling; others thought it pretty amiable. One or two found Iowa a thoroughly unsympathetic place as students and haven't had cause to change their minds. The good thing is that no one has signed any kind of confidentiality clause.

In successful writing workshops, certain habits of attention are developed. The workshop community is supportive, but it also puts its members under pressure to meet deadlines, exercise constraint, and of course, requires a whole range of human and social obligations. The best workshops blend routine and surprise through the steadiness of regular meetings and deadlines and the sometimes astonishing prose and poetry that enters the room. That's maybe the deepest wisdom this book has and which it approaches in many ways—an understanding that writers need to develop the habit of art but never at the expense of being fully available to the *aha!* moment.

Beyond all this, there's the greatest paradox of all—that a creative writing workshop invites you to join a community of practice and learning, yet leaves you to do your work in what Eudora Welty called an absolute state of Do Not Disturb. There you are in this oddly collegial world, yet there you are, too, entirely by yourself, staring at a blank screen or sheet of paper. As John Irving remarks, the writing life is very different from the team philosophies of filmmaking. "There is nothing collaborative about writing a novel; you're in it alone."

Finally, let's hear it for the teachers—those who do this thing that can't be done. These writers speak about teachers and mentors like Kurt Vonnegut, John Cheever, Ros Drexler, Stanley Elkin, Frank Conroy, Gordon Lish, Henry Bromell, Irving himself. Styles varied. Some teachers could be pedantic. Some were semi-missing persons. Some had favorites. John Irving clearly saw his role as aiding and abetting. John Cheever, notes Allan Gurganus, "ran his class like a cocktail party."

Some of those names get a mixed press, none more so, perhaps, than Stanley Elkin. My friend and colleague, the novelist Damien Wilkins, studied with Elkin in St. Louis in the early '90s in what he calls Elkin's "last great puff." "Heart, lungs, MS. It was painful for him to turn a page." Damien reveled in the high drama of Elkin's teaching. I have heard him tell several terrifying classroom tales. One particular Elkinism, repeated often, was this: "Give everyone the best lines."

That sounds like wisdom of the most useful kind. It even works for editors. *Give everyone the best lines*. This book does exactly that.

PART ONE
TO BEGIN, TO BEGIN

Chapter 1

THE CREATIVE ENTERPRISE

Glenn Schaeffer

In 1977, sixty days after graduating from the Iowa Writers' Workshop with a master of fine arts in imaginative writing, I was a stockbroker trainee in Beverly Hills. That vaunted zip code, later immortalized as TV's *90210*, was of course occupied by rich people, the kind that Scott Fitzgerald stated were "different" from the rest of us; and so I decided to make new friends there right away. Change my zip code. Begin with a predicament.

Other than a drive on Sunset Boulevard, I'd never been to Beverly Hills, despite having been raised in greater LA. The worst that could befall me, I figured, was I'd meet a Jay Gatsby, which, as my own story unfolded, wasn't too far from the truth—except the money was licit and the boom days were more than an illusory flicker on the horizon. After another few years, I was a financier on the Las Vegas Strip, that gaudy dream twin of LA smack in the Mojave Desert. I'd discovered a career developing the biggest entertainment stores ever conceived.

I mention this because I'm often asked how it is someone with an MFA in imaginative writing from the Iowa Writers' Workshop ended up in business and, more particularly, in the gaming business. The answer to that question leads, as in a tightly spun novel, to other questions: How did this book come about and why?

So let's start in Des Moines, Iowa, circa 1999, where, as president of Mandalay Resort Group, I made a presentation to the editorial board of the *Des Moines Register*—or to be more accurate, I was interrogated by the editorial board. It was a Sunday morning, and I'd come to convince the paper to endorse our company's bid for the slot-machine concession at the Prairie Meadows Race Track outside of town, what's now called a "racino."

At that meeting, I presented our credentials, with one little gem saved for the end, when I let slip how dandy it was to be back in Iowa. You see, I explained to the editors, I hold an MFA from *the* Writers' Workshop at the University of Iowa. Mouths dropped open. An investigative reporter was immediately dispatched to Iowa City to check out my dubious claim. This was back in that bygone era when newspapers still employed investigative reporters who searched out actual facts. I'm sure he figured to catch me in a whopper. Who could be more of an outlier than someone with a degree in imaginative writing atop a Las Vegas gaming company?

But it wasn't all that absurd. I'd long found that my MFA was excellent preparation for the business world. Like innovation in literary narrative, which aims to resonate in readers' hearts and minds, innovation in business is meant to evoke trust and spark desire. Creativity captures and holds the attention (or money) of others, whether signified as audience or customers. In fact, people depend on narratives to get them through life; neuroscience tells us that our brains are hardwired to organize our existential states as ongoing narratives, draft upon draft of them. Therefore, a concept in business, as in a story, must be told forcefully and simply, using consequential logic mixed with dramatic leaps. Writers who can convince us of the *real* through the artifice of the story are similar to entrepreneurs: Both start every day with the barest essentials, hoping to change us or our experience of the world, and struggle toward expression on the blank page, or the blank drawing board (infernally resistant media in either case). They are chronic drafters; for every one idea they keep, discarding ten or twenty or fifty. They'll think their next will be the best they've ever had—an optimism shaded by delusion that turns an inherently lonely occupation into a tickled prospector's journey.

During my era at the Writers' Workshop, the late Stanley Elkin, author of daring novels, happened to be a visiting professor. Now Elkin was a gentleman, except on the page or in the classroom. One afternoon, a classmate put a story up for "crit" that represented a chapter from his novel-in-progress. The theme of the piece was ostensibly antiwar, but with the folly and tragedy of Vietnam already exposed, its perspective was utterly passé. It was by the numbers. To prove it, Elkin challenged the writer by asking what "number" his chapter was.

"Three," this poor guy said.

"How many to go?"

"Seven."

"Okeydoke," Elkin mused, picking up said manuscript by its corner, like a foul dishrag. Then, in a Looney Tunes voice—Elkin was, among other things, a vaudevillian and could perform a fugue of cartoon voices, Donald Duck being his aria—he predicted the balance of the book, chapter by chapter. "And that's all, folks!" he concluded.

The writer was stunned. If someone can predict your book aloud by reading a random fragment, you're sunk. It was a mordant critique, and nobody else bothered to speak. The cartoon voice held the floor, period. In any lesser classroom, the story might have been an A, but it lacked passion. Craft without tongue, bereft of evocation or novelty.

There are no new stories, only new *tellings*, alive with resonant perspective. Life isn't pat or predictable; it's complex and fraught with secrets and codes and unexpected possibilities. My own mentor at Iowa was novelist Vance Bourjaily, by then perhaps past his peak as a creative artist, but he'd been a breakout kid with his early novels after World War II. He taught me three things he believed formed a primer for writing a literary narrative:

1. Your willingness to explore or confess all that you know about life *emotionally*. You must render yourself open, maybe painfully so, and deeply interpretive toward your own experience. Writing becomes a personal forensic. *Experience*, not belief or intellectual conviction, by turns prodigal and indecent and subliminal: *that's* what you transfigure and clarify into story.
2. Your realization of oppositional or pivotal conflict through dramatic dialogue, never exposition, and the nemesis gets the better lines, as in real life.
3. Your discovery of a resolution that won't be the same as the one you envisioned when you began.

Try writing after *that*, if it sounds easy. I was only twenty-two, on the shy side of life, learning that you earn the privilege to tell stories over the span of time and the course of devotional hours. Creative talent is honed through learning. It is improved through constant experiment, wherein visualization, interrogation, boldness, and originality become traits of practice, then action. Writerly habits that arrive at "insights" in narrative literature don't vary much from habits of experiment that generate authentic breakthroughs in business.

None of which was on my mind when I learned that the *Register's* investigative reporter had gone so far as to dig through the library archives to retrieve my MFA thesis, sixty pages of an unfinished novel I was calling *Holy Shaker*. I don't think he was particularly entranced. He also called Connie Brothers, the Workshop's program associate, and asked her what kind of student I'd been. Connie had started her job at the Workshop not long before Olsen and I showed up. And as I write this essay, she's still running the shop. "Oh," she told the reporter, "we remember Glenn well here. He was quite popular; he was outstanding . . . funny and bright." Bless her; she didn't mention no one thought I'd ever be a writer. I was too allergic to the life of solitude. Maybe I'd become an executive.

It so happens the *Register* endorsed our bid, though we didn't get the contract (there's no record the Prairie Meadows folks read my thesis). I like to think that my MFA carried a little sway; that the editors at the *Register* understood what so many these days seem not to get, that *creativity* is a veritable edge. The meeting in Des Moines and Connie's discretion reconnected me to Iowa and led, roundabout, to both this book and a new annex to the Workshop headquarters that bears my name.

Even though it might have appeared that I'd jettisoned writing for business, I had for years after Iowa nibbled away at one writing project or another, often in collaboration with Olsen. We'd met at Iowa and become good friends; though our paths diverged, we worked on various writing projects together, including a few essays on gaming that made their way into print and a novel that, close call, didn't. After my meeting with the *Des Moines Register* and realizing, to my dismay, that my MFA thesis had been exposed, I began to dwell, a bit obsessively, on the fact that if a reporter could find and read those sixty pages of *Holy Shaker*, well, who couldn't?

I soon resolved to rework *Holy Shaker* and, this time, polish it off and have the new and improved version retyped on some antiquated high-rag-content bond with an old IBM Selectric (perhaps on loan from the Smithsonian, with one of those nifty self-correcting buttons that were the ultimate in high-tech gadgetry way back when), to bind the typescript properly, and to slip this meta-version into the guarded library archives. The original would be excised in a feat of creative destruction.

I enlisted Olsen in the effort, not least because he'd been a professional writer and editor for all this time, and because he was hip to deceptions; and besides, we'd always worked well together on the page, owing to similar sensibilities toward the world sized before us. Olsen thought it would be a worthy postmodern caper, but demurred when I suggested we reenact *his* MFA thesis while we were at it. After writing five books and innumerable magazine articles, he was well past any writerly gloss on himself, he said. By contrast, I could still start out, even if under a ruse, or because of it—never a bad way to begin.

Our conceit was that any redacted version of *Holy Shaker* would be an absolute improvement. And one would think that a few decades of life experience might sharpen one's writing. On the other hand, there's something to be said for the swoop of youthful enthusiasm, the naive sense of possibility in one's early work, before you become more sophisticated and that giant delete tab inside your executive brain begins to peck at you constantly, about which more, and the entire matter of sustaining the creative process, in the chapters ahead.

The planning for this venture got us thinking about related issues, such as the institution of the Workshop in general: the "workshop method," the creative process, and the nature of the *grip* the Workshop and the desire to write seemed to have on us, so that thirty years later we were plotting a rendezvous.

In other words, we began to wonder: What the hell had we fledgling fabulists and pale poetlings been thinking out there on the steppes of Iowa? Then we decided to ask our former classmates. If there's one thing the MFA conferred, it's a lifetime Rolodex of authors—with whom Olsen and I made friendships that have endured across the years.

We started by calling up a few of our old gang, among them John Irving, Don Wallace, Sandra Cisneros, Jane Smiley, T. C. Boyle, Allan Gurganus, Michelle Huneven, Jayne Anne Phillips, Robin Green, and Joe Haldeman. Everyone has (mostly) fond memories of Iowa, while those that are less than fond—yes, there were the usual jealousies, the resentments that simmered after a writer trashed another's *note-perfect* opener, but such were the rules of engagement—are just as valued as "material." Perhaps some of our memories are now sepia-tinged by the years or blurred by those pitchers of beer at the Mill—the hangout for prose types on East Burlington—but a uniform sense among everyone we interviewed was how *collegial* the Workshop was. And so everyone we asked agreed to humor us. And they knew others we should talk to—say, you know so-and-so? Remember that time? And so-and-so would connect us to someone else. Over time, we ended up doing extensive interviews with nearly thirty classmates and faculty.

We've been rather flexible in how we define *our* Iowa class. Olsen and I both started in the fall of 1975 and left, virgin MFAs in hand, after the end of the 1977 school year, on a steamy July morning, chugging westward to California in my dingy yellow 1969 Falcon featuring its three chrome mag wheels and one undersized black spare, a doubtful journey. We included in "our class" those that overlapped ours at either end, roughly from autumn 1974 to spring 1978.

Our goal in assembling this book has been to create a compendium of reflections we wish that we'd had before we arrived naked in Iowa City—a book in which practitioners of writing call themselves straight up. While no small few of those we interview have led prosperous careers as literary writers, others went into teaching or journalism or advertising, some became editors, and one made the big time in television. A few of us departed the writing life entirely, at least for professional gain. One became an attorney, and two others became high-tech entrepreneurs. And I went into the gaming business, among others, a peripatetic.

In the intercepts that follow, we and our fellow workshoppers discuss how we got into writing in the first place, our experiences at the Workshop, and what we've learned about life, art, the creative process, and the lit biz in the thirty years since. If there's a prevailing theme in our book, it's that writers face doubt on a daily basis. Yet persistence spurred by hope is what leads writers to create until those lean, intoxicating *aha!* moments reveal themselves—until sentences find their shape, characters command the page, and stories bloom into being.

We also navigate the creative process and try questions as to whether or not imaginative composition can be taught and, if so, whether the "workshop model" is the most effective approach. Some of what we came up with in the interviews defies the conventional critique about workshops and Iowa in particular: that MFA programs impose a flat, institutionalized voice on impressionable writers. The Iowa model holds up well, if the accomplishments of its alumni indicate anything.

One hears now and then discouraging statistics about the "success rate" of workshop versus, say, med-school graduates. But such comparisons depend on what we mean by "success" in two endeavors that are incommensurable. For my money, authentic narratives are the rarest output, by one hundred to one. Poet laureates, for that matter, count success as one classic poem, something you can *look up* as Mark Strand once informed me. So there are your stats. Anyway, the success rate among the writers we interviewed is closer to 100 percent, if by *success* one means sticking with ideas and deriving pleasure from discovering *le mot juste*—the right word.

Regardless, I would suggest our cohort to date, as a slice of scribblers, is the most decorated in the history of American letters, insofar as having been enrolled at the same graduate institution at one time.

To become complete, writers must grow beyond their early successes and failures—which also corresponds to innovative conduct in business—and create in their own mood and voice harvest upon harvest. It is fruitful to remind ourselves that a prolific innovator in business like Steve Jobs has at bottom been a lyrical modernist. His humanist project trumps sheer technology. Thus he never runs out of room for growth. Innovation at its best, whether in the arts or in business, is the permission we allot ourselves to walk, in homage to the visionary poet and radical William Blake, through the dull delimiting door in the walled garden and into astounding perception.

The Book of the Dead Man (The Writers)

> Live as if you were already dead.
> Zen admonition

1. About the Dead Man and the Writers

The dead man has been licking envelopes from the past.

The dead man's mouth is full of old glue.

He registers the poets starving for a yes, the option-dollars left behind when a writer ran out of material, the trickle of royalties during writer's block.

He lines up the empty wine bottles, the shot glasses, the dead soldiers.

The dead man has made a pinch pot, a kiln god, a clay-footed statue of a famous author.

He remembers the young writer who rediscovered the Mayans.

It was the Dadaists had it right, the Surrealists who knew what was what, the Mayans, the Incans, the lost scribes of Atlantis.

The young writer thinks someone must have known how.

The young writer is cast out of himself and lives between what he was and what he may be.

The dead man and dead woman do the same.

Hence, the dead man ships his writings to the future.

He is still ten thousand fools, all the young writers at once.

He pitches the universe an idea of the sublime.

He opens his Shakespeare, what else? for a playmate.

2. More About the Dead Man and the Writers

The Sumerians had it, the Etruscans, they knew in antiquity what writing could be.

In lofts and basements, in woods or city, at the café or the tavern, the young writers live between old and new, between recovery and creation.

The dead man advises them to look past the words.

They open their Dante, what else? to feel what it is to be forlorn.

They roll and pitch on the deck of a rudderless self.

Are they self-similar, thousands more fractals of the natural world?

They gather with the like-minded to mimic, rebel and shape-shift.

They hunger for the wisdom of the dead, they fall for fools.

The dead man was one of you.

Like you, he was a part of the workshop in appearance only.

The dead man has gone to bed exhausted from finding words that could stay awake.

Then he recovered the Egyptians and Tibetans who wrote about him.

The dead man, like you, still writes into his ignorance.

That, and abandon, are the writerly attributes, but first he had a body.

—Marvin Bell

Chapter 2

WHAT POSSESSED US?

I t shouldn't be surprising that many successful writers seem to have some sort of compulsion that keeps them at it, or that *compulsion* seems to be a useful trait. After all, writing doesn't make much sense economically—only a very small percentage of writers make any serious money at it, not *serious* as in hedge-fund serious, of course, but serious as in enough to pay the bills and maybe to summer on Cape every other year or so. And writing's tough; most writers spend an awful lot of time staring at the blank page, waiting, perhaps *praying* to the Muse or to whomever for inspiration, or at least a good idea, or any idea at all, for that matter. And then when the idea finally does come, if it does, that pesky internal editor goes to work: "No, that sucks." And then, "No! That *really* sucks!" And then, "*No no no no!* Jeez, what the hell are you thinking?" And then if we manage to get past all that nagging and finish something and send it out in the hopes of getting it published and earning a little recognition and maybe even the promise of a check in the mail, the result more often than not is a terse rejection slip: Thanks, but it's not for us.

And yet we do keep at it, and the ability to keep at it—that *addiction*, perhaps—seems to make all the difference. Talent's nice, sure, but as Ted Solotaroff put it so well in "Writing in the Cold: The First Ten Years," a wonderful and wonderfully downbeat essay on the writing life and success in it, or the lack thereof:

> It doesn't appear to be a matter of the talent itself—some of the most natural writers, the ones who seemed to shake their prose or poetry out of their sleeves, are among the disappeared. As far as I can tell, the decisive factor is durability. For the gifted writer, durability seems to be directly connected to how one deals with uncertainty, rejection, and disappointment, from within as well as from without,

and how effectively one incorporates them into the creative process itself....[1]

But *where* does the durability come from? The drive? The *compulsion*?

Writing, or for that matter the making of art of any sort, can now and then be a deeply pleasurable endeavor—when the words are coming and that internal editor has, for once, shut up and the mind is fully engaged and time seems to stand still.

This pleasure becomes for some people an almost mystical experience, leading to the persistent notion throughout Western history that writers have been touched by divinity or the Muse, or touched by something. We *do* like to think writers are somehow special, gifted—and lots of writers certainly like to think of themselves that way, even (or especially) those who showed up at the Iowa Writers' Workshop in our years there to give a reading or teach a master class while roaring drunk and reeking of unwashed tweed.

But the romantic view that writers are somehow blessed or *special* is now apparently hopelessly out of date. Recently there have been books and articles that purport to explain the drive to make art in biological terms, "art" being used in the broad sense to include all the artistic endeavors such

We *do* like to think writers are somehow special, gifted—and lots of writers certainly like to think of themselves that way ...

as writing as well as painting and making music and so on. There is now even a branch of literary criticism known as "Darwinian literary studies." Instead of being "touched by an angel," say the Darwinians, writers have been touched, if not bludgeoned, by evolutionary pressures. Humans have evolved the capacity—in some individuals the *compulsion*—to make art because it's an "adaptive human behavior," a point made in two discourses on the Darwinian aspects of art making published in 2009: *The Art Instinct* by the late Denis Dutton, a philosopher of art, and *On the Origin of Stories: Evolution, Cognition, and Fiction* by Brian Boyd, an expert on Vladimir Nabokov.

The drive to make up stories and tell them seems to arise in every human society, and if the few hunter-gatherer tribes that still exist are any indication, then this urge goes far, far back before the historical record begins. Both Dutton and Boyd argue that the human organism evolved the ability and the desire to spin stories at least in part because it helped us survive. The human mind seems to depend on the formation of narrative to make sense of its world; all of us, as we take in information and try to order it so we can make our way through the day, are constantly making up stories. And Dutton notes that story fabrication is a low-cost, low-risk surrogate for experience that allows us to think strategically about what might have been and what might come to pass, to plot in advance how to deal with threats or to gain pleasure. And perhaps more to the point, says Dutton, to get laid.

Well, of course.

Dutton compares art making such as story weaving to the peacock's tail, an extravagant expenditure of resources that would seem maladaptive for a creature that needs to be able to hide or escape quickly from predators. But the tail is also a signal to a potential mate that here's a chap with the resources to waste, an important indication of good genes. Likewise, making up stories, in the Darwinian view, would seem to be an extravagant waste of resources that makes sense only as a mating display.

And maybe there's even something to this notion. Certainly an ostentatious display of writing skills worked amazingly well as a mating ritual for an awful lot of visiting writers at Iowa (especially, it seemed, the poets) who'd give a reading, attend the obligatory postreading party, and then be seen departing with one arm wrapped around a bottle of vodka, the other around a genetically desirable admirer.

But procreation was probably the last thing on the unformed minds of many of us students, with our bottle-lens glasses and braces, hunkered down with our books—Borgesian moles, as T. C. Boyle referred to this breed in "This Monkey, My Back," a delightful essay about this compulsion to write. Indeed, more than a few of us wouldn't have had a clue what to do with a sexual conquest in the extremely unlikely event one presented itself.

We asked everyone we interviewed for this book what possessed him or her to write in the first place. Every answer was unique, but patterns emerged. Few could point to a moment when they had become, inescapably, *a writer*. It was more often a drawn-out process of being attracted to the notion and gradually being sucked in. The writers we interviewed, our classmates from Iowa in the mid-'70s, tended to realize they were hooked only long after it was too late to turn back.

There have been plenty of studies of the genetic basis of addictions that suggest that some people may be predisposed to addictive behaviors, and so why not to writing, especially if it's an "adaptive behavior" as the Darwinians would have it? But one's genetic predispositions won't be realized without exposure to the addictive agent. For many of the writers interviewed here, that necessary addictive agent was books and more particularly exposure to books at an early age.

The booze usually came later, if not the sex.

❧

GORDON MENNENGA: It was in the third grade. I had rheumatic fever. They say that rheumatic fever is the "writer's disease." I was at home for six months, and I didn't have anything to do, so I read. I must have read two hundred books during those six months. I remember on the back of one there was a photo of the writer sitting on the front porch of his home looking very satisfied with himself. I thought, *That's the life for me.* I was really pissed that I was sick.

JENNIE FIELDS: Reading was an escape from my childhood into another world. My parents were anxious, volatile people, but they couldn't bother me when I was in my own little world of books. I read all the classic girls' books, *Anne of Green Gables*, *Little House on the Prairie*, an entire series of these books in one inhale. I read *Jane Eyre* in fourth grade. I didn't understand most of it, but I was just absorbed by it. I loved the beautiful words.

My parents knew I was writing, but fortunately they weren't that interested.

I wrote my first "novel" at six, though of course it was just a few pages. When I was nine, my teacher that year asked us to keep a journal, but I wrote something much longer: a story about a girl who gets caught in a flood, is separated from her parents, and has to make it on her own. Of course, she succeeds and helps others and becomes a hero.

Other students were turning in two or three pages a week, and I'd turn in seventy-five pages. The teacher just checked it off. I don't think she ever read it. The novel ended up three hundred pages, longhand.

My parents knew I was writing, but fortunately they weren't that interested. That was a wonderful thing because at that age, parents want to control everything in your life. My writing, however, was mine alone.

In high school, I started painting, and I got into the Rhode Island School of Design; but it was too expensive, so I went to the University of Illinois as an art major. Then in my sophomore year, I went back to my true love: writing. In art class they were making us draw circles without a compass—certainly *not* encouraging creativity—while my writing classes were. So I switched my major to creative writing, with a minor in studio art. University of Illinois was an amazing school for fiction writing at that time. Wonderful professors, so encouraging. Mark Costello, a short story writer, and Daniel Curley, also a wonderful writer. He ran the literary journal there, *Ascent*.

I still love to paint, especially watercolors, very saturated, fairly realistic, about light and shadow.

MICHELLE HUNEVEN: When I was very young and being read to, books exerted a tremendous allure; I saw that they contained treasure—in code. I was desperate to learn how to read and unlock the code for myself.

Once I began reading, I became deeply attracted to print, in particular the beautiful boxiness of paragraphs, which I was then desperate to duplicate. At the time, I was seven or eight and writing on that newsprint with the turquoise lines; I could eke out maybe a sentence or two at a time. How did writers make whole filled-in squares of prose, pages of beautiful square and rectangular paragraphs? This was something I was determined to do. I loved the materiality of words on paper and the worlds they conjured.

GARY IORIO: My interest in writing began at a very early age, second or third grade. My mom had an ancient Remington electric typewriter, and she would set it up on the kitchen table to do a little business for my dad. We lived in the Bensonhurst section of Brooklyn. I would dictate little plays (always plays) to her. "What does Bill say now?" "He says, 'Gee, Penny, wasn't the circus great! Let's play again tomorrow.'" Really. This stuff is pretty personal to me, but I feel that my next step at writing is a bit more universal.

I became a writing student. In high school English classes, we'd get assignments to try to write a short story or poem. My writings were very well received, so this acceptance led me down the path of least resistance. I decided I wanted to be a writer, and authority figures—teachers and parents—encouraged me and I performed. But there was no particular book or event that sparked this interest. I just wanted to do something I thought I could do well.

JOY HARJO: The only book in our house until I brought books home from school and the library (I was the oldest of four children) was the Bible. It influenced me, especially Song of Solomon. I loved the sensual passages and turned to them during boring sermons. I was an irreverent reader and shocked my mother by reading to her the story of Lot sleeping with his daughters. She couldn't believe that was in the Bible and thought it was my imagination. Everything was "just your imagination." It still is. In Iowa, I wasn't reading from the academic mainstream of poetry like everyone else. I read Amos Tutuola and Okot p'Bitek from Uganda and escaped to the International Writing Program where my friends were Leon Agusta and Denardo, a poet and playwright from Indonesia. And now I still read at the edges inward, from Tagore to Yeats. I return to Neruda, Lorca, James Wright, and Adrienne Rich. My poetic voice is somewhere between King David, Jayne Cortez, and Jim Morrison.

But being a writer was not in my original plan for life. The plan was something like this: I would be a painter like my grandmother Naomi Harjo, whose paintings and drawings of horses and tribal leaders hung in our home. Art was something I could do naturally. And creating art didn't require eloquence of speech or the ability to speak in front of the classroom or strangers. My only bad grades in school were awarded in speech classes because I was too timid to speak. Why did I take them then? The power of the word has always attracted me. I was first drawn to singing. My mother sang and wrote songs on an old Underwood typewriter at the kitchen table. Actually, I was obsessed with the mechanics of the typewriter and associated it with creativity, a kind of magic box for song lyrics. Jukeboxes also had a pull. Poetry was singing on paper. But I was not by nature a writer.

SANDRA CISNEROS: There were always a lot of books around our house, some from the library, and lots of Mexican comic books. You know, with bloody skulls on the cover or men getting hit with frying pans and busses going over cliffs.

My father was an upholsterer, part of that new middle class in Mexico after the Mexican Revolution, the son of a military man. My mother's family was more humble: poor country people, *campesinos*—peasants. My father should have been the more cultured one, but my mom was the one who introduced us to all the arts, to music and opera, and made sure we had library books. My father was into more popular art. He watched sports, soccer, the news. From him, I got pop culture, but I also got from him, because of his homesickness, a wonderful education about Mexico and how there the arts aren't separated from the everyday.

My mom was the big reader in the family, but she drifted away from novels and started reading all the books she heard on Studs Terkel, all these political books. She started reading Eldridge Cleaver, Erich Fromm, Native American stuff, all these political books. So she was much more politically well read than anyone else in the neighborhood. We had a photo of Spiro Agnew on our dartboard.

> There were always a lot of books around our house, some from the library, and lots of Mexican comic books. You know, with bloody skulls on the cover . . .

So the creative writing that I was doing seemed different from what my mom was reading or my dad's reading. I was a closet writer for years. I never let on. My folks didn't know. I was a girl, and so my father expected me to get married. He didn't mind me going to college because in his world, middle-class girls went to college to marry well. What puzzled him was that I went to college for so many years and didn't come out with a husband.

ERIC OLSEN: My old man was also an upholsterer for many years after he got out of the Army following WWII. Then he was a letter carrier. My mom was a seamstress for many years, but she'd been to art school in LA. It was all very working class, but with aspirations, in a working-class neighborhood with aspirations. Our house was full of books, and my folks were always reading something. There was a tradition back then of the working-class intellectual, I think, maybe a leftist thing. My father had been a Communist during the Depression. He'd read Marx, Engels, the whole bit, tried to organize the workers. Communists tended to be readers, I think. And my father had been to college back when most guys from his world never dreamed of such things, the son of immigrants: Better yourself in the New World.

My folks belonged to the Book-of-the-Month Club, and I remember every month a book would come, and it was always a moment of great excitement around the house. Of course, my dad made most of the picks. History mostly, some politics (but nothing even remotely left-leaning from the BOMC, of course) and nothing I was interested in, early on. My mom would order up the occasional art book, a novel now and then.

> **Our house was full of books, and my folks were always reading something. There was a tradition back then of the working-class intellectual, I think, maybe a leftist thing.**

My earliest memories of reading involve science fiction. In particular, a series of books for children about an eccentric scientist who was short but with a huge head. He might have been an alien, or an alien in disguise, but I don't recall for sure. His first name was Tycho, I assume homage to Tycho Brahe, the seventeenth-century Danish astronomer and alchemist. I can't recall the character's last name or the names of any of the books or any of the plots other than they were science fiction mysteries, and I loved them. Tycho was sort of a futuristic Sherlock Holmes.

JOE HALDEMAN: I started reading science fiction in the fourth grade, when my parents gave me *Rocket Jockey* for Christmas. I read it several times cover to cover, and my teacher finally took it away from me. Then she brought me several young adult novels from her daughter's collection, provided I didn't read them in class, and I was hooked.

Don't read much science fiction now; too busy writing it. My wife reads a lot and recommends things to me. I'm far too critical to enjoy most of them. For light reading, it's mostly crime fiction; I like Lawrence Block, James Lee Burke, Carl Hiassen, Elmore Leonard. Bobby Crais was one of my students; I pick his books up now and then.

Books by the Bed

JOE HALDEMAN: When I go to bed, I fall asleep immediately. The little stack of books I have there goes back a couple of years to when I had a cold and was stuck in bed—*The Viking Portable Faulkner, The Viking Portable Joyce, Love Among the Haystacks* by Lawrence, Fowles's *The Collector*, and *The Turn of the Screw and Other Short Novels* by James. Pretty classy stuff. But it's been years since I opened one.

ERIC OLSEN: I do remember vividly the pleasure of going to the local library and checking out the science fiction books by one writer, one by one, and then everything by another, and the sense of loss I felt when I'd read everything by one writer and there weren't any new books. I was too young then to understand that these books might have been written by someone who was now dead or in a care facility for the infirm or insane. But the whole world of science fiction lay before me, and I devoured the novels coming out back then: Asimov, Dick, Clarke, Spinrad, Heinlein, Simak, Bradbury, Leiber, Boucher, Zelazny, and to me perhaps one of the greatest novels of all time, *A Canticle for Leibowitz* by Walter Miller. I refused to read anything other than science fiction. I mean, forget *The Scarlet Letter*!—yes, they were making us read Hawthorne! Hell, they still make kids read Hawthorne!

I was reading this stuff throughout my childhood and into adolescence, and so you can imagine how it twisted me. I can still remember the opening from a Philip K. Dick novel: "The proton beam deflector . . ." et cetera, et cetera.[2]

So by the time I get to high school, I have a serious attitude problem, especially when it came to lit classes. They're making us read Hawthorne and *The Old Man and the Sea* and things by Steinbeck, and I'm wondering where the hell are the proton beam deflectors? Where are the mind-reading mutants with tentacles for hair? We're talking the 1950s, the 1960s, the Soviet threat, Khrushchev banging his cheap collective-made shoe on a podium, Sputnik, and nuclear attack drills in class and our teachers trying to convince us that we could survive an A-bomb blast if we just got under our desks quickly enough. I knew better, of course. I knew they were lying to us because I read science fiction! I knew about proton beams.

There was always something transgressive about science fiction. My teachers disapproved. I think my parents also disapproved, but they didn't say anything; at least I was reading, and they figured science fiction was better than me hanging out on the corner smoking cigarettes with the neighborhood punks. So it was natural, I think, that from science fiction, the next step for me was to get political. Our teachers were lying to us? Hell, so was everyone else in power! Science fiction was about heroes who paid attention to the man behind the curtain. The war in Vietnam was escalating. Kennedy, then LBJ, then Nixon were lying to us, and so from science fiction it was on to Marcuse, Fanon, *Soul on Ice*, and all that. Still no Hawthorne, though. It became a point of pride for me that I'd get lousy grades in English, and my grades in English were very, very lousy.

SHERRY KRAMER: I was a voracious reader when I was young. I read quickly, with total recall. When I was eleven, I read the first *Man from Uncle* book; it was called *The Thousand Coffins Affair*. I was so in love with it I memorized it word for word. I started reading the Russians in junior high. I was a huge Dostoyevsky fan and took Russian in college so I could read him in the original but never quite got the hang of it—I used to say that I hoped to master English so I'd be monolingual.

I'm a science fiction freak, a *huge* science fiction reader; that's my preferred genre, and it's also the place where some of the most vital conversations in America about God and faith have been happening the last twenty-five or thirty years or so, which is a constant draw as far as I'm concerned. Science fiction freaks look at everything differently.

In college I fell in love with the Japanese—Kawabata, of course, and Kenzaburo Oe and Kobo Abe—but I was most influenced by Mishima and read everything he wrote.

Then along with everybody else in the '70s, I had the incredible joy of "discovering" Borges and Márquez. These books changed all the ways I saw what could happen in a book, and not only that, they changed the way I understood change. After Borges, I understood that I couldn't take the surface of any story as a given, ever again. I was a poet back then, a bad one but still a poet. I'd been a bad lyric poet from the age of about seven, but when I was sixteen I discovered a Charles Bukowski poem inside a free paper in San Francisco, and so I became a bad poet in new and exciting ways.

> . . . when I was sixteen I discovered a Charles Bukowski poem inside a free paper in San Francisco, and so I became a bad poet in new and exciting ways.

ERIC OLSEN: Of course, genre fiction was frowned on at Iowa. One most definitely did not commit genre at Iowa, especially your first year while you were still angling for position in the pecking order and hoping to get a coveted Teaching/Writing Fellowship for your second year. As far as I know, Joe Haldeman was the only guy in the Workshop who was good enough to get away with committing genre when I was there. His novel about his service in Vietnam, *War Year*, had already been published when he applied to the

Workshop. It'd even gotten a full-page review in the *New York Times Book Review*.

JOE HALDEMAN: Jack Leggett would never have accepted me if he'd known I was writing science fiction. He detested commercial fiction, genre fiction—anything normal people read for pleasure.

My advisor, though, was Vance Bourjaily, and he thought it was cool that I was actually publishing and getting paid for it. (The first day I was at Iowa, I went up to the office and saw all the grad assistants running around making copies and such. I asked Vance what I could do. He said, "You're writing a novel, aren't you?" I said yes, and he said, "Go home and write.")

Most of the other professors were amused or bemused that I was writing commercial fiction. Only Stanley Elkin was not—he forbade me to write any science fiction for his class, saying that even the best of it was necessarily refractive and useless as literature. For him, I wrote a long Vietnam piece called "Spider's Web," which became the novel *1968* a couple of decades later. (I liked Stan a lot in spite of his attitude. He was one of the few writers there who passionately wanted to teach.)

T. C. BOYLE: There is a very fine distinction between these things, literature and genre fiction, but who cares? I don't want to come off as a snob, but I read books that appeal to me for language, what's going on under the surface. Mysteries give us the story, sure, which is the essence of everything we do, the starting point, but I need a whole lot more than that. I would rather read Pynchon on the airplane than Ross MacDonald or Michael Crichton. They might have ideas, but their writing doesn't appeal to me on an artistic level. It's as simple as that. And you know, mysteries don't appeal to me because they're confined by a formula. In a mystery, you know someone's going to get murdered, and someone's going to find out who did it, or not. The only variation seems to be when a new writer comes along with a detective who's Chinese or an American Indian or a woman. Those are the variations. That's great, and a lot of readers find comfort in that; but the writer I'll like, like Denis Johnson, is going to take you someplace you've never been before. That is what I love. I don't want to know what it's going to be. When I write anything, I don't know what it's going to be.

Books by the Bed
T. C. BOYLE: Robert Stone's *Fun With Problems*, Louise Erdrich's *Shadow Tag*, Anton Chekhov's *Ward No. 6 and Other Stories*, Sy Montgomery's *Spell of the Tiger*, Michael Capuzzo's *Close to Shore*, and Carol Sklenicka's biography of Raymond Carver.

DOUG BORSOM: As a child, I also read a lot of science fiction—Bradbury, Asimov, Heinlein, Clarke—and in the Workshop, I wrote a fair amount of science fiction; but lacking Joe Haldeman's courage, I stayed in the closet and sent the stories off to the pulps. As an undergrad, I read the usual suspects, though I also went through a period of reading eighteenth-century writers like Smollett, Goldsmith, and Sterne. At Iowa, I remember reading Italo Calvino and J. P. Donleavy in Vance Bourjaily's class and admiring them so much that I went out and read everything I could find by them.

I couldn't begin to emulate Calvino, but I could manage a shallow impersonation of Donleavy's style, and did so in a short story. Edna O'Brien, in Iowa City for a reading, included it among the student stories she commented on. I'm sure she recognized my clumsy effort at copying the style of her countryman, but she was very kind. Soon I realized that Donleavy could do himself better than I ever could, and that one Donleavy was sufficient. There are many writers I wish I could write like. But Conrad and LeCarre through his midcareer would have to be near the very top. And then Nabokov in the lotus position and illuminated from behind by shafts of light, floating above all the rest.

GERI LIPSCHULTZ: Well, I feel foolish saying all of this—but what the hell, yes, of course, Nabokov. Who else but Vladimir Nabokov, specifically *Ada*. And *Ulysses* by Joyce. Eventually Shakespeare and Neruda entered the mix. But for a while, I lived in *Ada* and *Ulysses*, passages became my mantra, and really the first book I started writing, the one that got me into Iowa, was so clearly a botched amalgam of both of these books . . .

BILL MCCOY: I played the bass guitar and figured I'd end up being a bass guitarist (I was making some money at it), but I knew I had to be in college and get a degree, and so I figured I'd major in filmmaking. I'd play some gigs, make some money, and study film. My advisor in the film department had written a book about the Marx brothers, so he was a sort of a writer, and he started encouraging me to write. He said the only people making money in the film biz were the writers, which was completely wrong, but neither of us knew that at the time. He encouraged me to take writing and literature classes in the English department, and the novelist Thomas Rogers taught the first lit class I took. He wrote *The Pursuit of Happiness*, which was a National Book Award finalist and got made into a movie. He was also, by the way, a graduate of the Workshop. His class just opened up books for me in a way they hadn't been before.

What I learned from him seems so obvious now, in retrospect . . . that books are an extension of someone's experiences, not words on a page. That books are people speaking to me in a certain way. Suddenly the whole process of literature became simultaneously demystified and more mysterious.

He had us read *The Red and the Black*. That's the one that really clicked for me. Here was a guy about my age, screwed up rather like I was screwed up, and he was a sympathetic character like I hoped I was. It was the first time I felt like I had a lot in common on a deep level with a character. Julien Sorel, of course. Now that I think about it, I probably felt that way about Holden Caulfield when I read *Catcher*, when I was twelve or thirteen, but I hadn't felt that way about a book again until I read Stendhal. I had figured that once you were a grown-up, you didn't feel about books in the same way.

> He had us read *The Red and the Black*. That's the one that really clicked for me. Here was a guy about my age, screwed up rather like I was screwed up . . .

DENNIS MATHIS: In elementary school, I was in a Junior Great Books program, and I fell in love with the Saturday-morning discussions of whatever books they gave us—*The Red Badge of Courage*, Plato, Jules Verne, *Wind, Sand and Stars*, et cetera. I liked being the dissenter in the group. I hated *Johnny Tremain*, though.

My brother was eleven years older than I, and he left his college books around where he knew I would snitch them. I read *Rabbit Run*, *The Centaur*, and *Pigeon Feathers* when I was twelve-ish. That's how I found out about the mechanics of sex. I didn't realize girls didn't have penises until I read Updike.

CATHERINE GAMMON: My mother used to tell me stories. She made up stories, stories about me, basically. She read *Alice in Wonderland* and *Through the Looking Glass* with me over and over. And at the end of her life, when she couldn't read novels or even the newspaper anymore, I read *Alice* to her. There was a lot of reading in my family, and there were walls full of books, all kinds of books, from European and American classics to contemporary politics and popular science and hard-boiled detective novels. You know, in the '50s there were those Heritage books with all the wonderful illustrations and beautifully printed limited editions. So as a child, before I could read these people, I was appreciating the physicality of the book and the illustrations and the type and the paper. And the flimsy paperbacks, too, with their seedy seductive covers. Later I was reading teenage girl historical novels and horse novels, and in high school, *War and Peace* and *Wuthering Heights* and *Metamorphosis*, but I didn't have a sense of writers, really, just books. I read Hemingway and Steinbeck and Salinger and Carson

McCullers and Truman Capote and Harper Lee, and they were all alive then, but it wasn't as if they were any more alive than Tolstoy and Emily Bronte.

In college, I was attracted to Dostoyevsky and Woolf and Joyce more than to living contemporaries. Beckett, too, and he was alive, but I read him as if he were not. As a kind of hippie, I read *V* and *Unspeakable Practices, Unnatural Acts*, and *Play It as It Lays*, but I had no sense of reading Pynchon, Barthelme, or Didion. I had no concept of a literary scene or a world in which writers knew each other and hung out together and got into messy affairs with each other. Until I got to Iowa, my idea of a writer was someone profound, brilliant, spiritual, and dead.

JANE SMILEY: My mother was the woman's page editor of the *Saint Louis Globe-Democrat*, now long gone. I visited her at work from time to time. I knew what she did for a living and saw her byline and everything. She hadn't written a novel but had written a memoir of experiences in World War II, though it wasn't published. Anyway, I knew people wrote, and I think my mom wanted me to be a writer, but I rejected that. I wanted to be an equestrian, but it was clear by the time I was thirteen I was going to be too tall for that. I didn't start writing until college.

I grew up reading a lot of book series for girls—*Nancy Drew, The Dana Girls, The Black Stallion*, and other series of horse books. This is what gets kids to read, and when these sorts of books are no longer interesting, they try others and expand their horizons. My daughters read the *Sweet Valley High* series. Now my daughter, Lucy Silag, who was in the Workshop, has published a trilogy of young adult novels.

ROBIN GREEN: I was a grandchild of immigrants, the first generation to go to college. There was some reading in my family but mostly a great appreciation of entertainment on TV, especially Sid Caesar. I do remember we got the *New Yorker* and that was highly revered. I knew somehow that my mother wanted me to be a writer, though I don't think she stated it outright, or even knew what that meant, only that it would be a great achievement and have great status, clearly an Old World view.

T. C. BOYLE: I grew up in a working-class family. My father was an orphan ... raised in an orphanage, educated to the eighth grade. My mom had high school only. There were no books around the house. I read the *Daily News* and watched TV, but then I began to read a lot but not what I was supposed to read. It was current stuff, what was happening right then. In the late '60s, there was lots of experimental stuff going on. In college, at SUNY Potsdam, I was introduced to Flannery O'Connor in a sophomore literature class.

Outside of class, I started reading nontraditional literature—Barth, Beckett, Genet, Barthelme, Coover, Márquez, Gardner, Cortazar, Pynchon, all that stuff. I think they hold up well, too. I don't reread them much, but I do now and then to see how they hold up. But there's so much new stuff coming out, and I'm reading new stuff all the time when it comes out. And I'm also reading a lot for whatever project I'm working on. I keep up with careers of people I like: Coover, all his books. Márquez, all his books, which I use several times in my classes.

DOUG UNGER: The single most impactful book on my youth was Gabriel García Márquez's *Cien años de soledad*. I was introduced to it in Spanish, in the cheap corner bookstall edition brought out by Editorial Losada, which my adoptive brother, Álvaro Colombo, found and read in 1969 in Buenos Aires, then passed on to me. The book was scarcely a year in print at that point and not yet available in English translation.

Though my Spanish wasn't yet entirely up to comprehending everything, I remember Álvaro lying on his bed, reading parts of it aloud to me, and both of us cracking up, especially at the incestuous emblem of the later Buendías being born with pig's tails, that passage and others, and I was hooked. So then I found *La hojarasca*—translated into English, later, as *Leafstorms*—and read that. Then *No One Writes to the Colonel*, and I kept going. I was seventeen years old.

Later, I found Roberto Arlt and his collection of little sketches called *Las muchachas de Buenos Aires*. I loved his ironic, darkly humorous style, slightly touched by fantasy and madness, and it was like discovering an as-yet-mainly undiscovered voice with the power of Dostoyevsky, applied to a culture in which I was living, so it opened up a whole new way of seeing the world. Also, Horacio Quiroga's tales of horror and madness in *La gallina degollada y otros cuentos* and *El regreso de Anaconda*, a political fantasy about a congress of snakes. I think my youthful reading of what only later I discovered were serious literary books in Spanish turned me into a different kind of reader, one who of necessity paid attention to language because they were written in a language I was still learning while reading the books. I missed a lot. But that meant there was so much to keep returning to, and so I did, time after time.

I was always a reader. I had read the beat poets, Ginsberg and Ferlinghetti, and some Jack Kerouac before that, and loved the sense of a rebellious, countercultural world they conveyed. And, for some reason, I sought out and read the Grove editions of Eugene Ionesco, *The Bald Soprano*, *Rhinoceros*, *The Chairs*, and other short plays. I was a pretty indiscriminate reader. I remember reading *The Bald Soprano* followed by Ian Fleming's *On Her*

Majesty's Secret Service, then Terry Southern's *Candy*, then Horace McCoy's *They Shoot Horses, Don't They?* in that order for no other reason than they were available in a ten-cent bin of used paperbacks out on a New York street.

In grade school, I read adventure novels, but not cheap ones. I read Kenneth Roberts' *Northwest Passage* from cover to cover in the fourth grade. And that big illustrated edition of Thor Heyerdahl's *Kon-Tiki* was one of my most treasured books, about his raft trip adventure across the Pacific to prove his ideas about pre-Columbian discovery. I don't know what any of this means, save that I didn't make connections of books I was reading with anything practical, or any idea of becoming a writer, or any sense of the so-called "literary." I read for escape.

> The first book that made me think about being a writer was *A Fine Madness*, by Elliott Baker . . .

The first book that made me think about being a writer was *A Fine Madness*, by Elliott Baker, but mainly because I identified closely with the marginalized existence of the crazy writer he describes.

While growing up—either in the United States, where my family home life was a nightmare of the alcoholism, violence, and clinical insanity of my parents, or in Argentina, where my family were all extremely civilized, cultured people but the country was a military dictatorship about to descend into the brutality of tortures, mass murders, and disappearances, then out West working on my father's ranch away from everything and everybody, then after that in Buenos Aires—I relied on books as my main means of escape. I let them take me anywhere they would, and I was greatly appreciative of them and thought of books as my best friends. They never let me down. I could never be lonely when I had them within reach.

GLENN SCHAEFFER: I'd always been a reader, but it got serious for me with *The Great Gatsby*. That was the game-changer. I was sixteen, seventeen. I was in high school, trying on identities; and since I'd read *Gatsby* three or four times, one of my identities was card-carrying intellectual. I was president of Honor Society and the academic officer on student council, a straight-A student. But once I'd been listed in *Who's Who in American High Schools*, I devolved into disobedience, for which I possessed a flair. As my erratic tendencies went from bad to worse, my guidance counselor suggested I was on track for continuation school. I had no idea what he was talking about—*continuation school*? Well, what the heck, I had time to kill before college.

This continuation school, what used to be called a reform school, happened to be an annex to the hospital in Pomona, California, where I

was born. It was a two-room affair, one large room containing library car-
rels, the other beanbag chairs, known as a "rap room" back in 1970. The
rap room was intermittently occupied by malefactors—druggies, serial auto
thieves, street enforcers, shoplifters. None was a stranger to me. Out back
was a pen walled off from the patients where you could walk in circles or
eat your sandwich on a wooden bench. I understood that it was modeled on
the rooftop pen at County. That was the progression at the time: continuation school, Chino Boys, County. San Quentin was the apex. Actor Steve
McQueen hailed from Chino Boys, local bad boy made good. A few of my
classmates ascended all the way to Q, the Show.

The alleged principal was a hippie with lank hair to his shoulders and a
ghost of a moustache. I presented my bona fides as truant and belligerent—
over the maximum days in absentia by California statute—and he signed my
papers. He was smoking a cigarette, simpatico. I needed only two courses to
graduate, so I decided first on US Civics, perhaps to ground myself better
with respect to the opposition. In four days, I'd wrapped it up on a nine-to-
five schedule. You read a textbook and took standardized tests. I aced them.

Back at Pomona High, word of my defection had spread, and one of my
AP teachers saw fit to tip off the superintendent of public schools. So there I
was, two weeks into my tenure on the farm, well into the advanced course of
Modern American Politics, when the hippie principal summoned me to his
office. I was expecting a decoration, but he wasn't smoking this time. He was
ticked, in fact. I was summarily terminated. Booted, 86'd. He told me I was
his worst case, there under false pretense. What was wrong with that? *That's
why it's called reform school!*

So then I had to meet the superintendent of schools, who informed me I
was misusing the system. They wouldn't accept any of my work completed in
reform school, and that if I didn't want to return to regulation high school,
I'd have to finish up in correspondence school.

We all went quiet for a beat. Correspondence school? What was that?

The superintendent solemnly explained that I'd have to take my courses
by mail, home alone, no proms or parades.

What? Why didn't someone tell me about this in the first place? You can
work from bed? Graduate in your pajamas? I thought, Isn't that what writers
do?

So I literally completed high school on the beach, solo. Forget classes;
mailed 'em in. More particularly, I made up my own reading list, consisting
of the usual fare: *Catcher in the Rye, On the Road.* Next I tackled the big boys
in small doses—Hemingway, Bellow, Mailer. I was so puzzled by Fowles's
French Lieutenant's Woman, I had to read it twice. Tricky narrator. I began a
journal of reading notes and commentary, primitively speaking; became an

adept body surfer and saltwater distance swimmer. On weekends I'd catch up with my school-trapped buddies, college-prep and athletic types, and I'd do riffs for them on what I'd been reading, like a walking Classic Comics. They were mostly amused. Some tried out the books for themselves. My face blazed with incipient skin cancer. I believed that books and beach light were good for me. Could I stretch them into a grown-up life?

ALLAN GURGANUS: My mother had a master's degree and had been a schoolteacher before she started having kids at thirty. But my father's family were landowners, farmer-merchants. Moneymaking was extremely important, like one of those semirapacious families in Lillian Hellman. Folks that know the price of everything and the value of nothing. Of course, it was also a very religious family. My father converted to fundamental evangelical Christianity when I was about nine, and that was a terrible loss to us all. I resisted his joyless version of the Lord. But the paradox is, having gone to church all my life, I absorbed much, much more than I could have ever imagined.

One of the many things I learned from sitting out those endless dreary Sunday school classes, taught by people unqualified to teach the Bible or anything written down, is precisely the power of reading aloud. Hearing the King James Bible read out loud over and over again, hearing those lessons while looking at those highly colored lithographs posted on every wall, made me understand that ordinary experience, common experience, throwing seed into the garden, or losing a valuable coin in the house then refinding it, had immense allegorical and metaphysical significance. These simple truths mattered immensely. Homely events, told simply, could take fire, light up. A local reality became a universal truth if treated properly. Fables matter.

GLENN SCHAEFFER: And there was *Gatsby*. I wanted my name on that book! It was short enough (what, sixty thousand words?) that I could read it through in less than a week. Then, one week, I decided that I would write it myself and practiced the first chapter longhand on a lined tablet, the way Fitzgerald often wrote, on his lap. When I discovered that the Huntington Library in Pasadena was displaying a holograph of *Gatsby*, I drove over there and compared our handwriting. That novel hadn't been inscribed, after all, by the right index finger of God. Here was Scott Fitzgerald thinking aloud on the page—cross-outs, margin notes, rampant misspellings. In a spelling bee, I'd have skunked him. But bit by bit, the thing added up. Creativity appeared to be incremental. You attacked the page in bursts, then faltered, by the looks of his working method. It was like I'd peeked behind the magic curtain.

ANTHONY BUKOSKI: My parents bought my sister and me books for Christmas and for our birthdays. I read *Huck Finn* in sixth grade, plus a lot of baseball players' biographies (Stan Musial's, for instance, he being Polish), and even a biography of President Eisenhower. *Huck Finn* was difficult going for me, given the book's dialects. I was proud of myself when I finished the novel. I also remember the wonderful feeling I had when I realized Mark Twain was actually alive earlier in the century. I must have thought authors were from the very distant past, perhaps five hundred or more years before I came on the earth. Then that February day, perhaps it was in 1956 or 1957, as I stared out the window, the knowledge came to me that Twain was alive fifty years earlier. The idea just hit me like a meteor. Books were a welcome present for my sister and me. I loved their feel, their scent, their colorful jackets.

Another book I read as a youth was *Robinson Crusoe*, a gift from my parents. These were unabridged books though for young readers, so the books often had beautiful artwork to accompany the narratives. I have in my hands now Tom Meany's biography of Babe Ruth, another one I read. The inscription reads "June 1958. To Anthony who cut the grass so diligently and faithfully. Mom and Dad." Reading the inscription brings tears to my eyes.

DENNIS MATHIS: My family was working class and Midwestern, plain vanilla. Back in the '70s, being plebeian disqualified a person from becoming a top-rank author, I thought. My father's side had a lot of aunts and uncles who were all brilliant in odd, unmarketable ways. Smart but not hugely successful at anything. Their father, my grandfather, who I never knew, was universally said to be "the nicest man in the world." It was assumed in my family that being nice trumped being rich. The family always valued a sense of humor. We laughed a lot. Anything that didn't make someone laugh was pointless; anything that did was brilliant.

Money, careers, success meant nothing to my parents. They assumed all successful people were snobs. My brother was an English major who went on to teach for thirty years at a community college, and my parents thought that was fine. When I started college, my father and I had a thirty-second heart-to-heart about my plans for my life. I told him I thought maybe I'd be an English major like my brother because I liked stories. I sheepishly admitted maybe I'd try to be a writer—picturing Updike. My father said, "Okay." That was it.

My father sold refrigerators and washing machines after the war. When he saw a television for the first time, he had an epiphany (the same one I had when I first saw the web) and got rid of all the appliances, sold TVs instead. We had the first television in Peoria. People crowded the street in front of the store to watch the Gillette Friday Night Fights until the local paper ran an editorial declaring the store a public nuisance.

Storytelling, for me, meant TV. Captain Video, Mr. Wizard, Arthur Godfrey and Jack Paar (my parents didn't care if I stayed up till midnight), *Playhouse 90*, *Secret Agent*. I spent my youth hypnotized by cathode ray tubes. When I was at Iowa, this was the self-image I clung to—I'd grown up having electric stories poured into my eyeballs, so that made me what I was.

JAYNE ANNE PHILLIPS: I'm from West Virginia, which is still a world unto itself. It is a storytelling culture—small, isolated towns in which everyone knows everyone, and all tragedies are connected—a populace of mostly Welsh, British, Irish ancestry. Steadfast, dour, "don't-brag" people. Secrecy. The powers of perception, observation, and memory go into overdrive early, and we were always surrounded by Rip Van Winkle mountains and dirt roads that went nowhere. Perfect for artists, except that so many artists in such places are claimed by life before they can isolate themselves in their work and deflect what kills the writing or drawing or whatever. Storytelling was everywhere, in the air, and I got caught up in it early.

My mother joined a book club for me when I was seven, things like *The Happy Hollisters* series and *The Boxcar Children*, and on it went. I spent most of my time reading. I remember when my mother bought *Uncle Arthur's Bedtime Stories* from a door-to-door salesman. It was an orange hardcover with a kindly gentleman and his grandchildren on the cover. Inside, the stories were all frightening, nightmarish moral tracts, a collection of religious tales and lessons: a young mother leaves her baby sleeping in his crib (Why? Errands? I don't remember) and comes back to find her house on fire; even firemen couldn't hold her back and she rushes inside. There was one about the terminally ill child who was told to raise his hand if he wanted Jesus to take him, so he props his arm up on his bedclothes. A brother and sister quarrel over an electric train and set the house on fire, and, well, you get the picture. They were stories from a Christian Twilight Zone. I was so attached to that book that my mother finally got suspicious and took it away from me.

> **Storytelling was everywhere, in the air, and I got caught up in it early.**

It seemed natural; I began writing as an extension of reading. I read everyone, highly contrasting voices, William Burroughs, Bruno Schultz, Chekhov, Kafka, and of course the Southern pantheon of Porter, Faulkner, Welty, Agee. I kept my own writing a secret for a long time, which allowed me to write what I wanted to write, without thinking of reactions or consequences. I never declared myself a writer to my family. They heard it from others. At twenty or so, I began telling my closest friends (writers themselves, usually) that I was a poet. Failed poets make the best fiction writers, I think.

DON WALLACE: I was reading from third grade on, seven or eight books a week. Whenever I found an author I liked, I'd read everything by that writer. I'd just go down the shelves. I ended up reading *Enderby* by Anthony Burgess when I was in the sixth grade. You know, the poet who farts and writes in the toilet?

I wasn't the most attentive student, but then this teacher in the eighth grade, Mr. Henderson, did three things that blew my mind. First, he assigned "A Rose for Emily" by Faulkner, and then he says he wants us all to write a short story. So I wrote a Vietnam story. This was in a time of great racial tension in LA. We'd had the Watts riots, and a lot of white people were running around with guns; our Boy Scout group was an armed gang; even the country club members were packing. "Rose" was about the South, my first taste of Southern gothic, though half my family was from Memphis. And here I'd written this story about Vietnam, complete with a dramatic face-off between two soldiers in a moonlit clearing. The teacher announced that most of our stories weren't very good, but there was one he found interesting, and that got my hopes up. Then he started reading a story by a black girl in our class. Her story was about racism experienced at a personal level, and I realized how puerile my little war story was.

My teacher did a third amazing thing. He read us *A Good Man Is Hard to Find*. That would have gotten him fired if it hadn't been the last day of school. It was mind-boggling, that ending, shooting the grandma. I went out and read everything by Flannery O'Connor. Most of her stuff wasn't that great, I thought. I read Hemingway's *For Whom the Bell Tolls*, with Robert Jordan lying under the bridge at the end, so I started writing the next chapter. My friend Dell showed up one afternoon and I was out, so he started reading the story and was sitting there reading when I got back, and he said it was pretty good; I should keep writing.

DENNIS MATHIS: Updike, of course, because of the scintillating prose and his center-of-the-country gravity. I had poor eyesight, and Updike's gasp-inducing similes were like suddenly seeing clearly. It opened my eyes to what words were capable of. I identified with the boy in *The Centaur*—there's a brief passage where he's shown grown-up, with a girlfriend in a dirty bed in Greenwich Village, and that became a glimpse of my own future for me. I remembered it years later when I was living in New York City, lying in a dirty bed with a girlfriend.

But I don't want to leave the impression I wanted to write *New Yorker* stories. My reading back then, even in high school, was very eclectic and bizarre. I loved contemporary world lit—Japanese, German, Latin American, anything exotic. In high school I did a paper on Theatre of the Absurd, Beckett and Ionesco, and such. Apart from *Pigeon Feathers* and *The Centaur*, I didn't like anything that was set in someplace resembling Peoria. I hated American domestic novels about marriage and infidelity in Connecticut. To me, "Waiting for Godot" was much more accurate to life in Peoria.

ANTHONY BUKOSKI: I remember reading Faulkner's "Barn Burning" and some other Faulkner works during my freshman year in college. I also read Algren's "A Bottle of Milk for Mother." I was really surprised and pleased by the story, for in it were characters with Polish names, something I'd not seen in literature before. It was like I was being validated in learning that people of my background could actually be a source of fiction. The bad thing was Algren, a non-Pole, often made his characters thugs, whores, dope addicts, as was Frankie Machine in *The Man with the Golden Arm*. "Machine" was an Anglicized Polish name.

I left college after one year, joined the Marines in the summer of '64 and in Vietnam read popular novels like *Peyton Place*, *The Bramble Bush*, and the like. I spent my last year and a half in the Marines at the base in Quantico, Virginia. Occasionally, I went to the base library to read plays by Tennessee Williams. He certainly had his negative Polish stereotypes.

I was home from the Marines in the summer of 1967, discharged honorably at the rank of corporal, and I lounged around that summer, bought a 1959 Austin-Healey and read Kerouac. I felt that I wanted to distinguish myself in life, be more than a mill-hand like my father or an insurance agent or some other unglamorous occupation. How to do this? I realized I wouldn't

> I spent my last year and a half in the Marines at the base in Quantico, Virginia. Occasionally, I went to the base library to read plays by Tennessee Williams. He certainly had his negative Polish stereotypes.

distinguish myself as a baseball player, for I hadn't hit in three years. But what else was there that was sexy? I know, I told myself, I'll be a writer.

ALLAN GURGANUS: I got sent to war. I chose a longer term in the Navy over a surefire Army or Marine death sentence in Vietnam. I got very lucky in a number of ways—I ended up on the USS *Yorktown*, a carrier with four thousand men onboard. This happened so long ago there were no televisions on the ship. Imagine four thousand men, ages eighteen to twenty-three, with a couple of alcoholic fifty-year-olds in charge, floating around in the South China Sea for thirty-five days on end without ever even seeing land! Imagine the mischief, the energy, the volatility, the typhoon-level testosterone and erotic swill among all those men.

> *Portrait* was the first novel I remember reading with the sensation of suspended breath, entering this world that seemed so familiar and alien and magical.

The Navy wisely put a library onboard just to keep us all from fucking and killing each other. There was a lot of fucking going on, usually in the showers after midnight. I felt much too terrified to be there doing that. (Decades later, the "straight" guys asked me where I'd been and told me what I'd missed.) Where had I been? In the library, every night till nine. That seemed the only game at sea for me.

My sole chance of staying sane meant finding something to learn, to do. I was trained as a painter. Had gone to art school for a year. But painting was not exactly a leading career option on this aircraft carrier. I had my sketchbook and I had a journal and I had license to check out books. Then I lucked out and found Henry James's *The Portrait of a Lady*. Our library was mainly cast-off books from some captain or other, a lot of Conrad, Ford Madox Ford's *The Good Soldier*. Someone was trying to put together a group of works with a military theme, but somehow Henry James and a few others slipped in. I was ready for something. *Portrait* was the first novel I remember reading with the sensation of suspended breath, entering this world that seemed so familiar and alien and magical. It got me thinking the way I had thought as a painter, back when I was looking at Cezanne and deciding, "I can do that," which was complete bullshit. But of course, what you don't know won't hurt you. And the ignorance of being nineteen years old constitutes the courage of being that age.

~

M ost avid readers never try their hand at writing, or if they do, they don't let on. What is it that provokes some of us to cross the line from reader to writer? There does seem to be a common trajectory in the lives of those we interviewed for this book that leads from a little natural talent for using words to an appetite for reading, to that fateful next step.

Sometimes, at a young age, an avid reader meets a real, live author, perhaps at the local library, someone with bad breath and dandruff and a hearty laugh, maybe, a vision for the young would-be writer of his or her own future self, who realizes that, gosh, writers are human, maybe I can do it, too. Or a young writer crosses that line when he or she writes something, shows it to someone whose opinion is trusted or respected—rarely a parent, of course—and gets praise for it, a moment of validation that is often so crucial.

DON WALLACE: I'm not sure when I decided to *be* a writer, but I wrote my first story in the fourth grade. Our teacher gave us an assignment to write about something that happened to us that weekend, and so I started writing about going out with the family on our cabin cruiser, and how the engine died and we were getting washed up on some rocks, and my dad's trying to restart the engine with eight-foot waves crashing over us. Finally, we clawed our way around Long Point and got into the lee and made our way to safety. When recess came, I kept on writing and wrote all through recess to finish. I became known throughout the school as the boy who wrote through recess.

ALLAN GURGANUS: You know what they say about heroin: the first hit is always free because the dealer wants to hook you. And I think the same is true of writing, for the chosen ones, and by chosen, maybe I mean singled out for special abuse.

The way the writing addicts you is this: It gives you something very beautiful on the first attempt. You're too innocent to know how good your prose is that first time out. Or how bad it is. You haven't had enough time to second-guess yourself and rewrite the energy out of it. But there is a colossal gap between that first inspired burst and what's next: earning your way into your own good services and your own confidence, continuing to write out the second inspired burst.

It always moves me to see even very, very gifted people who don't trust what they've been given at the outset. They revise themselves out of existence; they can become self-conscious to the extent that they are dubious about what comes easily. They suspect their own first hit, and that makes naturalness of voice so difficult for them.

The thing about a career, as I perceive it, is you're surviving that first meltdown, you're reconstituting yourself for a second run . . . it's like a gambler's luck, then you melt down a second time and you start up a third time and a fourth and an eighth . . .

JACK LEGGETT: Just before my dear friend Oakley Hall died, he struggled out of bed and tried to get to the keyboard or get something to write with, the essence of a man needing to set down in words just before the curtain was drawn on him. And then in the matter of Chris Buckley, he had a piece that was in the *New Yorker*, and he wrote the book about the last days of Bill Buckley, how he was also dying. Chris wheeled him out to his studio where his unfinished manuscript was, and he tried to press the keys so he could finish it, and he couldn't and, in despair, turned to Chris and dictated the last paragraph of a book he was writing . . . two guys that I had some relation with and here they both were in death . . . I don't know any other occupation where the impulse and *need* to write become so central in life. My theory is that it gives us a sense of something that's important, that makes life worthwhile.

ANTHONY BUKOSKI: Where'd I get such a notion that I might write? Perhaps my father's loquaciousness at the supper table fed what would eventually become a consuming interest. My dad was a laborer in a flour mill in Superior. If he worked the day shift, he got home around four-thirty. Before supper he had a bottle of beer and a shot of brandy. Under their influence, he'd open up with his stories. He'd been a merchant seaman both on the Great Lakes and the ocean, and he told stories about that. He told other stories of his youth. They were interesting, but sometimes he repeated the stories. Nonetheless, my sister and I had to wait until supper was over, then we had to ask whether or not we could be excused from the table. So I was captive for many years to a man who had to tell his stories somewhere, if only at his own table.

After the Marines, back at the University of Wisconsin, Superior, I tried off and on to write poems and stories. I became known among my friends as someone who wrote.

DON WALLACE: The turning point for me was my freshman year at UC Santa Cruz. It was a pass/fail program, but still, I almost flunked out. I hated it. I especially hated the English classes. The approach was all wrong. I went to my advisor and asked him what I should do, and he got me into a fiction class taught by Page Stegner.

I'd had to write something to get in, and I hadn't written any fiction since my finishing touches on *For Whom the Bell Tolls*. So I wrote a prose poem about two brothers free-climbing down a desert canyon on drugs and one falls off a cliff. All true except the fall. And Stegner read it aloud the very first class, and oh, I felt like crawling under the sofa (we sat on sofas at Santa Cruz). I saw clearly that I was out of my depth, and these upper-division students were seething over how this callow youth thrust upon their exclusive society. So I set out to write a real story, not a prose poem.

But a funny thing happened before my second writing class: I almost died. On a weekend ski trip, I severed my left bicep, crushed my upper legs, and suffered a concussion. I was laid up in my dorm room for two months and only showed up again at the very last class—looking liked I'd acted out my first story.

I'd like to be able to say people's expressions were priceless when I showed up for that last class, but my vision was still too blurry. Anyway, Stegner gave me a pity pass, which helped me keep my deferment and stay out of the Army.

Next quarter I took a poetry class with Naomi Clark, who paired me with a sensitive young woman writer, Noelle Oxenhandler, sort of a foil for a rude boy like me. (Noelle went on to become a writer, too.) We read Rilke's *Letters to a Young Poet*, and suddenly I was knocking out poems and wrestling with revisions for weeks on end. Naomi was impressed enough to urge me to send out my work. But I didn't have a clue what she was talking about. *Ploughshares*? What was that? With poetry, I never could get over this feeling that I was uncouth, a barbarian among the Illuminati.

I was a singer in a rock band, too, so I wrote and played rock and roll. But I did see a notice for a college poetry contest, and I entered some poems. I didn't win, but I did tie for second with Lawrence Weschler, who was the senior god of lit on campus at the time; and as I walked up to get the prize (which was a very Oxford bottle of sherry), I could see them all thinking: Who is this little punk? Now Weschler has his own institute at New York University. And I'm still a punk, I guess, still an outlier.

By nineteen, I was never not writing, but as a solitary and even furtive act. Every year after that, I won the fiction prize or took second in poetry. My senior advisor, Jim Houston, quipped that I just showed up at awards ceremonies for the sherry. It must have been true because when I went back for my twenty-fifth class reunion, people came up to me and said they still didn't understand: I was the biggest slacker there. . . . They didn't know I snuck off at six-thirty every morning to write a thousand words in a dormitory storeroom.

By then, I was totally a writer. I completely entered the writing culture of Santa Cruz, publishing in the local free rag and giving readings. I knew Ray Carver before he was Ray Carver, when people pointed to him as a cautionary tale of how not to get ahead in a writing career: publishing in the wrong small magazines, drinking too much, getting married, and not playing the teaching game.

GARY IORIO: At Hofstra University, I was an English major, prolific writer, and active in the literary magazine and workshop scene. But I was still a writing student. I remember one teacher at Hofstra actually said that he was sure everything I wrote would be published. Pretty seductive stuff for a twenty-year-old kid.

At the time I was reading Roth and the Northeast Urban Writers. We all read *Slaughterhouse Five*, but I was a little put off by anything close to science fiction. I discovered through a great professor at Hofstra the novels of Edward Wallant— *The Pawnbroker, Children at the Gate, The Human Season*, and *The Tenants of Moonbloom*. Hemingway wrote the best sentences. Joseph Heller and Norman Mailer wrote about a world I thought I knew. Dreiser gave me value for my time spent with him. As an undergrad, I also took a lot of literature in translation classes—Thomas Mann, Gunter Grass.

Books by the Bed

ANTHONY BUKOSKI: I keep on the table by my bed Thomas Mann's *Stories of Three Decades*, translated in 1936 from the German by H. T. Lowe-Porter. I eschew newer translations thinking that, by reading Lowe-Porter's 1936 translation, I am closer to Mann. I also keep nearby a novel John Irving recommended to me in 1975, William Goyen's *The House of Breath*, which I reread every few years and whose prologue I reread each year. I keep Gordon Weaver's novels and short story collections stacked near the bed. I've read nine of his books. A fine writer, he's gotten less recognition than he deserves. Because I review fiction for the *Minneapolis Star Tribune*, I have one or two books from them always waiting to read, currently Yoko Ogawa's novel *Hotel Iris*. Finally, I'm rereading Tennessee Williams. Within reach of my bed, I have the handsome Library of America edition of his plays from 1937 to 1955. I read four of his plays last semester in a course of Tennessee Williams and William Faulkner. I'll finish reading the rest this summer.

ANTHONY BUKOSKI: My senior year I became the editor of the college literary magazine *The Crosscut*, but my work was so awful, one time I even had to reject myself!

The next year, I went for the MA at Brown University. I was reading Poe, Hawthorne, Shelley, Keats, Chaucer, all the classics, so the time was well spent. I was laying a groundwork of reading. John Hawkes was teaching there, and I especially enjoyed *The Lime Twig* and tried to write a story following his style. I would see him in the English building and think, *So this is a* writer.

Once in a while I would show my dad a story I'd written. He'd say, "It's good, but I just wish you could write more like Jack Anderson." My parents-in-law in Lexington, Massachusetts, were, I imagine, befuddled by the fellow who'd married their daughter. "A writer?" they must have been asking themselves. "Who's he trying to kid?"

CATHERINE GAMMON: I had one teacher, in the seventh or eighth grade, who taught both math and English; and at the end of term in my yearbook, she wrote: "You certainly have a way with words. May it bring you every happiness." This was a kind of benign good wish, you know, but for a girl whose unhappiness was so deeply buried and definitive, it was a powerful seduction.

I was eleven when I first started writing a novel. I was drawing, and the drawing came with a mental story about the people in it, and a voice and words to begin came with it; and suddenly I was writing a novel, and I wrote it for years, all the way into college. It was set in Civil War times, completely imaginary, not out of my life, but of course it was full of my life; and it grew up with me, from eleven to eighteen, even though it was happening in another world. I lived in Los Angeles, in a sort-of-tract home, middle-class neighborhood. It was the mid-'50s. Nothing I read or saw in the movies was about that, so nothing I wrote was about that either. Once I started writing about a family escaping from Communist Czechoslovakia. What did I know? I saw something on TV, and it inspired me. I pretended to be sick for three days, which I was not, and I stayed home and imagined all these characters and wrote what I thought was the first chapter of what seemed to me my wonderful novel. Then my father got hold of it and called it "a crackerjack little story" and told me how to rewrite it into something completely different. After that my writing became more secretive.

ROBIN GREEN: I got hooked on the idea of being a writer in high school when the teacher read a funny essay I wrote to the class and everyone laughed. I think I was just better at writing than anyone in my small class, and so I thought of myself that way. Same thing with art class; I was good at it. I loved drawing and reading as a kid. It's what I did in my room. I suppose I liked to be somewhat solitary, although I did a lot of goofing off with friends, too.

I got a full scholarship to the Rhode Island School of Design but went to Brown instead. I was talented as an artist, but it was too great a leap, too impractical or something, to even think of being a visual artist. Don't forget, this was an era when a girl took typing so she'd be able to get a job as a secretary. And I wasn't going to be a teacher.

At Brown, in my junior year, I got into John Hawkes's fiction class with something I'd written. He loved some things I wrote, was critical of others. But the good short stories were very good. I wrote as if taking dictation then, in a blessed sort of state, in a beam. When I *tried* to write, it wasn't any good. Mostly I copied Hemingway; he was my favorite. He probably still is.

When I was still at Brown, I remember some big-shot editor from the *New Yorker* had come to visit, and he picked out a story I'd written and he read it in front of three hundred people. I was overwhelmed. There I was having something I'd written being read in front of three hundred Christians with blond hair!

They even made me editor of the Brown literary magazine. I really wasn't very good at it, kind of dragged my heels. But it did give me some visibility on campus, and people who weren't interested in me before now thought I was hip. So writing got me attention and admiration, and I think what happened after that is that I didn't write much because I'd gotten what I wanted out of it in that time and place.

I was overwhelmed. There I was having something I'd written being read in front of three hundred Christians with blond hair!

GLENN SCHAEFFER: I applied to UC Irvine because it was the best school closest to my aluminum beach chair. Known as Instant U for its instant enrollment of thousands and its instant tenured faculty, drafted in chunks from Berkeley and UCLA and the Ivy League, Irvine all at once became a number-one factor in comp lit and lit crit circles (and still is). Its MFA was likewise instant, also high-ranked, headed up by literary naturalist Oakley Hall and Carl Hartman, both Iowans who were my future mentors and steered me to Iowa. Richard Ford was an MFA student at Irvine when I started, and the visiting faculty included Ed Doctorow, Ron Sukenick, and William Inge. Books and beach light; what can I tell you?

My father, a PhD in organic chemistry from Berkeley, felt that all higher education was intended for the credentialing of chemists. I had different ideas. This led to tumult.

Finally we compromised. Freshman year I sampled a science (chemistry), a math (statistics), economics, core humanities, and playwriting. Ran the table, except for a hoary C in chemistry. Point proven. Other than chemistry, I had great luck at Irvine.

My sophomore year I was walking through the library and saw a poster advertising the first such-and-such essay contest, along with a $500 prize for the best essay about a singular "intellectual" influence, so I went back to my dorm room and wrote my submission—a letter to J. D. Salinger. I entered it and won the prize! Then I signed up for a playwriting class to be taught by the epic alcoholic William Inge—*Splendor in the Grass, Come Back, Little Sheba*—but he kills himself the week before class starts, and the class is taught by Bob Peters, a poet.

In that class, I wrote a one-act, one-man skit about a kid who wanders out of a psych ward into a city park and therapizes himself by standing there engaging anyone who walks by (off-stage, unheard) in solipsistic repartee, Hamlet as stand-up. Professor Peters told me it was the best piece of student writing he'd read at Irvine and entered the play in another derby, which I won, and this time the prize is $1,000. So now I'm up $1,500 by doodling in my dorm room, and I figure I'm on my way to the moon, no stops!

CATHERINE GAMMON: My father was a newspaper reporter and an editor, and although my mother didn't write poetry or fiction, she had a facility with language and a deep, well-educated intelligence and acute editorial skills. She had been a dancer and had an intimate appreciation of various arts, including literature. There was a sense of beauty that I think I got from her.

From the very beginning of writing for school, my parents were always giving me editorial input. My mother usually respected the boundaries of what a parent should enter into, but my father didn't. He was a self-educated man, and I think he had once had literary aspirations, but he didn't show that to me. I saw him as pushy and domineering. I was his only child at home—he had grown-up sons from an earlier marriage—and I felt him putting a lot of expectation on me. He gave me a great deal, but there was a point, and I think it was probably around the ninth grade when I stopped accepting the input. The act of rebellion was to write something and turn it in without getting any input from my parents first. And it was liberating to see how this small writing assignment that I had done on my own was appreciated by the teacher and the other students in the class. When I showed it to my parents after the fact, immediately my mother, as she would, interpreted it in a way that made her think she had to worry about me because she disagreed with what she thought I was saying, which was not what I was saying at all. I think she had a blind spot in her understanding when it came to me. She so much wanted me to be happy; she couldn't see me the way I was.

So there was this continued sense of being misread and misunderstood or interfered with, and I did an ordinary teenage thing—I began to make a secret life that my parents couldn't get at. That's normal teenage behavior except usually teenagers do it through dating, smoking, and drinking, but I was pursuing this secret imaginary life of writing. I even made my handwriting messy so my father couldn't read over my shoulder. I felt I was protecting the truth of my life, a place where I could be completely unfettered and true. I wasn't conscious of this activity as a spiritual practice then, what I would now understand spiritual practice to be, but I think it was my first effort to awaken or create a space for a spiritual life.

SANDRA CISNEROS: I was the artist in the family, but I wasn't the only one. My mother drew and sang. And my brother Keeks and I could draw. All seven of us kids were exposed to the arts thanks to my mother—public concerts in the park, visits each weekend to the museums, stuff that was free since there were so many of us. My father would bring home butcher-block paper from work, and we'd draw murals. Keeks and I would direct the projects. When I got older, though, I started, in private, writing poetry.

I liked to write, but I didn't know you could be a writer; I knew there were writers, but I hadn't a clue how they got that way . . . I never knew anyone who was actually a writer. I was a young Mexican American with no models in my life. I was inventing myself.

I was a closet writer throughout my childhood; no one knew. I wasn't rooted out from under the bed until high school. There was a moment when my teacher discovered I could read and perform well and write. I only became public about it in high school, then went underground in college because I was taking all the required courses. I never made any public declarations of being a writer, though. I never said I wanted to be one, even though I thought about it. My mom wanted me to learn to type and get a job as a secretary, something to keep my hands clean, she said, and so I took typing classes so I'd have something to fall back on. I'm really fast. Not accurate, but fast. I remember once recently when I was in the business center of the American Academy in Rome, and I was typing and someone there said, "Wow, you type really fast," and I said, "Yeah, I make my living doing this."

> I was a closet writer throughout my childhood; no one knew. I wasn't rooted out from under the bed until high school.

DENNIS MATHIS: I was a good artist as a kid and even into college, where I double-majored in studio art and English lit. An art professor visiting from New York City took slides of my paintings to Leo Castelli, who offered to give me a show if I had a bunch more paintings, but I was too lazy to contemplate that. In other words, I was dithering between art and writing as my dream career.

I didn't really settle on writing until I reread a John LeCarre novel I'd read when I was about thirteen. There was a scene where two trench-coated spies on an ominous mission on a rainy night knock on a door, and a little girl answers. Something about that event, the uninventable randomness of the little girl at that moment, made me realize that nothing else could conjure the kind of startled, elusive emotions that this fictional event triggered in me. From that moment, writing was to me the most important thing a person could do.

MARVIN BELL: The most interesting students at college were in the arts. I knew they knew something I didn't. Most were in the design department of the College of Ceramics at Alfred University: painters, print makers, graphic designers, potters. A few wrote poetry or fiction. Gradually, I came to know some of the more creative students. I had played cornet with all sorts of groups for years, but that didn't do it. Rather, it was watching the more creative of the students at Alfred. They had work to do that mattered to them and was exciting and exploratory, and so they didn't worry about what people thought of them. That was new to me. In the '50s, it seemed as if that was all anyone thought of: what others thought of them.

Pursuing any art throws one in with outsiders. Keeping at it *makes* one an outsider.

I always liked odd ducks. I got an amateur radio license as a high schooler and rode my bike to the homes of hams to learn about radio. The hams were always odd ducks. In college, I tended to sit around with people the party boys didn't care for.

I wrote for the campus newspaper and eventually edited it. I took up creative photography—before it was taught in schools. I photographed for some time. The creative photographers of that time were definitely odd ducks. I did a short film for a graduate class that, I later heard, some Polish Film Academy people liked. It wasn't *An Andalusian Dog*, but it was weird, even startling. And there were the Beats. A small-town boy from the '50s, with a father who had come from Ukraine, I was naturally attracted to the idea that the rough-hewn and weird could be artists, and that art was a field for outsiders. The artists had better parties, too, and the more exciting lives.

> Pursuing any art throws one in with outsiders. Keeping at it *makes* one an outsider.

After college, while living briefly in Syracuse, briefly in Rochester, then in Chicago, and finally in Iowa City, I edited and published a magazine of visual and literary materials, *Statements*, which lasted five years and put me in touch with poets through the mail. Literary magazines, the majority of them then referred to as "little magazines," came and went according to their editors' enthusiasm and finances, so it was easy to feel avant-garde. Then I took a class in Chicago with the poet John Logan and later joined a group of poets known as "the poetry seminar," who met with Logan. Then came the Writers' Workshop. Dumb luck, personal taste in people, a string of random chaotic events, as well as teachers and classmate poets—all those things counted. But the bigger thing is that I always liked finding ideas that fit. Poetry, for me, is another way of thinking. I like thinking. That takes words. But I like thinking beyond the words. That takes poetry. You should understand that, for most poets, as Cummings put it, "feeling is first." But there is common feeling and there is uncommon feeling. Moreover, the brain is inexorably tied to what we think of as emotion. In any case, I never felt it necessary to use poetry to prove to people that I feel deeply.

ALLAN GURGANUS: I also started out to be an artist, and I'd been praised for my drawing accurately and my skill at cross-hatching. But I think in art school, I saw where I stood on a scale of one to ten in terms of how original my talent was. Had I stayed a painter, I would have surely found something beautiful to do; I loved Bonnard and I loved the Dutch masters, and Manet and Velasquez, but I think my work would have been figurative. It would have been in a way more conservative than I think the best new work should be.

I had been to the Pennsylvania Academy of Fine Arts, and in one class, I recall, we drew from classical statuary. Here were these life-sized naked plaster gods and goddesses, the same ones sketched since Thomas Eakins taught in these very rooms. Especially on rainy days, it was very satisfying to have a faint blue-gray piece of paper and black chalk and white chalk. Your assigned task was to replicate the statue as you saw it. You studied it front and back and truly got to love it. The sculptures that I drew, well-known pieces, had a profound sedative effect on me. So, onboard the aircraft carrier, confronting written monuments, I adapted the art school method of copying Old Masters. Everyone who matters, no matter how many degrees they hold, is self-taught. I was a Writers' Workshop of one. This is how I studied literature: I'd write a page of Dickens, a final chapter and happy marriage from Jane Austen, the tone of a Virginia Woolf dinner party. I'd try to write a middle chapter out of a Henry James novel and then an opening chapter from Balzac. In this simple way, I taught myself how to write. But I later saw that all my training had been in nineteenth century prose. If one sentence opened with subject-

verb, the next sentence would begin with a dependent clause and the subject
and verb withheld till the end. It was very antique and very endearing and
insular and weepy. I was very earnest, militantly earnest, the way we self-
taught are. And I learned these precepts as I learned to replicate in charcoal
the back of Zeus.

This happened on an overcrowded warship, and the writing became a sort
of armor for me. I was writing in longhand because I was just then learning
to type in Radioman School. But longhand proved very comforting, and I
filled journal after journal. I still have them, but I can barely stand to read
what I wrote. I was just nineteen years old, an adolescent, but an adolescent
who's been sent to war against his will, completely isolated, living among
four thousand guys floating on a hunk of metal in the South China Sea.
Some of what I wrote sounds like a thirteen-year-old prepubescent girl sunk
in misery and self-pity, full of big words from vocabulary class, but there is
some gorgeous writing, too. Some of it emerged as piled-up Joycean stuff I
wouldn't do now, couldn't do now! Guys on the ship would see me writing.
"Hey, perfessor, whatcha doin', writin' to your old lady?"

"Just a few notes," I'd answer, cautiously.

"Hey, man, am *I* in it?"

GERI LIPSCHULTZ: I was supposed to be the musician in the family. I
played the piano. I had some talent, but no discipline. Somehow I needed the
language of words, in addition to my banging on the piano. I loved music,
but words drew me in for the kill, so to speak. I just wrote and wrote and in
fact used writing as a distraction from a terrible heartache.

It was my high school boyfriend—he broke my heart, but I don't blame
him. By the time I was ready to marry him (we'd been dating for seven years),
he'd had it with me. I mean, he'd *had* it. I'd gone from a preppy type—my
boyfriend was a football captain and I was the cheerleading captain—to a
hippie, but he didn't change. I tried everything to draw him back to me,
but nothing doing. And then my parents moved to Florida and dragged the
whole family down there, and, oh, it was awful. I refused to go. I moved to
New York City and wrote and wrote and wrote.

I started writing a novel to keep from killing myself. I know, it's a bit
melodramatic, but true. I saw a shrink and everything. It was messy. The
only reason I really couldn't kill myself was because someone in my extended
family actually did it—the reality is too awful, so I had to find a way out, and
writing was it. The words helped me heal myself. I know it sounds trite, but
there was something about being able to name the thing that I felt, something
about the power of transforming the thought into a word, getting it outside
of myself, legitimizing it, making it humorous, for God's sake.

Then I got into Iowa, and I was still heartbroken.

SHERRY KRAMER: In college, I thought I was a poet. This was at Wellesley. They say it is the most beautiful college campus in America, with its own lovely big lake and a massive topiary garden, and an arboretum with every plant, flower, and shrub mentioned in Wordsworth's poetry . . . that kind of place. I loved it. I took a year off from all that relentless pastoral beauty and went to Wesleyan to study poetry with Richard Wilbur, and he gave me a B and I cried for five days. It was the end of the world! But I didn't stop writing poetry. Nothing can stop that, I guess. A couple years ago, I realized that a bad poet is still a poet. So, that's what I am.

The next semester, I was taking a class in Zen, and the professor had us do a Zen project, so I wrote six haikus for my final report. The Zen professor gave me an A+ and wrote that she was stunned; she couldn't figure out how someone who sat so badly could write haiku like that. But my A+ in enlightenment couldn't even begin to take the sting out of that B in poetry I'd gotten—it was an early lesson in learning what Paul Valéry said: profundity is a hundred times easier than precision. I had no poetic rigor. Then I wrote a short story called "Toes," which was, as you can imagine, about toes, and submitted it for the senior English creative writing award, the Jacquiline Award for Excellence in English, and I won it and thought, wow, that's easy. So I stopped being a full-time bad poet and jumped ship for fiction.

> I cried for five days. It was the end of the world! But I didn't stop writing poetry. Nothing can stop that, I guess.

I still have a fatal attraction to Zen poetry. I tend to write haiku while I walk in the forests in Vermont, a pleasant habit. You can work on one haiku for an entire fall, I find; you don't need to use paper or anything, just roll it around over and over in your mind.

DOUG BORSOM: I started writing in the summer after I turned twelve. I thought books were powerful, so writing conferred power. Also, I loved books so much I thought their genesis should be similarly enjoyable. Well, I was only twelve. And I was a private child; it was appealing to me that writing was such an intensely private act.

My mother was fine with the idea of me writing. My father was less enthusiastic but okay with it. They both thought I should have some skills to land a day job until checks from the publishers and the *New Yorker* started pouring in.

DOUG UNGER: At the University of Chicago, I started out on a pre-med track, which I soon abandoned. One of the reasons was all the social upheaval back then. Also, I had a connection at UPI and started taking freelance photos for them. I was attracted to journalism, being out in the world and writing about things that were happening. I also took Richard Stern's (IWW, '52–'54) class in creative writing. I thought I had a story to tell. I'd been out with my brother, in New York, on the streets, that kind of stuff, and most of the kids I was with at Chicago had nothing like that in their backgrounds, so I started a novel about it, a really naive, weak first novel, but it was good enough that Stern took an interest in me. So I changed my major to general studies in the humanities and used my novel as my bachelor's thesis. Stern sent it to Random House, and Jason Epstein bought an option on it—$1,500! My first novel called *Fevertree*.

I hung around Chicago for another six months, doing journalism and taking photos. I covered the '72 presidential conventions as a cub photographer and photo messenger for UPI. That winter, Epstein gave me a call and said, "Why don't you come to New York and I'll get you set up?" So I went to New York. Epstein set me up ghostwriting the filler copy for one of Yvonne Young Tarr's cookbooks. So I ended up living in a garret, hanging out with the St. Mark's poetry project people, doing ghostwriting for one of Epstein's moneymakers, hack writing, starving half the time.

> Well, Jason finally rejected the novel, and we had a big confrontation in his office. I shouted at him. He shouted back and threw a two-pound copy of *Antaeus* at me. . . .

Meanwhile, I went through multiple rewrites of the novel, which Epstein never thought were good enough. Well, Jason finally rejected the novel, and we had a big confrontation in his office. I shouted at him. He shouted back and threw a two-pound copy of *Antaeus* at me; it knocked the breath out of me. He told me, "Go out and make a name for yourself." So I phoned Stern and asked, "What do I do?" Stern said he'd try to get me into Iowa. I hadn't applied yet, and it was theoretically too late to apply, but Stern phoned people there and told them to take a look at me. So I sent the novel, and two weeks later, I got a letter back saying I was in and with an assistantship working at the *Iowa Review*. Only then did I complete the actual application, the rest of it pulled off through insider connections to Iowa by Richard Stern, who I thank to this day for believing so strongly in my writing.

I left New York, went to my father's ranch in South Dakota to help him get his hay in and earn some money, then took a bus into Iowa City where I bought a panel truck, which promptly broke down. At first, I lived in the truck. It was hot, flies buzzing around everywhere, my manual typewriter set up on the front seat. That's how I started at Iowa—living in that clunker truck parked out on the street.

BILL MCCOY: After taking an undergraduate lit class from Thomas Rogers, I took a writing class from him, and that turned out to be another terrific experience. In the meantime I read his first novel, *The Pursuit of Happiness*, and loved it, and then I read his second and I loved that one, too, and so I wanted to be him, basically.

The stuff I was doing was a pretty apparent pastiche of Tom's work, but I wasn't doing it to suck up, but only because it was the way I felt at the time. He recognized what was going on, but he still felt the work was good in its own right; and then at one point, toward the end of my senior year, he asked me what I was going to do when I graduated, and I said I don't know, I hadn't thought about it. I said maybe I'd stay at Penn State and go to grad school. He said if I was going to grad school, I should go to the Iowa Writers' Workshop, and if I decided to apply, he'd write a recommendation. I did some investigating and thought Iowa sounded interesting, and so I took him up on his offer. And so Tom pretty much got me in. I didn't know at the time that he was also going there to teach in the fall.

T. C. BOYLE: After college, I was teaching to avoid the draft. I'd never had any teaching experience, didn't know anything about it. I went into it cold and did a lot of drugs, and being a crazy young hippie, I began to write stories and send them out. And a great miracle happened. Robley Wilson at *The North American Review* accepted my story "The O.D. and Hepatitis Railroad or Bust," and on the strength of that, I decided I could get into the Iowa Writers' Workshop, the only one I'd ever heard of. All my heroes had been there or taught there or had something to do with the place. I sent in a story called "Drowning" along with "O.D." and I got in. I don't know who read it, or how it all worked.

ERIC OLSEN: I think my interest in writing as a craft began in the late '60s, when I was involved in the antiwar movement. I had started out at Cal as a pre-med major, like just about every other freshman there, but the required class in organic chemistry—"orgo" as it was called not so fondly—disabused me of any notions I had about a career in medicine. And I was rather less than dedicated as a student in any case. Above all, I hated the required English courses. Even orgo was preferable to English 1-A, a survey all freshmen were required to take. It was taught by a distracted grad student, and you could tell he would have much preferred to be working on his dissertation, something about seventeenth-century English poetry or an equally relevant topic, I'm sure. Meanwhile, the war in Vietnam was raging. Young men just like me were getting shipped over there to be killed, and I got involved in the antiwar movement—it was Berkeley, how could I not? I had a student deferment and decided that it was chickenshit and that Cal was a big "nothing factory," a term that had some currency at the time. I decided I needed to throw myself full-time into the antiwar effort and dropped out and declared that I intended to go *mano a mano* with the Selective Service System. To say I needed some adult supervision back then is putting it mildly.

Soon, I was writing one-page antiwar screeds—"down with the man" and "hell no we won't go" and all that sort of stuff—that we ran off on a mimeograph machine in an office full of young Maoists and anarchists and Students for a Democratic Society and even a few Black Panthers who'd show up to skulk around now and then before they went off to sell drugs to white kids from good neighborhoods. It was all great fun; everyone writing screeds and running around stapling them to telephone poles and bulletin boards and raising clenched fists and shouting down with the man. What I wrote made absolutely no difference at all, but I remember how fun it was, a bit of a rush, really, to think that something I wrote might have an impact. And of course, thinking back, I realize that the "rush" was really from the fumes of the solvents used in the mimeograph ink; the room we worked in wasn't well ventilated.

> It was all great fun; everyone writing screeds and running around stapling them to telephone poles and bulletin boards and raising clenched fists and shouting down with the man.

As much as I enjoyed writing, or at least the fumes, I didn't actually try writing anything like fiction until I was a senior in college at the University of Iowa, of all places. This was after the war had ended and I had returned to school, dropped out again, returned. I was not a particularly dedicated student. It took me eight years of on-again, off-again college just to get to my senior year. And during all those years after the war, as much as I had hated my first English classes at Cal, I found myself drifting into classes again and again that had something to do with literature—what's considered *literature*, not just science fiction. All the time I had in the back of my mind, I think, fond memories of those heady days writing screeds in a room full of solvent fumes.

JANE SMILEY: I didn't start writing until college, my senior year. I started a novel about the Dostoyevskian lives of Yale students. There was even a tragic automobile accident in it. I was married then, and my husband and I were living with two or three other Yale grads in Upstate New York, living directionless lives because there were no jobs and no one had a plan (one guy in our house was writing and selling stories to romance magazines under a pseudonym, and another one was doing a lot of drugs and earning his living playing poker in the Catskills). I truly enjoyed writing the novel. I thought I could do this the rest of my life. When I typed it out, it was at least 210, 220 pages, a real novel, at least in terms of length. My senior advisor liked it, thought it was impressive for what it was, but he didn't offer to help me get it published, which turned out to be a good thing, and anyway, the very idea of publishing it was almost incomprehensible to me. Finishing it was enough. I got my degree and I knew what I wanted. I wanted to write.

JOY HARJO: I'll never forget the day that I walked into the drawing studio at the University of New Mexico to tell my drawing teacher, Nick Abdullah, that I was withdrawing from my studio art major to major in creative writing. It was a crossroads point. I was ending a relationship and I was still in love. The art studios were my refuge, the place on campus where I utterly belonged. I felt I had to make a choice. I could not both write and paint. I needed to focus. I was going back on a promise I made to myself when I was four years old.

The path to poetry was an unseen path, for me. At four, I made the decision to be "an artist." To me that meant that two-dimensional art, especially painting. I also loved music, but because my mother's path to music seemed stymied by circumstances, I didn't find an obvious handhold there. My grandmother Naomi Harjo Foster and aunt Lois Harjo Ball, however, were artists. They actively made art. I had seen their paintings, and we had some of my grandmother's original art and art objects she had collected on her travels. I aspired to be like them. They were educated, worldly, and came from tribal leadership. This choice wasn't so conscious at four years old. I didn't always analyze my choices. It was something I "knew."

> Poetry basically took me captive, took pity on me. Poetry basically told me: You don't know how to listen, you need to learn how to speak, you need to learn grace, and you're coming with me.

When I was four, I had no models for writers of poetry. It was not an option for me. My mother wrote song lyrics. They were not the poetry of Longfellow, Tennyson, or Frost. There were no indigenous writers known to me, no one like my family. It wasn't until I was well on the path of poetry that I learned that Alexander Posey, a minor American poet from my tribe, was my cousin.

Once I met and heard my first native poet, Simon Ortiz, and was drawn into the circle of writers and poets in the Southwest at that time—Leslie

Silko, Leo Romero, Ricardo Sanchez, and Gene Frumkin—and began to hear the live poetry of Anne Waldman, John Logan, and others brought in by the university to read, I decided to take my first poetry workshop at UNM with David Johnson. He led us to trust our instinctual mythic sense, and his enthusiasm for poetry was planted in us. Poetry basically took me captive, took pity on me. Poetry basically told me: You don't know how to listen, you need to learn how to speak, you need to learn grace, and you're coming with me. That's what happened. Poetry became my master. I immersed myself in poetry.

If I had not been a single mother with two children, I most probably would not have felt I needed to make a choice. Poetry was and is a demanding master. But raising children alone meant that my hours for study and practice were limited. It was only when my children were grown that I took up music. And I'm beginning to work with images again.

CATHERINE GAMMON: My father took some drawings that I did in school during the seventh grade to somebody he knew who had some kind of authority that he respected, and this man told him, "Oh, this is a talented child who should be encouraged." So he started having me go to Saturday art classes, which I basically enjoyed except that sometimes it felt . . . you know how when you're a kid if you're doing things that are different from other kids, it feels weird if you're caught at it? Anyway, after a few years there was a new teacher who had us do a still-life setup that felt like advertising art to me, and I was out of there. I had a very strong sense—and probably still have—that there's art and then there's commerce.

After that I started having private art lessons. That was very good, but I didn't know what to do on my own; I always had a teacher or my father looking at what I did. So writing was not only secret and private, it was completely my own, and when I wrote, I knew what to do next; I knew what the next problem was, what the next question was, what the next move was. If I didn't know, I didn't need someone to tell me, I just needed to explore deeper into what I had already done. Much later, I learned how to learn from feedback about the writing—from Lenny Michaels as a teacher at Iowa, from writing peers at Iowa and Provincetown. But I didn't need feedback to get going, or to find the next move, even if it was a wrong move. In art, I needed instruction; I didn't have any intuition at play. If you set me a problem, I could do a really interesting response, but to just start on my own didn't work.

When I was about to enter college, this difference wasn't so clear yet, and I still had art and writing both in mind. Then an art teacher at UCLA told me I had to choose; I couldn't do both at once. I don't know whether it was the right advice, but I thought he knew. I ended up going to Pomona College on scholarship and eventually majored in philosophy. My father wanted me to major in math or physics. So I took those classes my first year. I also took an art class, but I jumped the intro class, based on what I'd already done; I should have taken the intro class with my peers instead of going to a class that was too advanced for me in terms of its independence. It was also too advanced socially. These kids were smoking and drinking, and I hadn't started that yet. I couldn't connect with them and I didn't connect to the teacher and the teacher didn't connect to me and that was it for art for me at college.

During lectures, though, I was drawing, all over my notes. In freshman English, when we were studying *The Iliad*, I saw myself drawing the opening shot for a movie of it, and I started to think about film as a medium that combined what I thought were my abilities in image and language. Throughout the year, this idea got stronger, and I investigated how I could take a leave from Pomona and go to UCLA to study film. I gathered all the information and the necessary applications and had a conversation with the dean, but then I had to talk it over with my parents. When they said no way, out of the question— in part because they had never heard anything about this great interest that I had been so carefully nurturing, so how could it be anything but a frivolous impulse?—I just gave in and stayed at Pomona. I was still planning to go into film, and during my senior year, I was accepted to UCLA's graduate film program. Thankfully, life had another idea because I got pregnant and married and moved to Berkeley. Now my daughter's the filmmaker, and I'm a new grandma.

ALLAN GURGANUS: When *Portnoy's Complaint* came out, I was still in the Navy, still on the Yorktown. I paid retail for the hardback; it had gotten so much attention. It's not like I lived in isolation, living in a compartment with sixty other men, but I was dying for conversation when this guy named Douglas wandered on board and he had tortoise-shell glasses and blond hair that he parted on one side and he looked like a prep-school boy. It appeared he might have read something, and that was all I really cared about. I just wanted someone to talk with about books.

So one day I sat reading *Portnoy* in front of him, ostentatiously, you know, trying to provoke a conversation, and finally he said, "Oh, I see you're reading that new best seller." And I brightened up so, "That's right." And he said he had heard it was highly sexual and I agreed. And I felt so excited to finally be talking about *books*. And we went on and I ventured a few starter observations, and I heard him say, "Phillip Roth, is he Jewish?"

I remember thinking, *My God, this is where I'll be stuck for the rest of my life; even the people willing to talk about a book are absolutely brain-dead.* That short conversation left me almost suicidal. It seemed that literature, like sexuality, was a coded language that only I spoke. My goal was finding a conversational partner. And I think literature provided just that in a way . . . it felt like there was someone on the other side of the net. Literature itself could create community even for a man alone. I hollered. Its echo rolled back to me. And when at last I found someone who could really talk books for hours on end, it literally felt like being saved.

Well, the other guys on the ship considered my writing useful in some ways. I was by now called "professor." This acknowledged that I could help other men write letters home. No surprise, many of my shipmates were high school dropouts, functionally illiterate. Joining the armed forces proved the one job they could get. They were at least big and healthy and could take orders. So I wound up writing romantic, then erotic letters to women all over the world, wives and girlfriends and recently patronized Filipina prostitutes. It was very powerful training, far better than sketching plaster goddesses. I've written a novella about it. Jointly writing love letters for my favorites soon made for a powerful kind of erotic tie. Frequently I'd be writing sexy letters dictated by some man I really, really wanted sexually, someone I didn't dare approach. He would have shown me photographs of the girl back home. Often she was better educated than this beautiful lummox of a sailor. I would soon begin putting words into his mouth and his writing—very Cyrano de Bergerac. Together we'd be writing these wildly familiar letters that became increasingly erotically specific. I was interviewing the boy at hand about what he and his Roxanne had and hadn't done, and how that could apply to our next missive. It became a profound connection, and sometimes these guys—I would not call any of them potential rocket scientists—would simply bring their letters from their wives or girlfriends and hand them to me to open. We'd go off someplace quiet, "our" spot, and with full theatrical energy, I'd read Roxanne's letter back to him. It was very hot, this oblique foreplay stretching ten thousand nautical miles! And her letter might say, "Dear Rocky, I never knew you were such a poet. You made me so wet last night when I read, I soaked through my flannel nightgown and the sheet and mattress pad as you told me how you wanted my . . ."

It became this very heady kind of experience. And in a strange way, I look back and see that, though I could not find one literate man out of the

> **Literature itself could create community even for a man alone. I hollered. Its echo rolled back to me.**

four thousand I lived with, one form of literacy did join me to my literary dependents. I still feel a kinship with those pen-pal girls I turned on, at several removes. So in a way, my finding my own power in prose came about not only from imitations of nineteenth-century fiction, but while being the anonymous ventriloquist for these beautiful Billy Budds sleeping all around me.

When I got out of the Navy, I went to Sarah Lawrence to work with Grace Paley. I did have the wit then to see that she was, along with Cheever and Stanley Elkin, one of the great writers of the period. She was phenomenal as both a person and an artist. Though her life had been devoted to ending the Vietnam War, she never blamed me for having been shanghaied by it. There was nobody working then who had more purity and originality than Grace. And I showed Grace one of my ship-written nineteenth-century stories, and she said, "Oh, honey, it's excellent, as writing. But people aren't doing that kind of thing anymore. These are great sentences, as sentences, but hey, it's now more about . . ." I've always wished I had written down her exact words. She told me that these days the subject was how people get along, and what they have to do to stay alive, and what they sacrifice to survive, what they choose to save. By then I was what? Twenty-two? And I just said, "Oh, okay." And I trotted back to my room and spent two days writing what I think is the first real thing I wrote, "One Family, Repeatedly," which was later published in a now-defunct magazine called *Quest*. It was a series of vignettes about a—to say it was a dysfunctional family is redundant, of course—but about one tribe's betrayals and compromises and mythologies and romances. But before I hit the twentieth century, somewhat more than seventy years into it, I'm eternally grateful for my three and a half years of shipboard nineteenth-century rhetorical preparation.

Chapter 3

WE WERE SO DAMN POLITE

It started with that polite letter each of us got from the Workshop: "Dear Mr. Olsen" or "Dear Mr. Schaeffer" or "Dear Ms. Cisneros, we are delighted to tell you that you have been accepted into the Program in Creative Writing. . . ."

And we'd write back, politely: "Dear Ms. Landres" or "Dear Mr. Leggett" or "Dear Ms. Brothers, I plan to attend Iowa in the fall. I am very happy to have been accepted into the Program in Creative Writing and look forward to participating in the Fiction Workshop."

Or, "Dear Ms. Landres, I want to thank you for the time you've spent answering my questions this winter. Applying to a school can be confusing, but you and the people who handled my application have made things very clear. I look forward to meeting you."

Or, "Dear Ms. Brothers, As I am self-supporting (or rather, my wife pretty much supports us), I am interested in the job outlook in Iowa City."

Or, "Dear Ms. Brothers, Yes, I'm interested in the possible ditto room job!"

There followed an acknowledgment that the Workshop had also received our applications for financial aid. And then would come "a word about housing in Iowa City," which was, we were gently informed, "rather expensive and often hard to find," with the advice that we come out in June or July to scout around for a place to live—which few of us did. The letter then concluded with a warm, "Don't hesitate to write if you have any questions about the Workshop or if we can help in any way with your plans."

And then later we'd get another oh-so-polite letter—"Dear Mr. Olsen"— with the bad news about financial aid for that first year: "At this point in our financial aid considerations, the available positions have been filled. Because of the shortage of funds we are unable to offer you a definite award for next year."

Nothing here about maybe we didn't get any aid because we weren't deemed worthy. Of course, those of us who didn't get any aid for the first year assumed that was precisely the reason, but it was a comfort to think that the folks who ran the Workshop were so solicitous of our delicate writerly sensibilities as to offer an alternative and nicely nonjudgmental explanation: no money. We bought it, too, and so we'd write back politely: "At any rate, national depression or no, I intend to enroll at Iowa, and I thank the faculty for providing me the opportunity to study with them."

It wasn't until classes began that we met our fellow students and discovered that, budget cuts notwithstanding, some of them *did* get aid their first year. Perhaps some of us felt a brief *frisson*—a word some of our fellow workshoppers would use with what would seem a rather excessive frequency—of resentment, but it would pass quickly because what did we have to beef about, really? Hadn't we gotten into the Workshop? We were young. We were talented. We were on our way!

"We were the cream of the baby-boom crop," recalls Sherry Kramer, Fiction, Iowa class of '77 and playwriting class of '78. "We were sophisticated, well-traveled, rich compared to the generations before us. We even knew how to swim! No one knew how to swim before World War II. Now we all knew how to swim! Better yet, Nixon had resigned, the war was over, and we sure weren't going to make those mistakes again. And remember, this was before AIDS set in and put an end to all the fun. The worst thing that could happen back then was herpes. . . ."

And we sure were polite.

Such politesse would seem to be a bit at odds with the archetype of the writer we'd all grown up with, the freethinking, hard-drinking, none-too-clean, hirsute free spirit who had dispensed with bourgeois conventions—*who thumbed his nose at bourgeois conventions*—and lived in Paris and starved for art with a capital *A*.

> "We were sophisticated, well-traveled, rich compared to the generations before us. We even knew how to swim! No one knew how to swim before World War II. Now we all knew how to swim!"

"More and more of our students were coming from so-called 'good schools,' where they'd already benefited from writing classes taught by real writers," notes Marvin Bell, who graduated from the Workshop in 1963, served in the Army, then in 1965 returned to Iowa to teach until his retirement in 2005.

Bell had us nailed. It was true. We were arguably among the first generation of writers to enter the writing game through a process of polite application and polite acceptance, not by storming the barricades with our inexorable brilliance and bad manners. Most of us had taken at least one writing course as an undergrad, and it's no surprise that many of the teachers of these courses were Iowa Workshop grads. Iowa had been the first writing program in the country to churn out creative writing teachers with graduate-level degrees and even a bit of teaching experience. These men (and early on fewer women) then set up creative writing programs of their own, either modeled on Iowa or in opposition to it. By the mid-'70s, there already existed a well-established scouting system that channeled the best and brightest prospects—or so we liked to think—back toward Iowa City, or sometimes advised them to avoid the Iowa "factory" at all costs, which of course just made the place all the more enticing.

"They were sophisticated," Bell says of this new generation. "They were influenced by theories, they talked jargon, they adopted increasingly specialized aesthetics. They began to focus on their careers as we had not, and to publish while students, which had been rare in my day. They'd become professionals instead of the funky, counterculture community of my student days. We had no room after a while for the rough-hewn student from nowheresville. Our loss, I felt."

"One afternoon I was walking down a hall chatting with Vance Bourjaily," recalls Joe Haldeman, who entered the Workshop in 1973. "He'd just read my novel, *War Year*. He asked whether any of the other students were combat veterans, and I said not that I knew of. 'What are they going to write their first novels about?' he asked. 'Graduate school?'"

There was already then, as now, a sniff or two of condescension among the many critics of creative writing programs—and of Iowa in particular, big fat target that it is—that they produced "workshop writing," "domesticated writing." The poet Allen Tate, who ran the creative writing program at Princeton, complained that the "academically certified" creative writer goes out to teach others who are not writers, who teach others who are not writers. And one hears the same sort of thing year after year. The underlying assumption, of course, was that writers are born, not taught, and therefore MFA certification is worthless, a scam, a sort of academic Ponzi scheme.[3] In his thorough and now and then impenetrable discussion of writing programs, *The Program Era*, Mark McGurl writes, "Having conceived a desire to become that mythical thing, a writer, a young person proceeds as a matter of course to request *application materials*."[4] (The emphases are McGurl's.) The problem for McGurl is the apparent discord between the romantic ideal of a writer inspired, driven, unyielding, in touch with the Muses, railing against bourgeois convention, yet applying for admission to a writing program.

But apply we did, and how! We filled out that form, we licked that envelope, and we stuck on that stamp and sent in that application. And if we had any twinges of uneasiness about whether or not this was the right thing for a young wannabe writer to do, we quickly stuffed it. What were we supposed to do, after all? The romantic ideal of the writer suffering for art was being complicated by the threat of opportunity.

～

JAYNE ANNE PHILLIPS: I don't remember exactly how I first heard of Iowa. I was told by my only "creative writing" teacher at West Virginia University to think about applying to a writing program at Bowling Green in Ohio. But the idea seemed insane at the time. All I wanted to do was get out of school and travel.

I went to California and then to Boulder with Sasha, my dog, she of the golden eye and pink nose. Sasha went everywhere with me for twelve years, including (later) to Iowa, where she swam in the river while I was in class. When I came out of the English-Philosophy Building, she'd be right there waiting for me.

I went to Boulder initially because the poet Bill Matthews, whom I'd met at WVU, told me they were starting an MFA program at the University of Colorado. The program didn't materialize. I stayed in Boulder, waitressing, writing between jobs. I remember running into Gregory Corso after a reading at the Naropa Institute. The New York poets and Beat writers who founded Naropa considered Iowa boring and academic. Corso must have heard I was applying to Iowa because he grabbed my nose and twisted his fist. "Don't go to Iowa," he said, "you'll come out of there with your nose on all wrong."

I was sick with mono and went home for a winter to regroup, working as an aide in a rural elementary school while I applied to several schools, including the University of Montana in Missoula because of Richard Hugo. Montana rejected me. I wrote my first story, "El Paso," in order to apply to Iowa in both fiction and poetry. I was accepted in fiction and realized within the first months that fiction, for me, was a far more subversive and less limiting form.

JEFFREY ABRAHAMS: Iowa had the reputation. My writing teachers at Miami University in Ohio talked about Iowa all the time and used the Workshop approach in the classroom.

I was so naive. I had no idea how competitive it was to get into Iowa. I just assumed, based on my writing successes as an undergraduate, that I'd be admitted. I didn't even consider applying to any other creative writing programs.

I went too soon after college. At Iowa, there wasn't the warm mutual support I'd enjoyed at Miami. And Iowa was competitive in a way that diminished my passion for writing. The snarkiness that prevailed as the style of Workshop criticism was crushing. I didn't have the confidence necessary to laugh off all the bad behavior and posturing. Plus, there were lots of folks there who'd been out in the real world. They were especially skilled at cultivating relationships with the teachers and working a party. They'd read the right books and could engage in the right patter. There was an intellectual vibrancy among the older and second-year students that was intimidating. What could I possibly add to that? How could I stand out as I had as an undergrad? I should have spent at least a year out of academia; I think I might have taken better advantage of Iowa.

GORDON MENNENGA: Iowa was the only place I considered seriously, though when I was about to graduate from the University of Northern Iowa—I'd been writing plays, stories, and poetry there—I wrote to Richard Hugo in Missoula and said I was thinking of applying to the MFA program. I was a big fan of his. But Richard wrote me back and said don't. "Go to Iowa," he wrote, "I hate the sons of bitches here." So I applied to both poetry and fiction at Iowa and got into both. I thought I could do everything, but then after a couple of poetry workshops with Jorie Graham and Jim Galvin in them, I started concentrating on fiction.

JAYNE ANNE PHILLIPS: I had "studied" poetry at WVU with Winston Fuller, who liked Robert Bly and all the poets in the *Naked Poetry* anthology, all wonderful poets, if from a particular school. I'd published a few poems in little magazines like *New Letters* and *Io*, and my first small-press book, *Sweethearts*, was published by Truck Press the June before I went to Iowa. At the time, I was actually more interested in writing poems. I was accepted in fiction with some aid, and I initially planned to reapply in poetry.

I didn't really know anything or what to expect. At WVU, we turned in poems that were mimeographed in purple copies that we discussed in class, but it was a large class, thirty-five people at desks in rows; there was no seminar table or "workshop." I thought Iowa would be pretty much the same thing. I didn't care. I just wanted to write, rather than waitress. I had no illusions that the degree would help me get a job. It was just a way to keep writing for two more years.

Once at Iowa, though, I found I loved fiction, that the paragraph was so subliminally powerful, innocuous, and packed with dynamite. The reader is always aware of reading a poem on the page, but we read paragraphs without adjusting our expectations or armoring ourselves. We take in the words and point of view directly, into the voice of our own thoughts. We approach poetry and worship the words. We mainline fiction, and then feel the effects.

SANDRA CISNEROS: I also started out to be a poet. I had a poetry teacher at Loyola who'd been a student of Donald Justice at Iowa. He told me I just *had* to study with Donald Justice at Iowa. I thought this guy, my teacher, was interested in me because he thought I was a good writer. I was a good writer, but this guy sort of helped himself, too. We had an affair. I was very, very young, and I thought this is what writers do. You have to live and break rules and dance on tables and have affairs. I didn't know how to be a writer. But I did apply to Iowa for admission into the poetry program because back then I did what I was told.

> We had an affair. I was very, very young, and I thought this is what writers do. You have to live and break rules and dance on tables and have affairs. I didn't know how to be a writer.

ANTHONY BUKOSKI: I started hearing about Iowa in 1968 or so when I was an undergrad at the University of Wisconsin in Superior. Several Workshop alumni—Bob McRoberts, Bob Crotty, and Geoffrey Clark—had one- or two-year teaching appointments at Superior. I heard a little about Iowa from them, though they never encouraged me to apply. Donald Justice was also in Superior for a two-week summer workshop, and I knew, when I applied in 1974, that he was at Iowa. I was planning to go the academic route at first and get a PhD in English, so I applied to South Carolina, Cornell, Virginia, Louisiana State, and a few other places. But I'd been doing a little fiction, and so I also thought I'd try Iowa's creative writing program while I was at it. Somehow, and to this day I don't know how I could have been so lucky, I was admitted to the Workshop. I recall looking at an atlas a few weeks before packing up and heading to Iowa, looking at the wonderfully romantic names we would come to know better: Cedar Rapids, and even the name Iowa City, Iowa, with its alliteration, was equally appealing. A couple of years later, I waited on Donald Justice at Sears in Iowa City, where I worked in the complaint department. I think he came in for something for a bicycle. I guess even poets sometimes have something to complain about.

JOY HARJO: I believe I first heard about Iowa from Lawson Inada, my poet bass player jazz friend and mentor, as a possible place for graduate school. Simon Ortiz attended the International Writing Program, but

I don't recall him encouraging me to apply to graduate school there. The word among serious creative writing students was it was the place to apply. However, just as many tried to dissuade me. I struggled with the decision as I felt no kinship with or draw to the middle of the country, to Iowa, and place made a difference to me. I also knew that I had been raised up in an approach oppositional to what was considered the Iowa writing workshop poetry style. I came from a tradition in which words absolutely mattered and could change the weather or walk into the past or future, literally.

I had published a chapbook, *The Last Song*, from Puerto del Sol Press in Las Cruces, New Mexico. I had already developed an audience for my poetry in New Mexico and in ethnic literary circles. I knew that chances were, I most likely wouldn't be accepted. If I was, I'd decided I would go despite my dread of moving to Iowa with two small children for two years. I wanted the best creative writing program.

What I didn't want was most clear. I didn't want to be a waitress, which would have been the job available to me with a BA in creative writing. I wanted to write for two years and to get the mentorship I needed to explore poetry and literature. I wanted a writing community.

I applied to four schools: University of Montana to study with Richard Hugo, New Mexico State University, the University of Arizona, and the University of Iowa. I was offered support from scholarships to teaching assistantships at every school I applied for except Iowa. They offered me nothing.

I had no idea how the application process worked, though I was told later that some of the female students were picked on the basis of their photographs. Given the predatory atmosphere in the workshop between many of the professors and female students, that didn't surprise me. I often wondered if I'd been picked on the basis of a photograph and not my poetry, especially given my voice and style of poetry.

Books by the Bed

JOY HARJO: At bedside? Yeats, *Collected Works*; Robert Moss, *The Dreamer's Book of the Dead*; *Bhagavad-Gita*; Pam Uschuk, *Crazy Love*; *Cards of Your Destiny*, Robert Lee Camp; *Dictionary of the Muscogee Creek Language*; *The Virgin of Flames*, Chris Abani, and more.

DOUG BORSOM: I grew up in Hinsdale. After high school, I went to Case Western Reserve University in Cleveland to study physics. After a couple of years, I decided I liked literature better. I transferred to Knox College in Galesburg, Illinois. Once there, I discovered the college offered classes in creative writing. The professor, Robin Metz, was a sensitive and encouraging teacher. It was from him that I learned of the existence of the Iowa Writers'

Workshop. Metz had gone there in the mid-'60s. It had never occurred to me that such things existed.

My first big rejection as a writer was when the Workshop turned me down for admission in the fall of 1972. With the unreasoning confidence of youth, I decided to wait and reapply in 1973. I spent the interim writing and working second shift on the line in a refrigerator plant that covered twenty acres of former Illinois prairie. If you need a building that covers twenty acres, the plant is empty and available for lease—has been for years.

CATHERINE GAMMON: After a few years of marriage, I left my husband, and at that time I started writing again, this time a novel about the countercultural life I was living. Like the childhood one, it started with finding a voice for a character, but it took me a year of effort before that came, a way to write imaginatively about my present world without just writing reality with the names changed. I was still living in Berkeley with my daughter, in a semicommunal house, being a hippie pretty much. I remember once someone telling me I wasn't really a hippie because I read too much—I was really a beatnik, he said. That was before I sold all my books so the "family" could go dancing, which also meant drinking. Someone else said about the whole group of us that we weren't really hippies because we drank too much. We were certainly not the sort of hippies who didn't drink.

By way of that same hippie family, my daughter and I ended up living in Yellow Springs, Ohio, a few years later. I had two part-time jobs there, one as secretary at Antioch and one as a bartender, and I finished a draft of this novel, written all in longhand. On weekends I typed up that first draft on the office typewriter, revising as I went, and all the time I was drinking and partying and falling in and out of love. So my life was kind of schizo. I was reaching the point where I needed to get out of the whole counterculture thing, and I had the idea graduate school would be a way to do that. I had always been interested in the History of Consciousness Program at UC Santa Cruz, so I thought I'd apply there. At about the same time, I read an article by Gail Godwin in one of those slick counterculture magazines—*In These Times*, I think—about Iowa. She talked about how the Workshop had all these returning Vietnam vets and divorced women and people in their thirties with families and children. I was reading it, and this kind of little shock went through me that said, *This is what's going to happen.* I was twenty-nine, I had a daughter, I'd been married. The world I read about in that article sounded possible for me.

Just the month before, over the Christmas holiday, I had borrowed the typewriter from the office where I worked and retyped the revised manuscript. That's the only reason my boss at the time knew of my interest in writing and handed me that magazine to read about the Workshop.

So I applied. I also applied to Santa Cruz and thought I would see what would happen. I assumed I'd get into Santa Cruz, frankly, not Iowa. But Santa Cruz said no, and Iowa said yes; and after that, I thought, *This is what the universe wants me to do.*

DON WALLACE: I graduated from Santa Cruz with my degree in writing slash English lit, won the short story prize and got a novel excerpt published in *Quarry.* The latter got me an invite to my first fancy literary dinner, and a couple of weeks later, the hostess, an older woman and saloniste manque, knocked on my creaky Victorian's door and made me her lover. Only later did someone cue me in that her long-term partner, who had published a story in the *New Yorker* while still an undergrad, had just left her to go to Iowa. (No, dear reader, she didn't suffer that fate with me—she dumped me, in what I suspect was a fit of aesthetic revulsion over discovering that my latest stories were not about her.)

Iowa and grad school weren't on my radar yet. I hadn't noticed where my writing pals were going. I took a year off to write, to garden, and to sing rock and roll in my Victorian living room. I had a construction job I commuted to for a couple of months, building a mobile home park in a Nipomo bean field. When that was done, and I'd flunked my test as replacement lover for the *New Yorker* guy, I took a job as the AAA emergency night dispatcher for Santa Cruz County. Talking to truck drivers, EMTs, and cops on the radio, directing them to wrecks and assorted automotive disasters, I became a voice on the airwaves with my own handle, "Sergeant Serious," and worked a 20-button phone, all alone, for nine months. I'd sleep on a cot between calls and then, during the day, go to my desk and work on a short story about a writer who foresees the inevitability of getting dumped by a woman whose last lover got published in the *New Yorker.*

Books by the Bed

DENNIS MATHIS: Lots of cheap paperbacks by foreign authors, Penguin translations, etc. Kawabata, Mishima, Gunter Grass, Reinaldo Arenas . . . Anything that wasn't about wealthy people in New England worrying about divorce (which is ironic, considering how I was attracted to Updike's stuff, but I squinted my eyes and pretended Updike was writing about downstate Illinois instead of Massachusetts). I once asked my Bradley mentor for a reading list, and he reluctantly gave me a perverse list that included *Tristram Shandy*, Robert Musil (*Die Mann Ohne Eigenshaften*—the only German I know), Latin American authors like Borges and Cortezar (*Hopscotch*), and a couple stupid books I was already reading. He said, "You don't have to read these things, just know what the covers look like." Which ironically earned me a record score on the Graduate Record Exam.

DENNIS MATHIS: I grew up in Peoria, got my BA at Bradley University. I was lucky to have a mentor there, George Chambers, a slightly insane poet and experimental fiction writer who'd studied under Robert Lowell in Boston and then taught at Iowa when George Starbuck was director of the Workshop. He encouraged me to get an MFA in creative writing, if that's what I wanted to do, but warned me about Iowa—it's a factory. He had a low opinion of the conventional style that Iowa preached and the East Coast snobbishness, though he came from a Boston Brahmin family himself. As a result, when I applied to graduate school, Iowa was my third choice. I was accepted to CCNY. Anthony Burgess was there, and they published the tabloid-format *Fiction* magazine. I ate it up, but New York City was unrealistic for a kid from Peoria. The University of Illinois at Chicago also accepted me. It had a (supposedly) hip new program in creative writing. And Iowa accepted me and offered me a research assistantship, but I chose a teaching assistantship UIC offered instead—a big mistake. It was a terrible program and I dropped out. After a couple of years of working in factories, I reapplied to Iowa.

The first time I had applied to Iowa (I found out by reading my dossier; someone had discovered you could see your file just by asking, so it was cheap entertainment the first week of class), one of the judges (possibly Tom Boyle) thought I was a "genius" and wrote on the scoring sheet "Offer him a season football ticket and a university car—anything! Just get him!" But Jack Leggett was irritated by my sample, so other readers jumped into the debate and there were four pages of single-spaced arguments before Jack grudgingly gave in, and I was offered the assistantship. I didn't realize that any financial aid offer the first year was big stuff when I turned it down. When I applied a second time to Iowa and was accepted, this time there was no financial aid offer. I went anyway. I had a little savings from working in a film lab. I lived on food stamps at Iowa for a while.

JOE HALDEMAN: I didn't know much about Iowa when I applied, just a magazine article or two. I'd started writing full-time after my first novel, *War*

Year, was accepted. My wife, Gay, and I had a deal: I'd write for two years while she worked, teaching school. If after two years I wasn't making enough for us to live on, we'd reevaluate.

What happened, though, was her school's principal turned out to be literally a madman. She couldn't work there. We'd just come back from Mexico and realized we could live there fairly comfortably on what I made from writing science fiction short stories, let alone novels.

War Year had just come out and got a favorable full-page review in the *New York Times Book Review*. So I sent the book and review to Iowa and outlined my position: I could come to Iowa if they would offer me an assistantship; otherwise, I was headed for Mexico. I didn't apply to any other schools. They accepted me and gave me a "teaching" assistantship—just collect money for three semesters and then teach full-time one semester.

DON WALLACE: Then one day at the Santa Cruz Bookshop, I met a writer friend in the stacks who told me that my other writer friends had all applied to writing programs. Santa Cruz writers were supposed to apply to Missoula, I was told, because Iowa was snotty and East Coast. So I applied to Iowa, figuring all the really hot Santa Cruz writers would get into Missoula and then we'd be locked into doing the same stuff. And—this was key—even though I was in the midst of an intense, love-spawned, near-suicidal depression aggravated by working all night with car crashes and drunks who'd locked themselves out of their cars, I felt like I was ready for a real ass kicking in the prose department.

All my friends got their acceptances and rejections. I heard nothing. In late June a slim letter arrived, and I was in. I stood barefoot on the hot sidewalk of bucolic Santa Cruz and took my first long last look around me: my view of the San Lorenzo River, my forty-square-foot vegetable garden, my exquisitely faded gingerbread Victorian—and that of my brand-new girlfriend, who lived next door. I knew I was leaving a kind of Eden for the colder, harder unknown, but suddenly I couldn't get out fast enough.

> Santa Cruz writers were supposed to apply to Missoula, I was told, because Iowa was snotty and East Coast. So I applied to Iowa . . .

GLENN SCHAEFFER: As I mentioned, I'd taken writing courses from Oakley Hall at Irvine as an undergrad, and Iowa was always in the back of my mind. It looked to me at the time like an MFA from Iowa could get you somewhere, but then I thought, typically, that I'd go one better than an MFA. I decided to get a PhD in criticism. I thought (and I thought I'd invented this idea) I'd get a tenured position in an English department teaching literature and write novels on the weekends. I mean, how hard could it be?

I got accepted to the PhD program at Brown and UC Irvine. I couldn't afford Brown, so I stayed at Irvine, a big mistake. Something happened between the time I graduated in the spring of 1974 and the very next fall when I started grad school. The world of humane letters had been transformed by deconstruction! Everything that was solid had somehow melted into air, right there on the former Irvine Ranch. When I graduated with my BA, I was a confirmed New Critic. We did close readings of primary texts, mainly poems, and searched for that hat trick of metaphor, irony, and paradox. You discover paradox in a poem, then you know you've really *read* it. But when I started grad school, there was no room left for Cleanth Brooks. We weren't reading primary texts any longer. We didn't bother with books because the stuff we were reading was so *new*. Jacques Derrida was ginning it up in his bedroom in Paris, and then it would land in the hands of J. Hillis Miller at Yale several days later, and someone who knew someone would mimeograph it and send it all the way to Irvine, the outer ring in the emergent Theory Empire, and it would be distributed to the likes of us as if we were feral Irish monks meant to be the last keepers of the Word, to be killed by Norse, or retrograde New Critics, if caught. So we had to read this smudged incunabula that reeked of mimeograph solvents, and it seldom made any sense. The critical theorists put themselves on pedestals: we were doing philosophical work as important as anything that's been done since the Enlightenment. Novels be damned.

MARVIN BELL: I don't think the explosion of literary theory, which was at heart sociopolitical, pulled the rug out from under writers. Serious writers already knew that language is impure and temporal, subjective and relative. That's baby knowledge. Mostly the theories licensed literary critics to think of themselves as more important and, at long last, hip. Professors who couldn't boogie could now talk endlessly about the dance. And some poets wrote poetry to interest them.

I remember a colleague from the English department saying that he needed a subject for his new book but was having trouble finding a poet he could explain to readers. Within that remark is the unbridgeable distance between poetry and criticism.

Disjunction is the way the world comes at us now: ten things on a single Internet page, nonlinear movie time, a scroll and a sidebar on the cable news, the constant yapping by "commentators" during sports broadcasts, ads on our shirts. It's a jump-cut life.

In fact, our reception of the world is kaleidoscopic, a phenomenon that led me to create the poetic form known as the "dead man poems." "Dead Man poems" come at you sentence by sentence. The sentences are elastic, and the linkages come at you from many angles. So, for example, line fifteen may connect, not directly to line fourteen, but to line three or to lines twelve and twenty. Mere disjunction and such techniques as interruptions in syntax are simpleminded and lead to little. A kaleidoscope is not disjunctive. It assembles, disassembles, reassembles anew.

As for a definition of "beauty," who needs one? Here's a poem by e. e. cummings:

> mr youse needn't be so spry
> concernin questions arty
>
> each has his tastes but as for i
> i likes a certain party
>
> gimme the he-man's solid bliss
> for youse ideas I'll match youse
> a pretty girl who naked is
> is worth a million statues

GLENN SCHAEFFER: I hated it. This mutant version hadn't stood the test of time. What's with deconstruction? Was it literary knowledge or not? It wasn't a method, a discipline, or an aesthetic. I soon came to a conclusion: *Get me out of here!* I went to see Oakley Hall, who'd tried to warn me off the PhD. "I knew you couldn't put up with it," he told me.

What I could put up with was a story I'd written as an undergrad that Oakley especially liked, "Kicks," about a teenage underwear fetishist. But I needed more output to apply to Iowa, so I spent the entire Christmas break banging out a couple more stories and sent them with "Kicks" to Iowa and—still, to this day, this is the most important thing that has happened to me in terms of validation—I got in. I told Debbie, my first wife, "I'm going to be a wealthy, famous novelist!"

～

Such was Iowa's reputation at the time that it was, perhaps, a little too easy—at least for the excessively optimistic or fanciful among us—to assume a direct cause-and-effect link between an MFA from Iowa and literary fame and fortune. Almost from its inception as the first creative writing program in the nation—but maybe not first in the world, since the

Gorky Institute in Moscow may have Iowa beat by a couple years, and the poets of Kiribati have everyone beat by centuries—Iowa began to churn out one major literary figure after another. This was where Flannery O'Connor started *Wise Blood* and Philip Roth wrote *Letting Go*, and where Wallace Stegner, Paul Engle, Robert Bly, Marvin Bell, Oakley Hall, Bill Dickey, John Gardner, John Irving, and many, many others got their start. This was where John Cheever, Kurt Vonnegut, Robert Penn Warren, Robert Lowell, John Berryman, Stanley Elkin, and just about everyone else who was anyone important in the literary world came to teach, or at least to give a reading and then to party. And maybe, we all figured, some of whatever it was about the place might rub off on us.

Much has been written about the origins and development of the Iowa Writers' Workshop. There's a nice summary of this history on the Workshop's own website. Anyone interested in learning more should certainly turn to Stephen Wilbers's *The Iowa Writers' Workshop* for a comprehensive history of the program through the mid-'70s.

Verse making, or versification as it was also called, was first offered at Iowa in the spring semester of 1897. This wasn't such a terribly radical notion at the time; several universities around the nation were offering similar courses. This was back when it was widely believed in academia that students might benefit from the literature of one's own culture, at least, and to actually read a bit of it now and then. Students of literature were encouraged to read primary texts, too, and not merely criticisms of criticisms of those texts. Students back then were even encouraged to take seriously and examine what authors had to say about their own work! And even more incredibly, young gentlemen—and a century ago, it was invariably young gentlemen—were invited to dabble in a bit of poesy now and then themselves because in those quaint old times, some academics believed that one could learn something useful about poetry or fiction by trying to write it. Of course, it was also assumed back in that era that no young gentleman in his right mind would persist in versification beyond what little was expected in a class or two.

Then in 1922, the graduate college at Iowa announced that creative work—including poetry or fiction or "artistic production" or performance including music and art—would be accepted for advanced degrees. No one dared try this until 1925, though, and that was in the music department.

In 1929, one Norman Foerster (pronounced "firster"), an English professor at the University of North Carolina, proposed in an English department meeting that a dissertation for the MA degree could be a group of poems or other creative writing.[5] Before anyone at North Carolina could decide whether this was a good idea or not, Foerster accepted an offer from the University of Iowa to head up their School of Letters, where they were already doing just what he proposed.

As D. G. Myers tells it in his insightful examination of the workshop movement in general, *The Elephants Teach*, Foerster felt that literary scholars had "fallen out of touch with literary creation; as a result, poets (and poets' points of view) had been excluded from academic study."[6] In promoting creative writing in the academy, Foerster hoped to advance literary study of all types. He believed that creative writing was criticism's natural ally. It was a beautiful dream: Foerster the hopeless romantic.

With Foerster heading the School of Letters, and with his urging, and thanks to the already receptive environment at the University of Iowa, the university began development of a structured program that granted graduate degrees for written creative work, that had a permanent faculty, that brought in visiting writers, that sponsored readings, and that, in short, became what we know today as the Program in Creative Writing, a.k.a. the Iowa Writers' Workshop.

The first MA in English given to a student who produced a creative thesis was awarded in 1931. The next year, five such "creative" MAs were awarded, including one to Wallace Stegner and one to Paul Engle, whose collection of poems, *Worn Earth*, earned him the Yale Younger Poets Prize. And then in 1936, the Workshop as a formal entity was started under the direction of Wilbur Schramm, who stayed on until 1941, when Paul Engle took over as director.

All of which raises the question: Why Iowa? As the poet Robert Bly (Iowa Writers' Workshop, 1954–56) reportedly said, "It is just one of the weirdest things that in the United States our first writers' workshop would be in the middle of Iowa."

> In promoting creative writing in the academy, then, Foerster hoped to advance literary study of all types. He believed that creative writing was criticism's natural ally. It was a beautiful dream: Foerster the hopeless romantic.

But was it so weird? Couldn't we just as well ask *why not?* Despite the romantic notion of the writer working alone in his or her garret, writers seem to crave community, exchanging words with frank but forgiving colleagues who will warn you that you're about to embarrass yourself if you show that piece of crap to anyone else. Writers crave readers, too, because otherwise, what's the point? A writers' workshop is, first of all, an instant community.

It may seem a little odd that such an institution didn't first take root in a place like New York City, the center of all things literary, or so we'd been taught. But then maybe that's exactly why Manhattan didn't spawn the first program-based writers' workshop. What did New York need with classrooms for writers? It was already full of writers' communities of various sorts: coffee houses, salons, readings, and parties where a writer could get instant feedback, get drunk, and (if all went well) get laid. And New York was just a relatively short hop across the Pond to Paris, where you could do more of the same *and* with a change of scenery and lots of very good food and wine. Indeed, the vigor of the development of the Iowa Writers' Workshop derived in part from its outsider status, from *not* being anywhere *near* New York City. As Wilbers points out, regionalism "was the significant literary influence during the Workshop's emergence at the University of Iowa."[7] By "regionalism," Wilbers means the early twentieth-century literary movement that encouraged writers to look to their own locales for material and to cast off the dominating cultural influence of the east.

At the same time that regionalism took hold, a number of writers' clubs began to form in Iowa City to promote "literary culture,"[8] which included such activities as public speaking, debating, and declaiming—does anyone still *declaim*?—as well as writing. This was at a time when literacy was generally considered a social good, and the clubs

> Indeed, the vigor of the development of the Iowa Writers' Workshop derived in part from its outsider status, from *not* being anywhere *near* New York City.

attracted not only members of the community but students looking for a critical audience for their own work. Many of the university faculty were also involved in these clubs, and so there developed a "conversation" between the university and the community, with the clubs serving as a sort of early laboratory out of which the shape of the writers' workshop as we know it today emerged: roundtable discussions about a writer's work, visiting writers, readings, and upstart literary magazines.

The fact that Iowa had some of the richest soil on the planet didn't hurt either. Iowa was covered with prosperous family farms owned by folks who, maybe just a generation or two or three removed from Europe, held to the core values of the Enlightenment. They valued hard work and thrift, also education, and though they may not have had the time to read themselves, what with all the milking and planting and fence-mending to be done, by God their children would go to college and make even better lives for themselves! And so they paid the taxes that funded the development of one of the finest public universities in the land, the University of Iowa. They were happy to pay those taxes, too, because back then values like hard work and honesty and community and literacy mattered. Back then, dumb wasn't cool like it later became; back then, dumb was, well . . . *dumb*.

While the Workshop itself thrived, Foerster's vision for a sort of academic utopia where critics and creatives played nicely together withered. The title of D. G. Myers's book refers to a remark made by Harvard linguist Roman Jakobson when Vladimir Nabokov was proposed for a chair in literature there. "What's next?" Jakobson asked. "Shall we appoint elephants to teach zoology?"

Jakobson's question highlights the two issues that have enlivened debate about writers and writers' workshops from the beginning. One is the persistent, nagging, tiresome, unanswered, and perhaps unanswerable question whether or not writing can be taught (about which more appears in chapter four). Jakobson seems to have been of the school that holds that it can't be, at least not by writers. The other issue concerns the suspicion, if not outright disdain, that many academics have for creative writers in their midst. Most working writers, at least back when Nabokov was being considered for a gig at Harvard, hadn't been through the system of apprenticeship and acculturation into academe. They didn't have PhDs. Many of the best of them hadn't even been to college! And they didn't read theory. They weren't members of the club, in other words. And later, even those writers who showed up with MFA degrees in creative writing were viewed with suspicion because, as academics all seem to agree, *those* aren't *real* degrees.

The divide also was one of opposing worldviews at a deeper level. Myers summarizes it nicely as two distinct ways of accounting for a literary text. One is that the text is determined by large impersonal forces such as history, economics, the unconscious, gender, race, and so on, which it takes an academic to explain. The other is that the text is created by an individual human mind. "And the difference between these two is that the writer relies upon flexibility of judgment—the capacity for remaining detached, for shifting the attention, for imagining the possibilities—while the scholar commands a systematic method."[9]

By the mid-'70s, the tensions were becoming even more aggravated by battle cries from the deconstructionists and critical theorists. In 1968, the French writer Roland Barthes announced that the author was dead. And then the near-incomprehensible manifestos of Jacques Derrida, Michel Foucault, and the former Nazi Paul de Man began peeling hot off primordial fax machines in English departments on this side of the Atlantic in funky steaming rolls of thermal fax paper to be mimeographed and passed from hand to hand in a frenzy of being part of *what's happening now*. If the author is a dead concept, then the author's words have no fixed meaning! If text has no fixed meaning, then no method of analysis can have any claim to authority! If no method of analysis can claim authority, then criticism is an act of imagination! Suddenly the *real* action was in criticism![10] The critics were the *true* creatives: they hadn't been taken in by the outmoded ideal of meaning! *Writers were has-beens!*

It's no coincidence that the number of writers' workshops around the nation began to grow rapidly at about this same time that the old verities were crumbling. Writing workshops became the last bastion for folks who thought that literature had value and who liked to read it. And even sometimes to write it.

At the same time, the publishing business was undergoing a profound shift. We had assumed when we applied to the Workshop that we were throwing our lot in with a cultural institution as much as a business, one in which an editor cultivated a raw talent over a period of years, from one modest seller to the next until critical acclaim and a degree of economic security materialized. We'd grown up on 1950s movie scenes of genteel mentoring sessions over three-martini lunches at the Algonquin, or publishing executives savoring manuscripts over more cocktails in the club car on the five-twenty back to Westchester. But that lifestyle, if it ever really existed, had drowned itself in gin or been shoved aside by the snowplow of progress by the time we showed up in Iowa. Elderly editors who claimed to genuinely care about literature were already being replaced by marketing specialists practicing a new blockbuster-or-die business model as multinationals run by quants snapped up one prestigious little house after another and demanded a twenty percent return on investment.

Magazines that once had published short stories and paid reasonably well for them were cutting fiction inches or folding entirely. *The Saturday Evening Post* and *Colliers*, which had sustained the likes of Ernest Hemingway, Willa Cather, J. D. Salinger, and Kurt Vonnegut, were long gone by the time we came along. The per-word fees being paid for the few short stories still being published hadn't gone up in decades, while the cost of living was rising steadily. The days when a writer could hunker down in a cold-water flat in Greenwich Village and survive by knocking out the occasional story for this or that weekly magazine while he worked on his Great American Novel were wistful memories.

Workshops like Iowa's thus became a refuge for young, developing writers in the absence of more support from anywhere else. And, of course, once writers started teaching other writers and got paid to do it, the movement went viral. From the official founding of the Iowa Writers' Workshop in 1936 until the mid-'70s when we were applying to the Iowa program, there were only about a dozen programs offering the MFA degree in creative writing, many of them started and staffed by Iowa alumni. In all, including programs offering undergraduate degrees and PhDs, there were seventy-nine. At the time of this writing, there are 153 MFA programs and nearly 800 programs in total with more on the way.

The growing popularity of writing programs seemed only to aggravate those age-old tensions between academics and "creatives." Despite Foerster's grand vision of a world in which the critics and writers worked together for the good of literature, by the time we arrived in Iowa City in the mid-'70s, the divide was wider than ever. Indeed, aftershocks of a seismic shift in 1966, the "Battle Between the Hut and the Hill," that ended Paul Engle's twenty-five-year tenure as director, still rattled the Workshop. "Hut" referred to the Workshop's makeshift classrooms in Quonset huts by the Iowa River; "Hill" referred to the Department of English's offices on the hill above, at the center of the campus. The blowup had nothing to do with critical theory, though; it was just good old-fashioned academic infighting. Some things never change.

Paul Engle took over when Wilbur Schramm stepped down in 1941. Engle was dynamic, ambitious, and above all, a famously effective fund-raiser. Under his guidance, the Workshop grew in size and prestige. By 1965, though, Engle was ready, he said, to cut back on his duties as director so he could concentrate on his own writing projects. While Engle was out of town working on a film project (*Poetry: The World's Voice*), John Gerber, the head of the department of English, selected Robert Williams, a recent addition to the Workshop faculty, to serve as a de facto acting director.

All hell broke loose. R. V. Cassill, another member of the Workshop faculty, accused Gerber of trying to "annex" the Workshop to the English department—the *horror!*—and bring it under his control.[11] As a result of the brouhaha, Cassill resigned and accepted an offer at Brown, where he eventually founded the Associated Writing Programs, now the Association of Writers and Writing Programs (AWP). Williams shrewdly left Iowa and took a job teaching creative writing in California. Paul Engle resigned as director of the Workshop and founded a new entity within the University of Iowa, the International Writing Program.

Eugene Garber, a novelist and professor in the department of English, filled in for a year as director after Engle stepped down as director. Then in 1966, George Starbuck became the new director.

Like Engle, Starbuck was a poet—and the last poet to direct the Workshop, to date. Like Engle, he'd won a Yale Younger Poets prize. And like Engle, he had a knack for bringing in divergent voices to teach, including Ted Berrigan, Anselm Hollo, Richard Yates, and Robert Coover. "It's probably true that George was interested in breaking the stranglehold of well-made fiction and academic metaphysical poets," Garber recalls. "I don't know if his leaving was entirely his own choice, or if he threw up his hands because of too much resistance."

Starbuck was interested in breaking other strangleholds as well. While Engle, through force of will and a knack for working within the system—or simply working it—had carved out a place for writers to be writers *within* academia, a model that's been replicated again and again, Starbuck had a knack for going *mano a mano* with "the system." With the war in Vietnam raging and the antiwar movement at its most heated, the University of Iowa, in hiring Starbuck, brought into the house one of the nation's most articulate critics of the military/industrial complex. Starbuck even managed to get himself arrested with a number of students during an antiwar demonstration on campus, when students besieged the student union.

Starbuck left Iowa in 1969 to head the creative writing program at Boston University and John (Jack) Leggett came on board as acting director the next year and director in 1971. A former editor at Houghton Mifflin and Harper & Row, Leggett wrote both fiction and nonfiction. His best-known work is probably *Ross and Tom: Two American Tragedies*, a superb dual biography of two young writers who achieved early fame and success and then descended into Fitzgeraldian crack-ups.

By never quite being a part of academica, by basking in unresolved tensions, the folks in a creative writing program can enjoy their view of themselves as genuine outsiders . . .

"Starbuck kept it a place of individuality," recalls Marvin Bell. "Leggett oversaw the increased institutionalization that was probably inevitable. We went from a community of outsiders, tolerated by a bemused university, to an approved program, made more famous by its public successes in fiction."

Still, there were enough lingering tensions and resentments among the academics and the "creatives" to keep everyone happy. Mark McGurl, in *The Program Era*, makes the point that academic creative writing programs are examples of "the institutionalization of anti-institutionality."[12] By never quite being a part of academia, by basking in unresolved tensions, the folks in a creative writing program can enjoy their view of themselves as genuine outsiders, changing the status quo, but of course from within the comfy and nurturing confines of the academy, "inner outsiders." And their presence on campus helped to reinforce the academy's view of itself as a place that welcomes original thinkers of all sorts, however disruptive and annoying some of them might be.

But most of us were more or less oblivious to all of this when we arrived in Iowa City; we just wanted to be writers.

JANE SMILEY: I went to Vassar, where I wrote the novel I mentioned previously, the tragic Dostoyevskian thing about Yale students. When I graduated, my husband and I went to Europe for a year while I rewrote the novel. Then we both applied for graduate school, to the University of Virginia and to the University of Iowa. I used parts of my novel to apply to the writing programs at both. My husband got into both schools, in medieval studies. I was rejected. My husband was from Wyoming, so we chose Iowa, since it was on Route 80 and we could drive to Wyoming in a day and a half.

He started at Iowa in the fall '72, in medieval history. In the winter, I enrolled in an Old Norse class and then applied to the PhD program in the English department. This would have been the spring semester '73. Once I was in the PhD program, I took a class in writing from Stuart Dybek, who was a Teaching/Writing Fellow. I got into the Workshop in 1974, and for those years, I taught beginning literature courses for the English department, took workshops, and also took a variety of courses in medieval languages (Old Norse, but also Old English, Old Irish, Gothic, Middle English, and Old High German). After I got my MFA, I went to Iceland on a Fulbright, both to learn Modern Icelandic and to think up a dissertation topic for Old Norse.

But I soon realized my future was in writing, not in Medieval languages, though I loved what we read in Old Norse—the *Sagas*, but also the *Eddas*. It was pretty evident there were no jobs for a specialist in Old Norse. By the '70s, Old Norse had been almost fashionable for a century—the style of study was philological, but outside of that literary world, there were all kinds of new linguistic theories that were more fashionable than philology, and it wasn't clear how I'd go forward if Noam Chomsky was the model. When I got back from Iceland, my advisor (who was more interested in hiking than teaching) told me that medievalists were hired one per generation, so if you came along at the wrong time, you were screwed. It was clear to me my future was not in Old Norse. But my studies weren't wasted; I got *The Greenlanders* out of it—it was in Iceland that I heard about the medieval Norse colony on the southern tip of Greenland.

One day, I told my advisor I wasn't looking forward to writing my dissertation, and he said good, because he wasn't looking forward to reading it. So I asked Jack Leggett if I could turn in a creative dissertation made up of the stories I had been writing in Iceland, and he said yes.

My husband and I had split up early on—his true love was Marxism. He didn't think grad school was political enough, so he went to Montana to organize the workers, and I stayed in Iowa City and got involved with a guy who tended bar in the Mill. A typical Iowa City story: come with one person, leave with another.

T. C. BOYLE: I didn't know a thing about Iowa when I applied, but I'd been reading John Gardner and Robert Coover and Ray Carver, and they all had a connection with Iowa, and that's what got me interested. In my mind, it was the only program. I got in on the basis of a couple stories, including "Drowning," which was accepted for publication. I got $25 for it, which was wonderful . . . You know, getting $25 for the product of your own brain? You could buy a lot of beer in Iowa City back then for that. I remember Vance telling us once how he was filling out some kind of form after publishing his first novel, and it asked for his profession, and he wrote "novelist." He said it felt good. "Oh, you're a novelist?" someone asked. "Fiction or nonfiction?"

ROBIN GREEN: One year I entered a magazine short story contest. I think it was *Mademoiselle* or something. I didn't win, and I think it was then that I gave up the idea of writing. Talk about how to handle rejection! But still, after college I gravitated to jobs that had something to do with writing: a brief stint in the production offices at Houghton Mifflin, then I was Stan Lee's secretary at Marvel Comics. But it was the late '60s, and pretty soon I was in Northern California making jewelry.

Then an old college friend got me an interview with the publisher of Straight Arrow Books, which was part of *Rolling Stone Magazine*. This was 1970, I think. The publisher already had a secretary, but he said it looked from what was on my résumé that I could write, so he got me set up with Jann Wenner at *Rolling Stone*, and Wenner assigned me to write about Marvel Comics. I wrote ten thousand words. I was paid a nickel per word, which went up to a dime on my next piece. The story about Marvel Comics was my first piece for *Rolling Stone*, but it was held until the summer, so my first published story was about Dennis Hopper, who was then crazier than shit and very drugged out and living in New Mexico near Taos in Mabel Dodge Luhan and D. H. Lawrence's old place. It was a crazy scene and a good article.

So that's how I got into journalism. I never intended it, though I did apply my skills as a short story writer to the articles, telling them like stories. These were the days of the "New Journalism," so I was in step.

After four or five years of it, I got tired of magazine writing. It was 1975, and everyone around me was into drugs and I felt lost—I'd long before ended a relationship with the guy I went to California with, and I think I wanted to start my life over again and start it from the last place I'd started it, the last place I'd felt solid, and that was college and writing fiction.

I'd met some people who had been at Iowa—poets and trust-funders— and it sounded like heaven. All you had to do was read and write. I applied

> I thought school was irrelevant and boring. So first thing, I got a job at Iowa Book and Supply. That was irrelevant and boring, too, but I liked getting a paycheck....

and got John Hawkes to write a recommendation. I heard that Allan Gurganus didn't want to admit me; he thought my writing was thin. He was right, but I got in anyway.

ERIC OLSEN: I got into the Workshop thanks to Allan. Maybe he thought my stuff was thick. But I ended up in Iowa City in the first place because of Robert Williams, who'd graduated from the Workshop back in the '60s. Williams was teaching creative writing at a school in California where my wife was getting a master's in ed psych. Cheryl took a couple writing classes from Williams as a break from running rats through mazes. After writing a few stories, she decided writing beat the hell out of running rodents, so she asked Williams what she should do.

"Go to Iowa," he told her.

"Iowa," she told me that evening.

"Where the hell's Iowa?" I asked.

So Cheryl applied to the Workshop and got in, and we ended up in Iowa City one steamy August day in 1973. We didn't have a car, so we borrowed my grandfather's Chevy El Camino, a sweet, sweet pickup built on an auto chassis. It had a souped-up 327 V-8, four on the floor, and a Hurst shifter that let you downshift into first gear no matter how fast you were going. I remember how my grandfather squirmed an unlit, very soggy chewed cigar from one corner of his mouth to the other as he handed me the keys to his beloved El Camino and told me not to do anything stupid. Of course, he assumed I would as soon as we were around the corner and out of sight, but we managed to get to Iowa City with no mishaps, driving straight through to save money, stopping only for gas and burgers along the way. We had no idea what we were getting into.

At that point, I still hadn't managed to get a BA and had no great desire to return to school to get one. I thought school was irrelevant and boring. So first thing, I got a job at Iowa Book and Supply. That was irrelevant and boring, too, but I liked getting a paycheck and being around books, if only to straighten the displays after the students came in and messed them up. But then I was in an accident and needed surgery on my back. I didn't have health insurance, so I enrolled at the University of Iowa because students got health coverage.

By then I'd accumulated enough college credits from eight years of on-again, off-again attendance to enter Iowa as a senior. Thus I ended up back in school and, better yet, a school with what was, arguably, the nation's leading creative writing program. And I got surgery from a leading orthopedic surgeon in one of the nation's top orthopedic surgical units.

Meanwhile, my wife was in the Workshop, and I noticed that writers had pretty fun parties. I was doing a lot of physical therapy after the surgery and feeling very, very sorry for myself; I was thinking I could use a good party. Allan Gurganus happened to be a Teaching/Writing Fellow at the time, a "TWF" (pronounced "twiff"). The TWFs were second-year Workshop students—the stars—and taught undergraduate fiction or poetry. I took Allan's fiction writing class my last semester as an undergrad at Iowa. What I wrote is an embarrassment, but he gave me some encouragement, so I applied to the Workshop. I was rejected with considerable enthusiasm by a couple of Allan's fellow TWFs. "Many disconnected incidents, irrelevant allusions, referential statements which break the narrative flow and are distracting," wrote one. The other wrote: "This fiction seems a compendium of fact and artifact designed to bewilder and impress via complexity." I didn't realize it at the time, but apparently I was a postmodernist.

> **Meanwhile, my wife was in the Workshop, and I noticed that writers had pretty fun parties.**

Allan then suggested I take John Irving's graduate fiction class that summer (they didn't seem to care who they let in for the summer classes) and try again, perhaps this time with fewer referential statements and less breaking of narrative flow. I did, and John liked what I did and more or less shepherded my new application through the process.

SHERRY KRAMER: I didn't know a thing about Iowa. Not a thing. One of my teachers at Wellesley told me to apply, one of those professors who change your life. She was wonderful, so of course she didn't get tenure. I applied to Iowa right out of school. I sent in the three-page story about toes, mentioned previously. John Irving apparently liked it, so I got in—at least, I think it was his fault. One time a couple of us went in to the office and asked to see our files, and as I recall, his was the most enthusiastic voice on my behalf. I was the youngest person in the workshop at the time. Now I think there are a lot more people who go straight out of college, but not so much back then.

MINDY PENNYBACKER: I went to college on a studio art scholarship for women, but as a feminist and rebel, I found that the all-male painting and drawing staff was too sexist. (In retrospect, they simply weren't verbal.) I took a fiction class from David R. MacDonald, who was gruff but gentle, and who, having been born in Nova Scotia and having studied with the great regionalist Wallace Stegner, encouraged me to explore the relatively untapped literary landscape of Hawaii, where I came from. I switched to English Lit, and luckily the scholarship followed me.

I applied to Iowa because I adored Flannery O'Connor, and because Columbia never ever responded to my application, and because my mother, who, ahem, got pregnant with me while attending the University of Iowa as an undergrad, took a class at the Workshop from Paul Engle. Her fellow students included Donald Justice, with whom she and my dad played poker and smoked and drank, and all this, of course, crossed the umbilical cord.

> I applied to Iowa because I adored Flannery O'Connor, and because Columbia never ever responded to my application, and because my mother, who, ahem, got pregnant with me while attending the University of Iowa as an undergrad took a class at the Workshop from Paul Engle.

ALLAN GURGANUS: My inspiration for Iowa came about this way: I read Robert Giroux's introduction to the collected stories of Flannery O'Connor. It was that great, white book with the peacock on the cover. I found that she'd graduated from Iowa on June 11, 1947, the day I was born. I thought, *There it is, a hard fact ... not just the* week *I was born, but the very* day, *probably the* time *I slid into the world.* So I thought, that's the place for me.

I'd gone to Sarah Lawrence after the Navy and had won a Danforth that would pay for my grad education. I'd applied to Harvard for a straight MA in English, a scholarly degree. The same day, I applied to Iowa in creative writing, mailing off some of my short stories written for Grace Paley at Sarah Lawrence. I really thought of myself as a fiction writer, but I didn't know if anyone else did. I got into Harvard. Then I waited four more painful weeks, and when I heard positively from Iowa, that was the fork in the road. I sometimes wonder what would have happened had I not gotten into Iowa.

I got a look at the comments from one of the first readers, Stuart Dybeck. We weren't supposed to see what the first readers wrote, but I got a peek. He really pulled for me. That meant a lot because I admired his work. My stories were simply talented undergrad stories. I guess I would have admitted the kid who wrote those, but I'm not sure. They were very early and very different from what I would do later. I guess they work, those sentences, the sense of a struggle in their language—the prose at least had energy! Cheever used to say he could hold his hand over a manuscript and tell that central thing. It's all about vitality, need, and the magneto built into every single sentence, he said. It's about getting as many kinds of energy into as many different kinds of sentences as possible; and then to have it cohere as a whole.

ANTHONY BUKOSKI: As for how the application process worked, I don't remember what I knew or didn't know. Nor do I know who read my submissions. This much I do know: I once asked the Workshop secretary, who was very nice, to look at my file and tell me, if she could, what the committee on admissions had reported. She told me what Jack Leggett had written on one of my stories—that it was "eminently publishable." Not for a minute did I take this to be true, as my story submissions weren't very good. I wondered if he'd actually read what I'd submitted. Or maybe he was being snide, or merely going along with the recommendations of the Teaching/Writing Fellows, who, I later learned, read the submissions first. For Leggett to have said this was laughable, considering how awful the stories were.

ERIC OLSEN: Few if any of us had any idea how the selection process worked. I'm not sure how badly we wanted to know, just as it doesn't do to know too much about how the sausage is made. We got in; that's what counted. It was only when I got a TWF myself that I got an inkling of how the process really worked. The TWFs gave the admission manuscripts the first reading. Each manuscript was passed around among three TWFs, at least, or sometimes more if there was a big disagreement on some issue. From there they went to the faculty for the final decisions.

During the "season," hundreds of manuscripts came in. I hear now the Workshop gets eight hundred to one thousand or more each year. They had to be reviewed in a very short time.

So I'd take a stack of admission manuscripts to the Mill and sit at a booth with a pitcher of beer, smoking unfiltered Camels and drinking and reading the manuscripts. Now and then, Tony or Glenn or sometimes both would join me and I'd read them a particularly nice, or nicely awful passage. Sometimes I'd pass them a story to read while some local bluegrass band was playing too loud in the background.

> Few if any of us had any idea how the selection process worked. I'm not sure how badly we wanted to know, just as it doesn't do to know too much about how the sausage is made. We got in; that's what counted.

Maybe it was a little irresponsible, reading the manuscripts in a bar, sharing them with pals, dribbling beer on them, and scattering cigarette ashes all over everything; but it was fun, and I'm not sure the manuscripts got any less attention than they would have if I'd hunkered in my shared office, poring over every word.

DOUG BORSOM: I don't have a clear memory of what I submitted in '73 for admission to Iowa. The title "Perpetual Motion" rings a very distant, muffled bell. The Workshop may have the only copy in existence, which will someday make it invaluable, I'm sure.

The other story I submitted was a first-person narrative about a boy at a prep school who is propositioned by a fellow classmate. The narrator suspects that he attracted this unwanted attention because of his senior art project, which he thinks must have revealed something about him. The narrator then destroys his art project. If I had to guess, it would be this story that got me in. Not because it was good, but because of its subjects. I was unaware of the particulars of the screening process. I don't remember whether at the time I had any notion of what the process was.

It's nice to imagine that my rejection in '72 was due to a couple of loser TWFs, and that the insightful, sensitive, world-famous writing instructors would surely have recognized my genius, if they'd had the chance. Whatever, I had no juice in '72 and probably less in '73. My last semester at Iowa, a nice young woman who did the real secretarial work mentioned that I could look at my file if I wanted. They were all in a file cabinet in her office. Of my '73 submissions, Gail Godwin had commented, "Get him in," or something like that. So I guess I had made it past the TWF round into Final Jeopardy. I wonder what percentage of applicants who make it past the TWFs are admitted.

ERIC OLSEN: Fact was, we wanted to do a good job reading the manuscripts. I was particularly happy to think that what I might say about someone's manuscript might change a young writer's life; a little power's a heady thing if you've never had it before. Of course, the first readers wouldn't be the final word. I'm not sure our opinions mattered in the least, but I liked the idea that the faculty was backing us up and making the final picks. I hated the thought that I'd be the last word on dashing some poor bastard's dreams.

Each manuscript came with a cover sheet with little boxes with different ratings: outstanding, good, acceptable but undistinguished, and not worth accepting. Each reader was supposed to put his initials in whichever box expressed his own view. And below the boxes was space to write some comments. If I was the first reader to get a particular manuscript, I knew that a couple other TWFs and then a few of the faculty would be reading whatever I wrote, so I tried to sound as intelligent and insightful as I could. And if others had read the manuscript before it got to me, then my comments were in part a response to those of the other readers, and to the work itself. It was all great fun.

Most manuscripts were clearly not what we thought of as "workshop material." But a few clearly were, and I remember how exciting it was to come across something truly good. We found ourselves rooting for these young writers because we'd been in their place just a year before. Of course, each of us had our own ideas of what was good. I favored clear, simple prose with mostly complete sentences, *stories*, and nothing too self-consciously fancy. I had particular issues with stories with dead grandparents in them, or that were set in East Coast prep schools, or anything that seemed influenced by French critical theory. I guess I was a little conservative. Plus I was from California. No doubt I gave the occasional thumbs-down to this or that budding young genius whose prose was so brilliant and edgy that I just couldn't see it for what it was. But then I figured the faculty could spot the geniuses; that's what they were getting paid to do, after all.

We were already hearing about how workshops were factories for feckless prose, and writers going the workshop route would drab-down their work to keep from giving anyone something to swing at, but the stuff I saw was all over the place in terms of style and energy and subject matter. And quality. But when you consider how many very, *very* good writers come out of Iowa, you have to figure that the process, as haphazard as it may seem, must work fairly well.

Books by the Bed

GERI LIPSCHULTZ: I have, in Long Island, about seven skyscrapers of books piled around my bed, ranging from Dante to the relatively new book about Oppenheimer. Also *The Portable Oscar Wilde* and a book of Pound's and one by Jasper Fforde. I have Philip Larkin's collected poems, and Jose Saramago's *Blindness,* and this book by Anne Michaels, she's a poet, but this is prose, *Fugitive Pieces,* and an anthology that I taught literature with, opened up to, let's see . . . oh, it's a Donne sonnet, "Batter my heart . . ." and so on. And there's a book of Frost's early poems, opened to the poem about the woodpile.

In Athens, the skyscrapers rise and fall, depending upon a paper I might be working on. The most recent skyscraper is now in pieces, was comprised of books like Salih's *Seasons of Migration to the North* and Abani's *Song for Night* and Ngugi's *Grain of Wheat* and Achebe's *Things Fall Apart,* and soon there will be books of criticism that will replace the books that are on the coffee table in the study (also in skyscraper form). They will rise up to haunt me until I tear the goods from them, dismantle the skyscraper and return them unharmed to their cozy snoozing spots on a library shelf.

GERI LIPSCHULTZ: I had been taking a course in nonfiction at Columbia's School for General Studies when I got the idea that I might go to graduate school. I think it was J. R. Humphreys who told me about Iowa, although he said I'd never get in. I believed him, but I applied anyway, and I remember the day I got my acceptance. I was in the elevator in my building, opening my mail, and I actually jumped. The elevator jumped, too. Luckily, no one else was in it, and when I stepped off into the dull hallway, I opened my apartment door, stepped inside, and screamed.

Later, I got a peek at my folder, with the comments on my admission manuscripts. They ranged from the sublime to the ridiculous. One person wrote, "This girl can type," and someone else wrote something much better, most of which I forget, but ending with this, "I'm taking her name down because I know we will hear from her."

JENNIE FIELDS: In my senior year of college, I went to Greece to study archeology in a study-abroad program, and I was there when Papadopoulos was overthrown and rioting broke out. There was a curfew, but a friend of mine was in the hospital with a broken skull, and they were going to throw him out; they needed space for the injured. I was his only contact, and I had his passport, which he needed in order to maintain his bed in the hospital. I had to crawl through the streets to get the passport to him. Coming back, in front of where I lived, some soldiers in a tank saw me and started yelling, then shot the outline of my shape on the wall with a machine gun. My memory of it is like an action movie. I can only see myself in third person, as though I was lifted out of my own body. This was in November '73.

I planned to go to graduate school in '74. I grew up in a family where education was valued. And I wasn't ready to face the real world. I thought I'd like to teach, to be like the wonderful professors I had at University of Illinois. And I was reading Alison Lurie novels about university faculty members. At the time, it seemed like a great life.

> I knew the Workshop was the best creative writing program in the country. When I was accepted, I burst into tears. I had no choice but to go. . . . There I was: still stuck in the Midwest.

So in order to create a submission to grad writing programs, I went to an English bookstore and bought four books of short stories and force-fed myself on them, trying to think in short form. They were the classics: Capote, Updike, and so on. Then I locked myself in my room for an entire weekend and just read and read and read, and started writing.

My experiences in Greece became the seed for one of the stories I submitted for admission to Iowa. I wrote it while still in Athens, and it became my first published story. I named one of the characters in another story I wrote that weekend after a guy I'd loved in college but had broken up with. Twenty-seven years later we reconnected, and he's now my husband.

Finishing up my time in Greece, I thought, *Where's a cool place to take the GREs?* I chose Paris. When I think of myself back then, I was free as a bird.

I cried when I was accepted at Iowa. I'm from Chicago. I grew up there, went to school there, was desperate to get out of the Midwest. So I applied to Massachusetts, and when I got my acceptance letter, I thought, *At last, I'll escape.* But I also applied to Iowa. I knew the Workshop was the best creative writing program in the country. When I was accepted, I burst into tears. I had no choice but to go. . . . There I was: still stuck in the Midwest.

32 Statements About Writing Poetry

by Marvin Bell

(Work-in-Progress)

1. Every poet is an experimentalist.
2. Learning to write is a simple process: read something, then write something; read something else, then write something else. And show in your writing what you have read.
3. There is no one way to write and no right way to write.
4. The good stuff and the bad stuff are all part of the stuff. No good stuff without bad stuff.
5. Learn the rules, break the rules, make up new rules, break the new rules.
6. You do not learn from work like yours as much as you learn from work unlike yours.
7. Originality is a new amalgam of influences.
8. Try to write poems at least one person in the room will hate.
9. The *I* in the poem is not you but someone who knows a lot about you.
10. Autobiography rots. The life ends, the vision remains.
11. A poem listens to itself as it goes.
12. It's not what one begins with that matters; it's the quality of attention paid to it thereafter.
13. Language is subjective and relative, but it also overlaps; get on with it.
14. Every free-verse writer must reinvent free verse.
15. Prose is prose because of what it includes; poetry is poetry because of what it leaves out.
16. A short poem need not be small.

17. Rhyme and meter, too, can be experimental.

18. Poetry has content but is not strictly about its contents. A poem containing a tree may not be about a tree.

19. You need nothing more to write poems than bits of string and thread and some dust from under the bed.

20. At heart, poetic beauty is tautological: it defines its terms and exhausts them.

21. The penalty for education is self-consciousness. But it is too late for ignorance.

22. What they say "there are no words for . . ."—that's what poetry is for. Poetry uses words to go beyond words.

23. One does not learn by having a teacher do the work.

24. The dictionary is beautiful; for some poets, it's enough.

25. Writing poetry is its own reward and needs no certification. Poetry, like water, seeks its own level.

26. A finished poem is also the draft of a later poem.

27. A poet sees the differences between his or her poems, but a reader sees the similarities.

28. Poetry is a manifestation of more important things. On the one hand, it's poetry! On the other, it's just poetry.

29. Viewed in perspective, Parnassus is a very short mountain.

30. A good workshop continually signals that we are all in this together, teacher too.

31. This Depression Era jingle could be about writing poetry: Use it up / wear it out / make it do / or do without.

32. Art is a way of life, not a career.

PART TWO

COMMUNITY, CRAFT, AND "LEARNING" LITERATURE

Chapter 4

SAY *YES!* TO EVERYTHING

Maybe it's a good thing there was no Internet back when we were applying to the Iowa Writers' Workshop; we were spared the Workshop's buzz-killing disclaimer currently on its website concerning what can or can't be taught or learned there. Would we have been so enthusiastic, so positively gleeful about our bright prospects and what the future held when we got those acceptance letters if we'd read that the folks at the Workshop itself agreed "in part with the popular insistence that writing cannot be taught"?

Well, of course, we'd have been just as pleased with ourselves because we wouldn't have believed a bit of it. We all assumed we'd come out of Iowa better writers one way or another. What writers don't assume they'll get it right eventually if they just keep at it? And besides, we were facing the delicious prospect of two years to do nothing but write—well, we intended to do nothing but write, until we discovered all of Iowa City's swell bars. Afterward, for the rest of our lives, we'd have the right to say, "I was at Iowa," which we were sure would open all sorts of doors at big publishing houses in New York City and then maybe even land us a tenure-track position at some nice little liberal arts college in New England teaching creative writing to a classroom filled with really, really bright liberal arts majors.

But the Workshop's disclaimer does raise some questions: What gets taught at the Workshop, if anything, and how? What gets learned?

That "popular insistence" of course refers to all the carping about workshops that's been going on since the first workshop took shape in Iowa back in 1936. One of the Workshop's very own, Flannery O'Connor (certainly among its most noteworthy grads) famously pronounced, "The ability to create life with words is essentially a gift. If you have it in the first place you can develop it; if you don't have it, you might as well forget it." Nelson Algren, who taught at Iowa in 1965, was even crankier. After his stay there, he wrote a now-infamous article in the *Chicago Tribune* titled "At Play in the Fields of Hackademe" in which he declared that the Workshop "had not produced a single novel, poem, or short story worth reading."

Some folks consider O'Connor worth reading, though, and it seems odd that Algren could be unaware of all the other esteemed, prize-winning poets and prosers who'd also already come out of Iowa by the time he showed up. But then Algren reputedly lost badly at poker night after night after night during his time in Iowa City, which perhaps dampened his enthusiasm for the place.

Philip Roth, who also taught at Iowa, was somewhat less dyspeptic than O'Connor and Algren, explaining, not unreasonably, that "writing workshops have three purposes: give young writers an audience, a sense of community, and an 'acceptable' social category." But even Roth couldn't bring himself to concede that something might get taught or learned there, and in the years since, one observer after another has taken a shot at the idea that anything useful might go on in a workshop.

The Workshop's disclaimer does admit the possibility—and one can't help but sense that what's left unsaid is that it's an exceedingly *faint* possibility at best—that "talent can be developed." This passive construction, which would probably be blue-penciled as a rhetorical cop-out in most writing workshops, avoids dealing with such messy considerations as to what might be meant by "developed" and who's doing the developing, and whether or not the Workshop's faculty—its *famous* faculty at that—can be given any credit.

"But why do so many people dispute the value of teaching creative writing?" wonders John Irving, yet another famous Workshop grad who's written more than a few books most folks think are worth reading. "We don't discourage flat-out dreaming in other academic and/or artistic pursuits. I think the question about how writing is taught or if it can be taught is akin to beating off in a bathtub. Who cares how? Who cares if?"

> The Workshop's disclaimer does admit the possibility—and one can't help but sense that what's left unsaid is that it's an exceedingly *faint* possibility at best—that "talent can be developed."

"The question is meaningless," says Marvin Bell. "What does it say about us that people spend time arguing over a question that is theoretical and can never be answered and for which an answer would be neither interesting nor consequential? Real writers don't bother themselves with that question."

"After all," wrote Paul Engle, the Workshop's director for twenty-five years, who probably had to listen to this debate countless times, "has the painter not always gone to an art school or at least to an established master, for instruction? And the composer, the sculptor, the architect? Then why not the writer?"[13]

But the question may not be one that everyone necessarily *wants* answered, even if it could be. In the academy, in business, in the sciences, in politics, and certainly in the arts, everyone agrees that to be creative is a good thing. The myth of American exceptionalism is based on the notion that we're the people who come up with all those great ideas—always have, always will. Okay, so some of those ideas haven't been so great, like subprime mortgages, Reaganomics, trickle-down economics, and derivatives. The point, though, is that on the whole we are damned creative. And part of creativity's allure is its ineffable, mysterious nature. No amount of study, training, practice, or socialization seems capable of getting at the heart of the creative process. And thank God for that. Heck, if it was easy, then everyone would be doing it.

But setting aside the matter of how or if, this yes-it-can-no-it-can't disclaimer on the Workshop's website does summarize rather neatly the speculation about creativity and what it is, where it comes from, and how we can get more of it—speculation that's been going on as long as there have been writers to speculate. It seems to come with the territory; we're never quite sure what we're doing or how we're doing it—it is the spooky art—but by golly we're always looking for some edge, an angle, especially when facing that dread blank page and waiting for a little inspiration so we can do it more and do it better.

On Creativity: A Reading List

> *The Faith of a Writer* by Joyce Carol Oates, *Creativity and Flow* by Mihaly Csikszentmihalyi, *On Becoming a Novelist* by John Gardiner, *Shop Talk* by Philip Roth, *The Creative Process* by Brewster Ghiselin, *The Courage to Write* by Ralph Keyes, *Stephen King On Writing, Henry Miller On Writing, The Midnight Disease* by Alice W. Flaherty (on writing and depression, about which more later), *The Structure of Scientific Revolutions* by Thomas S. Kuhn, various editions of the *Paris Review* interviews with writers, *Ron Carlson Writes a Story* by Ron Carlson, plus several books by and specifically about the Iowa Writers' Workshop, all of which touch on the creative process one way or another. Among these are four excellent works: *The Workshop*, edited by Tom Grimes; *The Eleventh Draft*, edited by Frank Conroy; *The Iowa Writers' Workshop*, by Stephen Wilbers; and *A Community of Writers*, edited by Robert Dana.

No doubt the artists who, some thirty-five thousand years ago, painted the figures in the caves in Chauvet, France, the first recorded "creative acts" found to date, struggled with the very issues creative types have always struggled with, meaning above all they wondered where their next meal was coming from, when they weren't yearning for—*pleading* for—another good idea, for inspiration, for some little nod of recognition from what might have passed for the Muse back in the Aurignacian. No doubt they struggled with creative blocks, too, and tried to ignore that nagging internal editor going on and on and on about that line there, the one defining the haunch of that ibex, really, you can't be serious. And no doubt there were critics back then, too—surely there have been critics as long as there have been artists—one of whom probably held up a torch to view that new work daubed and brushed on the cave wall with red ochre and carbon black pigments, and who thoughtfully scratched at his lice and gnawed on the leg bone of some now-extinct mammal and opined, "Don't you think that auroch there—you do mean for that to be an *auroch*, I assume—isn't just a little, well . . . *derivative?*"

Philosophers, poets, visionaries, and maybe a few lunatics have been pondering the nature of creativity ever since. And what all of this pondering points to, again and again, is that creativity (whether in the arts, the sciences, politics, business, or even the military) is a process with several characteristic steps.

The Workshop's waffling disclaimer aside, the creative process can be practiced and honed and refined, and at least some aspects of it can be learned, perhaps most effectively in a *community* of people sharing their struggles and small triumphs along their individual wandering paths.

∾

JACK LEGGETT: I suppose you could revise that disclaimer so that it said we can't assure that the result of your stay here will be altogether gratifying, but it might be, and there are reasons that it might be.

MARVIN BELL: One of the secrets in life is that if you do anything seriously long enough, you get better at it. Good writing is contagious; one doesn't learn to hit a baseball by watching others strike out. Hence, the "teaching effect" accomplished by good writers who also teach. Hey, that's a useful term: "the teaching effect."

Teachers influence students, whether in person or through books. Students learn in the presence of teachers. Is it only coincidental that so many works of serious literature have come from alumni of the Iowa Writers' Workshop? Maybe nothing can be "taught," but anything can be learned. In the absence of models, there is little learning. Good writers who teach provide models for the writing life, which encompasses craft, knowledge, nerve, attitude, and even, sometimes, lifestyle. In addition, if enough good writers, young and old, gather in one place, good things happen. That is the essence of a workshop: that we are all in this together, students and faculty.

> Good writers who teach provide models for the writing life, which encompasses craft, knowledge, nerve, attitude, and even, sometimes, lifestyle.

ANTHONY BUKOSKI: Why does this question about whether writing can be taught so perplex the writing schools? What's the mystery? A writer needs the great desire to write, the desire and need to sit (or stand, as was the case with Thomas Wolfe) and write the sentences, the paragraphs, the pages. And I believe this can be taught and learned. A person, assuming he has a reasonable aptitude for reading and writing, can be taught to look for the odd angle of vision that might lead to the unusual turn of phrase or the imaginative image. This sort of thing can build upon itself, provided the student (or the nonstudent wanting to be "creative") is willing to try out the lessons taught, to try them and to apply them.

MICHELLE HUNEVEN: Creativity can be nurtured—but most importantly, I think, creativity has to be privileged. One's creative life has to be put in the forefront, ahead of social life, domestic life (grocery shopping, housekeeping, taking the dog to get her shots). At times (but not always), creativity must take precedence over personal life. Once creativity is in the forefront, everything else falls into place and a writing life becomes possible.

I started out with a mantra, which I stole from the great radical feminist theologian Mary Daly, who devised it when she really wanted to write a book, but found herself doing everything *but* writing. She realized that she had to put creativity first and the rest of life behind that. Her mantra (and soon mine) became "I have to turn my soul around." I probably chanted that for months before it finally took hold. And take hold it did.

But there's constant slippage. Life overwhelms. In between my first and second novel, I bought two houses. Then, between my second and third novel, I remodeled a home, met my husband, and eventually married him. All big adjustments. Eventually, we built a beautiful little shed in the backyard where I can close the door and write, a necessity.

Even then, constantly, I breathe to myself: I have to turn my soul around.

JOHN IRVING: An older, experienced writer can be of use to a young, talented writer. The older writer can at least save the younger writer some time. You can't (in my opinion) convert young writers to your method, or you shouldn't try; you can illuminate your method in an unpushy way, as a means of getting them to discover what their method is, and how it differs from yours. I don't have a method of teaching writing; I certainly do have a process that I have learned to follow as a writer, but I don't urge my process on anyone else. My Iowa students—for example, T. C. Boyle, Ron Hansen, and Allen Gurganus—don't write at all like one another, and they shouldn't. They never did! Everyone has something that you do too much of; maybe you do too much of it because you're good at it, but everyone does something to excess—even if what you do to excess is being a minimalist. You do something to an irritating or a potentially irritating degree; you should know what it is. Maybe you shouldn't back off doing it, but you at least should know what you do that irks people. (If you're going to piss people off, you want to be sure you do so intentionally.)

Cocteau used to say that young writers should pay attention to what critics say—only the negatives. Because what the critics don't like about you is probably the only original thing you have. Well, that may be true some of the time—or true about critics. But writing teachers aren't and shouldn't be critics; they should be trying to help you get better at what you already have a feeling or a passion for.

"You think you're funny, don't you?" I remember saying to Tom Boyle once. Then, of course, we both laughed because Tom Boyle is funny. Who would ever want him to stop being funny? I was just trying to begin in a place of common understanding: Okay, so you have this thing you do, and you do it well, but would it be better if you did it just a tad less—or might it be best if you just did it insanely nonstop and breathlessly?

"You really like this character, don't you?" Vonnegut asked me once. Maybe what that meant was, if you liked this character a little less, maybe we'll like him more, or if you like him a little less obviously . . . that kind of thing. You have to figure out what a writer's best thing is; you can always work constructively with that.

I coached wrestling longer than I taught creative writing. I had many young athletes who were never going to win championships; they just weren't good enough athletes, they weren't quick enough, or their balance wasn't good enough, but I could still teach them a few moves and holds that would work for them, that would protect them (to some degree) from the superior athletes. Wrestlers aren't all equal; writers aren't, either. But you can see what the gifts are and work with what the wrestler or the writer has. Some books are (to put it kindly) a lot more modest than others. Not all writers can do all things, but if someone has even a modest amount of ability, you can help him or her improve on it.

Books by the Bed

JOHN IRVING: Robert Stone's *Fun With Problems*, T. C. Boyle's *Wild Child*, Michael Ondaatje's *The Collected Works of Billy the Kid*, and Gail Godwin's *Unfinished Desires*.

JAYNE ANNE PHILLIPS: Writing, or any art, is a calling, rather than a career. People enter into an MFA program, not to "learn" to write, but to spend time in a mentor relationship with an accomplished writer, or a series of them, and to be part of a community for a scant two years that supports literature, reading, and the attempt to write. No one can "teach" anyone to write, but talented writers can find crucial support and encouragement, and learn to edit their own work (half the battle) within the academy.

In a culture/economy that basically views artists with suspicion or hostility, the academy has become a last outpost. The more MFA programs, the better, as far as I'm concerned, because those programs are encouraging literary readers, readers who care about contemporary literature. Many of those readers/writers will go on to publish their writing in one venue or another; a minority will publish a body of work.

SANDRA CISNEROS: I believe in workshops. I teach workshops. I just don't believe in the academic workshop. I believe in alternative workshops. We used to do workshops at community centers and in my living room. We'd do workshops in coffee shops, where we'd sit for two hours and read each other's work and not say a word until we were done. That's what we can do for each other.

> As writers, we're required to write alone. But I like to use the metaphor of writing being like cutting your own hair; there's only so much you can do yourself, then you need someone to help you with the back.

As writers, we're required to write alone. But I like to use the metaphor of writing being like cutting your own hair; there's only so much you can do yourself, then you need someone to help you with the back. That's what we do at the workshop; we cover each other's back. So you don't walk out with a bad haircut, so someone doesn't say, *Damn, where'd you get that bad haircut?* But you have to be with people you can trust. Believe me, if you can't trust those people—which is what happened to me at Iowa—how can you grow?

MARVIN BELL: There are many ways to "teach" it. I teach genius. I teach genius, not necessarily to geniuses. It takes jiujitsu. It requires knowing how to create momentum and knowing when to get out of the way. I confess that I hold subversive views about the teaching of poetry writing. Genius in the arts consists of getting in touch with one's inner wiring. Writing poetry is a way of life, not a career. The funky, vaguely disreputable Iowa Workshop of which I was a part definitely nurtured the creative. It had about it a certain loosey-goosey quality that encourages artistic growth. We were outsiders, then, which was definitive. Today, other things define writing communities. For better or worse, they are more sophisticated now, more knowing and known. They have become an accepted part of literary studies. They are less in love with chaos.

The Iowa Workshop "nurtured" creativity in the sense that it gathered creative people and left us alone to watch one another, gab, party, and do what we had to, each in our own way.

SHERRY KRAMER: Something special happens in workshop, in the sharing of work, and how it works, and how each word means something to the writer. A writing class can be a doorway to new ways of being in the world and organizing your place in it.

One of the most rewarding things about teaching writing is that at a certain point, you hand over the process to the students, and you're in the room, and yes, everybody values what you say, and how you focus their gaze and help reveal the pattern, but the class itself is in charge—it's a community, and it functions on its own terms. I've never been a fan of "guru" teachers, who always hold the secret keys to what's good and bad, who everyone is desperate to please. I like turning the class into the teacher. And I have only once been disappointed by the generosity and insight that my students have displayed when workshopping each other's writing—I guess there's always the exception that proves the rule.

In the theater, we have a saying: the director sets the tone. Everything that happens in a rehearsal reflects the director's values, and that model is absolutely accurate when talking about a writing class. And I like to think that the values that govern our discussions and the habits of generosity that are displayed will flow into my students' lives at school and after, showing them the way to create and live in all the communities that they'll be a part of.

SANDRA CISNEROS: I think that what you can do is teach discipline. We're solitary. We write alone. We need to communicate. Our families don't understand that all the time; they think we're nuts, but we're the only ones who have our acts together. We process our shit. We take that shit and process it to grow. I think you need a family of writers that will sustain you. Maybe that's what I've tried to do with my workshops; I think Iowa got too big, or maybe it was a family for some, but it wasn't *my* family. I felt homeless, and I created my own home with *House on Mango Street*. I want the writers at Macondo to feel this is their family, and for one week out of the year, we'll have sustained them, so they'll keep writing the rest of the year. That's what you can do with a community

> I think that what you can do is teach discipline. We're solitary. We write alone. We need to communicate. Our families don't understand that all the time; they think we're nuts.

of writers—sustain people for the long haul. Macondo[14] is a workshop that gathers writers who are generous, compassionate, and believe their writing can make nonviolent social change. In other words, the opposite of the Iowa Writers' Workshop.

JOHN IRVING: When I taught, I would tell my students that if they were going to be writers, especially if they were going to be novelists, they better know themselves well enough to be certain that they liked being alone. I said that writing novels was a solitary pursuit; I said that four, five, six years might go by, and you were all that time alone with these characters you had created. I said that, if they were truly passionate about their novels, they would realize that they were living with their characters more intimately than they would ever get to know anyone else.

I've said many times that what I enjoy about writing the occasional screenplay is that it is a social undertaking; you write screenplays for other people, often with other people. It is a relief from the solitary task that writing a novel is. I would hate to have to write screenplays for a living; if writing screenplays was the only writing I did, I would be very depressed. But as a vacation from the solitude of writing a novel, I like writing a screenplay because it is such a collaboration. There is nothing collaborative about writing a novel; you're in it alone.

Not so with movie people. When I won an Oscar (for Best Adapted Screenplay for the film of *The Cider House Rules*), now that was a party! It's a collaborative business, moviemaking, and those people know how to have a good time. I still felt like an outsider, or an interloper—the novelist and only occasional screenwriter—but the Academy Awards, and the parties after those awards, make you feel like you belong to a big club, like you're a part of a great, grand team. It's different; that's all I'm saying.

You have to like being alone with yourself to be a novelist; or, perhaps more strongly, you know that you have to be alone with yourself, which is why you are a novelist. Whatever feeling there is of a culture you are part of—well, if the feeling is even there, it's fleeting. The movie business is a culture, but novelists live on their own planets.

SHERRY KRAMER: The word "playwright" still has the old association to a craft attached to it: we're "wrights," we're makers or builders. We make a thing. When you want to make a thing, you study it or you apprentice with someone who knows how to make it. That, and the fact that our plays are not really plays until they're produced—and the language of "production" again indicates that we're clearly making a thing—these things free playwrights, as a rule, from thinking about the whole can-writing-be-*taught* issue. Instead, we say and hear things like, plays aren't written, they're rewritten—we live in a rewriting crisis, all the time, our play-developmental programs are all about that, to an actually destructive degree, so we're always talking about how to teach rewriting. Because so much of our rewriting happens, not alone, but in company—in rehearsal, in collaboration with a director, dramaturge, actors, designers, producers—rewriting in the theater almost seems a different art form from writing. And because a play does not ever "stay" produced (soon after it is "made," it slips out of that state and returns to its incomplete, unmade self), it also can and often does have this entire rewriting process all over again, with another full set of collaborators.

JANE SMILEY: We go to workshops for community, to meet like-minded people. Most writers don't succeed if they're just sitting in a room writing but not getting out. If you look back at the history of the novel, nearly everyone who succeeded was part of some sort of literary group. There is hardly anyone who thrives on being solitary. Think of Virginia Woolf and her circle; they supported one another and talked to one another and talked about literature. Thackeray and his friends, the same. People do it in New York City as a matter of course, so the idea that you would somehow not thrive in a more communal environment is absurd. In my experience of working with students who perhaps have been writing alone for years, they tend to develop the easy parts, but avoid the hard parts; we all do. A student who's good at plotting will go for plot, and if that student's not good at characters, the characters will be flat. So you need others to prod you and tell you your plot's fine, but the characters are flat.

MARVIN BELL: The better MFA programs today are still one of the ways young writers can find community and time and test themselves. It's not the lesser aspects of a literary scene that flatten creativity. It's the economic and political character of a society. Ironically, many of the attempts by American institutions to spread literature have paid for economic success with a public dumbing-down. We are required to promote support for the arts in this country by claiming it makes money.

SHERRY KRAMER: Imagine if your novel had to be rewritten with notes and suggestions from a new editor (or three or four) every one thousand copies. Exciting? In some ways, I suppose. Terrifying? Exhausting? Of course, most plays aren't rewritten for their fifth or twenty-seventh production but many are for their second, third, or fourth . . . and every production, including the twenty-seventh one, is a kind of rewriting of your work anyway, that's part of the peculiar dance that a play is. The text of your play can be frozen, but your collaborators will (you hope, you pray) create their own true version, a complete rewriting of it—the actors with their bodies and their voices, the director and designers with their choices—and they'll create a version of your work that is completely surprising to you and at the same time (when you're lucky) more like your play than you had ever imagined. And all these kinds of rewriting can, of course, be taught. We are always learning and unlearning and relearning how to rewrite our plays because we're always doing it in a different room filled with different people.

Books by the Bed
SHERRY KRAMER: Two *Wired*s, the only magazine I subscribe to. I'm still working my way through *2666*. Then I have a couple sci-fi books, they're candy, for binging when I want something easy and sweet, a Jack Vance collection and one of those huge best-of-the-year anthologies, I think 2004. I usually keep a Pema Chodron within reach. I always have a stack of plays by friends I'm trying to find the time to read. Philip Hoars's *The Whale*. The *36 Arguments for the Existence of God* by Rebecca Goldstein. And *Moby Dick*—I've decided, late in life, to take the plunge.

JANE SMILEY: And in a workshop, you have to produce, and so what if it's not perfect? If it's an assignment, you have to produce. At Iowa State, in Ames, where I taught, I had each student bring a draft every week, four drafts, four stories, sixteen weeks, and get input every week, so they got into the habit of doing their work. You can't be a novelist by being a perfectionist because if you are never satisfied, you won't get the book written. One of the things that I found so congenial about my group in Iowa was that they were very forgiving of one another. The real key was production, not perfection. . . .

So when you go to a workshop, it doesn't really matter what teacher you get. What matters is to write and to read others' work and make friends with others who are as interested in writing as you are, with the same aspirations. That's what's valuable. That's the good thing about a workshop.

JOHN IRVING: Maybe "community" is a better word for the Iowa Writers' Workshop—more accurate than "culture," I mean. The community of writers in Iowa City is a real thing. You can feel it, and it doesn't seem to be altered by changes of location: those Quonset huts down on the Iowa River, or the hotel-sized English-Philosophy Building, or the new digs nearer to downtown. I was never so much of the feeling that I was part of a community of writers as I felt, at various times, in Iowa City. And that's a good thing because the work of being a writer is pretty lonely.

I was never so much of the feeling that I was part of a community of writers as I felt, at various times, in Iowa City. And that's a good thing because the work of being a writer is pretty lonely.

~

Creativity refers to the ability to bring something new or useful or, in the case of the arts, something beautiful into being. Or perhaps in the case of certain schools of contemporary visual art, something the critics and sophisticated collectors think is *not* beautiful, since the idea that any work can or should be beautiful is a bourgeois expression of power relationships between the oppressor and the oppressed, according to the critical theorists, and so if you're truly in the know, the uglier the art (or the more incomprehensible the prose), the better.

We're all creative, though. Even the guy who does your income taxes can be creative (the more creative the better, if he can save you some money while keeping you out of jail). We tend to think that being creative is a good thing, and generally it is. The puny human species without a decent coat of fur or big fangs and talons has nonetheless managed to survive and thrive thanks to its ability to imagine new and creative ways of working itself out of trouble.

To be human, in other words, is to be creative.

In Shakespeare's *A Midsummer Night's Dream*, Theseus holds forth on the topic of poets, lovers, and lunatics:

... as imagination bodies forth
The forms of things unknown, the poet's pen
Turns them to shapes and gives to airy nothing
A local habitation and a name.

One hesitates to suggest that the Bard didn't have it quite right, but if he was expressing through Theseus his own view here, then he didn't, quite.

Strictly speaking we don't construct something new from airy nothing when we're being creative. Rather, artists innovate by drawing on common experience or from ideas that already exist that they've acquired through research or study. They often only reshape familiar stories and images and tunes, combine them with some new twist or view them from a different angle—what if the damsel in distress doesn't want to get rescued?—and thereby reenergize what has faded into the habitual, the clichéd. We make it *new*, as Ezra Pound demanded. Sometimes radically so, outraging critics and the public alike.

Still, at the heart of the creative process there often *is* an airy something: something a little ineffable, inexplicable and a little spooky—where the hell did *that* come from?—that usually strikes when we're not looking for it, while we're sweating to hammer into place an element we're convinced is essential but that doesn't want to fit, and then *aha!* the jumble of preconceptions and days (or weeks or months) of work tumbles into irrelevance and the remaining pieces fall into place. When all is going well, a work of art takes on a life of its own, the characters begin to write themselves, the story insists it wants to turn out a certain way—and the author is just along for the ride. Or so we hope.

> **Still, at the heart of the creative process there often *is* an airy something: something a little ineffable, inexplicable and a little spooky—where the hell did *that* come from?**

Writing about the creative process, C. G. Jung remarked, "The work in process becomes the poet's fate and determines his psychic development. It is not Goethe who creates Faust, but Faust which creates Goethe."[15] Or as T. S. Eliot put it, "the progress of an artist is a continual self-sacrifice, a continual extinction of personality."[16]

The irony here is that artists of all sorts are known for their outsized egos, but what they often crave above all else is to escape that ego, lose control, and be created. This is the heart and soul of the creative process.

～

ROBIN GREEN: Writing fiction and writing scripts are for me different. Script writing is a craft, so you can't have writer's block. I had it once when I worked on *Northern Exposure* for Joshua Brand and John Falsey, and Josh said, "Well, if you don't come up with a scene, then I will." I knew this wouldn't be good for my career, so I wrote the fucking scene.

So sometimes I force myself to do it, but I do it. It was worse when I wrote alone, but now I write the TV stuff with Mitch Burgess, my husband, and it's a very disciplined, work-a-day effort. It's a business: problems to be solved, to be worked out. It's a very focused, structured thing we're doing. After twenty years, we're familiar with its demands. Not that we're not back to square one every time. It's just that there's a definite format.

But I remember when I was writing fiction, sometimes I wrote as if taking dictation, in a blessed state, in a beam. When I *tried* to write, it wasn't any good.

ALLAN GURGANUS: Like taking dictation, exactly. As if the power of the universe is flowing through you, time passing very quickly. That's when you know you're doing it. I've had what seems about twenty-three minutes pass, and the clock later says those really lasted six hours. . . . It's so thrilling, exciting. You've been off in the other world.

Other times, you come home from a party, say, when you're a little snockered—a surfacey champagne drunk, not truly gut-and-gill gin drunk—and you're sitting in the dark at the keyboard at 1:00 AM, typing as fast as you can toward some new idea, with your eyes closed . . . I find the digital stimulation is extraordinary; as soon as my fingers begin to move, it's Pavlovian, the train of dreams ten little fingers can pull. And then you close the document without rereading it, and only in the morning do you go back and print it out—inevitably there are misspellings or mistypings. But you can see where it came from and where it staggered toward, half-tipsy. Then you enter the corrections and clean it up a bit and let it sit around like cheese getting moldy. You know you're onto something you would not have snagged during a usual workday after your usual breakfast and regular coffee. It's a wonderful feeling of possession, of faith in the abiding inward sources of fiction. It doesn't happen every day. If only it did. . . .

SANDRA CISNEROS: If you're thinking about the reader or the product, if your head's involved in it, you're blocking the potential for the story to take you someplace fantastic. If your *córazon* is involved, then, like Betty Davis said, you're in for a bumpy ride. That's where I want to go with my writing. Then the writing goes someplace I never imagined. That's the kind of writing I want to do. Don't think too much . . . then you'll be able to say something wiser than your years, bigger than yourself. That's what I try to tell writers, "Don't get in the way; step aside." When you sit with your writing long enough—I know from experience—you'll have to walk through a long valley of despair. But if you can get past that, and you're humble enough, and service-oriented, if you say to yourself, *I'm here to serve*, then your higher self, your spirit, god, light, or whatever you want to call it, will take you there. But you have to be ready for that to happen. And I think if you're steering the writing with your head, you're impeding it from happening. It's like Buddhists say, "You have to empty yourself to fill up with the everything of the universe."

ROSALYN DREXLER: I'm a worker. I don't wait for inspiration. I don't know what inspiration is. A certain connection happens as you get deeper into the work. You are not really there. You are a state of mind: at one with the creation (book or painting, etc.). Thus I think inspiration comes afterward, not before. However, a contract and a substantial advance in payment is a great inducement.

JENNIE FIELDS: First of all, I read a lot; it feeds my writing. If I don't read, I don't write. Last night, for example, I read a passage from Updike's *In the Beauty of the Lilies*. Just the fact that someone could write so exquisitely is exciting. It's the quality of his writing that stuns and humbles me. Hearing the music of the words summons my muses. When someone writes something wonderful, I want to write like that. I sit down and I'm writing.

I learned early on that the creative process in advertising comes from a different part of my brain; it's more conscious. With fiction, your subconscious does most of the work. When I wrote *Lily Beach*, there was a violent moment, and I was shocked when it happened. But looking back through the novel, I could see that I'd set up that moment all throughout the book.

> I start a book by getting to know my characters and giving them an insoluble problem that I then let them solve for me. I once read, and I think it's true, if you love your theme, you'll finish the book.

Still, it came as a surprise to me when it happened; my subconscious knew it would happen. *I* didn't.

I start a book by getting to know my characters and giving them an insoluble problem that I then let them solve for me. I once read, and I think it's true, if you love your theme, you'll finish the book. I don't always know what my theme is when I start. Partway through, as my characters show me who they are, the theme begins to reveal itself. I guess my theme is usually about women who don't believe they have the right to be happy, but I can't always see that in the beginning.

Because the writing comes from that deep, secret part of my brain, I can fall into the work and forget where I am. I lose all sense of time and place. It's the most Zen thing in the world: to lose yourself to what you are doing.

CATHERINE GAMMON: In therapy later I realized that part of the attraction of writing for me, as a way of exploring and expressing my creativity and myself and my spirit and my life, was that my body didn't have to be invested in the presentation of it. Early on, if I gave you a story I'd written, I couldn't be in the room while you read it. I could read it to you if I knew you really well. Later I was able to read to an audience of familiar people, and even later to many strangers, but initially, I felt like this writing needs a wall, a protection, and other people don't get in until after what's being said gets out of my body, separate from me in time and space.

Getting into Zen practice shed more light on this and kind of freed it up. Zen practice is a process of the body, of being present in the body, and the art of it is in the body. It's not just in your ideas or your thoughts or what your mind does or your imagination, and the stillness of it is itself a very high-energy act. The process is about stillness and finding stillness in the midst of activity, which is very challenging. But somehow for me it has helped to break down that wall between me and the reader or you.

Has Zen practice helped my writing? I don't know yet. Recently, it's mostly meant years of not writing. But writing and practice aren't separate. Before I really entered training in Zen, at various times I was practicing sitting and also writing, and there was a more direct connection. After I was sober, when I went off to arts colonies, I had the time and space to sit before writing, and then I would do that. When I was working on *Sorrow*, an unpublished and very dark novel, I was sitting in the morning on my writing days before I started writing, and the sitting in that situation had the function of getting the distance out of the way, that resistance, a feeling in the gut that you don't want to go there, especially if I was working on something troubled or difficult in some way. So the sitting would already have taken care of that, and I could go more freely to the writing. But that's not really what sitting is for, the purpose of sitting, and I knew that, and I felt the difference between sitting as a pre-writing activity and a larger sitting that is just sitting still in the midst of this life, for the sake of life itself, not just to get out of my own way in order to make a book.

Right now my life is so immersed in Zen training, it's like being a Sunday painter to sometimes have Fridays to write. But having those Fridays also feels like preparation for the time when I don't live in a Zen community anymore, when I'm not doing a full-time job taking care of some aspect of the temple or this large complicated community, when I will be practicing as a Zen priest in whatever way that might manifest and will also have real time for writing.

SHERRY KRAMER: The impulse to acknowledge the sacred or magical or nonrational aspect of writing is pretty strong. If writing didn't connect me with some part of the world, a connection that gave me great peace and joy,

I don't think I'd do it. It sounds both obvious and embarrassing to say it, but I feel really alive when I'm writing.

Now I have students and friends who I call self-torturers—they're people who never have that euphoric state, writers who are anxious, anxious, anxious at every step, from the doubt and worry about the work before it's written, all through the writing, and after it's done. I feel bad about this, but with students, once I figure out that this is pretty much their relationship to their work—that the anxiety and worry isn't a side effect of writing but a necessary precondition of it—I stop seeing it as something dysfunctional, and I try to get them to see it that way too. Everybody finds their way into the world of their work differently. There's no wrong way.

MARVIN BELL: At the heart of "being creative" is always achieving a point in which the nonrational, the nonlogical part of the mind has a chance to go to work. This is true of all creative writing, but it is true with a vengeance if one is writing the sort of poetry that tries to express the otherwise inexpressible.

I prefer to write when the pot boils over. Of course, over the years I have learned how to turn up the heat. I generally write very late at night, beginning after midnight, when the mind loosens its grip on the rational connections one needs in one's utilitarian life. I like staying up late, always have. I write in spurts, always have. If the energy of the language flags, I walk away, which means I lose a lot, since one can't always get back into an unfinished poem. Not if the poem has been pushing the envelope.

But I can write anywhere, and at any time, if I have to. Nothing stops me. The more I have to do—jobs, family, friends—the more I write. Energy produces more energy. And writing, when one is cookin', is an escape from time. Regardless, I prefer the late hours, and I think they encourage pushing the envelope. And sometimes I write to stamp out my brain. The idea is always to write with abandon. I tend to say *yes* to whatever comes along.

SANDRA CISNEROS: *Yes!* Say *yes* to everything! What's the worst mistake a writer can make? Thinking too much. Don't think. It's not about thinking. You think when you edit. When you create, say yes, yes to everything. When the bell rings and it's the Jehovah's Witness folks, answer the door and say *yes*. The guy at the door might be in your story. Maybe he'll leave a piece of paper that takes you to

> At the heart of "being creative" is always achieving a point in which the nonrational, the nonlogical part of the mnd has a chance to go to work.

the next chapter. Say yes to everything; nothing's an accident. Later is for the editing, but in the creation, be open, be gentle, like a mother; there's nothing you say no to. Trust that the nonsense you're writing will take you somewhere.

ALLAN GURGANUS: Exactly. Be generous with and to yourself. After that first draft, stash it away a while; work on other things (I believe in working on many units at once), let a little distance set in, and then reread it, ideally without a pen in your hand the first time, so you're reading it at exactly the speed with which you wrote it, not interrupting. Reconsider it from start to end, bemused with a kind of teacherly or parental patience.

Of course, I can say but not always do that. I'll maybe get two paragraphs in, trying to read it like that, impartially. Then I'll go ah, that so sucks, and I whip out the pen. . . . You have to take a macro view before you get into the dental-assistant details, the overcleaning; if you go too fast to the incisor-brightening, you might be working on the teeth of a dead man. Or you'll use up all your ingenuity on sentences that will prove redundant in the long run.

T. C. BOYLE: For *Talk Talk*, I had to know about ID theft, and so I got every book I could on the subject, how you do it, the horror stories, the cases, and so on. But it wasn't long until there was no depth to the story. It's about your identity; how do you know who you are? You have language. That's how you can name yourself, how you can think. I happened to go to my dentist when I was researching the book. He was divorced and had his eye out for the ladies, and he said, "The most gorgeous woman in the world was sitting in this chair before you, and you know what? She was *deaf*." Then he got out the jackhammer and the drill, and I realized that my heroine would be deaf. I began to see the possibilities. If my character were deaf, she'd have a special language, different brain patterns. The deaf from birth are from a different culture, with different brain patterns to make that special language.

DON WALLACE: Poems came out of my emotional weather. I'd walk and chant them in my head until a chain was formed that would last until I got back to the typewriter. From a poem I quite deliberately reverse-engineered my first real story at age twenty: of knocking around the streets of Long Beach with a Chinese high school friend, Bob Wong, and how our paths forked at the place where class, race, pride, ambition, anger all swirled together. It ended with the metaphor that tied the poem together: our friendship had been like a drop in the pan in Bob's father's Chinese restaurant, sizzling until it vanished. (I later heard Bob didn't particularly appreciate my appropriating his life—I didn't even change his name—and I'm still waiting to run into him to apologize.)

Because of that unity, coming from an existing poem, with the ending secure in advance, the story caught the ear of the fiction editor of the free weekly in Santa Cruz called *Sundaz*. Two weeks later I was a published author.

Once I had a calling, I quickly became disciplined, a daily grinder. A morning person, I liked having something done and in the bank, psychologically speaking, before the rest of the day, before the "regular" work of being a student, and later, before the actual grinding jobs I would hold for the rest of my working life.

Though a grinder, I am careful to leave myself open to visions, inspirations, fugue states and Dionysian interpenetrations, and, yes, hangovers. (I stopped the obligatory writer-drinker thing in the late '70s, turning to jogging like so many other Americans in thrall to our Puritan—and in my case Scottish/Swedish—heritage. I now walk long distances again to spare my knees, and the ideas and thoughts rush in as before, exactly the same as when I was eighteen).

Books by the Bed

DON WALLACE: Not having had an end table on my side of the bed for a couple of years, my bedroom reading tends to drop to the floor and join a pile of loose newspapers, yellowing copies of the *New York Review of Books* and the *Times Literary Supplement*. A writer's rats' nest snapshot of a month ago (before Mindy launched a surprise cleanup) would have come up with *Na'Kua'Aina: Living Hawaiian Culture*, which was helping me with a documentary film I'd been writing; R. W. Thompson's *Battle for the Rhine*, an out-of-print paperback that gave "Band of Brothers" a lot of its pith (and has a really strange, almost autistic third-person point of view that gives it much of its interest); *The Enthusiast*, a new novel by my old UC Santa Cruz writing pal Charlie Haas, about a hack magazine editor whose career bears some resemblance to mine; and Judith Freeman's *The Long Embrace*, in which she traces—or stalks—the strange marriage of Raymond Chandler, who fell for a woman without knowing she was twenty-two years his senior. Chandler lived in thirty-five places in a dozen years in Los Angeles, including a lot of places I once called home: Signal Hill, Long Beach, Idyllwild. These give an idea of the intellectual squalor in which I blissfully wallow.

DOUG UNGER: Let yourself go; give yourself the freedom to make mistakes. It's impossible to write a novel sentence by sentence perfectly. In the first draft, write some messy sections, take wrong turns, and accumulate enough material to have something to work with. I saw John Irving doing that, when he revealed to us his process while working on *The World According to Garp*. He let us in on his first drafts and then his revisions in a way I never saw any other writing teacher do before or since. And I really learned a lot by witnessing this. He was an extremely generous teacher in how much he gave of himself as a writer by revealing his creative process. And he was generous to me personally.

Also, I learned a great deal from Lenny Michaels, in the opposite way, how he'd write a paragraph that was so tight, it was like a passage in baroque music; but in his case, it was like a musical score from a good piece of jazz or blues, how he felt the rhythm of every sentence, in every paragraph, every word, yet in revisions still left room for improvisations. The combination of both sensibilities, of such tight control and the impulse to freedom, makes for good writing, and students need to know this.

ALLAN GURGANUS: I do a lot of reading out loud. That's a huge, huge part of what I do, trusting my ear as an editor, imagining reading it to another person. Or actually reading it to a real live friend. I have people here who allow me to come over on short notice and corner them. Amazing how effective it is. Writing is so abstract, so algebraic—reading it aloud renders all that into real sound waves, makes it into physics. Tremendously important.

It helps to imitate how your characters speak, how people talk in a completely different language from the way they use for writing. The way you write about both is a third lingo. The more distinct a character's spoken and written language is, the more opportunities you have for comedy and tension. You hear shortcuts, you hear how many articles and prepositions people leave out. Hand gestures become surrogates for dropped lines. It's hard to write all that in silence.

DON WALLACE: Several of my long projects, novels, have had historical roots. I discovered that reading deep into a subject and a time and a place replaced the childhood way I had of creating worlds in my head. In addition to histories, I'd read nonacademic stuff, old novels and old newspapers, journals; I'd latch onto found objects with some physical connection to the period. For my latest work in progress, an old friend who combs estate sales for rare books and sells them on eBay sent me a great old dictionary from eighteenth-century England, as well as sailors' journals and other eccentric texts. When I read this stuff, I'm in heaven, my brain making up stories right and left out of the wonderful ricocheting details and vocabulary.

Certainly there's a danger of the research getting in the way and supplanting the actual creative writing: I don't want to be James Michener, after all, though I am grateful for the award I received in his name from the Copernicus Society. But for my first novel, *Hot Water*, which is about the then-unimaginable world of professionalized bass fishing, I kept a three-foot stack of press releases from lure and boat companies by my desk. Whenever my writing ran dry, I'd just pluck one up and—"Worm blood? What the hell is worm blood?"—I'd be off on another riff . . .

DENNIS MATHIS: Even terrible books are worth studying. While I'm reading a sentence, my mind is rewriting it better. That's more fun than passive reading. Sometimes I can't come up with a better sentence, and then I take time to savor a well-made sentence, a crafty foreshadowing or something. I'm a very slow reader. I need eye surgery, for one thing. I have a condition that makes printed words swim like minnows. So I don't read unnecessary books unless they capture my imagination . . . or I'm avoiding something else I should be doing.

Actually, one of the books on my table is a three-book compilation of John LeCarre's early novels, found on the "last chance!" shelf. One of the novels has the scene I mentioned before, where the spies knock on a door on a rainy night, and a little girl answers.

ANTHONY BUKOSKI: How does one stay inspired? I'm always inspired. My life has beautiful, troubling, perplexing things in it. I want to write the things out of me in order to understand them. Done with one story, an inspiration comes to me. Sometimes the inspirations get backed up. I am like the writer in Sherwood Anderson's "The Book of the Grotesque" preface to *Winesburg, Ohio*. "You can see for yourself how the old man, who had spent all of his life writing and was filled with words, would write hundreds of pages concerning this matter (of grotesques). The subject," Anderson writes, "would become so big in his mind that he himself would be in danger of becoming a grotesque. He didn't, I suppose, for the same reason that he never published the book. It was the young thing inside him that saved the old man."

I view writing as a craft I've been entitled, blessed really, to pursue. I'm honored to be blessed this way. I don't take myself as seriously as some—no fainting spells, no beret wearing, no absinthe drinking, no posing, no analyst telling me what is wrong that I can't write. If I find myself particularly confused or hard-pressed about writing, I remind myself that I am always just trying to learn to write. Confused for a moment, indulging myself in "frustration," I remind myself this kind of thinking, this "suffering," is for "real artists," whereas I'm a simpleminded grandson of Polish peasants lucky enough to be interested in writing. I guess this is my pose: the Polish peasant pose. I don't take myself too seriously. I don't indulge myself. In fact I tell myself I'm not a good-enough writer to be bothered by writer's block. Then I get back to basics. I imagine such an attitude wouldn't set well with the "smart set" whether they be in Duluth—where there is indeed a "smart set" of visual artists, filmmakers, poets, et al.—in New York, Paris, wherever they may congregate in the service of "art." But, again, this attitude, the peasant attitude, serves me well.

Finally, I have no tricks to recommend to one needing inspiration. Or perhaps I do. Given my ethnic background, a sure way for me to be inspired is to listen to Chopin. I don't rely on this often, however, for I am always inspired to write.

JACK LEGGETT: Ordinarily I'm at the computer writing daily, and I've now got two what I deem to be publishable, saleable, even rather good novels if that's a reliable assessment (everybody that's finished a novel thinks it's publishable, better than anything anybody else has done). For the most part, I'm very grateful for my experiences in writing; it made a career in publishing, in education, and allows me a certain grace in retirement. So whether or not I'm published—I won't say I'm indifferent to that—but ideally I should be writing just to please myself. In other words, it should be enough . . . to get it as perfect as I can get it. That's the satisfaction and it's what I believe to be the ultimate gratification in the writing life.

MICHELLE HUNEVEN: I get inspired often by the dictionary or by odd bits of research. I love it when I look up a word and the etymology or the connotations leads me to another, close line of thought and thus puts a new bend or depth in the narrative.

Also, reading great fiction inspires me. I am never so alert and engaged as I am when reading a superb book. I think, if I can give some tiny portion of the literary pleasure to others that this book is giving to me, all those solitary hours of work will be justified.

ALLAN GURGANUS: I think everyone has his or her own inherent flaw or flaws they must come to terms with. One of the challenges, starting out, is realizing how your major tendencies to tell stories are successful and unsuccessful. Like shortsightedness or deafness in the left ear, these

require a daily compensation, a bitter realism about your standing imper-
fections.

For instance, one of my flaws is a love for beginnings; I adore starts
that come like a drum roll leading to a trumpet call leading to *cancan* girls,
leading to the coming up of the curtain leading to a single actor on a park
bench alone onstage. I like the setting of the stage, the puppet mechanics of
the opening. Once upon a time remains my favorite opening.

After that, it's just flying, grabbing everything that comes into your
head as fast as you can type it. Starting a
new story is a little like calisthenics for
me; it feels hydrating-oxygenating to
start something new. Usually you've heard
something that sparks an idea, or you
have some strong first sentence or maybe
even just a title has appeared, wanting
something under it. You go into a kind of
trance as you're hurling words onto the page, and see how they'll look in
print; you're dictating to the printing press.

You go into a kind of trance as you're hurling words onto the page, and see how they'll look in print; you're dictating to the printing press.

This can become a vice, though. You might be led from one beginning
to another; it's like having promiscuous sex seven nights a week; you don't
finally know whom you're waking up with. . . .

SHERRY KRAMER: I always keep what I think of as the mother lode,
which is the first full draft where I made it all the way to the end. That's what
I refer back to when I'm working. I might have a dozen drafts, or two dozen,
but all those in-between drafts can sit forgotten in my computer. It's the first
impulse that I need to be in touch with, not all the ways I've illustrated it
or obscured it or (worst of all) taken all its mysteries and made them clear .
. . the first draft is the treasure map. I don't ever doubt that it's the truest—
maybe not the best, of course, because a lot of the time it's not fully formed
and transformed, but it's the *truest* representation of what the work wants
to be.

DOUG UNGER: Lately, I've been working on an essay about poetic inspiration. It's something I've been writing, actually, for some five years by now,
in bits and pieces. I use three writers as examples: the great poetic primitive,
Thomas Wolfe, who let himself get so lost in his trance state when he was
writing that he might not notice when someone else was standing in a room
with him; or he'd be talking to himself, muttering, pacing two hundred feet
up and down a hallway in the Hotel Chelsea, and then he'd sit down and in

a rush let the words come out with his pencil and paper, pages flying off his desk every which way and landing on the floor.

Or I think of Jorge Luis Borges, who, in another kind of meditative state, would very consciously (later in his life, when he had gone completely blind) sit in a chair, with his blind eyes closed, rocking back and forth while he was stroking his cat. After about two or three hours of this, he'd have a complete paragraph or a stanza of a poem memorized in his head, and he'd call for María Kodama (his companion, whom he later married) and he'd dictate, whole, a passage he was writing. I've had two long conversations with María Kodama about this.

Or I think of my best friend and brother-in-law, Ray Carver, in those last great years when he was living out in Port Angeles, Washington, often all alone, writing poems. He'd call me up and, amazed, meaning to share his astonishment at what was happening with his writing, he'd say how the poems were coming to him, two a day, maybe more sometimes, big, whole, complete, and beautiful. He described the experience like pulling up fish, one after the other, like catching these incredibly wonderful steelhead or salmon from his secret fishing spots, and he was having this most incredible fisherman's luck—luck was just what he called it. He was in that state, too, that meditative and inspired condition of the imagination when it is very open to the world.

~

Different writers on the topic of creativity divide the process into different stages and give these stages a variety of names, but the heart of the process in most if not all of these accounts is the inspiration or the illumination or the *aha!* Sometimes it's a *moment*, a fleeting glimpse of a good idea—a brilliant idea, or so it may seem at first glance—to be worked out on the page (at which point it often seems not quite so brilliant). Sometimes it's a prolonged state of mind like the athlete's "zone," or the "flow" described by Mihaly Csikszentmihalyi,[17] when it does seem as if we're taking dictation or the work is writing us, when we forget where we are, when the hours pass unnoticed, or rather become compressed into one glorious *now*.

But such moments rarely come without some coaxing, without courting the Muse, as it were. So we should not overlook the first stage of the creative process: preparation or practice, as it's variously called, that is, making oneself available to a good idea, should one come along.

One doesn't create something *new* without knowing what's *not* new, and so this preparation stage might involve study. This concentration on a particular problem or the study of the current knowledge or thinking in a specific field might involve formal training, consideration of the status quo or the "dominant paradigm," as Thomas Kuhn describes it in *The Structure of Scientific Revolutions*.[18] Or this period of study might be much less formal.

All of that reading writers were doing as kids and all of the reading we're doing now is part of this first stage of the creative process. And so is that morning cup of coffee and perhaps a cigarette or two, and a few moments going over what one wrote yesterday—and of knocking one's head against the wall wondering, What the *hell* was I thinking?—all as a way of getting back into the proper frame of mind. The preparation stage might take a few minutes, or it might last for days or weeks or years, depending on the nature of the project.

As Kuhn describes it, such preparation might lead to dissatisfaction with the dominant paradigm, or at least some gnawing sense that whatever one knows, or thinks one knows, or has thought or done to date about some problem or issue, isn't entirely accurate or complete or adequate. Such a sense of something not quite right might then lead to a period of deliberate, conscious questioning. In the arts, this is of course the artist's perpetual striving to *make it new!* Often, perhaps of necessity, a work of art is a reaction to or *against* what came before. Thus modernist movements in art, architecture, and literature began first with dissatisfaction and disillusionment, and then reaction to—or against—the bourgeois sensibilities of nineteenth-century Europe.

Writers likewise struggle to be different from those who came before, or to protest against them. Or on a more day-to-day level, it's a struggle against who we were yesterday, and laboring over the same paragraph again and again the next morning in an attempt to capture who we are and what we know *now*. And that doesn't suck.

Preparation doesn't always lead to that longed-for *aha!* Sometimes there's no transcendent moment of illumination at all, rather just a lot of hard work day after grinding day that, in the end, turns out to be not half bad.

How creativity happens is more than a little capricious, in other words, which is why poets, painters, musicians, and novelists have a well-documented history of drinking too much, chain-smoking, fidgeting, and now and then going insane while trying to court a muse. Indeed, there are statistical if not clearly established causal links between creativity and conditions psychologists politely refer to as "serious mood disorders."

In 1974, during her residency in psychiatry at the University of Iowa, Nancy Andreasen did a study of students and faculty at the Iowa Writers' Workshop and found that 80 percent of the participants suffered from either depression or what was then called manic depression (bipolar disorder in today's terminology). And no wonder: If your income, your sense of self-worth, your very existence (or so it sometimes seems) depend on something as fickle as having yet another stroke of genius when you have no idea where the last one came from, you might be excused for suffering mood swings and chronic anxiety. Or as Plato put it: "He who approaches the temple of the muses without inspiration, in the belief that craftsmanship alone suffices, will remain a bungler and his presumptuous poetry will be obscured by the songs of the maniacs."[19]

But let's not get the wrong idea here. The creative process has distinct pleasures that can far outweigh the agonies, which is why so many of us stick with it, often well beyond the point when common sense says it's time to get a real job. For some, the struggle itself can be powerfully therapeutic, the cure rather than the source of psychological malfunction. In many cases, individuals prone to mood disorders may be attracted to creative endeavors precisely because such activities help. Thus the observed incidence of mood disorders in creative types may not be cause and effect in the presumed order, at least not in all cases. Virginia Woolf, for example, who ultimately committed suicide, stated that she could not have survived as long as she did without her writing.

The search for something *new* can also put an individual at odds with the dominant currents of his or her culture—or at least its economics. Accepting a creative calling can require immense self-confidence and persistence. As Rollo May points out in his classic *The Courage to Create*,[20] courage is at the very heart of creativity, since to be creative requires us to see reality in counterintuitive ways, to not be satisfied with something perfectly acceptable to everyone else but rather to strive toward an ideal. Creativity requires placing a bet on oneself and sometimes doubling-down despite self-doubts and that nagging internal critic the best writers learn not just to tolerate but to rely on.

And if the inspiration doesn't come today, or the next, or the day after that or for weeks or months? If we stick with the *process*, at least we're getting words on paper. The point is that whenever you're working on something, you're making yourself available to a great new idea, and even if the Muse does forsake you, at least you've gotten some work done.

~

ALLAN GURGANUS: Just work every day. And only write about things that interest you profoundly. Otherwise, why do it? Dramatic things. I keep a kind of casual journal. I just had the experience of writing in longhand a kind of inventory of what I'm working on, where it is in its development, a kind of storekeeper's stocktaking; it proved very helpful. A sort of "note to self." Anything you can do to give yourself some outside reinforcement: "I am writing this book, I have had this problem, but now I feel clearer about character A." Give yourself an alternative forum for talking about these things, like group therapy. It affords another kind of reality, gives the whole process a kind of medical dignity.

If you write every day, badly or well or hideously, you're spared ever being, technically, stopped. I think the hardest part of writing is the starting and stopping. My way is to just continue, and thus the quality comes and goes, but at least you're writing.

MICHELLE HUNEVEN: I get up, go out to my office, ding about with e-mail and the news for a bit, then read something—usually fiction I admire—until I get itchy and want to make fiction myself. I work until I get something solid done, sometimes till the early afternoon, often till much later. Sometimes, despite an entire day in the office, I'll have very little to show for it.

I have blocks. I get stuck. I vow I'm not going to beat my head senselessly against the same scene, but I often forget this vow. Sometimes I'll be stuck on the same three pages for a month. *OY!* I'm not sure, though, that deeper work isn't being done at the same time, a kind of subterranean accumulating and organization. So while I'm trying to get a dialogue straight, an entire novel is taking shape.

DOUG UNGER: I don't believe that creativity can be lost. It's possible to write a dull story, or to fail at writing a passage in a longer book, or make a false start. It's possible to write badly, and I think it's actually necessary to write badly sometimes in order to write well; that's just a part of the process. The key is to recognize when one is writing badly, as it is also to know when one is writing well. Hemingway called it a "built-in shit detector" and I think, actually, when people speak about being blocked or their creativity being lost, it's that the means of judging what they are writing has been confused somehow, or it has shifted away from what's beautiful, or effective, or right in the writing. Along with a capacity to recognize when one is writing badly, it's important to know when the words are right, all the sentences are falling just the way they should. That's the best feeling in the world. Sometimes, writers can get discouraged and lose self-confidence. But I think the creativity is always there. It's how to use it, how to access it, how to maintain a discipline to keep on writing that's most important. Writing is a practice. Creativity is a practice. One has to keep practicing.

JAYNE ANNE PHILLIPS: Every writer has his or her own relationship to writing. Mine may not be theirs. Thinking about that relationship is part of the process. Whatever I'm working on has to be extremely compelling to me, so compelling that I can put it down for weeks or months at a time, and pick it up and reenter it. Of course, I have never stopped thinking about it.

I don't "plan" my work; I enter into a story or novel through the first line, which at the end, of course, may not be the first line.

JOHN IRVING: I write last sentences first. I work my way backward from the end of the novel, which is the first thing I know, to what the first chapter should be. By the time I actually write the first sentence, I have a virtual road map of the whole novel—either in notes or in my head. And in eleven out of twelve novels, that last sentence, which I wrote first, has never changed. But I don't know anyone else who writes a novel this way. Why would I think this is a "method" worth imposing on young writers? I sincerely doubt that this "method" would work for anyone else.

I think if something happened and I had to teach again, I would be inclined to do it the way I did when I knew nothing about my own method, when I was still figuring it out. Just be patient, be kind, try to figure out what the strengths and weaknesses of the individual writers are; after all, if writers aren't individuals, then no one is. I didn't tell T. C. Boyle the same things I told Ron Hansen or Allan Gurganus; they were and are totally different writers, and I noticed very distinctive things in each of them. What good would generalizations have done them?

> I write last sentences first. I work my way backward from the end of the novel, which is the first thing I know, to what the first chapter should be.

SANDRA CISNEROS: You need to do whatever you can to keep the work going. It helps if you have a trust fund; it helps if you can do without a lot of sleep. But you have to be obsessed; it's not discipline, but obsession.

Right now I'm trying to do the opposite of *Mango Street* . . . I want to do something small and tight. But it's not as if I sit down and write plots or something and see where it leads. I don't feel like I have a plan when I write. For instance, I had an idea for a conversation, so I sat down and started writing a screenplay. I figure the end will evolve out of the process. Right now, I don't have anything definite in mind, just a vague situation; I'm never sure what I'm writing until I'm halfway through it, and even then. . . .

T. C. BOYLE: When I sit down in the morning, whatever I'm working on, a short story, I go back to a little before where I left off, depending on how I feel. Some days I go backward. It's a way of getting out of the world, of letting the subconscious work. I suspect a lot of writers do that, but I don't know; I don't hang out with other writers and don't talk to other writers.

That's why I try to work every day; you need that everyday propulsion to get through it. But every novel since *Riven Rock* has been interrupted at some point because I tour so much. I've learned to live with that. I'll bring materials with me when I'm on the road, so I don't lose track and it doesn't get stale.

MARVIN BELL: Late night is my space, as I mentioned. I can write in any physical space, especially if it's night. I don't need a study made for writing, and indeed I wouldn't feel comfortable in a room with all the advantages. I sometimes stream jazz or alternative music or doo-wop or classical music on the laptop, but not always.

Get up early or stay up late. Think of oneself as being a writer every day. Write something, anything, almost every day. Welcome the arbitrary beginning. It's not what one begins with that matters, as much as the quality of attention one gives to it afterward. Surrender to the materials. Don't try to satisfy some vague standard or ideal. Rather, try to be interesting to yourself. Stop thinking of literature in the usual ways. Think of the piece at hand as a dance. Writing being a metabolic activity, allied with the breath—*inspiration*! For a writer, the act of writing is kinetic, a dance. Again, the idea is always to write with abandon.

DOUG UNGER: My personal approach to a writing space is that it's in my head, not in the physical location. I've had to learn to write almost anywhere, anyplace. Lately, I've been writing a lot on airplanes, booking a window seat in coach and settling in to type away until I go through two laptop batteries. I can make it through half of a draft of a new story on a long flight, or two scenes of a screenplay, or rewrites on an essay. It's a hell of a way to work, I suppose, but I've always worked that way—wherever I can set up, at whatever kind of space, on any uncomfortable chair in hotel rooms while traveling.

I think it's important to learn how to write wherever and whenever you get a chance. I recall a story about Isaac Babel, how he wrote some of his later short stories while on the run from the Czarist police. He had to sit down on tree stumps and pen off a story, then mount up and keep moving. Or I think about Caravaggio and some of the truly great smaller paintings he did when he was being hunted by the Papal

> My personal approach to a writing space is that it's in my head, not in the physical location. I've had to learn to write almost anywhere, anyplace. Lately, I've been writing a lot on airplanes.

Guards—he was able to make a painting in a few hours—beautiful, seductive portraits.

I tend to live a life filled with distractions, phone calls, people in need of this or that, and a dozen projects with deadlines going all at once, so I've learned to steal time wherever I can, in my office at the university. Fifteen minutes here and there, or I take a weekend day and work from 9:00 AM or so until around four in the afternoon. In other words: These days, I catch fifteen-minute sessions at the university office, in between phone calls or drop-ins or student appointments, or I come in extra early and get a whole hour, which puts me in a good mood all day. I've come to believe that I'm the kind of writer who needs to be surrounded by chaos to make some kind of order from. I prefer to work at home, on my old wooden door for a desk. It's more comfortable there, and hey, it's my home, right? Still, it's a home always busy with people, so there's plenty of chaos to make order from.

ANTHONY BUKOSKI: I need quiet above all. When I write, I put cotton in my ears. Last May, I bought a headset that blocks out sound. Understand that this headset has no electronic wiring for pumping in music. The headset is to block out noise when a person cuts the lawn or works near heavy machinery. It is awfully tight and hurts my head sometimes. So there I have cotton in my ears and a headset. I also own two Sleepmates, a machine that, when plugged in and turned on, makes a humming sound and has two speeds, faster humming and slower humming.

> If I can have a quiet place, or if I can make the place quiet, then I am content and can write. Nothing else matters, really.

I just don't like noise, barking dogs especially. If I can have a quiet place, or if I can make the place quiet, then I am content and can write. Nothing else matters, really. And I live in the country, so it is already pretty quiet.

Does this sound crazy? I don't mean it to sound crazy.

GERI LIPSCHULTZ: By way of a space, a setting, in which to be at your best as a writer, I think of the Dickinson poem, "To Make a Prairie, you need clover and a bee and reverie. The reverie alone will do, if bees are few." So I need solitude, a window, a clean tabletop, a chair, the tools (typewriter, computer, pen, paper), and reverie. If I have an idea, if I'm buzzing with the idea, all I need are the tools. But I must say that I find the idea of a retreat (a week or two away from family obligations) especially appealing.

I confess that I keep a journal and have since the time before Iowa. I have too many journals. And I keep track of my dreams, which is not to say I write them down each night. I used to memorize dialogues that I overheard, as if it were a ping-pong game. For the first ten years, I would buy special paper, special equipment. Sometimes I would "dress up" because I'd read somewhere that other writers did such things. Dame Edith Sitwell apparently used to lie in a coffin for her inspiration. Proust smelled apple peels. I have no coffins around, but I do enjoy smells, although I don't keep apple peels in my drawers, as Proust apparently did. Sometimes I tack up quotes, but usually I get tired of them. Pictures, too.

Well, kids changed my writing habits; I went from novels to stories. I would start writing at night and I'd go into the wee hours. I usually start writing a story by hand, in one of my notebooks, and then I go to the computer.

DOUG UNGER: At home or in my office, I write in a very messy room with papers and books piled up, books I use to think with when writing will be all around, amid piles of papers, previous drafts, two chairs stacked with books and papers, so I tend to write out of this chaos of information. It looks sloppy. But as chaotic as it seems, I know where things are in all the mess. So I tend to write out of a shifting mess, and then about once every six months, I clean it up, and then I can't write. It'll take about two weeks for me to get back into the zone. On the other hand, I'll use those two weeks of being frozen because I've cleaned up to start an essay or a grant application.

I get up in the morning, have coffee, think for thirty minutes, and I do a prayer and a meditation, then I'll get to work. I'll be able to put in at least an hour, or an hour and a half, or three or four hours on a good day, then I have to run off to teach or meet a student, or do something else that takes me away.

GERI LIPSCHULTZ: For months and months, I avoided writing. I had decided I should go back to get my PhD, and as I look back, I see the nature of my procrastination. I think I was in a spot where my life really had changed. I was changing. It was in my head but something was not quite digested. I was still too far outside what I was doing, so I really wasn't in a position to write.

In the last year, I have managed to write some new work, and I found myself really revising the old work, really seeing it anew. I'm excited when I have time that I know I can devote to my own writing. I find myself multitasking much more than I did during my first year as a doctoral student, and part of this multitasking amounts to writing. I've also been sending out work, both fiction and proposals for nonfiction. I've had a little success, and that's always an easier vibration for me. It's easier to write when the fire's going, when you're simply stoking the fire. At any rate, there's no typical day.

For the last twenty-four years—since I had kids—I would carefully hoard my writing time because I needed at least two hours for anything to "happen." I am still aiming to get up at 4:30 AM, William Stafford style, so I can work with nothing interrupting me. I've not yet succeeded in making that early morning time habitual. I'm still someone who finds herself writing into the night. When my children were growing up, I would typically— when I'd manage to find an hour with no one about—feel this jubilation. I would rush upstairs and go back and forth from the computer to the couch with a notebook. When I do have something happening, I'll write late into the night, 2:00 or 3:00 AM. When I was younger, I'd write until sunrise.

ALLAN GURGANUS: My ideal schedule is to go to bed before midnight; I like to be asleep by eleven forty-five, then wake up at six, have some strong coffee and an apple or . . . I'm all about oatmeal these days (get that choles- terol down), and by six-thirty I'll really be working. That gives me three and a half hours before any offices are open. The telephone answering machine is the writer's best friend; you can hide behind it. To work until one-thirty or two, that's a dreamy day, but I get maybe only the central four hours of that—filet of day, that pure protein at the center of all the starting and stop- ping, where you're totally concentrated.

JOY HARJO: When I'm home and settled, I get into a routine of writing every morning for three to four hours. I find that if I set up a daily appoint- ment, I get into the flow quicker, easier. But I travel and that breaks the rou- tine. I keep trying. I write sometimes late at night. I practice music in the late afternoon. And business . . . the business of setting up gigs, interviews, bookkeepers, gigging, family, home . . . that's another story.

DOUG UNGER: At Iowa, I used to work all night long, from about ten at night until sometime around four or five in the morning, then I'd come home, sleep a few hours, and go off to do the classes, workshops, editing and teaching, and the extra jobs where I'd put in a few hours. I kept up that pat- tern of night writing for years, all the way through when I started teaching at Syracuse, when I'd see my wife and daughter to bed, then head off to write.

Sometimes, I'd write at school, where I've been known to sleep in the office. Connie Brothers actually had to ask me not to sleep in my office at Iowa. (For a time while a student at Iowa, about three months, I lived in that office in the English-Philosophy Building, a.k.a. EPB, sleeping on a couch; and it was easy, really, with a shower and a locker to use over at the gym, and three squares a day at the Student Union). Connie caught me waking up to go to the men's room to wash up, early one morning. I told her I'd been writing all night, which was true, mostly. She told me to go home—really, she ordered me to go home, which wasn't so easy to do, since I hadn't paid rent for some time on the room I was supposed to be renting. When I came back later that day, Connie had disconnected my telephone, reasoning (correctly) that I'd probably have to find myself a more appropriate place to live if I didn't have a telephone with which to stay in touch with people. About a week after that, I moved out of the office and moved in with the actress Amy Burk Wright, who I had just started dating. Later, we married.

Around the mid-1990s, though, I couldn't pull the long night hours anymore and be worth a damn the next day. I started getting up in the morning; then I'd be at the desk around 9:00 AM and keep working until sometime around noon.

DOUG BORSOM: I keep a pad and pen on the bedside table. My wake-up-in-the-middle-of-the-night sessions are the most fruitful. Who knows what's already gone on while I've slept? And maybe the infinitesimal decrease in the solar neutrino flux caused by the planet's shielding makes us all just a fraction smarter at night. Nah. Whatever the reason, the night is better. The pen and paper are for recording after the fact. They are not part of the process of coaxing the *aha!* moment.

Most of my writing is near-future or present-day science fiction, though I think of it as fiction with science fictional elements. Despite my technical background, it is not hard-core sci-fi. There are sometimes technical bits, but they are decidedly subservient to the other story elements. I'm not interested in hardware, just what people do with it.

T. C. BOYLE: I write into the afternoon. I used to write late at night, then when a student at the Workshop, I started writing earlier, starting with *Water Music*, until I was working in the morning. Now I find I have to putter around a bit first, so I start writing at ten-thirty or eleven and work to three or so. Or I might work all day on something. Today, I just finished a new story. I'm working on stories now because I just finished a novel. I'm very rigid about it . . . I won't look at the story until I'm done with these five or six stories, the next book after this novel I just finished. Now I'm taking some notes, jotting down some thoughts.

> I used to write late at night, then when a student at the Workshop, I started writing earlier, starting with *Water Music*, until I was working in the morning.

SHERRY KRAMER: I remember when it was impossible not to write a new play every month or two, but that doesn't happen now. Part of that is the nicotine . . . or the lack of it. I stopped smoking over ten years ago, and it was a disaster for the writing for several years. I went to my doctor and asked him for something that would rev me up and calm me down at the same time. He said, "Sherry, if there were a drug like that, don't you think I'd be on it?"

So without the speed and clarity that nicotine brings, I've had to muddle on alone, but in the end, writing is still pretty much the same. One moment you're minding your own business, living your life, the next you're visited, sort of like an annunciation, by this *thing* you have to write about. And all of a sudden everything in your life seems to be showing you how to see this thing in a way that it is absolutely vital that you see it, the world starts showing you this pattern, it's laid out everywhere you turn, and every day it gets more important to find a way to write about it, and you follow the scent, and you keep focused and open, and you find it, you find this trap door in the world that is the way into your new world, and that's it, you're down the rabbit hole.

Books by the Bed

JENNIE FIELDS: I have books by Richard Russo, Sue Miller, Ian McEwan (*Amsterdam* and *Saturday*), Joyce Carol Oates (*The Falls*), and all of Edith Wharton. I go back to Stegner and Carol Shields, Anne Tyler, Colm Toibin. And *Revolutionary Road*.

JENNIE FIELDS: For years, because my life wouldn't allow me, I wasn't one of those people who sat down at the same time every day and wrote; but when I had a project in the works, I would try to go over what I was working on a few times a day, like fifteen minutes at lunch when I was at the office, or if I had ten minutes, I'd pull up my manuscript and start working on it, and that would keep me thinking about it the rest of the day. When I was young, and my daughter was little, I'd often write from 11:15 to 1:30 every night, while she was asleep.

Now that I've quit advertising after thirty-two years to write full-time, my life has totally changed. I take three- to five-mile walks every morning, and I write every afternoon. I can see what a fantastic difference consistency makes. My book is the focus of my work life. I don't have annoying clients, two-hour commutes, or anything else weighing on me. In the last two weeks, I've written fifty pages. Maybe this is a fluke. I hope not. I certainly can't expect that output consistently. But it's such a dream for me to be able to focus on what truly matters to me now. Also, I have to say, it makes a big difference to me that I've already sold the book I'm working on because it's great to know when I'm finished with the first draft, there will be someone there to "catch it," to help me shape it. Someone who cares.[21]

SANDRA CISNEROS: I try to structure the days I write so I don't have to go out of the house. I try to go directly to my writing. If I clutter it up with voices, I don't write. And I don't write every day. I'm very bad about that. The problem is for me, every time I leave the house, it takes me time to be able to write again; as many days as I've been away, that's how long it takes me to get back to writing. I don't write very much. Jack LaLanne once said something about working out that I think applies to writing. He said he didn't like working out, but he liked having worked out. I don't like to write, but I like having written.

The real writing for me is finishing it, polishing it. It's like spinning straw into gold, it's creating from that straw and working hard on it for weeks and polishing it and arranging it, making it the best possible, and putting your name on it. The stuff we put in our journals, that's not writing. I tell people it's like fishing, the more hours you fish, the more fish you'll catch. If you go fishing just once in a while, you get little fish. It's about getting up early in the morning when it's cold and doing it every day. That's writing. Going out once in a while . . . that's not writing.

> I try to structure the days I write so I don't have to go out of the house. I try to go directly to my writing. If I clutter it up with voices, I don't write.

~

The words "inspiration" and "conspiracy" come from the same Latin root *spirare*, to breathe. *Inspiration* means to breathe in. In the case of writing or the other arts, it means to take in whatever the world or the Muse presents by way of material, to say yes to everything.

Conspiracy means to breathe together. Inspiration is private, conspiracy is public, communal, and the arts include both. A third stage of the creative process, as we've been describing it, what we're calling verification, is going public with that private insight, making sense of the results of that inspiration, and communicating it. What good is a good idea, after all, if you can't express it (and maybe make a buck off it)? As Joyce Carol Oates puts it in the introduction to her book, *The Faith of the Writer*, "Since writing is ideally a balance between the private vision and the public world, the one passionate and often inchoate, the other formally constructed, quick to categorize and assess, it's necessary to think of this art as a craft. Without craft, art remains private. Without art, craft is merely hackwork."[22]

In the sciences, experimentation, observation, and analysis are used to test and verify a hypothesis. In the arts, verification is more a matter of expressing one's own insights, clearly, artfully. And while the heart of the process might be the *aha!* (if it comes), the real work takes place after, when we try to make sense of it. And what writer hasn't had a brilliant idea that, the next morning after the head clears, seems transformed into a piece of crap, which itself, a day or two later and of its own volition, has transformed itself once again into a work of pure genius?

The creative process is rarely a progression from one step to the next, but often a messy series of loops when learning might be stymied by impasse, which might lead to insight, which leads to an attempt to express the insight, which is itself a sort of learning that might lead to more impasses, a time out, another insight, and more attempts to express that insight.

If there is a part of the creative process that can be taught effectively in a writers' workshop, and learned, it is most likely this part of the creative process, the public, communal stage when we're all working together in a sort of grand conspiracy against the blank page.

It's in a workshop—two years to do nothing but read and write and hang out with other writers and talk about writing and obsess about writing and find out how others work, and to try out what works best for us—that the true shape and dimensions of our own individual creative processes emerge.

~

GORDON MENNENGA: I think there's a presumption that all writers work in the same way, the same energy for what they do. That's not true. Scott Spencer, who wrote *Endless Love*, was once asked why were there five years between his novels. What happened? And he said, "Well, it takes me five years to write a novel; that's my pace." There are no guidelines....

Each writer needs to find the way he or she works best. And that's one of the problems with workshops, I think. If you go at the wrong time in your career, a workshop can get in the way of that process of finding out how you write best, for good or for ill. If you have a lot of promise, and you're headed toward direction A, and you go to the workshop and you're told, no, go in direction B, and that doesn't pay off... can you go back to A? Some people, I think, got terrible advice there.

The worst advice I ever got? Mary Lee Settle read two of my stories and said, "Don't write like that." So how was I supposed to write? Like her, she told me. She wanted these epic-quality novels with lots of symbolism, decorated sentences, Southern writing. She was very limited in what she thought was good, and she let it show. It took me a while to get over that, as I thought I was going in an interesting direction. She didn't like short sentences; she didn't like explicit writing. She liked subtlety and the romance of language. I wasn't into that. I was into Ray Carver kind of writing, I'll admit it. "A man with two hooks for hands shows up at your house" and that sort of thing. And she just didn't like it at all.

But Ros Drexler liked it.

The best advice? To keep writing no matter what.

ANTHONY BUKOSKI: I don't think my habits have changed over the thirty or more years I've been doing this. I still compose longhand. I still use a typewriter for later drafts. I still think that writing one page of typed prose in a day is a good day. This means I have written two pages longhand, then typed and probably retyped the page. Sometimes I can get two pages done before my mind gives out. I have never been one for sustained writing the way my friend W. P. Kinsella wrote or the way I remember Joe Haldeman telling me he wrote. They'd sometimes work all night long. I recall seeing Joe, a fine man who was always patient with me, sitting bleary-eyed drinking coffee in that bar whose large window faced the street Iowa Book and Supply was on, Dubuque. He'd been up all night, and here I'd be, well rested, toddling off to teach a class as a teaching assistant. I wished I could have been Bill Kinsella or Joe for their tenacity.

ERIC OLSEN: Someone who knew me from our years back in Iowa gave me a photo of me sitting at my desk in my apartment on North Gilbert Street. I'm holding a cigarette, a Sherman's (a pretentious sort of cigarette that poets smoked), my face is obscured with smoke, and I'm wearing a flowered shirt with a vest, which is what I always wore, and behind me is an Underwood manual with a yellow second sheet sticking out of it—didn't we all compose on yellow second sheets back then?

The problem with a computer, for me, is the ease of editing. I don't know when to stop, so I end up going in circles, like driving around looking for an address that doesn't exist because I copied it wrong. You know you're in the right neighborhood, but you can't quite find where you want to be. On a computer, I just keep going around and around and around. I've tried going longhand for a first draft, then to the computer for a rewrite. But my handwriting's so awful I can't read half of what I scrawl. I have an Olivetti portable, which I used to carry around when I was doing journalism and I was on the road a lot. Sometimes I think I should compose on that first.

> The problem with a computer, for me, is the ease of editing. I don't know when to stop, so I end up going in circles, like driving around looking for an address that doesn't exist because I copied it wrong.

DON WALLACE: The electric typewriter itself gave me energy and ideas, humming away, like the guy in the library whose leg is jiggling so fast it shakes your end of the table twenty feet away, making you nervous, making you weird. When I left for college, my father had rather mysteriously given me a typewriter (electric was a very new technology at the time), an Adler Satellite, not one of those office IBMs that required a typesetter's approach to spaces and margins. Growing up, doing high school journalism, I'd pecked at an old manual Remington.

JOE HALDEMAN: I have a screened porch, a so-called "Florida room," behind my house in Florida. I work there for a few hours in the morning dark, starting around four or four-thirty. The room has no electricity, so I work by the light of several oil lamps.

I write in longhand, fountain pen, in bound blank books. I don't like pencils or erasers. If I change something in ink by crossing it out, the original is still visible. Sometimes I was right the first time.

I write slowly, and my first draft is very close to the final version. I'll typically write between three hundred and five hundred words by the time it starts to get light. Then I quit for breakfast, and later in the morning (after e-mail and diary), I type the day's work into the computer, changing a word here and there.

Sometimes I continue writing on the computer, beyond the handwritten text. If it's less than a paragraph, I just write it into the bound book. If it's a couple of paragraphs or more, I print it out and paste it into the book.

We travel a lot, so I often work in hotel rooms (bad) or campgrounds (good). An extreme case was *Forever Peace*, 868 handwritten pages done at sixty-six different desks (and campfires, cafés, and counters) in twelve states and ten foreign countries.

In the past month, I've added a gadget to that process: Dictate, a speech-recognition program that types out what you're saying with an astounding degree of accuracy. So instead of typing out my handwritten text, I just speak it into the computer, which provides an interesting intermediate step in rewriting.

> I write in longhand, fountain pen, in bound blank books. I don't like pencils or erasers. If I change something in ink by crossing it out, the original is still visible. Sometimes I was right the first time.

ALLAN GURGANUS: Hugh Kenner wrote a great book about the typewriter and the impact its invention had on literature, *The Mechanic*

Muse.[23] Kenner swears that Eliot's *Wasteland* could not have been written without the advent of the typewriter.

When you look at *Wasteland*, you see it defies being written in Victorian-Edwardian longhand. I mean it's all about the use of the space bar. It is like early twentieth-century Russian experimental painting: White on white. It participates in subtraction, not the additive impulse of the heroic nineteenth century. And the Hollow Men of the poem emerge from this spatial sense of negation that a machine makes possible.

I don't think we yet know what impact computers will have on writing. But I do feel glad I came into writing when I did, first learning to type. When I was in the Navy, they taught me to touch type, seventy words a minute. I still can't type as fast as I think, of course. But I'm getting there, if only because my speed of thought must be slowing as I get older.

I still own my first Hermes portable. I bought it because J. D. Salinger had written *Catcher* on one. I got the same model. I bought a manual typewriter rather than an electric because I was that sure there'd be a nuclear conflagration. There would be no electricity, but I'd still be able to type. Even though I'd have radiation sickness, I'd be clattering away . . . I even bought a big stock of ribbons.

I've been thinking of getting my Hermes refurbished, if only to type letters, so they'd have those little quirks, like the o's all charmingly clogged. Puts you in mind of Kipling in India, Hemingway in Spain.

I think slowing down may be a good thing for a writer, especially in short stories. In a novel, there's lots of "forward spillage" that's narratively necessary and enriching. But maybe for a shorter form it's good to build a work one perfect sentence at a time, slow it down that way.

At first, I only wrote longhand, but lately, I've been doing essays on the computer. I've had a sort of relationship with the op-ed page of the *New York Times*. You'll get a phone call on a Wednesday morning saying, "You know, North Carolina's just been hit by a flood. You're now our go-to flood guy and your hometown is underwater. What do you think about this?" So you rush to your birthplace and you wade in and look around, taking notes, and you come back and write it all on your computer, and by Thursday you get them 1,500 words. I wouldn't recommend it as a way of making a living, but the impact of such a piece when it works is incredible. Sometimes the things you get are what you would never find or ordinarily invent: wonderful images like a submerged traffic light still going from red to green to yellow. I saw it with my own eyes. Or a Lexus in a basement garage, brand-new, underwater, with the lights going through every permutation, turn signals, lights to dim, interior light flicking on and off, as if a scuba ghost sat at the controls. This was during the Hurricane Floyd flood of '99.

In writing for the *Times*, since all editing goes on online, there's no point in writing it longhand and then transferring it to a computer. Maybe it's a guilty pleasure; I'm not sure it's ultimately productive, but the assignment is almost irresistible.

Now with e-mail, concurrently as you're composing, you're getting *bing, bing, bing*, the messages are coming. E-mail is my favorite technology that's happened in my lifetime. Seems I've been waiting my whole life for the Internet.

ANTHONY BUKOSKI: I sit on a chair with a throw pillow on my lap and a record album atop that. I write longhand with a pen. I use paper that has writing on one side, old quizzes, and so on. I try to fill the reverse side with my writing.

In grade school, the Sisters told us that the paper we wasted in our lives would be used to help burn us in hell. I am not laughing at them for saying this. They taught a valuable lesson about conservation.

After I fill the back of the sheet by writing with my pen, I transfer the handwriting with an inexpensive electric typewriter. Here again I use scrap paper. I don't own a computer, though I have one in my office at the university. A typewriter has served me well. You can get one for about $140. To be at my best as a writer, this is what I need.

GORDON MENNENGA: I think fiction was better when it was physically harder to write. Margaret Atwood wrote about her favorite pen. I have my students write a piece in longhand, then type it, and we talk about the differences; they said they thought harder about word choices writing longhand.

There are some studies of boys, if they're made to use their other hand for more things, they become better readers and writers. Girls don't seem to have the problem. There's a fairly strong correlation between being left-handed and creative.

GARY IORIO: I use a computer now, and it has changed my process. In the mid-'70s, I was influenced by Leonard Michaels, and started being a bit of a minimalist. I did it because of the difficulties of typing stories over and over. I kept things simple and clean. This year I started using a computer to stretch things out and add a little resonance to the brevity. But it's too damned easy to edit; I edit in circles. You need to get

> . . . I'll take a yellow legal pad and a blue Bic with me and try writing longhand. I'm trying for a new slant on the story. I thought if I get off the computer that might help. And I like the Bic with its visible ink supply.

off the freaking page. I have a sixteen-page story I'm working on, and I must have printed it out five times!

This weekend I will blast off to Montauk, and I'll take a yellow legal pad and a blue Bic with me and try writing longhand. I'm trying for a new slant on the story. I thought if I get off the computer that might help. And I like the Bic with its visible ink supply.

ALLAN GURGANUS: I use different colored pencils, so I'm keyed to canceling my previous edits. One beauty of this is frequently an early draft is better than I thought it was; it's like a dog that has to have one of those megaphone-shaped tubes around on its neck to keep it from biting and reopening a wound.

Sometimes you think you need to utterly rewrite. But you find: Hey, this isn't bad; I need just three new words here, rather than start over. That's what D. H. Lawrence did; he'd finish one draft in longhand, put it in a drawer, then take out a whole new ream of paper and start over again without looking at the first version. And that explains his novels, both the brilliant things and the sloppy repetitions, the circles. It's not really an efficient way to work, but it was his, no choice.

I go through a ton of paper. My attic is loaded with drafts. I need to do some penance and go out and plant dozens of young trees.

SANDRA CISNEROS: I edit a lot. I write, then edit. I edit as I write; I'll write a paragraph, then edit. I don't write in a linear fashion. I write what I call "buttons." That's because I don't know any other way. If I'm writing a story, rather than going beginning to end, I just write scenes and don't worry about what connects them. Maybe dialogue . . . all out of sequence. I imagine I'm going to die in eight hours, so what part of this story do I need to write today that I haven't written because it's going to be published posthumously? I might just write some dialogue between a mother and daughter.

If I'm in a funk and tired about this book, I'll write about someone who's tired. I just use it as a place to go off from, then write it and rework it until it's beautiful, and then I have this little button. And my job is done. And then the next day I work on another button, and then I put them together and start to see patterns. So I don't work in a linear way. But there are moments when what I've done today takes me to tomorrow.

ALLAN GURGANUS: When I'm working, I go back and forth between my original handwritten first draft and later versions. I look at the first try and I can plainly see how I've overcomplicated it in later drafts. At times I've torn it up by the roots, given it a wig, then a hair transplant. It was often better the first time, but I need to try four others before trusting that inaugural thrust.

If I'm lucky, I come back to the freshness of the first draft. For me that's all part of the process, that back and forth, which is probably why I haven't published as many books as I might have, but I'm very proud of what I've put out there.

You can publish a book a year, and you can have a baby every ten months. But pretty soon, you're having idiots. And, as a loyal mom, you yourself are often the last to know.

I see how long a writer's productive life can run. Cheever was sixty-five when we worked together at Iowa. He lasted quite a long time after that. He finally quit drinking, and he had the great joy of publishing *Falconer*, which I don't think was his best book, but it sure got lots of attention. He was on the cover of *Newsweek*, and he loved the last-minute fanfare. My friend Elizabeth Spencer, a wonderful writer who lives here, had a musical based on *Light in the Piazza*, her novella from the '60s, and here it is forty-four years later and she's winning all these Tonys. She went on an ocean cruise, and she's enjoying the hell out of life; and it's wonderful to see people live long enough to see their work come around.

> You can publish a book a year, and you can have a baby every ten months. But pretty soon, you're having idiots. And, as a loyal mom, you yourself are often the last to know.

I don't think Cheever would have thought he was just starting out at sixty-five, though, partly because he'd come so close to dying from his heart ailments, and the alcohol was such a force in his life and it didn't make him happy. Both Carver and Cheever, who were at Iowa at the same time, had some good years once they stopped drinking, but also perversely they both got cancer at roughly the same time. I've wondered sometimes . . . I'm not arguing against alcoholics stopping drinking, but I do wonder if the combination of quitting smoking and stopping drinking after having done both daily for fifty years is, you know, a shock to the system. It seemed so cruel that Carver was just at the peak of his powers when he died so young.

DENNIS MATHIS: It's just hard work to me, making something from nothing. I suppose sometimes I get into that alpha-wave mode where things come out of my fingers without passing through my brain. But writing is so damned linear and tedious for me, like stringing teeny little beads into a long, long, long necklace. I prefer painting, where you can use a big brush (or preferably a paint roller) and cover wide swaths all at once. And also because

I'm so slow at writing, especially when I habitually look at yesterday's writing and throw it away. I am not prolific.

Books by the Bed

JAYNE ANNE PHILLIPS: Stacks of application portfolios for the Rutgers Newark MFA Program, which I designed and direct.

JAYNE ANNE PHILLIPS: As to blocks, life provides them; they aren't in my mind. I tell students to stay in their chairs—at the computer—with the work. I read my own lines, repeatedly sometimes, until I know where to go next. Frank Conroy used to tell us in workshop that we should begin every day by reading the last page we'd written, and then continue. And if that doesn't work, go back ten pages, or fifty.

For me, material dictates form. The book teaches me how to write it, just as it should teach the reader how to read it.

JENNIE FIELDS: One of the hardest things for me is to keep that inner editor at bay. When I was younger, I didn't have that problem; I was probably too stupid to have that inner editor. I think with experience, you get better, but also too conscious. When you're young, you have that youthful bravado, but that goes away, and you have to force yourself to take chances.

On days when my inner editor becomes a tyrant, I step away from the manuscript, read something, go for a walk; otherwise, I'll do more damage than good.

When my daughter was young, I'd write fiction at night, but I could never do advertising at night. The one thing I see common to both is that ideas happen when you're least aware, when you're falling asleep, on a train, in a funk, when I'm on the elliptical trainer, or walking; I walk everywhere: it's wonderful thinking/creating time.

GORDON MENNENGA: I don't think younger writers tend to get stuck as much as we do when older; they're too innocent.

I give a reading every year. I make a deal with myself that I can read only new stories, so I have to write, and that keeps me alive. Maybe if everyone had to give a reading every year, you'd come up with something. Nothing like the looming threat of embarrassing yourself for motivation.

I think if you're too long away from writing, the internal editor gets stronger. A lot of other things get in between you and what you're trying to do, not only the editing thing but other excuses and problems.

One thing that helps me, when I'm stuck, is to change my circumstances. Once I wanted to send a story to the Nelson Algren contest. This was 1995, just after I'd moved with my family back to Iowa City. I was going in circles. I couldn't write it, so I drove from Iowa City to Boulder, Colorado (I love driving and thinking), and got a hotel room and started typing and eating takeout French cuisine; and when I left Boulder, I had the story done and I sent it in and got an Algren award.

DOUG BORSOM: When I'm stuck, first I distract myself from the problem with other writing, reading, my schoolboy Latin or Greek, math problems (I also do math problems when I'm stuck on a math problem, but simpler ones in a different area). I feel like I need something that will keep my mind focused but away from the obstruction.

The one thing I will *not* do is go on the Internet. Vast quantities of time disappear and the experience is diffuse and fragmented. I might as well drink bourbon.

When I do reapproach the obstruction, it is typically in the middle of the night or while I am on a solitary walk. Then I'm obsessive, turning the thing around and around mentally. If walking, I often talk to myself, though it's more like semi-subvocalizing, with the volume knob up only a fraction. The advent of cell phones and those little wireless in-ear headsets has made me less self-conscious and conspicuous. I tend to be unaware of what's going on around me.

I never try to tackle the blockage at the keyboard or with paper before me. Wrestling with it in my head, divorced from the mechanics of writing and from the context in which the problem first arose, seems to liberate my thinking a bit and make it more agile. The way after an argument with someone, once away from the verbal combat, we can think of all the things we should have said.

JOY HARJO: We are all creative beings. We are creating our lives, history, politics with each of our thoughts, our dreaming, our behavior. Can one's creativity be lost? I've lost it along the way . . . Another way to see it, I've learned by watching nature. Last year in New Mexico, the plum trees were outrageously fertile. Fat boughs dropped plums in plentitude (sorry, couldn't help that) everywhere. This year, there were none. Next year, there will be tentative plums. This year, it was pears. All of us have our cycles. A natural part of the creative cycle is the not-creative.

MARVIN BELL: Can creativity be lost? I suppose one can lose the confidence, the illusions of youth, the energy, the need and will to write—whatever it is that encourages creativity in the arts. But lose the creativity? Not really, barring some physical catastrophe. One might come to a point in one's life

Writer's block comes from one's wanting only to write good stuff. Well, the good stuff and the bad stuff are all part of the stuff. No good stuff without bad stuff.

when the writing is no longer necessary. One might quit for conscious reasons. But can one tap into one's more creative side again at any time? Absolutely. For a writer, it only takes the need to write again, and then enough writing until the machine is sufficiently oiled. Creativity creates.

Writer's block comes from one's wanting only to write good stuff. Well, the good stuff and the bad stuff are all part of the stuff. No good stuff without bad stuff. Better to write to be interesting than to satisfy critical "standards." In the end, time and hormones take care of most aesthetic dilemmas.

DOUG UNGER: Don't force it. Never force ideas. Let them happen, let the work happen, let the story come into being on its own terms. This is something like the difference between prayer and meditation. Prayer is the sending out; meditation is the opening up and receiving. Sustaining the imagination is a practice and a discipline, like meditation. One learns how to open oneself up to what comes, letting that play in the mind, take shape, then to do the work of putting it skillfully into words, which is another discipline entirely.

SANDRA CISNEROS: Yes, writing is such a spiritual act, but it's very difficult trying to be God every single day, and what we're being asked to do seems impossible, so tap into all the help you can get.

When I say writing is a spiritual act, I don't mean in terms of any religious denomination. I do mean by this opening ourselves up and humbling ourselves to the point where we get inspired. And what I call the "light," others call the higher self, or inspiration or the zone, or whatever. But I do see it as some divine source we're capable of channeling.

I think I saw it as a child, but didn't have a word for it. You see that little symbol for the Holy Spirit, the dove above an apostle's head, and you're a kid and you say, What's that? and they say, That's the Holy Spirit, now shut up. But they never really explained it, that the Holy Spirit was God, and we're all capable of being God every day for a few seconds.

As a child, I often had religious experiences, but I didn't know them as such. I thought they were normal. You know, you go and sit in a tree and all of the sudden the tree is talking to you. That's not normal, but to me it was. I used to have a little statue of saints in purgatory standing in flames, with chains around their necks and arms, their faces looking up as if saying, Get me out of here! That's how I feel about my writing.

When I sit down to write, I do this nondenominational thing, with respect for all denominations and agnostics and atheists. Call on your higher self, or if you believe in spirits, or your ancestors, call on one person who loves you completely, imagine that person and smile at that person, and imagine that person smiling at you, and then inhale that smile and send that smile back on the out breath. Do this mentally ten times 'til you are in the light, and when you have your work to do, and it's hard, and it's bigger than you, do it with your spirit ally, with their help . . . do it today. And if your goal is to write one page, ask for help with that one page. Ask for wisdom and guidance.

Best of all, most importantly, ask for humility. Be humble because we're always blocking guidance with our ego, and it'll open up our channels to guidance if we can get our ego out of the way.

And then ask for courage because what we're going to be asked to do will seem impossible. But we're never asked to do anything we're not capable of doing.

I ask for humility, courage, and then to be able to work to honor the community.

You can adapt this meditation. It's a very empowering meditation, and humbling, too, because it reminds you that you're one person but you're connected.

JAYNE ANNE PHILLIPS: I have often said that writing is a practice, and that practice is certainly spiritual, in that it requires discipline, concentration, surrender. But it comes at spirituality from a completely opposite direction: through language, rather than despite language or through silence, the attempt to pass through/beyond language and judgment. The writer "works," stays in the chair, within the material, moving toward those moments when we gain access to something larger than the self, larger and deeper than anything the self can know.

> I have often said that writing is a practice, and that practice is certainly spiritual, in that it requires discipline, concentration, surrender.

MARVIN BELL: As in some forms of meditation, one distracts the conscious mind with elements of craft so that the subconscious can float upward, as it always does if given an open lane. So, for example, a poet may be writing a sonnet, attending fiercely to meter and rhyme. Meanwhile, something new may be happening to what we call "content." T. S. Eliot said something like, "Form is the meat with which the burglar distracts the watchdog while, with the other hand, he lifts the jewels."

ERIC OLSEN: When I'm going to work on fiction, which for me is a somewhat different process from nonfiction, I'll light a St. Jude candle. I get them for $1.69 at the local Safeway. St. Jude is the patron saint of lost causes. St. Frances de Sales is the official patron saint of writers, but St. Jude seems more appropriate, if you ask me. He had his head lopped off in 65 CE in Lebanon.

St. Jude is often depicted with a flame around his head, or coming out of the top of it. This flame is meant to indicate that he received the Holy Spirit, along with the other apostles. I think of the flame as symbolizing that inspiration we all hope and pray for. There's something rather writerly about that flame, and the decapitation that's a little like a rejection slip for all your troubles.

I blow out the candle when I'm done working for the day. Thus these candles can last for days, or weeks, a sorry commentary on how often I work on fiction.

The idea of the candle is to remind me that . . . well, I'm not sure. Maybe that I'm not writing fiction because I hope to sell it and make a buck (as if!) but because, well, I guess because I can't help myself.

Anyway, it's my little attempt to set the time I work on fiction apart from other time.

I have the candle right in front of me at my desk, and also a *retablo* of St. Jude hanging on the wall, so I'm always looking at the poor guy no matter what I'm working on, and at least thinking about my fiction, even if I'm not working on any at the moment. I think it's helpful to have nagging little reminders.

ALLAN GURGANUS: You can't write all day. I read all the *Paris Review* interviews from Hemingway to Nabokov. The one thing they all had in common: they couldn't work more than four hours a day. If you're really writing well, with the concentration required, four hours is an eternity day in, day out.

It gets harder to concentrate as you get older. I now take breaks every hour or two. First, your life is more complicated than it was when you were younger, and there's more intervening. And then your quality of memory and your focus, all that stuff . . . It's almost like the level of sexual energy and level of cerebral ferocity that is required, it lasts just so long. So what do you do the rest of the day? Not booze, and not finding your fifth wife.

Morning is the best for me. Some writers write later. Yeats was totally nocturnal. Some people don't wake up until everyone else is asleep. But I am literal as a rooster. Hangovers are the enemy because anything that interferes with waking clarity must be expunged.

I want to go to work immediately after dreaming, so the dream is continuous with the writing.

~

If there's any one thing we might learn in a workshop, it's to be open to the possibilities for ideas, insight, or inspiration—that is, to be available, to say yes to everything. This can be a pretty tough thing to pull off when sunk in the depths of writer's block (and who hasn't been?). Blocks are part of the creative process. So are frustration and desperation, since the search for something new usually hits some rough patches, if it doesn't grind completely to a screeching halt. Besides, the Muse is nothing if not fickle.

Successful writers seem to have faith in the process and to accept the blocks as part of that process. Often in the lore of creativity, the breakthrough insight—that big *aha!*—comes only after dashed hopes, and gnawing frustration, when the soul begs for mercy and release.

Many creative laborers structure a time-out into their routines, trusting that it is a forgivable variation of productivity. Einstein, for example, was a devoted practitioner of the long walk, during which he says he did some of his most productive thinking. So were Darwin, Wordsworth, Coleridge, and plenty of others.

"When I first came to the Workshop years ago," recalls Marvin Bell, "we had our offices in old barracks by the river that runs across campus, and my office was just down the hall from Kurt Vonnegut's. Sometimes I'd walk by his door, and he'd be inside doing chin-ups from one of the pipes hanging down from the ceiling. At first I figured he was crazy, then one day I realized he was thinking."

For others, the time-out is sleep, and what is sleep, after all, but the penultimate time-out? The philosopher and mathematician Bertrand Russell would often work on a problem to the point of exhaustion, then give up and go to sleep. He claimed that the solution would frequently come to him in a dream.

The history of science is filled with other tales of dream-inspired breakthroughs. In 1920, the physiologist Otto Loewi was stumped. He'd been searching for insights into the conduction of nerve impulses in frog legs, but to no avail. Then one night he dreamed of bloody frogs. He turned on the light, jotted some notes about the dream, and went back to sleep. In the morning, he discovered that his notes were an indecipherable scrawl.

But the next night the dream frogs visited him again, and this time when Loewi woke up, he rushed immediately to the lab, where he conducted a dream-inspired experiment establishing that nerve impulses were transmitted chemically, a discovery that won him the Nobel Prize in 1936.[24]

About the same time Loewi was dreaming of frogs, Frederick Grant Banting dreamed of an experiment that, when he carried it out, led to the first effective treatment for diabetes. Banting was, like Loewi, awarded a Nobel Prize.[25]

A productive time-out might simply be the time you spend *away* from the work, remaining open to the possibility that anything you do, anyone you meet, anything you see or read, might provide a good idea: Say *yes!* to everything.

The literature about literature is full of anecdotes about the little moment in the midst of unrelated activity that leads to an idea that grows into a major work. Joyce Carol Oates writes at length about this in *The Faith of a Writer*. She recounts stories of James Joyce's epiphanies; E. L. Doctorow happening to see a sign with "Loon Lake" on it; John Updike coming upon the former site of a long-gone Pennsylvania poorhouse and getting the spark of an idea for his first novel, *The Poorhouse Fair*.[26]

When a deadline is bearing down (and when is one not?), it requires a leap of faith to believe time away from your desk can be productive or that you *should* answer the doorbell because the Jehovah's Witness you know is standing there with his pamphlets and spiel at the ready might be the solution to a becalmed imagination, but when we consider what might be usefully taught at a workshop, this faith in the mystery of creativity might be one of the most important.

The value of downtime in preparing the creative mind to be open to possibilities it might otherwise reject is supported by recent findings in neuroscience. During intense study, when you're in the midst of puzzling out a math problem, say, or composing the next clause in a complex sentence, the left hemisphere of the brain (the right hemisphere in left-handed people), which is the seat of verbal, rational, sequential thinking, is doing most of the work. But there comes a point when this side of the brain simply runs out of gas—"pattern exhaustion," it's sometimes called. If you take a break from intense focus on the problem and shift to an "autopilot" activity—walking or a napping or shooting hoops or a warm shower—you give the right hemisphere of the brain, seat of the intuitive, "holistic," nonrational, nonsequential, nonverbal faculties, an opportunity to weigh in. It might come up with something the left brain is overlooking, maybe even something brilliant.

New research into the source of the "insight experience" even locates increased activity in the brain just before that blessed *aha!* in a small fold of tissue on the surface of the right hemisphere. One hesitates to think that the Muse is in fact a little bundle of neurons—it does take some of the romance out of it—but the findings are suggestive. This area of the brain seems to be involved in, for one thing, the processing of metaphors, a function that requires reaching out for remote connections between seemingly unrelated concepts. Mark Jung-Beeman, while at Northwestern University studying the insight experience, noted that these neurons in the right hemisphere are more "broadly tuned"[27] than those on the left side, with longer branches and more dendritic spines. Less intimately associated than neurons in the left hemisphere, they appear to collect information from a larger area of the brain. Relaxation, a time-out, therefore seems to be organically essential in giving this broadly distributed network of associations a chance to perform.

So the creative process artists have described over the centuries based on observations of their own working patterns—a loop of study, practice, impasse, time-out, then inexplicable insight—is reflected in the very structure and function of the human brain.

"The relaxation phase is crucial," Jung-Beeman adds. "That's why so many insights happen during warm showers." Researchers also point out another ideal moment for insights, that moment just before sleep comes or just after waking, when the drowsy brain has undergone a "reset" from the previous day's preoccupations and is mobilizing to equip itself, from an inventory of disassembled patterns, with whatever it might need to deal with a fresh day's challenges.[28]

Perhaps the Muse is nocturnal.

~◡~

ALLAN GURGANUS: Dreams are allies. Sometimes when I am dreaming, especially just after dawn, I can control the dream as a movie director would. I can add barking dogs to the action, or change the landscape, or introduce a new character. Fascinating. Oddly enough, the so-called invented reality of fiction writing can prove far harder to control.

My story, "It Had Wings," starts with the image of a naked angel falling into a backyard, starts with the sound that body makes as it hits new grass. That came right out of a dream. I mean, *verbatim*. I registered the sound of flesh meeting grassy ground as "thwunk." That was like taking dictation, writing down that sound.

But I think, apart from the dream images that you bring to the work, there's some sweetness of the unconscious mind that you want to continually attach, involve in the conscious process. I think the best writing is writing that lifts up forceful from the unconscious. You can shape and trim it, but the source runs deep as a well.

Whether you're writing about how you lost your virginity in the dormitory or how your grandma's Siamese cat died, it doesn't matter; what happens once that given is put into motion is the crucial thing. All the support you have from your dreaming self . . . that's the great ballast, the savings account, and that's the difference between a perfectly reasonable logical short story and those quantum moments that are absolutely unaccountable, memorable because irrationally right. But I must be as habitual as possible in my schedule as an invitation for precisely those crazy bits of happenstance to come calling.

> My story, "It Had Wings," starts with the image of a naked angel falling into a backyard, starts with the sound that body makes as it hits new grass. That came right out of a dream. I mean, *verbatim*.

SANDRA CISNEROS: I routinely incorporate dreams into my work. Or it would be safer to say I use dreams for everything, not just writing. I use my dreams the way some people use meditation, I suspect; I call it horizontal mediation. I just lie down, and it solves everything. It can be something simple, like the title to a story, or maybe it's something more significant.

One time, I was going through a period when I was making some significant changes in my life, and I had the same dream several times. At first, it was puzzling. In the dream, I was leaping from a train, making weird cartoon hairpin leaps off the train and then back on. What was that about? Finally, I realized that I was on track; a time of change is scary, but I was on track. I was doing the right thing. I felt much better about what I was doing, thanks to that dream.

So, take a nap, but first ask for guidance while you sleep. Close your eyes, it's wonderful. I have a big bed in my office.

And if you can sleep with a little dog, so much the better because they're full of spirit. Animals remind you to be present . . . if you can be around them, that's good. Take a nap with as many little dogs as possible.

And then when you get up, don't talk. Go directly to your writing. Go from being horizontal to writing as soon as possible without talking; that means not getting on the phone, not putting on your shoes, not going out of the house. It's very good.

And if you don't have any little dogs? Surround yourself with things of the spirit. Sit next to a tree. A tree has an energy like a dog. Or even a rock.

If I have to wake up with an alarm clock, though, the dream's gone. It only happens when I can wake myself, quietly. The dream is like a telephone wire with birds on it; if the alarm goes off, they take flight. The longer I can stay in that sleep/waking stage, the more of my dreams I can recall.

And if you can sleep with a little dog, so much the better because they're full of spirit. Animals remind you to be present . . .

I was the same way when I was a little girl. My mom thought I was just so fussy because I didn't want to talk when I first woke up. But I wasn't fussy; I was recollecting what I just dreamed.

Or try to walk, a walking meditation. Don't talk. That scares away the light.

ERIC OLSEN: Not long ago I was thinking about a ghost story, a screenplay. I figured there weren't enough ghost stories and so I should write one. But what to write? I read a bunch of ghost stories and started jotting ideas, but nothing came together.

Then one night I had this very strange dream. It was more vivid than my usual dreams, and it had a coherent narrative, unlike my usual dreams, which are mostly gibberish; and when I woke up, I remembered it all clearly. In it, two ghosts were telling me their story, and even as I dreamed, I knew this was the plot of my screenplay. The dream was so unusual, I figured it had to *mean* something. I thought it was a sign. I thought it was sent from wherever such things come from, inspiration from who knows where. It didn't matter. What mattered was that I'd been given a story just when I needed one. A gift, or so it seemed. The two ghosts in my dream even gave me an opening scene, certainly enough to get me going! So I sat down and started writing and got that opening scene down and even a few more scenes . . . and then as usual it came to a grinding halt. So now I keep a notebook by my bed, just in case the ghosts revisit with, say, a nice plot twist . . .

DOUG BORSOM: When I was doing mathematics and working on a difficult problem, it was constantly in my mind, sloshing around behind my eyes. I would wake at night and lie in bed going over the problem. This sometimes led to ideas for new ways to attack it. The same happens when I work on a story. I carry it around with me all day, and at 2:00 AM, I'll stare at the ceiling and run through a scene.

The thinking in each case is very different. The math thinking is much "harder" because it's abstract and there isn't a narrative scaffold. But the *aha!* moments are similar in that they typically involve making an overlooked connection: "Of course! The sum of the log of the function is bounded by the integral of the log of the function with respect to t, and that, in turn, is bounded by another integral whose solution is trivial." Or, "Of course! The narrator spots Sanford crossing the town square and offers him a lift. Not out of kindness, but because he wants to place an obligation on him. That fits perfectly with what I want to do in the next scene."

But all I'm saying is that the stage setting that encourages the thinking, whether for writing or math, is the same. The source of the revelations themselves is still mysterious, coming out of the inky depths like the answers in a Magic 8 Ball.

DON WALLACE: In the beginning, in my late teens and early twenties, writing was like tapping into a buried pipeline. You'd be digging down into a soil of loose associations, and your spade would sever the pipe and a geyser would splatter you in the face as it shot up: whoosh! Late at night or early in the morning, I'd write a short burst, usually as a break from the all-consuming social interaction of the dorm or shared house I lived in, often in the uncomfortable knowledge that I was avoiding studying. In that sense, writing was a liberation and an escape, and I swear the paper seemed to light up as I punched the keys of the typewriter. That was probably the goose-necked lamp peering over my shoulder, but I'll take it.

> Once enough latent images and observations had accumulated in the hopper, my subconscious began telling me their story. And then I'd feel possessed with the need to write it down . . .

Was there a process, a place where the ideas came from? Not from sitting in a chair, at first (that came later, with age and deadline pressure). Often walking, often lying in bed late at night or upon awakening.

To be honest, not a few ideas came on the heels of a late-night blowout, in the fragments of a hangover so all-consuming I was literally unaware of it and thought I was having a vision or a visitation. Later, emotional states themselves, without stimulants, could do the trick, open the doors of perception. Whether hungover or clear-eyed, there'd be a moment when an idea, which is to say a linked set of observations with some kind of zinger at the end, a kicker or unifying image or epiphany, would announce itself. Not with a blare of trumpets, exactly, but maybe with a *ka-pow!* or a *boinggg!* it would enter my consciousness almost fully fledged. Often it presented something like a puzzle of how people I knew were acting, what their motives were, and how from another perspective those actions and motives produced another thing, a whole that was an expression of a universal. Anyway, this riveting moment would unfold in a series of pictures and, often, with a little voice-over narration.

It sounds mystical, and I used to think it was, and still do, but also I always knew it was a process of creation by association. Once enough latent images and observations had accumulated in the hopper, my subconscious began telling me their story. And then I'd feel possessed with the need to write it down, and that sometimes led to a long scribble or, if I managed to make it to the typewriter while still in its grip, a long machine-gun-like burst. The loud echoing shock of typing—we don't have that anymore. The closest thing is overhearing your kid playing Halo or Doom with the sound cranked up in the next room while you're, like, trying to work.

ANTHONY BUKOSKI: I take a lot of long walks. I try to get in twelve hundred miles per year. Another way is to listen to Chopin, as I mentioned, or to Count Michael Oginski's magnificent polonaise that, in English, is called "Farewell to My Country." Oginski also wrote the beautiful Polish National Anthem, which inspires me to write.

Yet another way to sustain this writer's imagination is for me to read another writer's story or novel. If I am impressed by it, I then want to make something similarly beautiful. Movies make me want to do this. Two of my great favorites are Lena Wertmuller's *Seven Beauties* and Krzystof Zanussi's heartbreaking *A Year of the Quiet Sun,* a Polish film.

Anger, too, has helped me sustain the imagination. I get angry at real or perceived slights that occur, or have occurred to me, and I think to myself that I will succeed at what I am doing no matter the emotional, psychological, or physical cost. This is an unhealthy way to proceed. But if you get angry enough, then nothing will stop you.

ERIC OLSEN: Most of my writing is nonfiction and I do it for a buck, so I have to produce something, with or without an *aha!* I can't afford the luxury of writer's block, so I just get on with it without her (I assume the Muse is a her, since wouldn't we be inspired to bet on football and drink more beer if the Muse were a guy?).

Still, even when writing nonfiction, now and then all the pieces fall together in new and exciting ways. I'll be wrestling with a lot of material—facts, data, graphs, interviews, whatever—a real mess, and I'm wondering how to organize it so it makes sense and is at the same time a good read, and the struggle gets harder and harder, until, typically, I'll feel a little restlessness, just an inkling of an idea about how to make it work. These little moments often occur when a particular fact suddenly jumps out at me, and what had been a hodgepodge of other facts crystallizes around it.

I learned a long time ago that I can't grab for it, though. Instead, I have to look away. I usually get up and get a cup of coffee, or turn on CNN for five minutes, check out the Dow Jones average. Or I take a book off the shelf nearby and start thumbing through it, often an art book (art books with lots of pretty pictures seem to work especially well), something to distract myself from that inkling because, again, if I grab for it, it'll skitter away.

It's an actual physical sensation, like restless leg syndrome, but this is more like restless psyche syndrome. In those moments, writing nonfiction for a buck can be every bit as exciting and fulfilling for me as trying to write fiction.

Years ago I did an article about running and creativity, how exercise promotes creativity. It was called "Pumping Irony," a pretty cool title, even if I do say so myself. Unfortunately, it wasn't my title; it was suggested by my poet friend Jeffrey Abrahams. I interviewed Marvin Bell for it. This was back when Marvin was running marathons. "When I feel an actual metabolic change, a physical sensation," he told me, "then I know I'm working on something I'll keep, a poem that's substantial and original."

Howard Gruber, a psychology professor at Rutgers, said, "One thing creative people have in common is energy. You frequently find that creative people go for a lot of walks."

"When I sit around with other poets and we talk about the times we feel like writing, often it's after having done something physical," Marvin told me. "One of the secrets of life is oxygen; the more you have, the better able you are to do everything, even write a poem."[29]

GLENN SCHAEFFER: A couple of years ago, a friend of mine, the director of an art gallery in LA, was putting together a show of African movie posters. I collect these posters and some of them were going to be in the show, and so he asked me to write an essay for the catalogue. So I started writing it and I didn't get very far before I came to a grinding halt, out of ideas. I just didn't know what to say, and I'm running out of time and getting a little desperate. I happened to mention the problem to an artist friend, and he says, "I've got a couple books you ought to look at." So he goes into his office and comes out with about a dozen books about African art, and I flip one of them open and there's this photo of a *nkishi*, an African power figure, and—bingo—suddenly all the pieces of that essay, a real sprawl, came together in my mind and I knew

> I spend a lot of time in bookstores—and I find just what I need. You wander through a bookstore and it's like the book you need at that point calls to you.

exactly how to write it. It was that image of the *nkishi* that brought it all together.

Randomly, when I'm feeling stuck, I start looking through books, books I already own, tossed on my shelves. Or I repair to a good bookstore and start browsing—I spend a lot of time in bookstores—and I find just what I need. You wander through a bookstore and it's like the book you need at that point calls to you.

ROSALYN DREXLER: Books do appear mysteriously on library bookshelves. There are no writers. There are only clerks who fill in the spaces between books with other books so that they do not lean on each other and bend out of shape.

I discovered that writing could fight my battles for me to some extent: could go straight for the jugular. One night I stayed up writing down every nasty thing my parents said to each other during an argument. I was so upset. I loved them so much. I wanted them to stop. Next day I presented the "transcript" to my father. He tore it up and threw it down the dumbwaiter. My writing had had the desired effect.

DOUG BORSOM: For me, the first *aha!* moment is when the idea for a story bubbles up. The verification is in the writing. Sadly, my success rate is pretty low. I start all cranked up, but as the pages increase, so do the obvious shortcomings. I cut. I rewrite. I take a break from it. I experience incremental *aha!* moments. Sometimes it works out, but too often the story falls into a death spiral. It's painful. It's frustrating. I've put aside stories for a year, more, and when I came back to them, I've felt the same surge of enthusiasm I had at the start but still been stymied. Once I start a story, I nearly always finish it. It's a rule I try to hold myself to. Sometimes I'll finish a story multiple times (a very bad sign). But once a story starts to smell, it's unusual for me to be able to save it. This knowledge does not stop me from trying.

The incremental *aha!* moments that occur at least a couple of times in the writing of just about every story—I have a recurring one, where the sudden insight is familiar, but each time occurs in a new context. That is: "The reason you're struggling with this passage is that, contrary to everything you thought, it is not necessary." And "not necessary" is synonymous with "needs to be cut." I can't tell you the number of times I've wrestled with something for hours, days, only to get the *aha!* that the Muse has been trying to send me: "This does not belong in your work."

You might think I would learn, but I don't. Each time I have to earn the insight. I have no algorithm for differentiating between the sort of blocking passage that will yield to an *aha!* moment and one that needs cutting. I have to flail away at all of them.

The complement to the *aha!* moment at the start of the story is the one that goes with its completion. It can be awful when I know I'm somewhere near the end but feel as though I'm not yet there or have perhaps overshot it, or that what I have isn't right. It's like a hair on your tongue you can't quite get at.

Stories that stink, that I can't fix, these remain in a sense forever unfinished. I can never quite give up on them. They just go in the (now electronic) drawer against the nebulous future day when maybe I'll return to them and be able to make them right. Not too different from the copy of *Studs Lonigan* that has waited so many years on my shelf. Someday. Someday. But not this one.

GERI LIPSCHULTZ: There's inspiration everywhere. Learn everything you can. Keep an open ear. Kafka said that when he wrote, the world came to him. Kafka didn't have to go out of the house, but I do. I have to have a balance of in-the-world and out-of-the-world. I guess you could say, "Know yourself," because the thing you know keeps changing. I would also try to be forgiving of people like us who give you advice.

Chapter 5

LIGHT THE TORCHES! GET THE MONSTER!

The assertion in chapter one that "our class" was, pound for pound, the most productive, most published, most awarded class in the history of writers' workshops, all-time, everywhere (despite the fact that we had been not insignificant drags on the class average) isn't one that can be easily tested, which perhaps is just as well. Now and then, whenever we'd try out the notion on former classmates, or those from other classes and other programs, the responses were usually a hedge, "Well, I dunno about *that* . . ." with some thoughtful head scratching, and then other classes at Iowa would be proposed as the best ever, if you really wanted to start making such comparisons. Sometimes an alternative best ever from another school would be offered, often that celebrated group of writers at Stanford in the early '60s that included Ken Kesey, Robert Stone, Tillie Olsen, Larry McMurtry, and Wendell Berry, an amazing cohort for sure. And who knows? Pound for pound, maybe they could have whupped our class.

Still, if one were to tally the publications, awards, and other plaudits for "our class" during the past three decades, the list would be impressive. Our class has had a significant impact on contemporary American letters, no question, and a significant impact on class after class of the young writers they've taught, mentored, or influenced through their work. More significant than other classes? Who knows? But our class was pretty darned good. So what factors contribute to such a bumper crop?

Maybe it was the times. "A certain amount of turmoil and confusion is likely to call forth creative energies," writes Edgar Wind in *Art and Anarchy*.[30] "As we know from the uneasy lives that were led by Dante, Michelangelo, or Spenser (not to speak of Mozart or of Keats), the outward circumstances under which great art is produced are often far from reassuring."

Of course, by the time we showed up in Iowa, things were politically much less tumultuous than they'd been just a short time before. Nixon had just resigned and the Vietnam War was ending, leaving us with no clearly defined focus for our youthful energies and righteous indignation. There was a collective sigh of relief, but also a sense of being set adrift. Who could we hate now that Nixon was in comfortable exile?

In the arts, though, the habit of questioning authority was spilling over from politics into fiction writing, where "experimental" writers violated traditional rules regarding plot, character, and even punctuation, just to see what would happen. In 1969, a year after Barthes declared the death of the author, Ron Sukenick declared the death of much more, writing in *Death of the Novel and Other Stories*: "The contemporary writer—the writer who is acutely in touch with the life of which he is part—is forced to start from scratch: Reality doesn't exist, time doesn't exist, personality doesn't exist."[31] That became a sort of manifesto for some of us, but there were plenty of other options if you were still a little hung up on things such as punctuation, clear writing, and meaning. Gabriel Garcia Marquez's *100 Years of Solitude*, published in '67, offered a lively alternative to postmodern irony, nihilism, skepticism, and malaise: magical realism. And Gordon Lish was busy carving out of Ray Carver's maximalist drafts one minimalist masterpiece after another, while the New Journalism sought to break down the once-sacrosanct barriers separating nonfiction from fiction—and why not, since the author was dead and so were meaning and reality and those quaint bourgeois notions of the value of verifiable objective fact?

It was heady stuff.

But the times were the same times for everyone, not just a few residents of Dodge Street in Iowa City or off the I-80 exit ramp in Coralville. Was there something special about the Iowa Writers' Workshop?

If anything set Iowa apart from the dozen or so other workshops in operation at the time, it was probably its ability to attract, as full-time staff or as guest lecturers, the best-known working writers of the time: John Irving, Kurt Vonnegut, E. L. Doctorow, John Cheever, Leonard Michaels, Rosalyn Drexler, Jorge Luis Borges, Raymond Carver, John Hawkes, Judith Rossner, Anthony Burgess, Robert Anderson, Marvin Bell, Donald Justice, Carolyn Kizer, Stanley Elkin, Stephen Becker, John Updike, and more. This couldn't have hurt; good writers are sometimes—though not always—good teachers, and sometimes just seeing literary greats in the flesh and realizing they were as insecure, dependent, and fallible as we were helped us fight off despair and enabled us keep typing. But the Workshop has *always* attracted the best teachers and visitors; did any more of their insight leave an impression on "our class" than classes in other years?

From the start, first as the country's *only* writers' workshop, and later and for years after as the widely acknowledged *best* writers' workshop, Iowa attracted applications from no end of talented, dedicated, and ambitious young writers. The Workshop didn't really have to do anything to be excellent but accept the talents that applied. Its selection process was probably no more rigorous or perceptive than that of any similar program at the time, and no doubt plenty of young geniuses were rejected and a few klunkers got in, but when you have a large population of the best and brightest to choose from, and you have a comparatively large program so you can accept a wide sample of them, you're bound to get it right fairly often.

One hears a lot of snark about "workshop fiction" and how workshops tend to breed a sort of middle-of-the-road, risk-averse writer. But those who screened the admission manuscripts came from all camps themselves, so those who were selected for the Workshop in the mid-'70s were all over the map in terms of style and content. No one would have confused Tom Boyle's early experiments in a sort of fragmented metafiction with Sandra Cisneros's sharp-edged, inner-city sketches with Jayne Anne Phillips's willowy, unpunctuated new Southern Gothic prose-poems; or Olsen's tries at mythical magical realism with Schaeffer's quirky LA realism or Anthony Bukoski's northwoods realism.

"One of the ironies of the talk about writing programs is that Iowa was sometimes used as a straw man by people who claimed such programs produced look-alike art of no ambition," notes Marvin Bell, "whereas in fact, Iowa was very much the opposite of that. Among the hundreds of my former Iowa students to have published books of poetry are Michael Burkard, Marilyn Chin, Rita Dove, Norman Dubie, Albert Goldbarth, Robert Grenier, Joy Harjo, Juan Felipe Herrera, Mark Jarman, Denis Johnson, Larry Levis, David St. John, and James Tate. There is a wide range of methods in just that little sample. By the way, my former poetry students include a movie star, two well-known playwrights, several successful novelists, a pool hustler, two Zen monks, two professional basketball players, and a former assassin."

The selection process at Iowa arguably wasn't orderly enough to result in the kind of homogenizing consensus that invariably favors middle-of-the-roaders.

The selection process at Iowa arguably wasn't orderly enough to result in the kind of homogenizing consensus that invariably favors middle-of-the-roaders. Many of those in "our class" who couldn't resist having the Workshop secretary pull our admissions files discovered a chaos of conflicting opinions, arrows pointing to opposite ends of the accept/ reject scale, and standoffs sometimes resolved only by the insistence of one determined dissenter. But what mattered most was that we did get in.

~

JAYNE ANNE PHILLIPS: I drove out to Iowa City in my great big car, some kind of Chrysler, with my dog, Sasha, who had already survived several cross-country trips. One time she drank a whole orange juice can of cooling bacon grease in the middle of the desert, with no ill effects.

Iowa City was pretty and less gentrified back then. I moved into two rooms I rented in the back of the Means Real Estate office, or maybe it was insurance. Mr. Means weighed about three hundred pounds. I could always hear typewriters through the wall, and phones ringing. The apartment was actually a big square kitchen, a tiny bathroom with a shower and a narrow porch that had been closed in. The porch looked out on the parking lot of the agency, and I had a free parking space for my big car.

The next year, I lived way out of town on a farm, briefly, and then in the top two rooms, third floor, of a very funky boarding house. I had no door, or I had two doors, one into the bedroom, and another into the living room/ kitchen. The bathroom was downstairs, shared with many others. They made do with newspaper. I seldom used that bathroom. One of the guys in the house sure looked homeless; Fred Ayeroff used to say that guy carefully arranged the sticks and twigs and bits of leaves on his clothes and hair each day.

I knew a wonderful artist who finally moved one of the doors so that I actually had an apartment with (one) door that locked. It was a home improvement.

GLENN SCHAEFFER: My wife and I showed up at Iowa with our raggedy belongings in a big old U-Haul, towing our jaundice-yellow 1969 Ford Falcon behind us. I had a sense of mission—I was going to spend two years, like being away in the Army, and I was going to come out of Iowa as a formed writer.

Oakley Hall had been my mentor at Irvine. He asked me to write him about my experiences at Iowa, and so I did, an expanded riff, and he sent me back a brief note like he didn't quite know who I was. Well fine. I was his first charge to ever attend Iowa. They admit, what, twenty-five out of a thousand applicants? My report on Iowa, I think, was that you get out of it what you need; it has as much to do with where you are as a person as it does with your potential as an artist, and that our peers would be more important to us than the faculty in our development as writers, assuming we evinced any development. One of the Workshop's advantages is scale—it's a sizeable concatenation of talents; something's there for everybody to feed off in a cast of forty or fifty.

My wife and I both got jobs waiting tables at the Ironman Inn in Coralville just days after we arrived.

SANDRA CISNEROS: I didn't know anything when I got to Iowa. I had no concept of self, low self-esteem; I'd never been away from home by myself, so what did I know? I was like a little fifteen-year-old, as far as worldly experience. My father and brothers had protected me completely. They'd walk me to the bus stop, which people did in poor neighborhoods in Chicago. So of course as soon as I met that poet who paid some attention to me, I thought, *Wow, I was the one*. I didn't know how to be a writer except to be bad. But the word apparently was out by the time I got to Iowa. People saw me as so-and-so's little bimbette instead of seeing me for who I was. So when people looked at me, I thought I had lettuce between my teeth or something.

MICHELLE HUNEVEN: I was a naïf! I had an exalted view of writers and writing. I didn't know writers could be competitive. I always assumed the work was all. I had no idea that a writer would consciously make connections, sell herself, make herself known to those in power, strive, etc. Iowa brought writing and writers down to earth for me. At the same time, I thought the Workshop would be a world of writing, that I would live and breathe writing, meet other writers and talk about writing nonstop— and that is pretty much what happened. Except I wasn't working all that well and was easily distracted. My habits left much to be desired. I was awfully young when I went to Iowa, a young twenty-two, and I wish I'd waited a few more years. I was a little stunned by the intensity, intelligence, and competitiveness of the workshop, and I didn't really have all the tools to take full advantage of what was being offered. That said, it was a world where writing fiction was the most important thing, and over the years, I have yearned for that environment again.

JENNIE FIELDS: I was also from Chicago. I don't drive, so I took a bus from Chicago to Iowa City, and I found a place at 404 South Governor Street, a cute little apartment building owned by farmer and wife who'd gotten rich as God selling off acreage to buy buildings. They were the salt of the earth, wonderful people. The wife would come by and say, "I was thinking of you and so I baked you these cookies." I think I paid about $150 a month for the place.

Jack Leggett, the Workshop director, lived in a house on the next block behind us. I couldn't see him working, but I could see the lights on in his house at night and sometimes hear voices in his yard. I loved it that even though I was alone in my little apartment, there was a sense of a family living behind me, which I found comforting. That showed up in my first novel, *Lily Beach*. It had nothing to do with Jack, but the idea of Lily looking out on her professor's house was in the novel. I'm such a Peeping Tom. Writers are observers, thrilled by life going on around them.

ERIC OLSEN: My wife had applied and been accepted late, so we arrived in town just a few days before classes started, with no place to live. But my old man had been a letter carrier, and I knew that letter carriers knew where all the vacancies were even if they weren't listed—letter carriers generally know everything going on along their route. So we drove into Iowa City and just started circling the blocks, looking for the letter carriers, and every time we saw one, I'd yell out the window, "Hey, know of any vacancies?"

Of course, at the start of a new school year, there weren't any, but one guy pointed me to a place on North Gilbert, just down the block from John's Market, still there, and maybe a block and a half from Hamburg Inn number two, also still there. The former tenant, a grad student, had just moved out. The apartment, a one-bedroom, one-bath affair upstairs in an old Victorian, wasn't listed because the landlady wanted to paint it before she rented it again. I told her we'd paint the place for her, plus we weren't given to rowdy ways and misbehavin', even if we were from California. I know the El Camino looked bad, though. I'd made the mistake of parking in front of the house, and I saw the landlady giving it a hard look, then me, figuring anyone drives a car like that was bound to be given to errant behavior on Saturday nights, but I explained that it was my grandpa's car, and he was the one given to rowdiness of an evening, not us. We couldn't have been more well behaved, we insisted, and the sad fact is, it was the truth. So the landlady took a chance on us.

We lived there all four years. We loved the place, and it was great having a good bar and a good grocery and a good hamburger joint just down the street.

JOY HARJO: The reality for me was a gray concrete married student housing complex, the rare appearance of the sun, no assistance from the workshop—I was supported by a university program that assisted minority students and was given a class to teach in American Studies in American Indian culture and literature.

I struggled with a chasm of loneliness. The workshop culture was a foreign culture to me. I felt I was an outsider, but I wasn't the only one. We were all struggling with ourselves in that place and time, which I learned only many years after the fact, when comparing notes with other former students. Even those I had perceived as the insiders carried similar struggles and doubts.

But at the time, I perceived most of the students as from the East Coast with advanced degrees in literature. There was a small circle of students who appeared in tight relationships with the faculty, who always had pat approval no matter what they wrote or said. They knew the intimate language of the workshop and came up through the same literary worlds. The workshop climate was bent on criticism and language surgery. I felt pressured to mimic the style. The first semester I locked my spirit away and wrote copy. Then I began to break free.

> I struggled with a chasm of loneliness. The workshop culture was a foreign culture to me. I felt I was an outsider, but I wasn't the only one. We were all struggling with ourselves in that place and time . . .

GERI LIPSCHULTZ: I was pretty scared when I arrived in Iowa City. I suppose I had as much to learn about life as I did about writing. Perhaps that was true for everyone, but looking back, I see how young and vulnerable I felt. I thought lots of the other writers there had committed themselves much earlier than I had. Even though I had been writing for many years, I never thought, not even for a moment, that I might become a writer. I thought such an aspiration was beyond me.

I arrived with no place to stay, just a tent, a dog, and a car that I bought from my uncle, a used-car salesman in Florida. I'd been waitressing down there in a job my father set up for me. They had moved from New Jersey that year, the year I got out of college, and I ended going down that summer to work so I could buy a car. It was my very first, a terrible car, a Hornet. I asked my uncle, "How many miles on it?" and he told me, "As many as you want."

GARY IORIO: My best friend at Hofstra, Jim Amodio, was a playwright. He applied to the Iowa Playwrights' Workshop and got a conditional acceptance. They sent him to the drama department for an MA, but allowed him to participate in their workshops. I have no idea how I got into the fiction workshop. I just stuck three stories in an envelope and sent it in and crossed my fingers, and a few weeks later I got a letter from Hope Landres that I was in. Sorry, no financial aid. But still, I was floating.

My friend and I drove out together a few weeks prior to the start of classes to look for a place to stay. It was on that drive I saw my first crop duster.

We stayed a couple of nights in a motel in Coralville and then found an apartment we could share that fall. I wasn't married at the time. My buddy and I were both twenty-two years old and had never lived away from home. The joint we found was an apartment complex outside of town, 1100 Arthur Street. The rent was $145 a month, and we both got jobs at Iowa Book and Supply. We loved Iowa City!

When we got back there in the fall, we met a neighbor from the complex, Tom Boyle. I remember Tom's wife and his dog. Jim and I had a party for the Iowa Book and Supply crew that fall, and Tom Boyle was one of the few workshop people we invited.

DON WALLACE: When I arrived in Iowa City, I had one name, that of the older brother of a Santa Cruz classmate named Dave Givens. His brother John, it turned out, was a big deal as a second-year Teaching/Writing Fellow, and he couldn't have been more welcoming. In fact, he invited me to a "second-year only" party at his house before school began. I arrived in my infamous shit-brown Pinto with the exploding gas tanks and walked along John's lakeside house in the fall leaves, thinking happy writerly thoughts.

A grimace of disgust contorted her face. "There are too many people here from the West Coast. You've taken the place of a good writer from the East."

A woman standing in some sort of cognitive trance whirled around as I rounded a tree.

"Who are you?"

I gave my name.

"A first-year student? Who invited you?"

I explained.

"Where are you from?"

I said California, from Santa Cruz.

A grimace of disgust contorted her face. "There are too many people here from the West Coast. You've taken the place of a good writer from the East."

Later, she was pointed out to me as another second-year hotshot and TWF.

Word got out that students could request their admissions file and read the reader comments on their submissions—an irresistible voyeuristic offer for writers. When I got to the office, the good-hearted office dynamo and secret power of the Workshop, Connie Brothers, blanched at my request. "No, Don, don't do it," she urged. Well, of course that settled it. I sat on the bowlegged sofa and opened my file with trembling hands . . . having already received a battering in the workshops, my ego was not in great shape, and I was perhaps hoping to receive some belated encouragement. After all, they had admitted me, right?

To my surprise, my file's cover letter was by the TWF at the party, who'd been first screener. Her verdict: no, no, no. I was pathetic, illiterate, beneath contempt.

How, then, did I get in? Apparently John Irving, at that point departing Iowa after several years of teaching, stopped by to say good-bye; next thing he knew, he was reading one of my stories, all he had time for. "Admit him," he scrawled on the last sheet.

The rest I paraphrase from memory, no doubt unreliably, but something to the effect of "He sounds like an older person . . . uncertain grasp of grammar . . . but he has something to say." I was all of twenty-two.

JOHN IRVING: I taught at the Iowa Writers' Workshop from 1972 until 1975—three academic years. It was the best teaching-writing job I ever had; the students were good, and because they were busy doing their own writing, they pretty much left the teachers alone to do theirs. That always seemed to me to be the point of the place: the teachers and the students were there to write.

The hardest part of the job was the admissions process because no one ever agreed about which students to admit—or which students to single out as the most worthy for the Teaching/Writing Fellowships. (What do you expect of writers? Certainly not that we could possibly agree about anything!)

Allan Gurganus was my student. Allan also studied with John Cheever. Tom Boyle—T. C.—was my student. Ron Hansen, too. These young writers were super-talented, and they were workaholics. As a fellow workaholic, I was very fond of them—and their work.

I had published my third novel, *The 158-Pound Marriage*, in October of '74, my last year teaching at the workshop. It was published to resounding silence, as they say. It sold fewer copies than either my first or second novel, and it got almost no reviews—and those that it got (as I remember) were argumentative, for the most part. I was writing *The World According to Garp* in '75, but I was a long way from finishing the novel, which was to be my fourth, and my first best seller. (*Garp* was published in '78.)

ANTHONY BUKOSKI: My wife, Elaine, and I had arrived in Iowa in early August and found a place to live in the Carriage Hill apartments, a couple miles from downtown. I was so happy to return to the Midwest from the East Coast, where I'd been in grad school and teaching. I was excited about seeing big-time sports at Iowa, and excited, most of all, by the prospect of joining the Iowa Writers' Workshop. I grew more excited after our first group meeting, where Jack Leggett introduced the fiction workshop teachers: John Irving, Vance Bourjaily, Jane Howard, and himself.

ERIC OLSEN: I first set eyes on Tony Bukoski and encountered several others who became close, lifelong friends at the orientation session Leggett hosted in the English-Philosophy Building, Workshop HQ. I remember Tony very clearly from that meeting because he was wearing a stingy-brim straw hat and had a toothpick stuck in the corner of his mouth, which he'd shift from one side to the other now and then, and he looked decidedly not like a writer. Maybe that's what appealed to me right off. Plus he was sitting at the back of the room, and I'm a back-of-the-room kind of guy myself; I'd get as close to an exit as possible, so I could escape if I had to, before I started to snore. Clearly, Tony had the same idea and so we hit it off. I found myself wondering what sort of fiction he wrote. From the looks of him, I figured him for Southern gothic. I mean, how was I to know he was a Pole from the heart of the heart of the north?

GARY IORIO: There was also a big get-to-know-you picnic at Vance's farm, Red Bird Farm. This is funny, I remember having a good time, but the only guy I really remember meeting there was Tony! Maybe because I'm a hardcore heterosexual, I can't recall what he was wearing. I don't recall a stingy-brim straw hat. Wouldn't it be funny if Tony wasn't even there, though? Maybe I'm not such a hardcore heterosexual after all. Other than family, Tony Bukoski is one of the few people I've truly loved; he stepped up for me on many occasions. Life was good; I felt like I belonged in Iowa.

When I returned in the fall of my second year, I was destroyed because of the death of my sister in a car crash during the summer. I felt like I didn't belong anywhere. I thought I was abandoning my mom. I felt detached from the Workshop. The personal impact on my second year colored my experience. But Tony and his wife, Elaine, were good at pain management. Shortly thereafter, he was an usher at my first wedding in 1977. And this year, when I felt like an old fool because I was starting to write again, he said to me, "Hey, Gar, shit, you're still a young man!"

GERI LIPSCHULTZ: I remember my first party at Red Bird Farm, meeting everyone in both workshops, having some sense of the scope of my new experience. I remember looking for morels there, and just walking the grounds, and I remember when the sheep got out of the fenced-in pasture, and we got up and herded them back when there were stars and a crescent moon glaring at us.

ERIC OLSEN: At my first orientation meeting, I also first set eyes on Glenn Schaeffer, but Glenn was one of those guys who sits in the front row with his hand up to answer all the questions (correctly, of course) so we didn't meet until later. In fact, Tony introduced us. Tony was always putting people together. "Kid, you gotta meet this guy," he'd say and drag you across a street or across a room to meet so-and-so, someone Tony was sure you'd just love to know and you'd love his writing and you'd be best friends.

Glenn didn't look any more like a typical writer than Tony, not that I'd presume to say what a typical writer looks like. But typical writers tend not to look like used-car salesmen from Tulsa or, in Glenn's case, like a body-building surfer from LA (which he was) who read Whitman and Fitzgerald and Hemingway and was trying to write the next *Gatsby*. I didn't know anything about his reading habits at the time, but just from the looks of him, I figured he spent most of his time in the gym or on the beach, so his fiction would be clean and efficient, and simple, clear sentences, with lots of light in it. I mean, how was I to know he'd been reading Foucault and Derrida? And in the original, ferkrissakes!

I seem to remember also meeting Don Wallace at my first orientation, or maybe it was later, at a party or maybe even in class. Neither of us could be expected to remember the details. . . . I do remember his ponytail and Hawaiian shirt, a California stoner if there ever was one, my kind of guy I figured. I assumed from the looks of him that Don would be one of those guys reading a lot of that experimental stuff that was going on then, stuff that dispensed with plot or coherent narrative, or even recognizable sentences for that matter, stuff by Ron Sukenick, guys like that. Metafiction or whatever they were calling it.

Of course all my assumptions about everyone were completely wrong.

ANTHONY BUKOSKI: During the orientation session, I did sit in the rear of the room, I believe. Somehow, perhaps before or after, Glenn and I chatted. I liked him right off. He reminded me of Jeff Bridges, the shape of his face. He was enthusiastic about being in Iowa and, I thought, enthusiastic about life. Youthfully exuberant.

Later, I got to know his wife, Debbie; he called her "Little," and so did I. I'd go to their Coralville apartment off and on. We'd talk about life. I heard how Glenn had attended a tough high school, which I assumed precipitated in him the desire to stay fit, to lift weights, to box.

One time, Glenn fixed it in his head that we should go see the Iowa State Fair in Des Moines. I wasn't crazy about going during a terribly hot Iowa summer, but Glenn just had to go. We set off in his car one morning early, got halfway to Des Moines, and the car broke down on the interstate. A trucker pulled over and radioed to a gas station, and we arranged to have the car towed to a filling station on the highway in the middle of nowhere. And it was hot. We sat under the lone shade tree. We tossed back and forth the football that Glenn had in the car. We ate snacks, drank Cokes. I'll bet the car wasn't ready for a good five or six hours, during which we sweltered and complained. We made it back safely—but no Iowa State Fair.

Another time, he insisted we go to a quarry where he'd heard people swam "nekkid." "Oh shit, man, it's too hot to drive fifty miles for that," I told him. But he wouldn't be convinced. This time we went in my car. The scummy water of the quarry was refreshing, but I recall these hippies would allow their dogs to come in the quarry water, and the hippies themselves looked none too clean. This nude swimming was amusing for a half hour as Glenn and I swam near to each other and whispered, "Look up on the ledge to the right. See her?" That grew boring. Can you imagine growing bored looking at a half-naked babe sunbathing?

> Another time, he insisted we go to a quarry where he'd heard people swam "nekkid." "Oh shit, man, it's too hot to drive fifty miles for that," I told him. But he wouldn't be convinced.

ERIC OLSEN: I'd already been in Iowa City for two years before I got into the Workshop, and so I figured I knew my way around by then. By the time I got into the Workshop for the session beginning the fall of '75, I'd already been to a few Workshop parties with my wife. I was happy to go because there was always free beer . . .

The new students and those now starting their second year were all at the same first-of-the-year meeting, and like everyone else there, I suspect, I was busy checking out the designated Big Dogs, the rising stars, those anointed with the TWFs the year before, or those who didn't get the TWFs but it was all agreed should have. And I was busy checking out the new meat, trying to suss out who looked like they'd be the new generation of Big Dogs, who looked like the competition, and who might be friends and allies—that is, who were the weirdos. I felt distinctly like a weirdo myself, an outsider. I figured I was the only one there who felt like an outsider, who didn't belong. Of course, we all felt like outsiders. We were writers, after all.

Even if we weren't aware of it, I think deep down most of us understood that it was our peers who would matter most to us both in the Workshop and then after. Sure, we might learn something from the faculty, and we'd need to suck up to them now and then the way students have always sucked up because you never knew but that one of them might open a door or two into the publishing world, a letter of intro to some big-shot editor at a prestigious New York publishing house, but these people were all ancient. They had liver spots! How could they possibly function?

Even if we weren't aware of it, I think deep down most of us understood that it was our peers who would matter most to us both in the Workshop and then after.

In fact, they were all quite a bit younger than we are now.

DON WALLACE: I moved into a large house with a bunch of other workshop people, some new like myself, others second-year old hands. It was a nice introduction, meeting and talking over writing as I'd imagined it would be, even before our first class, with housemates Michael Maguire, Mary Bunker Petersen, and Linda Lappin. The neighborhood was cozy, with the Olsens—Cheryl and Eric—around the corner, and a very hospitable Southern poet across the street, Mark Van Tilburg, a descendent of a Western writer, Walter Van Tilburg Clark, whose works I had read and written about: *The Ox Bow Incident, The Track of the Cat*, etc.

DOUG UNGER: Before I went to Iowa, I'd been in New York City with the St. Mark's poets group, hanging out around them, and we were all living in cheap East Village cold-water apartments or apartments with no water, just one step above the gutter, and I understood that's the way real writers lived. All I wanted was to write a great novel. I was very interested in writing as a countercultural activity, a way to jab at the establishment.

Now I see writers in workshops who expect an MFA to be their ticket to a middle-class existence. That seems to be the goal. Or they want to write the big book that hits the best-seller list and gets the movie deal and makes them rich.

I never had that in my head when I was writing in New York or at Iowa. Maybe I'd have been better off then if I had, but I just never thought of it like that. I don't think some of the real successful members of the Workshop when we were there thought that way either. I don't think Tom Boyle thought that way; he was working at the *Iowa Review* and writing those quirky stories with that highly developed sense of language that he has, writing away, living a modest grad student existence.

Well, I was just a kid when I got to Iowa. I didn't know what to expect. I was so young I didn't know what a gift it was that I was even allowed in to the Workshop. My expectations were arrogant, at first—I expected my great talent to be confirmed and to be declared the young genius, I suppose, though I was hardly aware at the time that I was such an arrogant young punk.

Very soon, though, after getting to know my fellow writers there, and realizing how good they were, many of them writing much better prose than I was, I understood that it would be a lot of hard work and would take a great deal of luck also for me to succeed or even to keep going as a writer. It was a very humbling experience.

ANTHONY BUKOSKI: I was twenty-nine when I arrived in Iowa City; I would turn thirty in October, my second month in the Workshop. I suppose I was a bit older than most other Workshop students. By then, I'd served in the Marines in Vietnam, taught high school for three years, gotten an MA at Brown. I always felt I was fortunate to come to Iowa at twenty-nine; I was ready to study and to learn.

The Workshop is a great place for someone with discipline. Without discipline, or the discipline to write, a person could just enjoy the scenery and the nightlife and while away the two years. Heavens, you didn't have to do much of a thesis, and no classes were graded, so few expectations were made on a person, except those he made on himself.

Don't get me wrong, though. My discipline could have been better. But I was honored to be in the Workshop. Coming from a nowhere college in a nowhere place, I was eager to succeed.

I wouldn't say my age or experience helped me too much at Iowa. Not at first. I didn't realize that my life and my experiences in Vietnam and elsewhere could become the material for fiction. Again, what helped me so much was the feeling I had of gratitude that I had been accepted and that now others would read, with some seriousness, what I submitted on those Workshop Tuesdays.

DOUG BORSOM: I was walking in downtown Iowa City when I first met Tony. Somehow, he knew who I was and recognized me. He'd been out running, and he came over and introduced himself. He had me admire his ironlike calves, which I did. He told me how much he had liked "In Wheat," a short story I had put up, and I told him that in addition to his calves, I had really liked a short story of his, "Route of the Zephyrs"—I truly had.

I had been offered a "research assistantship," an RA, by the Workshop for my second year. The "research" part of it consisted of running off worksheets on the ditto machine in the Workshop office, and so I pretty much saw everything that came in, including Tony's story.

You hear about the so-called "workshop story," but the only pattern I detected in all the worksheets I read running them off was in the quality of the writing. Even when our stories didn't have a lot to say, they usually said it well. Beyond that, they were all over the place. Think Joe Haldeman, Doug Unger, Allan Gurganus, Tom Boyle, Gary Iorio, Tony Bukoski, et al. In statistics, there's the concept of standard deviation, a measure of dispersion of data points from the mean of the data set. The droplets from a garden hose nozzle set on broad spray have a big standard deviation. When the nozzle is adjusted for a solid stream, the standard deviation is small. To me, Workshop writing was, stylistically, a water balloon the instant after detonation of a cherry bomb.

You hear about the so-called "workshop story," but the only pattern I detected in all the worksheets I read running them off was in the quality of the writing. Even when our stories didn't have a lot to say, they usually said it well.

The great thing about running off the worksheets was that the ditto room was just across from the office of the director, Jack Leggett, and the office of his assistant at the time, Hope Landres, so I was at the center of the hub and somewhat included in things, rather like a harmless, slow-witted little brother, I suppose. Leggett and Hope were always nice to me, and I was invited to many of the parties for visiting writers. I suspect it was pity: they felt bad that I had what they considered such a lowly task, running the ditto machine.

DOUG UNGER: I lived a bohemian, outcast life as a student. We were involved in all sorts of underground activities of one sort or another. I remember a séance that Leonard Michaels had at Jane Smiley's house, in which Brenda Hillman and Chase Twitchell and I (and I think Allan Gurganus might have been there, too) and several others were sitting around with candles lit, very stoned, trying to decide what the difference was between writing fiction and writing poetry, and finally we determined that writing poetry would tend to make you more physically beautiful, and that writing fiction would tend to make you ugly.

For a time, on the sly, I was dealing pot, and was kind of popular with the faculty, which I thought at the time might have had something to do with how I got a TWF my second year, but don't print that, please—thinking that shows how much I doubted myself and my writing. The next year, I understood the process better, and that our collective, perceived quality of the writing and not personalities is what really counted.

DON WALLACE: Like Olsen and Schaeffer, I came in a kid from the West, a bit guileless, idealistic, ready to write and read and do this workshop thing with my peers, who would be, like me, idealistic and open and, above all, fair. I came in expecting it might be tough; I was ready for tough. Although Santa Cruz, where I did undergrad, was a fairytale place and the NorCal scene certainly wasn't too rigorous, I had come from a much tougher place before that, Long Beach, an inner-city place, and I'd worked in agriculture and in the oil fields.

So I had done the Hemingway thing working in manly occupations, and part of me believed in keeping a tight jaw and not mouthing up the writing game with cheap talk.

The other part, however, came out of the '60s—I'd been around black, brown, yellow, and gay liberation as they were bubbling up, and women's liberation, and furthermore in college had studied Ezra Pound and William Carlos Williams and James Joyce under Norman O. Brown, the Marxist-Freudian classicist—*Love's Body*, anybody?

It was the writing part of me that was most guileless and idealistic. It was where I put cynicism aside and really listened to the world and my soul. And I wanted others to be pure about it, too. I wasn't religious, I wasn't a vegetarian, and after years of protest starting at age fifteen, I no longer thought radical politics had any answers. My spiritual side was my writing, leavened with a healthy dash of California pantheism and nature worship.

You know, I thought I was pretty experienced for a twenty-two-year-old. For someone who'd walked to high school through a daily gauntlet of Crips and Bloods, junior Black Panthers, Venceremos and La Raza, and cops who'd just as soon bust you as talk to you, someone who'd worked in a lake of crude oil up to his neck, who'd been beaten and gassed and jailed by Tac Squad goons, going to class with thirty of the best young writers in America shouldn't be too intimidating, right?

CATHERINE GAMMON: I arrived at Iowa with the feeling I was going to write what I could based on what I learned and see what happened. It was all an exploration to me. I didn't have any specific intention when I went. I went to see what I would find. I didn't even know if I was going to finish the program. I didn't know if I had any reason to have a writing degree, since I didn't have any particular aspiration to teach. I just wanted to go see what I could learn and what it would be like. But once you're in the culture there, you want to teach because all the best writers are teaching. They all have TWFs or whatever, and so you end up thinking you should get a TWF, too.

DOUG UNGER: I knew enough that if I was going to do it, I better learn how to do it well because I left Chicago thinking like most young writers that anything I vomited onto the page was God's gift to literature, and I was disabused of that soon enough. I understood that I would have to learn how to write a hell of a lot better than I was at the time, and I meant to do that.

My whole first year I spent trying to rewrite the novel that had been rejected by Jason Epstein at Random House. Hundreds of pages of rewrites, and what I understood at the end of that process is that I had written it to a standstill, and it was only then, late spring my first year at Iowa, that I woke up to that fact . . . that there was a different level of story and style to the writing I aspired to do, and that I would have to work as hard as I could for the rest of my life to live up to anything even remotely close to my aspirations.

> . . . I left Chicago thinking like most young writers that anything I vomited onto the page was God's gift to literature, and I was disabused of that soon enough.

GERI LIPSCHULTZ: When I got to Iowa City, I had a hard time finding a place because I had the dog, but Hope Landres, the director's assistant, told me I could stay at her house for a while, which I did. Our dogs didn't get along, though. Then Hope set me up with Julie Mishkin, in the poetry workshop, and we looked for a house together. We needed a place with enough room for my dog and for her and her then-boyfriend, another poet. We found a place in Solon, on Lake McBride, the man-made lake. Where we lived was across the lake from where people went swimming. Also the playwright Lee Blessing lived there for a time, and that summer, Louie Skipper and Corny Guest moved in, along with a PhD student in literature who is now a published poet, as well—Ed Hoeppner.

There were lots of good times there, lots of parties. I remember one time when Jim Galvin had W. S. Merwin out there, and we were all talking and—this is probably not for the record—passing around a joint, and Merwin was amazing, profound, very gracious. My friends from New Jersey, Maggie and Terre Roche, the musicians, came by once and played at a party. They'd been on tour somewhere . . . it was before their sister Suzzy joined them and they became the trio, the Roches.

I remember having wonderful conversations sitting at the table with Louie and Corny and Julie and Jim and Lee. And lots of talks in front of the fire, all of us, talks about poetry, and I remember Vance was out there once, and that was when he told me that I was a good-enough writer but I didn't know "the importance" of what I had to write. It had to be so important to me that I'd be willing to scream it out in front of a crowd of strangers. Was it that important? he asked me. Or something like that. . . .

We did a lot of cooking out there, and I remember finding out there were mice in the kitchen and staying up all one night to catch them, and cooking Julie Mishkin's recipe for moussaka. I remember fishing out in the lake, the first time ever I fished, and then preparing the fish, scaling it and whatever, and then grilling the fish and eating it and feeling that feeling that I just ate something that was alive not even an hour before—that was a first—and the lake right there behind us.

I remember camping out in the snow with Louie and Ed, terribly drunk on retsina and ouzo (we'd been to a great Greek restaurant in Cedar Rapids). I could go on like this.

The folks around there didn't much like us, though. They didn't like renters. Or poets, maybe. Later, someone shot our dogs.

~

If there's any one thing that might have contributed to the quality of "our class," it's probably the simple fact that if you throw a lot of talented folks together in one place and give them the freedom to work and play together, not always nicely but nicely often enough, good things are going to happen. But then this is the case for every workshop class, not just ours. Maybe thanks to sheer chance, more than the average number of talented rookies applied those years, the admissions process worked a little better than such processes often do, and the economic environment was a shade more hospitable, allowing a few more of those accepted to take advantage of the opportunity. Beyond that, the mere fact these gifted people were in the same rooms together created a feedback loop, lifting all of them toward their highest potential.

Contrary to the Workshop's reputation as a haven for cutthroat opportunists and bloated egos, all of us, no matter which side or sides of the geo/politico/aesthetic debates we were on, enjoyed a remarkable collegiality and generosity of spirit at the Workshop. Indeed, it turns out that many of us, looking back at our time in the Workshop, share the impression that the real work of the Workshop was done outside the classrooms, as we shared our work with one another over beers at the Mill or George's Buffet, or joints in a cabin on the shore of Lake McBride. At the end of the day, we all found ourselves rooting for one another because we were all in the same boat, up against the same horror: the blank page. And we're still rooting for one another because even after thirty years, the blank page is just as daunting and just as frightening as ever.

But most of us didn't have a clue as to what we'd gotten ourselves into when we showed up for our first classes.

~

JAYNE ANNE PHILLIPS: My first teacher at Iowa was the playwright Robert Anderson, author of *Tea and Sympathy*. He was a very nice, very genteel man with pure blue eyes and white hair. I don't remember much from his workshop, or even who was in it. I do remember that the first longer story I ever wrote, an early version of "El Paso," which later appeared in *Black Tickets*, was the first story of mine discussed in workshop, so that must have been in Anderson's class. The draft I put up for the workshop had almost no punctuation. It was a long stream of language, in titled monologues. Everyone hated it. Some students said they "resented having to read this stuff." One guy, in disgust, said, "Why are you making us read this shit?" I was not crushed, however. I was actually encouraged at the intensity of their reactions. I figured I was doing something right. I did, however, add punctuation.

The draft I put up for the workshop had almost no punctuation. It was a long stream of language, in titled monologues. Everyone hated it.

I loved working with Fred Busch, who began his workshop on my story "Lechery" by saying the title in a delicious, leering way, which defused some of the tension.

CATHERINE GAMMON: I'd never taken a writing course before Iowa. My first writing workshop was with Lenny Michaels, and I boldly put up one of the chapters from my novel; not the first chapter, a very deep-in chapter. The first workshop. I didn't know what I was getting into. This was a little chapter that I thought was so wonderful and expressive of what was happening at that point in the novel, blah blah blah, and it seemed self-contained enough to put up like this. And it was extraordinarily vulnerable in every conceivable way, and Lenny pointed to and picked at each place.

Lenny was very precise about the words, the rhythms . . . word by word by word. His energy and his attention were really superb. But what I really remember most from it all was a kind of spiritual integrity about the precision with which everything was considered. You couldn't get away with something; you couldn't just kind of slide around something. I think it was—this may sound odd—a kind of Zen. There was a precision about the way he went through the worksheet, the word, the image, the sentence. That's what struck me.

The worksheets were anonymous in his workshops; you didn't put your name on the manuscript. And Lenny didn't let anybody say anything; he did all the talking. Or he usually did. There might have been some student comment when my chapter was up because I'm remembering at a point in the discussion where Doug Unger asked about some repetition for the sake of rhythm; it was obviously a musical repetition, and Lenny objected to it. And Doug said, "So you mean there shouldn't be any excess even for the sake of rhythm or music?" And Lenny said no.

I received all that really openly. I took it all in and I wrote a short story that I put up later while Lenny was still there, and he raved about it. I felt like in the several weeks Lenny was there, I'd learned everything I could learn from a teacher from him.

ANTHONY BUKOSKI: I had Jack Leggett's fiction workshop my first semester. My anxiety rose, as one would expect, when I prepared my first story for submission, "Route of the Zephyrs." I had no idea whether it was any good. Someone, though, told me I had an admirer, a second-year Workshop student who wasn't in my class with Leggett, but who'd read the story and found it quite wonderful. This helped so much.

One day I met him, Doug Borsom. He really was enthusiastic about the story. His encouragement, I can tell you, became a formative experience. As it turns out, the story was given a lukewarm response in Leggett's class, so it was good that I'd met Doug. One student in the class thought the protagonist in my story was a transvestite. Where that came from I have no idea. One or two others liked the story. Imagine smart people actually taking seriously something I'd written? It was pleasing and nerve-wracking at the same time, and finally demoralizing. I naturally assumed—don't we all when we are naive about our writing?—that everyone would love what I'd written.

After class, back in the apartment, I sat at the kitchen table while Elaine fried pork chops on the stove, thinking I could either just pack it in or I could enjoy myself at Iowa for two years doing nothing or doing just enough to get a degree, or I could fight harder to learn to write. I could somehow raise my critical standard, improve the writing, and hope thereby to earn the respect of my colleagues. I remember clearly the kitchen table with the overhead light on, the pork chops on the stove. I decided to fight harder.

Later, early in the second semester of my first year, in John Irving's class now, I put up my "Hello from Thure." When the class came to consider it, along with a story by John Givens, Irving was so excited about both stories that he did a little jig, I remember. That gave me confidence that I sorely needed. To this day, I am grateful to him and to Doug Borsom. The small things we do for people can pay rich dividends.

JAYNE ANNE PHILLIPS: I loved the general excellence of the faculty at Iowa, and simply having the time to write, as I'd come out of two years of waitressing and doing other jobs in California and Colorado, taking breaks in between to do my real work. I had never actually been in a formal workshop before I went to Iowa, though my first chapbook, *Sweethearts* (twenty-four one-page fictions, published in five hundred copies by Truck Press), came out the summer before I moved to Iowa City. The reading series was important as well, the sense that accomplished writers were constantly coming through. I remember being asked to take John Cheever out to lunch. He was so self-deprecating and witty, in a sad, serious way.

Books by the Bed

ALLAN GURGANUS: *Something I've Been Meaning to Tell You,* early stories by Alice Munro. *Everything Ravaged, Everything Burned,* Wells Tower. *The Account of Mary Rowlandson and Other Indian Captivity Narratives. The Stranger Beside Me,* by Ann Rule (a childhood friend of Ted Bundy's investigates serial murders only to start suspecting she knows the killer). Harry Crews's brilliant memoir *A Childhood. Air Ships,* genius stories by Barry Hannah. The 1897 Sears and Roebuck and Company catalogue. And *Middlemarch,* for the twenty-fifth time.

ALLAN GURGANUS: Cheever was an amazing guy, in a very vulnerable position but very endearing in his isolation. I got to know him well in a short time because, I think, he was lonely. We remained friends for the rest of his life. There he was living at the bleak university hotel, eating breakfast downstairs in a dining room Edward Hopper would have painted. Ron Hansen was in the class and so was Tom Boyle. Jane Smiley was a presence and lots of other very gifted writers. It was an exciting time at the Workshop, but then it always is.

I wrote a short story, "Minor Heroism," which I put up in Cheever's class. Didn't change it all that much on the basis of what was said in class, but it was helpful. I found it helpful that John read it and liked it so much. I had read Cheever's work on the *USS Yorktown.* The library was stocked with works that had military titles, including "The Brigadier and the Golf Widow."

Cheever ran his class like a cocktail party. He'd begin with some gambit from his own work. He would say it used to be possible to write a story that began: "It was one of those mornings when people sat around saying 'I drank too much last night.' All right, Mr. Gurganus, it was one of those mornings when . . . give me something."

And most people in the class, being Midwesterners with a tradition of keeping silent, not talking on order, proved too tongue-tied to say anything. Much less this idea of writing out loud on cue . . .

He was a very different writer than I, but we shared a class consciousness. We were both from shabby genteel traditions. And, of course, there are no experts at unshabby gentility like those of us left on the margins. I'd gone to Sarah Lawrence; Cheever's wife had gone there early in its history. I was writing about the alcoholic country-club people of Virginia and North Carolina, and he was writing about Westchester. I had been educated back East and had a certain kind of conversational style that was unlike many of my classmates'. It was a wonderful opportunity in a way.

Cheever gave us weekly assignments on top of whatever else we were writing; I did everything he asked. It amazes me to think that people were in a class being taught by John Cheever and they had never read his work; they didn't know who he was. I am still dumbfounded by how little many writers have actually read. Only in America. Every person sees himself as Columbus, the first. You go to Argentina, they can tell you every poem, by heart, written by any Argentine since the beginning of literacy. Here? People study with a master of prose, professing to be writers, and they are not even curious enough to read their mentor!

Cheever's reputation was, like his person, in decline. We all thought that Barthelme, Coover, and somebody called Ron Sukenick were the greatest living writers. I am embarrassed to say I once complained to Cheever that it was hard to be writing in an age of geniuses like these practitioners of metafiction. "Well, Allan, I know what it was like. When I was young, I was up against James Joyce." That shut me up.

Many of my classmates just considered Cheever a broken-down, 110-pound has-been in size 6 Weejuns. But having read him, and fully knowing his scale of artistry, it seemed to me an amazing chance to figure out what I could do and how any of that lined up with what he could do.

I published some of the weekly exercises I wrote; one that Cheever assigned us came to seem sort of prophetic. This was in 1973, and the task was "Write a love letter from a burning building." One of my own students was in the second World Trade Center when it was struck. He was on the phone describing the results of the first plane crash when the second one came right into his and ended him.

He was issued two thin bath towels every week. I mean his room, where he held all his student conferences, was where a traveling salesman might go to commit suicide.

Anyway, John was in a weird state, having just had a heart attack back East. He couldn't stop drinking. His doctor told him if he continued, it'd

Jeffrey Abrahams

Douglas Borsom

T.C. Boyle

Marvin Bell

Borsom (handwritten)

Department of English ● SOUTHWEST MISSOURI STATE UNIVERSITY · SPRINGFIELD, MISSOURI 65802 (417) 831-1561

August 31, 1975

Dear Jenny,

Guess what? I got a job after all. S.M.S.U., which stands for Southwest
Missouri State University, Bible School, and Learning Emporium; offered me
a job after at the last minute. I'd received a letter from them saying "no x
thanks" to my application and I wrote you accordingly. Well on Aug. 16
Mike Harris was down visiting me in good old tropical San Diego and S.M.S.U.B.S.L.E.
called and said one of their teachers had quit unexpectedly (I suspect foul
play). They flew me out that Sunday, I was interviewed Monday and hired.
Classes started here Aug 25 which gave me all of a week to prepare my
scholarly approach and develope a full routine of classroom jokes and learned
prattle.

I'm teaching two xixx classes in composition; teaching the offspring of
Missouri plow-jockies how to write good. I've got another class in the
short story- something like a core-lit course at Iowa. And then I'm teaching
a night class of (get this) creative writing. I've got 11 classroom hours each
week for which they pay me $8,700. Summers and holidays off. While no great
shakes, this does beat working for a living. The arrangement here is cute.
I'm hired for three years and then I'm out. That way they avoid having to pay
me be more than a minimum wage. This is the regular English Dept. policy so each
year the school hires several English teachers. You might clue some of the
second year students in on this if they're interested in this sort of work.

Now let me sing the praise of S.M.S.U.B.S.L.E. A week here and you begin to
believe Iowa's claims of being the Athens of the Midwest. Springfield is
a delightful town of 120,000 located right in the paunch of the Bible belt.
They've got a school in this town called The Baptist Bible College which does
nothing but crank out thousands of religious fanatics each year. On my first
day xexx here I was asked by a prof. "Air yew a hippy?" Note the quaint
dialect (I'm xxx sorry I can but approximate it on paper) not to mention the
sophisticated sentence construction. I'm spending my evenings under a sunlamp
developing a redneck. The country around here is beautiful (see how well I
describe things after two years in the Workshop?) Lots of trees, lakes, and
gently rolling hills. I xxx believe Springfield calls itself the gateway to
the Ozarks. I guess town's about 400 miles south of Iowa City so I'll be
visiting up there one of these weekends. That's all for now. Would appreciate it if you passed this letter on the Cheryl and Eric Olsen.

sent 9/15 (handwritten)

Doug (handwritten)

answered 9/16 (handwritten)

Letter from Douglas Borsom to the Workshop secretary, 1975

Connie Brothers, Iowa
Writers' Workshop
Program Associate

Jennie Fields

Anthony Bukoski

Jayne Anne Phillips

THE ARCTIC EXPLORER

DEPARTURE

Posing in full dress uniform at the bow of the little brig
Endeavor, rigid as the mast looming behind him, he raises a stiff
arm in acknowledgement of the small send-off parties spotting
the Queens' shore of the Narrows. With his perfect posture, im-
maculate uniform and manicured moustache, he looks very much the
Hero, a reincarnated admixture of Henry Hudson, John Paul Jones
and Sir Walter Raleigh. His solemn eyes scan the bandless, ban-
nerless shore: a paltry crowd, he reflects, for an occasion so
momentous. After all, he is sailing cheekily off into the fri-
gid unknown, beyond the reaches of men's maps, to probe regions
whose very existence is but rumor. Yet such, he supposes, is the
lot of Heroes: all but ignored by the complacent present, revered
by posterity. Glebe cows. If it were up to them Kentucky would
be a wilderness still.
Beyond the Narrows, the open Atlantic, rolling pleasantly
underfoot to a gentle June breeze. Captain John Pennington Frank
(M.D., U.S.N.) breathes deeply, closes his eyes, and removes his
cap to let the seabreeze tickle through his hair—as he does so,
the last spangles of confetti are sucked up in the wind and shot
away to starboard (this the confetti that his mother and two un-
married sisters had solemnly flung at him just half an hour earlier when the brig had been launched at the Brooklyn Naval Yard.)
Like Ishmael too long aland, he feels the salt breeze animating
all his old sailor's exultation: Ah! The open sea! Adventure!
Man against the elements! It is then that the brig pitches forward and an icy slap surprises the Captain's blissful countenance.
The lids snap—to like the surprise of a stroke and he lurches forward against the rail, while the cap sails out from his hand in a
graceful arc, to be sucked down by the frothing waves below. He
recovers himself and glances furtively about before digging out
the handkerchief, thankful that none of the crew had been watching.
The ceremonies over, and the voyage begun, the Captain retires to
his cabin, where the crisp and neatly-lined pages of the logbook
await him.
Of course he knows nothing as yet of the Arctic Night.

CAPTAIN'S LOG, JUNE 2

Set sail from NY harbor at 1100 hours Eastern Time. Momma,
Evangeline and Euphonia saw us off with a not inconsiderable
crowd. As we passed the Narrows, quite ten thousand I should
think turned out to cheer us. It was heartening thus to witness
the deep reverence and good will the people of this great country
show for our venture.
My party consists of fifteen: eight officers (myself included);
five crewmen; Phillip Blackwarp, cook; and Harlan Hawkins, cabin
boy. Our stores include a large supply of navy ration salt beef
and pork, hard biscuit, flour, some barrels of an exsiccated potato,
two thousand pounds of pemmican, a quantity of dried fruits, and
twelve barrels of pickled cabbage. (Surreptitiously, I laid in a
supply of party hats and whistles, to cheer the men during our winter

First page of a T.C. Boyle worksheet, 1973

Anthony Bukoski
711 Carriage Hill
Iowa City, Iowa 52240

Approx. 7,500 wds.

HELLO FROM THURE

A Short Story

by

Anthony Bukoski

    It happens every winter in Two Heart that someone is caught
after dark where he does not belong, in among the big firs, or out
along the frozen muskeg of the river. So be it if that is the way to
learn, only around here a boy had better be careful of Big Thure.
You may have seen his house. The picture of Thure straddling the
peak where the snow has yet to reach was sent all over the country.
It is a photo supposed to show the rest of the world how the weather
is here in Two Heart. What they do not know is that it is the same
year in and year out and that there is nothing unusual about last
year.

First page of a story by Anthony Bukoski, 1975

Anthony "Bruiser"
Bukoski, ready to spar,
Iowa City, 1976

Photo by Elaine Bukoski

Letter from Sandra Cisneros to the Workshop, 1976

Photo by Ray Santisteban

Sandra Cisneros and Barney
Fife (aka Barnitos)

Photo courtesy Pace Wildenstein Gallery

Rosalyn Drexler in her
studio, mid–1970s

The Rented House

Leigh carried her washed and sleepy children up the stairs, one straddling each of her broad, lean hips. You didn't appreciate hips until you had children, she thought. Then they became shelves for soft, terryclothed bellies. They took the weight off your arms and balanced you. Because the stairway was unfamiliar, she had to walk slowly. The children's feet slapped against her thighs. The little girl reached out and started playing with Leigh's ear, rubbing her small finger along the secret inner ridge. A chill curled down her spine, shaking her shoulders. The children pushed at her arms as though to steady her.

"Tomorrow, can we see the lake?" the girl asked.

"I don't know what Daddy has planned."

"Daddy said we could see the lake," the boy said. "Daddy said he get bat-ries for my truck."

Leigh reached the top of the stairs and bent to let the children down, their stomachs straining, their feet wiggling before touching the floor.

"Is this my room? Is this the room here?" the girl asked.

"Yes." Leigh flipped on the light. The yellowed paper was spotted with morning glories. A moth danced precariously near the light globe. Near the ceiling, the corners of the walls were covered with a fine white mold like sugar.

"Does Roy gotta sleep in the same room as me?"

"Yes. Roy. Get off the floor."

"I don't want him to sleep in the same room as me," the girl said, bouncing down on one of the beds so it cried.

"Roy. Get off the floor. These floors are dirty. Not

First page of a Jennie Fields worksheet, 1975

Catherine Gammon

Robin Green and Emmys

Allan Gurganus

Minor Heroism:
Something About My Father

Imagine him in his prime. A fairly rich Virginia farmboy newly cured of being a
farmboy by what he called Th'War, meaning the second one. He'd signed up in Charlottesville
when most of his fraternity had done it as a group and up till then he had been somewhat
humorlessly typical. He had been hung up with the rest of them in the fraternity of the
university that Jefferson designed, and he was lean and carefully prepared as all the
very best Virginia hams. And it would seem to follow that, in 1942, my father began being
made more valuable by several years of smoke. But this smoke was not the curative
Virginia kind, it was the high flying smoke of German cities burning. My father had
become a tombadier. He had become a minor hero in the Second World War and a major hero
in the Commonwealth of Virginia. He was photographed as Betty Grable stood on tiptoe to
kiss him. He was tall, he still is, but it is easier to imagine him in the uniform of
an officer in our Army Air Corps than it is to watch him wear his civies of today.

Heroes should have looks. His were better than most, better than wholesome. It was
one of those faces that fit handsomely into photographs and under a brimmed cap. It seemed
to know in every pose that captions would be under it eventually. His profile, nearly
as good as a Barrymore's, was better for being blunted slightly by boarding school boxing,
its two almost aristocratic angles democratised by one quick left. With very combed
blond hair waving back in the way hair did then, his was a face that even from the front
told much about itself in silhouette. Many of the photos still exists.

When I was a child in the years closer to that war than these are, people bombarded me
with accounts of my father's valour. They told me in front of other children how, though
everybody's father had certainly helped with it, mine had done more than most to insure
that the Nazi plot to rule the world, to rule the very ground on which this birthday party
was now taking place, had been crushed by the Americans and something about the Freedom
and the Wrights who could worship in whichever way they chose. They said to me, do you
know what your father did? I was told he'd been the reason people had written "Welcome
Richard!" numerous times on broad banners made of sheets that would stretch all the way
across Main Street and never be needed again for rolling Red Cross bandages.

But, before the war was won and he came home, there was the business about what they
made my grandmother do. She was a remarkably shy woman, even for then. In Virginia,
in 1942, shyness was less unusual than it is today. Both her parents' families had been
equally distinguished and austere and, as if to commemorate this, she parted her hair

First page of an Allan Gurganus worksheet, 1974

Allan Gurganus in Iowa City, 1974

Joy Harjo

Joe Haldeman

Gary Iorio   Michelle Huneven

Sherry Kramer

John Irving

Geri Lipschultz

Bill Manhire

John Leggett

Dennis Mathis

Bill McCoy and his wife Sharon, his son
Gavin, and Olive the dog

Eric Olsen

Mindy Pennybacker

Gordon Mennenga

Sandra Cisneros, 1976

Mindy Pennybacker, picnic
at Red Bird Farm, 1976

Annual Workshop
picnic, Red Bird
Farm, 1976

Don Wallace, Workshop
Prom, 1977

April 7, 1975

Mr. Gleen Schaeffer
110 1/2 Pearl Avenue
Balboa Isdand, California 92662

Dear Glenn,

At this point in our financial aid considerations the available
positions have been filled. Because of the shortage of funds we
are unable to offer you a definite award for next year. If aid
becomes available we will notify you immediately. We hope this
will not interefere with your plans to come to Iowa in the fall.

Sincerely,

Connie Brothers
Administrative Assistant

Photo by Eric Olsen

Glenn Schaeffer

Photo by John H. Irsfeld

Doug Unger

Photo by Mindy Pennybacker

Don Wallace

Jane Smiley

First page of a Jane Smiley
worksheet, 1975

Jane Smiley
Bromell GFW

HER KIND NURSERY

a short story

"Dog!" he said, "Dog! How!" She sucked in her cheeks
and closed her eyes, panting like a dog. It was no use. Another
scream roared out of her. It might have been ridiculous after all
their discussion about this natural childbirth thing, if each
scream hadn't been so searing. They began deep then jumped rather
than climbed into the higher registers. She was clutching his
fingers or he would have ground them into his ears. Where were
the doctors? the nurses? Oh, she won't be ready for hours, they
said, and here she was, bellowing continuously and arching off
the bed in agony. More than anything he wanted to knock her unconscious. Now she was calling his name, "Paul! Paul! Paul!"
she cried, "She's coming! She's coming! Get the God-damned doctor!" But she wouldn't let his hands go. When he disengaged one,
she grabbed it again. "Don't leave me!" Oh my God! There's the
head! I can feel it going!" Paul yanked his hands away and ran
into the hall. A resident was walking by, a stranger on night duty.
"The baby's coming!" shouted Paul, "Get your ass in here and give
my wife some dope! What's the matter with you fuckers!" The res-

be a death sentence. His family had essentially washed their hands of him, which I understand; it must have been very frustrating for them. And so there he was, living at that bleak university hotel, the Iowa House, drinking scotch out of the glasses they provided, the toothpaste glasses. He was issued two thin bath towels every week. I mean his room, where he held all his student conferences, was where a traveling salesman might go to commit suicide.

T. C. BOYLE: I had John Cheever my second year in the Workshop. Allan Gurganus was in Cheever's class. Cheever was very drunk all the time. You know, about all Cheever and the others gave me was, "You're on the right track, kid, keep it up." That's all you can do sometimes, all you need to say. I never needed any structural analysis or whatever. Somehow, and I don't know how, my work seemed to come together.

Anyway, I never got much advice from anyone; they were more like a coach, and I needed a coach, and Cheever was very gracious, very generous. So was Vance. Vance rolled his own cigarettes, and the entire class would come to a halt for five minutes while he rolled them.

I was writing stories then like the one that got me accepted into the Workshop, stories that played with the notion of narrative, and little sections you could mix and match, and I kept writing those stories and I was getting tired of them, and one day I said to Vance, "Vance, I'm tired of this."

And he said, "Do something else."

He was absolutely right. So I did something else, but I needed to hear it from him.

JENNIE FIELDS: To be honest, I was disappointed by the faculty when I was at the Workshop. They weren't nearly as involved or instructive as the faculty I had as an undergraduate. I rarely felt inspired and sometimes thought they were coasting. But when you're around fellow students saying brilliant things, you couldn't help but be inspired by them.

I did like Henry Bromell. I was inspired by him as a writer and a teacher. He cared and had something to say. Henry was young, and he tried to share what he had recently learned. I remember him talking about dialogue and what made dialogue sound real. That stuck with me.

ANTHONY BUKOSKI: Iowa was a great place for me. I thought the place was wonderfully supportive, especially once you knew at which skill level you were. You adjusted your friends accordingly, and I made wonderful friends there. There were, say, the Jane Smiley, Allan Gurganus types who were clearly superior to everyone else and knew it. Then there were other groups and finally mine.

Class structure notwithstanding, I thought so many fellow students were just wonderful to me. Even when a story wasn't very good, I found people like Joe Haldeman, Doug Unger, John Givens, and others to have been helpful and kind.

I was not so kind at times when criticizing others' stories. I made a few snide comments. But I rarely received that kind of treatment back. And remember that I got off to a good start when Doug Borsom got the word to me that he liked my first-ever class story submission. I have fond memories of the Workshop.

MICHELLE HUNEVEN: I made important connections and lifelong friends at Iowa. I loved conversation there—a mixture of gossip, storytelling, and talk about books. I'm teaching now, at UCLA, as a lecturer—which means part-time and without real faculty responsibilities or privileges or pay. But I've been there for several years now, and I'm crazy about the students, who are smart and mature and eager.

I always tell them, "Look around you at your classmates. These are the people who are going to help you along your way. These are the connections you need to make." I became good friends with Robin Green, who went on to write for many of the greatest television shows, including *Northern Exposure* and *The Sopranos*. She'd been a journalist at *Rolling Stone*, and after she finished at the workshop and before she went into TV writing, she went back to work in journalism. She got me started writing for the now-defunct *California Magazine* and introduced me to her old friend Ruth Reichl who was running the food section and was the main restaurant critic at the *LA Times*. I wrote for *California* until it folded and wrote restaurant reviews for the *LA Times* for a decade. Through Robin, I met many people who remain close friends and editors.

GERI LIPSCHULTZ: One of the major things I learned at Iowa was that I still had a lot to learn. I wish I'd had more under my belt before I went there. I remember that there was a separation among the poets, fiction writers, playwrights. At the time, and still now it is true, I write drama, poetry, fiction. I remember wishing I could settle on one—I felt so different from the others in this respect—because the poets thought fiction was just too long, and the fiction writers said they didn't really understand how poetry "worked," that it was "too complicated," and there I was, this relatively young, foolish girl, who knew neither but loved both. I learned not to speak up in class.

SANDRA CISNEROS: At Iowa, you had to claim citizenship in either poetry or fiction, and I was between. Because I had studied with a poet, I had to declare myself a poet, but I wanted to claim both and I didn't quite belong in either. Plus I was reading the "Latin American boom" writers, Puig and Borges, and Juan Rulfo, and here I was tossed in with the poets, and I never felt comfortable with them. They seemed very pretentious and very upper class compared with where I came from. And they were writing the kind of poetry that was antithetical to the sort of poetry I wanted to write, a poetry that could be understood by anybody, cab drivers, single moms, the woman behind the counter at Dunkin' Donuts, and that I'd grown up with, the Chicago gritty working-class poets, but I didn't discover this until I was reading Nicanor Parra's anti-poems, and I thought, *this is what I am.* I want to write anti-poems, anti–upper class, anti–ivory tower, anti–pretty poems.

So Iowa was an experience where I found out what I wasn't, where I discovered my otherness, and pulled myself away from who I was studying with and the kind of poetry I was reading to declare myself and what I was. It made me very uncomfortable.

I felt more comfortable in the fiction workshop, and I started writing *House on Mango Street*, but it wasn't part of my thesis. Don Justice said of sections of what would become *House* that I showed him, "Well, you know these really aren't poems," but Bill Matthews encouraged me to keep writing them. I wish I'd been a little older at Iowa; maybe I would have had more guts to say, hey, I'm a fiction writer and a poet, I'm going to do both, or I'm trying to fuse the two, because that's what *House on Mango Street* was, something experimental, in the footsteps of the boom writers, Puig and Borges and Rulfo.

> So Iowa was an experience where I found out what I wasn't, where I discovered my otherness . . .

Fortunately, I started making some friends, Dennis Mathis, a working-class kid from Peoria, and Joy Harjo. These were writers who were reading the same experimental stuff I was reading, and who were living hand-to-mouth like me, and they took me in and I felt comfortable. And when I could, I crossed over into the fiction camps and sat in the fiction classes. If I knew Dennis was in a class, I'd go sit in. I did a lot of thinking when there; I'm at my best when I get mad. First reaction: I'll show them, I'll quit! This time I didn't. I wrote a book.

SHERRY KRAMER: I applied to the Fiction Workshop, got in, and wanted to be in the Playwrights' Workshop too. So after I got to Iowa, I went over to the Theatre building and joined the Playwrights' Workshop. This was something that happened fairly often back then, but mostly with poets, not fiction writers, a half dozen or so poets came over to the Playwrights' Workshop and stayed to make their life in the theater.

A theater MFA is a three-year program, not two, so I stayed in Iowa City three years, and ended up with two MFAs: one in fiction in 1977, one in playwriting in 1978. The only downside to getting the double MFA is that after you fulfill the requirements of both programs, you don't have time to take much of anything else, so I missed out on a lot of what both programs had to offer because of that. I would have liked to have taken courses in set design or studied with Miriam Gilbert over in lit.

As soon as I started really writing plays, I realized I was more interested in plays than fiction. I didn't understand much of what went on in the fiction workshop. The stories that were supposedly the lousy stories, I couldn't tell the difference between them and the stories I thought were wonderful. It was a value issue, in the end: The things that were valued were not things I understood as having value. A lot of what was praised seemed to me to be style for style's sake. I was just beginning to struggle with the issue of how much "meaning" could be carried in a work of art, and I naively believed that it was possible to calculate and judge this. I was impatient, in both workshops, when pieces that seemed to me to be about nothing but surface were praised. Or maybe my obsession with Mishima, Kawabata, Kenzaburo Oe, the Japanese, maybe that just didn't translate well into what people in the Workshop were writing then.

Okkie Brownstein, who headed the Playwrights' Workshop, accepted all his first-year playwrights provisionally. He took six and told us he would drop two or three of us at the end of the first semester. This was his thing, no one else at any other program I've seen before or since does this. It's something that's just not done—people uproot their lives and come to a program . . . and then to be dumped? I've taught in playwriting workshops where it would be a kindness if we did that sometimes . . . but we don't.

William Inge wrote a scathing letter responding to a fund-raising plea, which used to be on display on the third floor of New Dramatists, the playwrights' organization in New York, in which he ranted about how helping someone become a playwright was like helping them into hell. But Okkie was selective about who he helped into hell, and I trust he'll be rewarded in the afterlife for it.

The thing with young playwrights is, you're not just looking for voice, or tone, or that spark, because, as it turns out, there are plenty of playwrights who write pretty good plays who really can't "write" all that well. And plenty of playwrights who can "write" well who can't write great plays. What you're looking for is the dramatic instinct, and that's a difficult thing to see sometimes. So you need three or four plays to see if it's really there or not.

GARY IORIO: My workshop experiences at Hofstra were good but different from those at Iowa. The teacher who ran the workshops at Hofstra was Sam Toperoff. He opened his home to his students. We read our stories, poems, and plays in his living room. Sam was an excellent teacher. After we discussed our writings, if we thought something had merit, Sam would, on his own time, edit our work. Every word of my application to Iowa was "blue-penciled" by Sam Toperoff.

My first class experience at Iowa was also a good one. Jack Leggett was my first writing teacher, and I thought he was off the charts. Before our first class, I asked if I could submit a story for the first meeting. He said that he thought it would be a good idea to just go over the ground rules of the workshop at the first writing class. Leggett's ground rules were simple: support and nurture.

At the first class, we did discuss a student's story, a good story, but one that was very much a work in progress. Jack had made the good choice to use this story as an entrance into the "workshop experience."

That was my favorite writing class at Iowa because of my classmates. These people could write! John Givens, Tony Bukoski, Jennie Fields (I think she was in the class), Jonathan Penner, and I (I had a tremendous ego).

Joe Haldeman was also in the class. I already knew his name. Before I got to Iowa, I read a book review of an autobiographical first novel by a Vietnam vet. The review was good, and I was dying to read the book. My library in Long Island didn't have a copy, and I put it on the back burner. Naturally, at my first workshop class, I met Joe Haldeman. Within the week, I found *War Year* at Iowa Book and Supply. A good experience, with a good book and a good guy. Leggett did a good job, and I was very prolific that semester. I wrote like a lunatic.

BILL MCCOY: The first thing I submitted on the worksheet was a bit from what I'd been working on in college with the novelist Tom Rogers. It was heavily influenced by *Lolita*, a little drunk on wordplay, a little self-consciously clever. It pretty much got savaged. I remember there were some who said nice things, but others seemed to go out of their way to say disparaging things.

Because I felt like I'd kind of waltzed into the Workshop without real literary credentials—and also because I was coming straight from college, and almost everybody else seemed to have had some sort of life experience that made them fuller human beings—I took the criticism pretty hard. I felt like a pretender who had been exposed. I spent most of the first semester rewriting and rewriting the first piece, trying to make it something acceptable. Finally I gave up. The stuff I started writing in its place was very different, and not much better. But at least I'd taken the first step of trying to figure out who I was through writing.

Later, I'd write a story called "Pretend Dinners." Bill Kinsella read it and went on and on, saying if he were writing a story with this title, it would be this and that, and he went on to describe *his* story. This story, he said of mine, was okay. He was a little dismissive, but he kept saying how much he loved the title. A few years later, I see a Pushcart Prize collection, and I'm flipping through it, and I find a story called "Pretend Dinners" by Bill Kinsella. It's within the rules. Who says you can't pinch someone's story title?[32]

GLENN SCHAEFFER: It's not that I didn't have success at the Workshop. But I spent most of the first semester at Iowa trying to rewrite a story I'd written at Irvine, "Kicks," which had gotten me into the Workshop in the first place, thanks to Allan Gurganus. Oakley Hall at Irvine had told me "Kicks" was good as far as it goes, but to be professional, it needed to be raunchier. Write it for *Playboy*, he advised me. So at Iowa I was determined to make it *raunchier*, reading up on de Sade because at twenty-one I hadn't had any lowdown sexual experience of my own to draw on. But it didn't happen. (Neither the story nor the mungy lowdown.)

So the first piece I put up for workshop was something I finally dashed off in a weekend, "Notes on Being Nasty." It was in Vance Bourjaily's workshop, and it got some good discussion. It was a longish story about a prank caller. My character begins a relationship with the caller, a random urban predator. This infernal caller says something that strikes him, infects my character, and he tries to keep the joker on the line. The joker would call back; they'd make dates to talk. We were getting to the psychiatric problems of my narrator. I'm telling this now better than I wrote it. Then Vance took it apart, but fairly. He taught me about dialogue: Never do exposition in dialogue; it's for dramatic conflict and the bad guy deserves the better lines. The secret sharer needed the better lines, even as my flawed narrator increasingly misbehaved himself. That's the best thing I learned in the Workshop, how to distribute those incriminatory lines. Then Vance told me it was an impressive story in concept, work on it some more, but I didn't. I didn't like the story after he went through it and showed me all my faults.

MINDY PENNYBACKER: I remember that advice, and Vance rolling a cigarette in class with tobacco all over his tongue, telling us what he'd learned from a screenwriting stint in Hollywood. In realistic dialogue, characters talk at cross-purposes, Vance said. He paused in his licking and looked up. "People don't just say what's really on their minds," he said. Except in workshop when they hate your stuff, I thought, but then workshop had little to do with real life, thankfully.

The class I loved most and that's probably had the most impact on my writing and lack of worldly success over the years was the Proust seminar taught by Henry Bromell, who later vanished into TV writing, which might have been Proust's fate if he'd been born a century later, with the miniseries *Paris Vice*.

DOUG BORSOM: I was in Jack Leggett's workshop my first semester, and the first story I put up for a workshop at Iowa was "Mary," about a man who flees his wife and life in Cincinnati and drives to LA to stay with an old college friend. To get the painful part over, I submitted the story early in the semester. The reception by my fellow students was lukewarm, but Jack was very enthusiastic, so I came away with a good feeling. Reading the story now, I can't imagine what Jack saw in it, and why the other students didn't trash it.

Jack had a sort of professional cheerfulness. One time, a couple of us invited Leggett out for a drink, and he was quite nice about it. He spent a couple hours with us in some Iowa City bar. He told us that contrary to our earnest belief, getting a first novel published would change nothing. *Nothing*. Bummer.

I recall having stories savaged by individuals, but I also remember praise. I remember sitting in a workshop where a story by Dan Domench was getting the crap kicked out of it. I had liked the

> He told us that contrary to our earnest belief, getting a first novel published would change nothing. Nothing. Bummer.

story and kept defending it until Dan turned to me and said something like, "Please stop. You're only making this worse."

JACK LEGGETT: What I found was no matter how awful the manuscript, if you asked when everybody was gathered round, what kind of things can you say about this manuscript, *somebody* would volunteer *something*, and from that you could go on. From there it was just "Well okay, but what about the . . . ?" "Add to that." "Do you want it to . . . ?"

It seemed to me that the job was to get everybody, or most people, talking and to educate them that you don't need to trash somebody else's stuff, but you don't want to lie. "This is a piece of shit" may be accurate, but it didn't get things going, so Rule Number One: If anybody considered it a piece of shit, I wouldn't agree with them. There's nothing so bad there isn't something good in it.

DON WALLACE: When the time came to pick our classes, there was a rush for everyone to get into Henry Bromell's class. He was very young, elegant in a louche sort of way, scruffy, and angular with a scraggly beard but with those nice East Coast clothes. A book of his short stories, all published in the *New Yorker*, was on its way. Compared to grizzled veteran writers, he seemed to be what we all wanted to be. Anyway, I got into his class through a lottery and, being a blind enthusiast, submitted a story for the first class. Why not? I was writing all the time. Iowa had already unleashed me, in a way. And I believed in going with your freshest stuff, not some old and polished piece that had already been workshopped into submission.

So the story I put up, "Face to Face," was about a rock climber with a degenerative condition caused by a head injury who was about to go up a cliff face just as a winter storm hits. He was with an old friend who was essentially helping him to commit suicide. It was told in a communal voice, the voice of a group of unnamed and unidentified back-country hikers on a fishing trip in the Sierra Nevada. They meet these guys at their camp, and it's weird and tense and threatening and only a year later, on a return trip, they understand what was going on when they see a body swinging in a sleeping bag way up on the cliff face. In a way, a very Walter Van Tilburg Clark kind of story, though I wrote it before meeting Mark Van Tilburg across the street.

> Compared to grizzled veteran writers, he seemed to be what we all wanted to be..

Probably this was a story not suited for Henry Bromell's strengths—his stories were delicate, *New Yorker* demographic fragments about a family of a State Department employee posted overseas.

ERIC OLSEN: I was also in Henry Bromell's class my first semester in the Workshop. I'm a little vague on the details, though. However, I kept a notebook back then, and I see from some of my jottings that I submitted one story the main character of which was a corpse. I know, what the hell was I thinking?

"That winter," the story begins, "the body went on display." The story was set in a small mining town in northern California during the gold rush.

I put up a second story that featured the painter Raphael and involved a dragon, or a dream of a dragon, or Raphael's hallucinations about a dragon or something or other. I'd been reading the magical realists at the time, with some C. G. Jung and Robert Graves on the side. I guess I couldn't help myself.

Bromell seemed to like the stuff I was turning in, at least based on my jottings in my notebooks. I think I got away with a lot early on, playing the myth angle. I think some readers figured my stuff must be profound with all the myth stuff going on, even if it didn't make much sense. Or maybe not making sense added to the gravitas. Plot and meaning and such things were dead, after all. Ron Sukenick said so. So did Roland Barthes.

Anyway, I have a scrawled note that Bromell even said he was going to send one of my stories to the *Antioch Review*. My notes don't say which story. It's hard for me to imagine either story being even remotely suitable for *Antioch*. And I guess Bromell had second thoughts himself. A later entry in my notebook indicates that Bromell hadn't sent in either story, and I scribbled a little comment about how nice it would have been if he had let me know. So it seems I sent both of them to the *Antioch Review* myself, according to my notebook (I've no memory of this whatsoever). There's no reference later to any results, so I assume the *Antioch Review* just dumped them in the trash.

My notes from that time also mention an hour-long talk by a visiting William Gaddis, during which he apparently talked about how he didn't have anything to talk about. At the party after, I noted in my journal, refreshments consisted of three half gallons of Almaden Chablis and a single bag of potato chips. My notes also include some rude comments about the host and his cheap refreshments.

But in fact, there are more entries in my notebooks from those days concerning my forays into boxing than adventures in various workshop classes. But then of course the Workshop and boxing were intimately linked in my mind. They still are.

My notes from that time also mention an hour-long talk by a visiting William Gaddis, during which he apparently talked about how he didn't have anything to talk about.

ANTHONY BUKOSKI: I think it was Glenn who had mentioned an interest in boxing first, and I took him up on an offer to meet upstairs in the old gym for a sparring session. Man, he took it to me; Glenn could fling leather. I don't mean he raised welts on my head or left bruises on my body, but he would bull in, head down, and I was unprepared for his attack, even though I am taller, heavier, and have longer arms. I was disappointed in my performance.

Olsen joined us later. I never could escape the wrath of Eric's wonderful left jab. He had this sullen quality—well, I came to realize he might have been shy or introspective or in pain from his back. He was still recovering from a back injury. Or perhaps he just wasn't one to blather on the way I do. When he did laugh or grow enthusiastic about a topic, it meant something; whereas I was enthusiastic, but too often scatterbrained about too many things. I believed him to be loyal to his friends. I believed, too, that like all of us trying to find our way, he was troubled by various things. One thing troubling him was his future as a writer (could he support his family and write once he left Iowa?), and of course another terribly troubling concern—and something from which I've been free—was the physical pain he was often in.

ERIC OLSEN: It was Tony's contention that all writers should know how to box, and that MFA students, the guys anyway, should be required to spar three rounds at least once a week. He said it was good for the soul. So every Friday afternoon a few of us would convene in the Field House—the original Field House that looked like a gigantic warehouse, not the fancy new Field House they have now—and try to hit one another upside the head. Whup up.

Tony was a big Marine who'd lost his front teeth in a fight with another Marine in Vietnam, and with these credentials, he was feared in the ring. He'd pop out his dentures and insert a mouthguard, a somewhat intimidating gesture. He had good legs, and he could hook off a jab, a neat trick. In fact, the only time I was ever off my feet while attending the Workshop was at the end of one of Tony's hooks. Flash knockdown.

> It was Tony's contention that all writers should know how to box, and that MFA students, the guys anyway, should be required to spar three rounds at least once a week. He said it was good for the soul.

Glenn was the best of us in many regards. Never mind that I had three inches on him and twenty pounds, and Tony had forty. Glenn had played football in high school, and he lifted weights, and he simply had tremendous raw strength. It helped, too, that Glenn had a wee mean bone inside him; it must throb when he fights. If you saw him strutting around—he tended to strut, and still does—in gym shorts and T-shirt, you'd know he was an athlete who'd done his share on the iron pile. Yet in the ring he lacked finesse and couldn't hook off a jab at all. He was also a little short on wind, I suppose because he was a weightlifter and trained himself for explosive bursts. He'd bring it furiously and dangerously for thirty seconds or a minute—seldom two—then his tongue would appear in the corner of his mouth and next he'd go flat-footed and have to be reminded to pull his tongue back in or it might get clipped off, at which point he'd wave a glove and say, Let's take a breather.

But if Glenn hit you, *mother*, it hurt. If he squared you upside your head, say, you'd hear a barely audible *crack* and then—I'm serious—you'd see stars. I saw them myself. Stars. I'd heard of such things, but didn't believe it until one day Glenn conked me and I saw them, so I covered up and backpedaled and let Glenn punch himself out on my elbows while my head cleared.

It was a good, honest punch, a pure punch that tells you stories about yourself, that you can take a hit first of all, and that after you've covered up and the roaring in your brain has subsided, and after the inevitable little hesitation while you ask yourself what the *hell* you're doing in here, after all of that, and after you've concluded it wasn't so bad—that punch and *crack* and those winking stars—you discover you can straighten up and come out from behind your gloves and answer back, much as I imagined Pound might have answered Hemingway in Paris. Hemingway, that bully....

At any rate, I like to think I learned some things about writing while sparring in the wrestling room on Friday afternoons, something about gutting it out even if I was on Queer Street. I liked to think I exhibited style as a boxer, with a good, quick, accurate jab, which I'd stick in my opponent's face, and then sometimes I could hook off the jab and cross off the hook and it would usually take my opponent a minute or two or even a couple rounds to figure out—even if my opponent was Glenn or Tony who *knew* already but still had to figure it out again each Friday afternoon—that I didn't have much behind my jab or hook or cross, that all you had to do was take a couple on your gloves and then step inside and go to my ribs, then my head. I'd practiced a lot of Asian martial arts, so I was a defensive fighter, mostly, a counterpuncher.

> **At any rate, I like to think I learned some things about writing while sparring in the wrestling room on Friday afternoons, something about gutting it out even if I was on Queer Street.**

Back then, I sometimes wondered in my darker moments—and I still do, I suppose—if there was some relationship between my boxing style and my writing, if my writing was merely a stylish jab with nothing behind it. I think deep down we each saw correspondences, or we thought we did, to the other's writing in the way he boxed, just as deep down we refused to believe there was any link at all between our own frailties as boxers or as writers. Boxing can be character.

GLENN SCHAEFFER: Boxing can be reduced to three punches, starting with the jab. You can't get hurt if you position your fist on the point of another man's nose at 120 mph. And yet again and again you see fighters, *professionals*, who can't throw the jab. You watch these pros, their hands come down, they don't jab, they drop rounds, they bottle themselves, get the jack whumped out of them. So you *know* what you're supposed to do and you just can't do it. And you can tell yourself every minute "let your hands go free, let your hands go free, let your hands do it, let your hands think" and you can't do it. It takes abnormal confidence; you must conquer the fear that inhabits your soul to do it. Yogi Berra said you can't think and hit at the same time. Baseball and boxing—you have to quit thinking so much. You don't *think* baseball, you *play* baseball. Indecision kills you. Same with writing. You'd hear things about what you're *supposed* to do in writing, but you don't always see it done, even at the highest level. And then when you *do* see it done, it's such a thing of beauty. It comes from somewhere, that beauty. And I keep reading to see how writing's done. Narrative consists of three elements, too—dilemma, conflict, and resolution, which are inflected by point of view or dramatic irony. Include the exercise of sex and power, and whamo, you *can* become champ. When narrative's done well, which is almost never, it's transporting. Like firing a strong punch.

> Narrative consists of three elements, too—dilemma, conflict, and resolution, which are inflected by point of view or dramatic irony. Include the exercise of sex and power, and whamo, you *can* become champ.

ANTHONY BUKOSKI: Why did I find it appealing, yet threatening, to slip on the gloves those years we were together? There is that moment of truth when you see what kind of shape you're in. There is the moment when you see whether you can take a punch and recover.

I also think that it is not unpleasant to be punched sometimes. It is not always, even often, pleasurable, but when you have been hit right, you go a little numb in the head. For me that was good; you're worry free, and you know exactly what to do next. Maybe this is why I always liked the "Bayonne Bleeder," Chuck Wepner. Maybe—this gets weird—it has to do with being hit by your father. When you get it in the right way, you become a boy again.

ERIC OLSEN: Generally, Tony and Glenn and I didn't talk much with other Workshop students about our Friday afternoons in the wrestling room, at least any more than we talked about our desire to be Ernest Hemingway.

Our Friday afternoons weren't exactly a secret, either, but they just weren't something we were sure anyone else would quite understand.

I remember one afternoon in the locker room, the playwright Robert Anderson (*Tea and Sympathy, I Never Sang for My Father*) was dressing in his whites for tennis and watched with decided amusement as Tony and Glenn and I wrapped our hands in linen tapes like veteran boxers and rinsed the gym-bag funk off our mouthpieces in the drinking fountain. After that, whenever Anderson saw me, he would give me that special, soft, and understanding smile we reserve for good-natured fools and ask, "Taken any good shots to the head lately?" Eventually we expanded our club to include other misfits, from hard-fisted recovered winos to Alaskan bush pilots to free-range martial artists, with Tony as matchmaker.

One time we contemplated asking John Irving if he'd like to come up and box. He was working on *Garp*, and we'd see him on warm afternoons jogging along the Iowa River wearing nothing but his red Speedo and running shoes, but there was something about him, a certain quality, so that Tony never booked him.

JOHN IRVING: I spent many more hours in that old Field House (because the Iowa wrestling room was there before they built Carver-Hawkeye) than I ever did in those Quonset huts along the river or in the EPB (English-Philosophy Building). I wasn't boxing then, but I was still wrestling, every day.

Later, when I lived in New York, the boxing room at the New York Athletic Club was on the same floor as the wrestling room, and I had a friend who'd been the middleweight champion of Ireland. He taught me to box and I taught him to wrestle. When I finally stopped wrestling, I took up boxing and kickboxing at a Tae Kwon Do club in Toronto, where the master was a former freestyle wrestler on the Iranian team in the time of the Shah. I also tried some boxing with the local karate master here in Vermont.

I can hook off the jab, and cross off the hook, but I just can't hit very hard. I tend to use the jab-hook combination as a means to get close enough to my opponent so that I can trip him. A wrestling move; after all, everything today is mixed martial arts!

But I never liked Hemingway. His prose came from journalism, and everything that smacks of minimalism oozes from it. I also never liked what he wrote about; there was nothing new in it. It was faux tough-guy prose and tough-guy stoicism. And he was a blowhard, wasn't he? A braying loudmouth who wrote sentences short enough for advertisements. When I first went to Iowa as a student, I told Vance Bourjaily that I thought of myself as the anti-Hemingway; this was probably why I chose to work with Vonnegut—Kurt was so *not* Hemingway, Kurt was the antimacho man.

ERIC OLSEN: Very soon during our boxing careers at Iowa, Glenn and Tony and I began to analyze other writers not according to their writing, but according to what we imagined were their boxing skills. When Kurt Vonnegut came to give us a master class and tell us how hopeless it is to be a young writer living in America—he vouched that advertising was the next game—we agreed he'd be one of those fighters who liked to mix it up inside. He'd be dirty in clinches, all elbows and thumbs, yet cut easily and bleed a mess, which wouldn't bother him in the least, and he'd try to wear you down. When John Hawkes came through town to give a course, we concluded that however impenetrable his experiments in prose had become, he'd fight straight up, out of the book, with a clean sharp jab, a decent hook, and the ability to put them together, though like me without much power. He'd play it fancy.

I think Vance Bourjaily loomed largest in our imaginations. There was something about him . . . the way he could roll a cigarette with one hand, maybe. We knew Vance would be aggressive in the ring, one of those fighters who'd crouch low, rolling sideways like a crab, looping wide punches that would miss more often than not so that by the late rounds he'd be woefully behind on points, and then he'd decide he'd had enough of this ballet, come out of his crouch, and . . . *bang*.

> Very soon during our boxing careers at Iowa, Glenn and Tony and I began to analyze other writers not according to their writing, but according to what we imagined were their boxing skills.

GLENN SCHAEFFER: There was also Norman Mailer, bard of boxing and protégé of champ Jose Torres. At the time, not a weekend went by that Mailer wasn't in the news for punching someone in an expensive Manhattan restaurant. Word was he even trained for these bouts. And his latest book, *The Fight*, about the Ali-Foreman "rumble in the jungle" had just come out. Mailer seemed to be in fighting trim, if a little long in the tooth. He and Vance were New York pals from way back, and Vance proposed that I box Mailer at an exhibition at Iowa—Vance asserted that *theirs* was the *baddest* generation. I considered this proposal and how it might suffice as my MFA thesis, a participatory treatment and literary meditation à la Frederick Exley, *Fighting Norman Mailer.* That could have been good. *Patricide as a Motive in American Literature.*

ERIC OLSEN: Vance was in grand spirits at Red Bird Farm when that subject was broached. He was roasting a pig. We were all drunk. I believe John Falsey (*White Shadow, Northern Exposure*) egged it on. A dreadful idea,

I suggested. Mailer was in his fifties, and Glenn was full of heat. If matters in a ring were to escalate, there was every possibility that Glenn would maim Mailer. Then he'd have to move to Bolivia, I told him. And if he somehow lost, against all the laws of probability and common sense? Bolivia again.

ANTHONY BUKOSKI: One time, it was February, I think, Glenn and Eric and I drove from Iowa City to Milwaukee to see the USA boxing team fight the Soviet team at the Mecca in downtown Milwaukee.

We arrived the morning before and checked into a hotel that had seen better days. It was called the Antler Hotel or the Hotel Antler or maybe just the Antler. We walked around downtown that afternoon. The lake was frozen. As we were walking, we came upon two young, old-looking men wearing identical blue Windbreakers. They were speaking a language we didn't know. Their faces had been busted by too many blows, it looked like. They were talking quickly, arms gesticulating. Then they turned and hurried off. We naturally assumed they were Soviet boxers. This made the afternoon more exciting.

ERIC OLSEN: There was a Duchamps urinal displayed at the art museum downtown, as I recall, and we went to see that, too. How could it get any better? Boxing *and* culture. . . .

ANTHONY BUKOSKI: The ring was gorgeous, elegant even, that night. The ropes seemed woven of white silk. The canvas was spotless. We saw a great night of boxing. If memory serves me, Tony Tubbs, who would later go on to have a fine career as a pro heavyweight, was on the card. I also remember a Woody Clark or "Clarke" with an "e" being on the card. There was a redheaded middleweight from Akron, Rusty Rosenberg, who came out and looked strong, until his crafty Russian opponent, ten years older, bopped him and he sat down in the ring with a heaving sound. At the end of the count, he merely shook his head at the ref. Fine with Rusty, just sitting there under the lights.

Afterward, we sat in the hotel lounge. A chanteuse was on that night. We liked her, a blonde who was not old by any means. She had written a song, "Santa Monica." To this day, I can sing the first few bars of her composition. We told her Glenn was from LA. This didn't impress her. We decided to ask her to come to our room for a nightcap. "You ask her," Glenn said to Eric. "No," Eric said to me, "*you* ask her." "No, you," I said. We went up alone, the three of us, three expendables who used to ask each other, "Do you think Hemingway would have liked us?" Not that night, he wouldn't have.

GLENN SCHAEFFER: Driving back from Milwaukee, we stopped in Madison for lunch at a Greek place, one of those student hangouts with a big glob of lamb turning on a spit in the window. Dirty snow was piled in the gutters. It was a grim, freezing day. We had greasy lamb and plenty of beers and walked outside to go to the car, and the next thing I knew I was down on my hands and knees, simultaneously hocking in the gutter snow and thinking how this could pretty much become the writer's life for me—it was how writers often served their craft, I knew. It was how Fitzgerald had behaved, certainly; it was how Richard Hugo behaved; it was how Charles Bukowski did, and Frederick Exley on the jag his whole time at Iowa. And it was how Larry Woiwode, most recently, had behaved when auditioning for a teaching role. Gravitas wasn't in the cards. With any luck, I was to be one of a long line of literary pukers.

ERIC OLSEN: After a workout, we'd towel off (we didn't bother to shower; we were fiction writers, after all) and then make our way to the Mill downtown. Over time that became our real workshop, a little sparring, then to the Mill to drink and talk about art and life, just as we imagined Hemingway and Joyce and Pound had done in Paris, and our faces and bodies were sore from punches that were clean and good and the beer was clear and cold and true, like a trout stream in Spain.

~

As Marvin Bell observed, we were hardly like his generation of rough-edged boho outsiders fresh from the Good War or Korea, but rather we were well scrubbed and maybe too bourgeois products of a system of scouting and vetting from undergraduate creative writing programs. But the beauty of the Iowa Writers' Workshop back then, and probably now, is that it provided ample opportunity for us to acquire some rough edges and begin to get a better sense of not only who we *were*, but of who we were *not*, and to feel perhaps for the first time a little like the proper outsiders all writers should be.

> ... It provided ample opportunity for us to acquire some rough edges and begin to get a better sense of not only who we *were*, but of who we were *not*, and to feel perhaps for the first time a little like the proper outsiders all writers should be.

Once classes began and we got to know one another, schools and schools within schools and various alliances and cabals began to form and reform, often around nothing more substantial than aspiration. Soon enough, we had the minimalists versus the magical realists versus the pastoral realists; the East Coasters versus the West Coasters versus the Midwesterners;

would-be Hemingways and the macho followers of faculty member Vance Bourjaily, who hunted and fished, versus the East Coasters who tended to gravitate toward Workshop Director Jack Leggett; with the major divides perhaps best exemplified by the two Ray Carvers: the Ray Carver who was published in *Kayak*, and the Ray Carver edited by Gordon Lish and published in *Esquire* and the *New Yorker*. It was not enough to admire both Ray Carvers; you had to pick a side. And what if you liked them both? And what if, deep down, you wanted nothing so much as to be published in the *New Yorker*, even though you were from the West Coast and thus were obligated to publicly express nothing but disdain for the magazine and its effete East Coast ethos?

And the folks who ran the Workshop helped to promote additional distinctions between us—*class* distinctions between those who got invited to the *best* parties and those who didn't. But as annoying, frustrating, and as fundamentally unfair as this system of preferments might have seemed—hey, we were all paying the same fees, after all—it did help to strengthen in many of us a further sense of *otherness*, plus a dollop of justifiable anger, which for a writer can only serve to focus the mind and energize the prose.

You could get drunk and stoned and laid—or try to—at the Workshop, too, because, it seemed, that's what writers did. At least that's what many of the famous writers we knew and admired seemed to do when they came through town. We also fought battles over who got to have their stories read by visiting writers and agents; the Workshop system of granting financial awards was accused of being fixed; a student with glossy headshots and a PR packet upended genteel tradition; and another ran off to San Francisco with an Amish farmer and paterfamilias. Meanwhile, "outside," in the real world, in New York publishing, the old manners were being shoved rudely aside by our current commodity-driven world, where demographics, gender, ethnicity, and above all, marketability are the yardsticks by which literary talent is measured and presented to the American public. We were being told, now, that only woman over forty bought novels, so deal with it. It was all great fun, that is, and some of us even managed to get some work done through it all.

~

JANE SMILEY: I do remember that Barbara Grossman and I and a few others used to go to Dick Bausch's house regularly and have extra workshops; we were willing to meet all the time to try to get somewhere. That was one of the ways I found the Workshop quite appealing and worthy; it wasn't about competition, but about all boats rising...

Books by the Bed

GLENN SCHAEFFER: *The Interrogative Mood: A Novel?* Padgett Powell. *The Financial Lives of Poets,* Jess Walter. *Curse of the Mogul: What Went Wrong with the World's Leading Media Companies,* Jonathan Knee. *The Pound Era,* Hugh Kenner. *Manhood for Amateurs, the Pleasures and Regrets of a Husband, Father, and Son,* Michael Chabon. *Catching the Big Fish: Meditation, Consciousness, and Creativity,* David Lynch. And various issues of the *New Yorker, Vanity Fair, Frieze, Art Forum,* and *Art + Auction.* Two copies of Malcolm Lowry's *Under the Volcano,* forever unread, and novelist David Markson's essay on same.

GLENN SCHAEFFER: You hear how cutthroat the Workshop is, but that wasn't my experience. I was never with a group of aspirants less competitive than my fellow workshoppers. You wanted a bunch of snarks, try getting a PhD in lit crit at Irvine. At Iowa, we knew it was a boot camp and that we were going to be shipped out and go to war for cultural or market stakes and some of us would get promoted and some annihilated, but we were in this thing together. At Irvine, it was plain cutthroat. Clued in ahead of time, your classmates would go to the research library and check out all the recommended texts and hide them for the trimester so you couldn't review them. I had to buy a library card at USC to get my work done. At Iowa, the biggest neurotics weren't the students; they were on the faculty—the screwballs brought in to lead us.

JANE SMILEY: I found my classes with Allan Gurganus and Barbara Grossman and Meredith Steinbach and Dick Bausch to be quite supportive. It may be that classes before us or after us were more cutthroat, but not ours. We had Henry Bromell, who didn't encourage us to compete with one another, but there were other teachers who privileged some students.

In that period, the teachers tended to be men of a certain age, with the idea that competition was somehow the key, the Norman Mailer period. The story was that if you disagreed with Norman, or gave him a bad review, he'd punch you in the nose. You were supposed to get in fights in restaurants. That was the model, and maybe it was a New York thing.

Gordon Lish came, and he was hard on you, and Ted Solotaroff was into that, too. Stanley Elkin used that "who do you think you are?" teaching method, which was supposed to arouse your pride and challenge you to greatness, but the teaching style I preferred was more cooperative.

By the mid-'70s, we students were shifting from that macho school, even if our mentors were not. It just wasn't an Iowa City thing; we were a group of like-minded people, why fight among ourselves?

SANDRA CISNEROS: I don't have good memories of it at all. I was going crazy trying to write something people didn't say was awful. I showed *Mango Street* to Bill Matthews, and I'd show it to my friends, Dennis Mathis and Joy Harjo. I showed it to Donald Justice, but he wasn't very helpful.

It took me a long time to not be angry; I just think now, what a jerk I was. But it really kind of made me feel, this is what I don't want from a teacher. As instructors we have lots of opportunities to abuse our students because they look up to us. I just felt there was a lack of respect and lack of honor there.

I had fallen in love with one of my teachers at Loyola. He fell in love with me and wanted to divorce his wife. I was in Iowa when I got a call from my mother saying his wife had called my home, and he was trying to divorce her. My family was very traditional. My mother said, "How can you lower yourself?" That's when I went to the park and wrote his wife a letter and said I'm going to break off this relationship, I'd been trying to.

I was going through stuff like that. Wouldn't that be a good writing assignment, write a letter to your lover's wife, to break off the relationship? That letter was perhaps the most honest piece of writing I did at Iowa.

JOY HARJO: I have remained friends all this time with one of the first people I met at the beginning-of-the-year workshop picnic at Jack Leggett's house, a visiting writer, playwright, and novelist, Rosalyn Drexler. She was irreverent and brilliant, and an outsider of sorts to the literati of the writing workshop.

ROSALYN DREXLER: Iowa was the first place I'd taught at, ever. Also, the first time I'd been on my own for a long time. The freedom was heady. I was experiencing the same things my students were: accomplishment, friendship, a bright future ahead of us. It took some courage for me to accept an offer to teach at the Workshop. I'd never gone to college. And these were the crème de la crème. I was like, "Oh my god, these people are so smart." I don't know how I got in there. Maybe Ted Solotaroff recommended me. Or maybe my friends in the literary world like Donald Barthelme, John Hawkes, or Norman Mailer recommended me.

In any case, in the middle of it, I said, "I don't know how to do this. I've never done it." So I spoke to the head of the department, John Leggett. I told him I wanted to quit.

He said, "There's nothing to it. Look, I'll tell you what to do." And he told me what to do: They all have to go and copy their stuff; they write their critiques, you don't say a word until they've all read their stuff, and then they read their critiques, and then at the end you say a couple of things; that's it. You help out on what they read or you encourage them.

So that's what I did. It was mainly supportive, and bore into the questions of form, content, and what is the best way to say what you want to say. Examples of other writers who were admired or disregarded as fashion changed were discussed. Maybe Barthelme and Vonnegut were "hot" at the time. I don't remember. Maybe if Proust had been in my class early in his writing career, it would have been next to impossible to guess that he would produce works of genius later on.

So my bit of advice is, if you want to be a writer, write. Write anything. Only write.

A creative writing program lends authenticity to hidden desires. There, one is encouraged to write it out, to share, and to experience what it means to be a writer. You begin by playacting, then it becomes real.

JACK LEGGETT: It was at Vance's invitation that I came out to Iowa. Vance had been Engle's anointed successor to head the Workshop, but he didn't really want it. So when I came to Iowa, the head of the Workshop was George Starbuck, a poet. I recall that John Gerber, head of the English department, was not happy with George. He was a typical poet; he was someplace else, doing his work, and trouble was always landing on Gerber's desk. Starbuck had fallen in love with his secretary and decided to take her back to New Hampshire, where he was from, so there was going to be a vacancy, which Vance obviously didn't want.

I rather enjoyed Vance because he was fun . . . I was then a senior editor at Harper and I know it occurred to Vance it would be good for him and others to have a book editor on the faculty. So I arrived in Iowa City, and in the course of my first semester as a visiting writer, I went to a couple of football games with John Gerber to cheer the Hawkeyes. Gerber liked me. I was sort of more proper and dependable than the usual drunk visiting writers they had in. So next thing I knew I was on the search committee to find a new Workshop director, and at a search committee meeting, somewhat qualified people would be proposed and I'd come up with some reason to turn them down, until it occurred to me that maybe the reason was that I wanted subconsciously to keep the directorship for myself. So I ran down to talk to Gerber about it. He said, what do you want? I said, I want time to work. He said, if you take the job, you needn't show up until after lunch. That was the best deal anybody could have offered. I said, John, I'll take it, and it was ultimately because I was given my mornings free.

JOHN IRVING: I was a student in the Iowa Writers' Workshop from 1965 until 1967. I took a class or two with Vance Bourjaily, who was teaching in the Fiction Workshop, and one from Marvin Bell in the Poetry Workshop. The course with Marvin was more about how to read poems than how to write them. I was never a poet. I'd earlier had some interest in the theater (as an actor, never as a playwright), and for the duration of my time as a student at Iowa, I was writing my first novel, *Setting Free the Bears*. I had started my actual first novel when I was a senior at the University of New Hampshire, but I had thrown it away by the time I arrived in Iowa City. I had written very few short stories before becoming a novelist; to date, I have written more novels, twelve, than I ever wrote short stories. I'm not a fan of short stories.

> Did Kurt have a "method"? Not that I could tell. Did he have a formula for how you should write a novel? No. He was very patient and kind, and he circled a lot of words on my manuscript.

I met Kurt Vonnegut in Iowa City; I'd read all his books, which were not easy to find then, and I believed he was underrated—and unfairly categorized as a science-fiction writer. Many of my fellow Workshop students, especially those who hadn't read Vonnegut, dismissed him as unworthy of their precious time. It wasn't hard to get into Kurt's fiction workshop.

Nelson Algren was teaching in the Fiction Workshop then, too. I thought he was an asshole. He was certainly a blowhard and a pontificator, but he had some students firmly in his thrall; he was a recruiter. Kurt just shuffled around; he didn't care if you took notice of him or not. He was both a mentor and a teacher. I loved the guy.

Did Kurt have a "method"? Not that I could tell. Did he have a formula for how you should write a novel? No. He was very patient and kind, and he circled a lot of words on my manuscript. You like these kinds of words, don't you? he would scribble in the margin. He was right. He didn't say that the words I liked were bullshit, or that I liked them too much, but I got the idea.

He circled the semicolons, too; those he openly disliked. He said various things about them, such as "Everyone will figure out that you probably went to college somewhere; you don't have to try to prove it." (Or words to that effect.) I pointed out to him that I loved everything about the nineteenth-century novel—including the semicolons. He said, "I guess you went to college, all right."

We watched the Six-Day War together in his kitchen. He invited me to come watch the war because he knew I didn't have a television. He told me that he thought capitalism would be kind to me one day. I had no idea what he meant. Years later, I asked him, "Did you mean that you thought I was going to write best sellers and make a lot of money on my writing?" Well, of course that's what he'd meant! he said. What had I thought he meant?

Bourjaily was a gentle soul and very old-school about realism and solid, no-nonsense prose. Algren, as I said, was a pontificator, and because I never listened to what he said, I can't tell you how he taught in his workshop, or if he had a "method" or a formula. When you think someone is just a bullshitter, you tune out, which is what I did with Algren. He used to try and bait me into a fight with him. "A boxer can kick the shit out of a wrestler"—that kind of thing.

I just said, "Depends on who's better," or, "I doubt it."

There were some talented students in the workshop in those years. John Casey was there and Gail Godwin. We were Vonnegut people. We didn't write anything like him, but we loved him. He was one of the father figures I latched onto in my life—they were all either writers or wrestling coaches. I am lucky to have met Vonnegut. We were neighbors when we both lived in Sagaponack, in the Hamptons. He used to ride his bicycle over to my house in the morning for a cup of coffee. I miss him.

JOY HARJO: The first worksheets were traumatic. Sandra Cisneros and I were in the same poetry workshop. We were the only two students whose poetry didn't appear on the worksheet for the first month. I wanted to quit the workshop but had invested too much time and money and decided to stay it out, at least a year.

I realized that poetry had many cultural forms and faces, that mythological impulses were the same at the root, but only those classical expressions pertinent to the dominant culture would spark recognition and kinship in the writing workshop. I still see this at work, at Iowa, and in the American poetry academy. (Yes, there is one.)

My friendships with other students made my completion of the degree possible: Sandra Cisneros, Dennis Mathis, Pam Durban, Kambon Obayani, and Jayne Anne Phillips. I also spent as much time as possible at the International Writing Program and their events.

JEFFREY ABRAHAMS: Once I got to Iowa, I got sucked into not writing like I wrote, but trying to figure out what teachers wanted. That was my undoing. And I didn't break out of it until my second year. You succeed as an undergrad in so many ways . . . how to get A's as an undergrad, but when I got to grad school, all those talents that served me as an undergrad didn't work at Iowa. I thought I needed to write the Iowa style, though I couldn't figure out what it was, and then having failed that first year to do what I was trying, the second year I just did what I did, and that was great. But it took the first year to get me to that point the second year.

GORDON MENNENGA: I sometimes recommend Iowa to my students, but I warn them it's very competitive. It can be very isolating, and you're on your own and you better be able to sit down by yourself and work. Everyone there takes it very seriously, and if you think you can use that to make you a better writer, then go for it.

I think at Iowa, most people walked into a workshop on the day their story was going to be discussed with fear oozing out of their pores. I don't know if that's good or bad. I've heard that it's like the Marines. If you want to continue that analogy, the Workshop can turn you into one tough-ass writer. I had a great time.

> It can be very isolating, and you're on your own and you better be able to sit down by yourself and work.

ROBIN GREEN: It was a mixed bag for me. As in my profession now as a TV writer, I liked my fellow writers well enough. Some, a few, have become lifelong friends. But there was and is for me a competitive vibe. It's business. Maybe it's something I bring.

But Iowa was pretty much a repeat of Brown; that is, I wrote just enough to be praised in class (Lenny Michaels's class; of course that's why I liked him, 'cause he didn't like anybody's stuff and he liked mine), and to get a stipend the second year. I loved Lenny Michaels's class. I loved meeting and reading Ray Carver. I loved reading Proust for a whole semester with Henry Bromell. That was really something. Heaven.

JOE HALDEMAN: Ray Carver and I got along well. We were close in age and temperament, which is to say fellow barflies. I loved his writing and he liked mine. He was also a great wounded soul, and everybody wanted to nurture him, or at least buy him another drink.

Another one was William Price Fox. He put together a two-semester screenwriting workshop that was priceless guidance when, a few years later, I came to write a couple of movies.

Stephen Becker and I got along famously. He was the only writer at the workshop who was writing exciting stuff about interesting people. He seemed to love my stuff, and we eventually wasted some months trying to collaborate on a science fiction novel, *Hard Water*. Neither of us was a good collaborator, but we wound up close friends for the rest of his life. (He's the only person who ever made a deathbed request to me. He said that religion was the greatest enemy of civilization, and I should take the goddamn gloves off when I got into the ring with it. Heard and obeyed.)

JOY HARJO: The workshops at Iowa were particularly brutal. Competition was rife and set us against each other. When I taught creative writing, I kept the high standards, but made a kitchen-table community. I've come to believe that, at best, workshops make a community of kindred souls who are working on the same large poem, the same large story. The workshop can be an inspirational resource, a crafting hot house.

I have begun to question the effectiveness of them to really teach the art. Writing is something we learn on our own, and there are always those students who make it through a program with a degree and still can't write and will never be writers. But that's not the sole purpose of creative writing programs. What we are teaching is the art of communication, of language, an investigation of the soul, of human behavior.

JAYNE ANNE PHILLIPS: The destructive or nonproductive thing at Iowa, to my mind, was the sense of competition between students. Most arrived with or without aid the first year, but everyone was basically in competition for better aid the second year, for the famous Teaching/ Writing Fellowships, which allowed the recipient to teach fiction writing to undergrads. Iowa was famous for its competitive atmosphere, and maybe a little proud of it, at that time, anyway. The idea was that talent would rise to the top. Students gossiped viciously about one another. Some writers told me they'd hated Iowa, took them years to recover, they'd stopped writing, etc. That wasn't my experience, but I found the tastes of the students rather conservative, while the instructors were supportive and mostly incisive.

> Iowa was famous for its competitive atmosphere, and maybe a little proud of it, at that time, anyway. The idea was that talent would rise to the top.

Iowa was also a fish bowl—a small town. Nothing was happening but the Workshop (as far as the Workshop knew), and the community was not at all diverse.

JENNIE FIELDS: The Workshop had issues when I was there. For instance, my first year, they decided they wanted a "woman" teacher, and they brought in Jane Howard, a journalist. She didn't write fiction at all. It was so embarrassingly wrongheaded. The rumor was that they'd asked Hortense Calisher to come to Iowa because they needed a "female faculty member," and she said, "When you need me as a writer you admire, call me. I'm not coming just to be a 'female' faculty member."

For me, the benefit of being at Iowa was spending time around amazing young writers. At Iowa, I gleaned the majority of my education from my peers who certainly could be harsh critics. I was surrounded by ideas, writing all the time, pushed by the quality of others' work. It inspired me to be better.

ANTHONY BUKOSKI: I loved seeing the Hawkeyes play football, basketball, and baseball, and watching single-A baseball, the Midwest League Cedar Rapids Reds (later the Giants, now the Kernels). I enjoyed the parties and the taverns in Iowa City. I made so many friends.

When I first came to Iowa and went to readings the Workshop sponsored, I felt a little distant from the writers the Workshop brought in, people such as Constance Urdang and Donald Finkel, who I must say I'd not heard of. I'd begun thinking by October of my first semester that the readings weren't for me, that mainly these writers were from some close, insider group of New York writers.

But Jennie Fields begged me to try one more reading. I didn't expect much when I heard Raymond Carver would read. I don't believe I was familiar with his work. Then, after he kept us waiting what seemed like twenty minutes, in strode this tall, hulking man with a shock of hair falling over his forehead, the forehead on a red face. He was wearing a cowboy shirt, a white one with swirls or something on either side of the front. Probably it had pearl buttons. I think he might have had a gut on him. He wore blue jeans. Geez, I liked him right off. He looked like someone I might know back home. Alas, he was pretty drunk.

However, I liked him even more when he read a poem about Bukowski. I remember pretending the Bukowski he was reading about was really the Bukoski who was listening to him. After a little while, Jack Leggett suggested that Ray was perhaps a little too drunk to continue and maybe he could read another time. The reading ended after a half hour.

But I was full of joy. This was a great memory. Unfortunately, it had to be built around someone's misery. To me, the reading was so romantic, the drunken, tortured artist and all that.

GORDY MENNENGA: The real workshop was the community. Ross Howell, another workshopper, was a neighbor, and we talked about fiction all the time. We'd go fishing every evening, and while we fished, we'd talk. Then we'd get to class, and there was a different tone entirely. The discussions in class became more brittle, and everyone had to put in his two cents' worth, and half the time you wanted to ask, have you actually read my story? People complained about things that didn't matter, and left the important stuff untouched. In class, comments got too personal.

Talking with my friends, we were talking about our work. There was a lot of posturing in the workshops, who said what about your story and was this person now your friend or your enemy? Sometimes a teacher saw through that crap and sometimes they didn't.

The weirdest class was Ros Drexler's. She was great, a breath of fresh air. You didn't pull all of that literary shit in her class. You know, you start talking about Proust and she'd go, Who? She didn't let you go negative, either.

BILL MCCOY: I thought most of the visiting teachers were terrific. The writer who was most useful to me—not in getting my so-called career going, but in terms of just getting my head on straight about writing—was Ros Drexler. She was very encouraging. I was at a point when I felt no one liked my work, and it hurt; but she was very encouraging, and I enjoyed writing for her because I knew she enjoyed reading it.

I will always treasure one particular piece of advice she gave me. She suspected, correctly, that I was overediting myself. So she gave me an assignment: to stay up all night writing, with the goal of a completed story by sunrise. "After two-thirty, you join the company of the immortals," she told me. So I did, and that story got by far the best reception of anything I'd submitted up to that point. It became sort of a turning point in my attitude toward writing.

Another visiting writer was Mary Lee Settle. She was also extremely encouraging. She really fought hard against that whole idea of your fellow workshoppers as your rivals. She really encouraged the idea that we were in fact a community. She also gently encouraged me not to be quite so much of a snob. She once said at a party that one of the most valuable things she did for her writing was to watch the most popular television shows. When I asked her why (no doubt with a note of disdain in my voice), she said, "Because that's where you find out what people's fantasies are."

I think there were some people there who wanted everyone else to fail. As a whole, I think, with a number of exceptions, a lot of the atmosphere was about seeing how much discouragement your potential rivals for aid the second year could take, a zero-sum game. I kept trying to find ways to make people happy. Then at one point, because of Ros, I realized I wasn't going to please anyone, so I might as well please myself, so I achieved a sort of peace with my writing.

Books by the Bed

BILL MCCOY: Simon Gray's *The Smoking Diaries*. It's really smart, well-written, funny, heartbreaking at times. *This Is Craig Brown*, by a satirist who writes for *Private Eye* and several other English magazines—because he cranks this out, he's gotten good at what he does. And something by the American John Krich. And a terrific Brit writer named Jeffrey Bernard, sort of a very rough Brit equivalent of Bukowski, but Bernard is more elegant and funny.

ERIC OLSEN: Ros was incredible. She's a painter, a playwright, a novelist, a singer. I think she'd been part of that whole Andy Warhol "Factory" scene. She also did a stint as a power lifter. She wrote the novelization of Stallone's *Rocky* under the pen name Julia Sorel. She wrote scripts for Lorne Michaels, and she taught at Iowa for a year. Unfortunately, I didn't take her class, but a lot of my friends did, and they thought she was terrific. Also, she was a pro wrestler, Rosa Carlo, the Mexican Spitfire.

ROSALYN DREXLER: Speaking of wrestling, let's not. I hated it. The fake blood, the body slams, the cries of pain. I got a novel out of it, though, *To Smithereens*, about to be reissued. A reviewer for the *New York Review of Books* loved it.

DOUG UNGER: I learned most from my peers from watching Allan Gurganus perfect his stories and from watching Boyle dream up his original and electric language. I learned from watching John Givens, who was the really hot writer there then, and from Bob Pope. I learned quite a bit from Jane Smiley because she was writing these long, out-of-control pieces in first draft, and then she would take something out of these longer drafts and they'd really start to come together into such truly marvelous writing. She was learning how to discipline her own writing, and I remember that vividly.

> I learned most from my peers, from watching Allan Gurganus perfect his stories and from watching Boyle dream up his original and electric language.

And I also learned from a couple of the teachers there, a great deal from Irving—how to let yourself go in the early stages, and how not to critique yourself while writing big blocks of first draft, how to write a lot, then work hard on what to cut out and what to leave in. He was working on *Garp* at the time.

The Iowa experience was exhilarating for me. And then I met Amy Burk Wright, a talented actress, and we fell in love. I moved in with her, and our house on Caroline Court was an artistic hub the likes of which I had never been in before. James Dickey would phone in the middle of the night, and Ray Carver would turn up, and all sorts of poets, writers, and playwrights would hang out there. This was the sort of place where spontaneously you'd read the pages you'd written that day and other writers would read to you, and they would respond, so you'd get immediate feedback and understand what worked and what didn't. Our house became a community scene, party central. We put on a party for Ted Solotaroff and one for John Irving, and we put on the John Hawkes party at my old roommate Bruce Pitt's place. Our parties were open to everybody—big bashes to which everyone was cordially invited.

I wasn't a big drinker then, more pot, and I'd keep things low-key at the parties, to keep my head clear enough, and then at eleven or so, off I'd go to write until three or four in the morning and then I'd sleep until the afternoon, then go to workshop. About drugs, drinking, and writing back then—I was rarely stoned when I wrote, soon found out that writing under the influence is often bad writing, and I could never write while drinking. In the mid-'80s, I gave up any use of illegal substances, including pot; and I haven't taken a drink of alcohol since early in 1997.

I'd make some extra money washing dishes at the Mill, or going in later and cleaning up; so I had all these little extra jobs, and I was also part of the marijuana scene, and that provided a lot of social connections, including with Anthony Burgess when he visited. I got close to him immediately, when a certain professor I won't mention by name very quietly passed the word that Anthony Burgess was interested in getting some really good hashish. Burgess was an insomniac, and he liked to smoke hash at night and write music, but only hash, not marijuana. Amy and I knew a guy who had some really primo hash, who lived quite some ways away, halfway to Chicago. We drove up there and I fronted almost a whole month's pay. What I did then, I'd take this little piece of hash and—I was working on yellow second sheets at the time, on an early version of what would later become *Leaving the Land*—and I would take a discarded page from the manuscript and wrap the hash in it and tie it up with a green string like a little birthday gift and pass it to Burgess in his office.

I made sure there was no charge to him because I admired his writing so much, and I was able to do enough retail that I could take care of his needs and break even. Burgess and I talked, especially about process—he had just finished *Enderby's End* and was working on *Beard's Roman Women*, as I recall. I was amazed at how he said he would write fifty, then a hundred pages for a book before he knew where it was going; and when he knew, he would just toss out everything he'd written and start over again.

He started inviting Amy and me to his house, and we got to know his wife, Liliana, too, who was a brilliant woman. So we got to go to parties with the president and the Iowa Foundation people, and they could never quite figure out why we were there—mere graduate students, after all, the only students ever invited to those high-profile events.

My rancher father blew into town from South Dakota one week, and Burgess joined us for lunch. They matched drink after drink at the table and became friends right away. Soon, they ditched the rest of us. My dad and Burgess went on a carousing, drunken tear around Iowa City that lasted two days; my father told stories and laughed about that until the day he died.

GLENN SCHAEFFER: For me, the real Workshop was a certain booth by the kitchen at the Mill, where I could watch the band, and my classmates would come by and we'd drink beer and talk about writing. Bob Pope, a star TWF two years ahead of me, was waiting tables there, while he published stories in top literary journals. Formally out of the Workshop, he'd still pick up worksheets and read them, and one time Bob walks up holding one of my stories and says, "This is kind of interesting." I lived for that.

Another time, I put up a story that wasn't inspiring too many wonderful responses, and Joe Haldeman jumps in, "Hey, this is a well-written page," and proceeded to read a patch aloud. These are the things that stick with you. Almost everything I'd written was given more than an honest reading. I made lasting friendships at Iowa, as many as anywhere else, maybe more. I was interested in what Jane and Bob and Allan and Tom thought. I didn't bank on what the faculty thought.

> For me, the real Workshop was a certain booth by the kitchen at the Mill, where I could watch the band, and my classmates would come by and we'd drink beer and talk about writing.

So you know, there were occasional nights at the Mill when we'd hoist a facetious toast to ourselves—"Another week gone by at the World-Famous Workshop where, entirely due to us, nothing worthy was written."

Of course in my usual acquisitive way, I *was* trying to calculate how to get a TWF, and so I took Leggett's workshop. I figured he's the director, so he makes the decisions; let him get to know me. Plus I figured Vance wouldn't feel strongly enough about me; though Vance seemed to regard my writing, and I made my mark during discussions, I didn't hunt or fish or play guitar.

ERIC OLSEN: We were all trying to figure out how to score some good aid and, above all, a TWF, the big prize, affirmation that you were on your way.

I'm not sure any of us had much of a clue as to how the various awards were doled out. Was there an official process of review and vetting? An objective process that invariably awarded the prizes according to merit, and not according to who kissed whose ass? Well, deep down I'm not sure any of us really hoped for a system that was objective, since, deep down, didn't each of us harbor deep-seated insecurities? Better if we could just suck up to the right people. . . . But who were the right people? Who knew?

DOUG UNGER: I felt there was an elitism that I was being excluded from, for unjust reasons. Still, I told myself I didn't care because I didn't think success depended on that kind of thing. The whole idea of networking one's way to success I found repulsive, disingenuous, false, and wrong. In truth, networking did count then, and does now, at least somewhat, no matter how much we wish it were different. And at Iowa, I saw that it really did help young writers to get linked up with agents and editors who came through on a regular basis.

Finally, I did make a connection with Ted Solotaroff, who later became my editor at Harper & Row and a lifelong friend, but I came to his attention only because of a worksheet he picked up and did a class on. Ted would have published it, too—told me he intended to publish it in the next issue of the *American Review*—but then the *Review* went belly up. That would have been the ideal thing for me, to have a piece in the *American Review*, a magazine I read almost every page of and had admired for years. That would have been my personal definition of an outstanding success, that my fiction had finally reached a quality truly worth something out in the world.

DENNIS MATHIS: Updike was coming to read and do a guest workshop, and Jayne Anne Phillips, as usual, was the pick "up for workshop." Though I liked Jayne Anne and loved her gutsy, scrambled writing, this time I was furious at the unrelenting favoritism toward her as the current Workshop star—the whole Workshop star system in general that left crumbs for the rest of us—and I wrote Frank Conroy a long, eloquent letter of complaint and slipped it under his door. Conroy was teaching there that semester, a last-minute replacement gig, I think; this was years before he became director.

Conroy apparently took my letter to heart and sent my story, late, to Updike. I skipped Updike's workshop out of humiliation because of the letter I'd written (I'm not sure what I intended Conroy should do about my grievance, but contacting Updike wasn't it, which taught me a lesson about complaining), but all afternoon people kept coming up to me and saying, "Updike is looking for you."

After his reading that night, I walked up to Jack Leggett's front porch for the after-reading party and someone said, "There you are. Updike is looking for you." So someone took me to him, and Updike led me through the house looking for a place where we could talk. We ended up in Leggett's bedroom, squashed up between the bedroom door and the closet door, toe-to-toe. Updike went through the notes he'd scribbled on the envelope flap, giving me a personal critique for half an hour. Mostly he corrected my spelling. But at the end, he said it reminded him of his own early stories. I still have the envelope flap.

JENNIE FIELDS: The thing that seemed ridiculously unfair was that there were parties after readings, but they weren't open to everyone. Either you got invited or you didn't. It was offensive; here you were paying to go there, only thirty writers, and they didn't invite everyone? It smacked of cliquishness that was truly offensive and wrong in every way. Before I left, things changed. But certainly, early on, it wasn't a very nice world.

ANTHONY BUKOSKI: I saw some shameless ass kissing going on. I suppose if you are built that way, then you need to do that. I couldn't. Maybe I should have learned to cozy up to people who could possibly help me. I guess I wanted to do it the old-fashioned way. I should say that I might have gotten on better as a writer had I kissed some ass.

DON WALLACE: All during our first year, there was a growing resentment, mostly among first-year students, as we became aware of the machinations behind awarding financial aid. It sounds so bureaucratic, "financial aid." But that's how the world beats you down when you're on the outside looking in.

At Iowa, what they called "financial aid" was really entree, access, permission to write, a green light to the publishing world. If you didn't get aid at Iowa, you'd missed the cut. And they let you know it. Agents came to visit, and nonaid students never heard about it. Big-name authors came to read and do workshops and met in the director's cozy brick home with the aid recipients, not the unwashed wash-outs.

> All during our first year, there was a growing resentment, mostly among first year students, as we became aware of the machinations behind awarding financial aid.

If the Workshop powers didn't like you at all, sometimes they told you not to come back for the second year. Can you imagine a cash-machine MFA program doing that today? Can you imagine the ego-crushing blow that would be to a young Carson McCullers, a young Emily Dickinson, a thirty-nine-year-old Marcel Proust, still living with his mother and writing a long difficult novel in half a dozen volumes?

I was unaware of the aid competition, a white-water rapid waiting for us downstream, when we started at Iowa. Eventually rumor cued us in, that and hearing bitter drunken tales at parties of the shunned.

Well, suck it up, right? Nobody said it would be easy. Maybe you just aren't talented, ever think of that?

GLENN SCHAEFFER: Second semester, first year, in Leggett's class, I wrote a story about a whacked bodybuilder and put it up for workshop, and as soon as Jack walks in, his first statement is, "I guess there's a fashion in contemporary literature for the incomprehensible and preposterous and we have a booming example of that today—anybody want to visit the scene of this crime?" Or that's how I remember it. And one of my classmates, George Lewis, a comedian, erupts in mock panic, "Light the torches! Get the monster!"

You know who spoke up for me in that class? Jane Smiley. She was sitting in the back of the room. I knew she'd been posted on a Fulbright to Iceland or Greenland or an outland reportedly colder than Iowa. She praised the story's "invention." Kim Rogel wanted to publish it front-page in the *Daily Iowan*, where he was editor-in-chief. I sent it to Ron Sukenick at *Fiction International*, and he accepted the story straightaway. Too bad; it never got published because his journal went under.

Well, I walked out of the class knowing that I wouldn't get a TWF. I thought I was in the running until then. I had *intended* to get a TWF. That's my *brand*, ferkrissakes! Just like when I'd go to my bedroom when I was an undergraduate at Irvine and I'd write something and I'd get a cash prize! But I walked out of that class and thought about quitting, until I decided it didn't matter. I started thinking ahead, about year three and forever after when I wouldn't be at Iowa anymore. It would be up to me to channel my abilities into sharper expression in due time. I decided to leave with an honorable discharge. I could never have written a story that Jack liked (although I was granted an instructorship in Rhetoric). And I didn't have any beef with who received which awards.

DON WALLACE: Let me dip that madeleine. One first-year writer, who shall remain nameless, was an ardent reader of Proust and had undergone a weird form of humiliation for this fault. She had dared disagree in class with Jack Leggett on his interpretation of a story of hers and cited Proust as a source of inspiration and as justification for a certain narrative tone. After that she was labeled "the Proustian"—a definite insult in the Age of Carver.

The following semester, a Proustian reference, a character's name, came up in another student's work, and when the Proustian pronounced the name, her French pronunciation was ridiculed by the teacher, Henry Bromell, and his favorite student, who had lived in Europe. When the Proustian protested, they mocked her. Small, petty stuff.

The Proustian didn't take it lying down, making it clear that she was fluent in French, had read Proust in the original, living and studying for over a year in Tours, which is the source of the pure Touraine accent of literary French. Predictably, this only goaded Bromell and his followers to step up their prep-school mockery.

To many of us who weren't favorites, it was indicative of how the put-downs, the junior-high clique behavior, had become overbearing. But we never would have expected her to be the spark of the Great Writer Riot of 1976.

The next visiting writer happened to be John Hawkes, a popular choice because of his provocative hipster stance and French-influenced modernist prose. The awards would be announced in a week, but word had already leaked out about who were the anointed, and thus the stakes were raised for his visit, and we all worked mightily to produce stories for his workshop, to be chosen by the man himself. We also hoped that a story by one of us, the nonelect, would be selected and praised over one of the anointed.

The Proustian thought she had an ace in the hole: she knew Hawkes and had known him for years. He was the protégé of one of her mentors in college. She'd spent time with him in France. She'd even declined his advances on a couple of occasions, yet it hadn't affected their teacher-student relationship. And so she considered that maybe, this time, she had an inside track on getting her story discussed by someone not under the diktat of the Workshop nomenklatura.

She was disappointed, then, not to have her story picked. But when the workshop gathered, she attended. When Hawkes arrived, he paused on his way to the podium and did a double take. Calling out the Proustian by name, he insisted on a big hug and a chat despite the sixty or so waiting writers. "How have you been?" asked Hawkes.

"Fine," said the Proustian.

"But why didn't you submit a story?" he said, bewildered.

"I did."

"I never saw it. And I saw them all, read every single one."

The entire room heard it. And as everyone in the room had submitted a story, with only three chosen to be discussed, there were fifty-seven students thinking the same thought at the same time: the staff had culled the entries, leaving only the favorites.

The very nice office manager, who actually ran the place and had to walk a wobbly tightrope, swooped in and moved Hawkes along. Later, after Hawkes had dealt with the first story, she crept up to the Proustian and handed her a slip of paper: the address and time of a party for the elect.

In the hallways after the Hawkes workshop, the Proustian reached a decision. She gave the address to any and every student who wanted it. The face of the Workshop director when he opened the door of his house and found twenty-five uninvited students was a wonder to behold, but he was gracious and welcomed everyone. It was a rockin' good time.

The next week came the announcement of the aid winners. It was the list of favorites we'd already heard of in rumor. Appended to the list was a personal letter from the director, Jack Leggett, justifying the process and ending with a fatal line:

"Even Marcel Proust, were he a student at the Workshop, would have been denied aid, on the grounds that his work did not show sufficient promise."

Chapter 6

THE CRAFT THING

Later, after we were out of the Workshop and Schaeffer went into business and was getting rich, and Olsen was trying to make a living as a freelance magazine writer and most definitely not getting rich, while he tried to finish one false start of a novel after another, after he'd had some experience working with agents and editors and trying to make absurd deadlines and trying to get paid by deadbeat magazines for work he'd turned in, and suffering all the other indignities and aggravations associated with being a writer, Olsen began to think how nice it would have been if the Workshop had clued him in a little about the "real world," had offered some advice in business practices, maybe, which might have saved him some grief while he was learning the hard way.

Many years after Iowa, he had the opportunity to sit in on some graduate-level art-theory classes for painters and sculptors taught by Dave Hickey, the art and culture critic—a genuine MacArthur Foundation "genius"—and got an inkling of just what it was he wished the Workshop had offered. In his classes, Dave would usually spend the first thirty minutes or more talking about "professional practices," how the culture and business of art collectors and galleries and dealers really worked, and how a young artist could function and maybe thrive in that culture. Dave always gave very precise and practical tips, like always saying "thank you," because young artists, like young writers, depended on the kindness of strangers. Or always wearing the same outfit to gallery openings so that collectors would have an easier time remembering you at the next one.

And then in his Texas drawl, he'd also remind his students why it was they make art: "It's to get laid!" And then he'd laugh and then light another cigarette and have a coughing fit. . . .

And then in his Texas drawl, he'd also remind his students why it was they make art: "It's to get laid!" And then he'd laugh and then light another cigarette and have a coughing fit and take a sip of his quad skim latte and begin a discussion about Foucault's take on Velazquez, or whatever was the topic for that evening.

This was the sort of stuff Olsen wished he'd gotten at Iowa—not the Foucault, certainly, but the little tips, the practical advice, emphasized perhaps with a snide comment or two, and even a coughing fit: This is the world you're getting yourself into, kid. You sure you don't want to get a real job, make your folks happy and save yourself some grief? The sorts of wisecracks that would make us want to be part of that world more than ever.

Years later, when Olsen was peripherally involved with a graduate writing program, he foolishly suggested some classes in "professional practices," such as how to find an agent, how to work with an editor—why editors seem to think they have to do what they do to a perfectly good bit of prose, and why these days they don't do much of anything—how to read a contract, the economics of publishing, and why your publisher, assuming you get one, won't spend a dime to publicize your book even though that makes no economic sense at all. Nuts-and-bolts stuff.

Olsen even suggested a class or two in editing. Editing was at the time—and this is ancient history, since these days editing seems increasingly obsolete—a decent way for a young writer to make a buck or two before those royalties start rolling in. Plus, a little practice in editing can be helpful to one's prose, though you have to be able to switch from edit mode to writing mode or too much editing will screw up your writing, which Olsen learned the hard way after he became an editor.

But Olsen's suggestions were not greeted with a great deal of enthusiasm, to put it mildly. The prevailing view was that a workshop should be a refuge from the "real world." Young writers, he was informed in no uncertain terms, should be "nurtured" and "protected" from the real world so they can concentrate on their art. It wasn't just this particular program where such a notion held sway; like so many other writing programs in the country, it had been founded by Iowa Workshop grads, and so, for better or worse, it was modeled on the Workshop and held to its core values, such as the underlying assumption that art is fundamentally a sacred or mystical endeavor that you don't want to mess up with too many practical distractions, no matter that however sacred and mystical art may be, a guy still has to pay the rent.

Ironically, the Iowa Workshop, when we were there, imposed on its students quite bracing doses of real life. What was the process by which awards were doled out for the second year, if not a bitter dose of real life? Wasn't that process for dishing out perks every bit as opaque, capricious, and arbitrary—or so it seemed to us at the time—as the way we imagined manuscripts were chosen for publication? And therefore wasn't the Workshop's system of giving awards excellent preparation for what awaited us "out there in the real world"? And wasn't our reaction to the capriciousness of that awards process and to those rejections essential to our growth as writers? Didn't our reactions tell us something important about ourselves?

Many of us had been stars as undergrads, and maybe we'd even had work published in campus magazines, one triumph after another. And getting into the Workshop in the first place was still more affirmation. But only a few of the truly anointed received any sort of aid coming into the first year. That was a bit of downer. But we got over it. And toward the end of that first year, everyone had the opportunity to apply for aid for the second, and for plenty of us, those who didn't get the juiciest plums, a TWF or at least a TA, the process was perhaps the first real taste of genuine ego-shriveling rejection: good preparation, that is, for life as a writer.

There were three levels of financial aid—plus no aid at all—all involving some labor for the university. And the award you received was, we were all sure (and feared), indicative of the faculty's consensus opinion as to who was best and who had the best shot at writing success later. At the bottom rung of the ladder were the research assistants. The RAs did things like run off the worksheets or run the tape recorder during readings. The TAs (teaching assistants) taught freshman-level rhetoric if they were lucky, or what was sometimes called "bonehead English" if they weren't. Good experience if you were aiming at a teaching gig after Iowa, and who wasn't? At least until the royalties started rolling in.

> . . . The process was perhaps the first real taste of genuine ego-shriveling rejection: good preparation, that is, for life as a writer.

And at the top of the ladder, the Teaching/Writing Fellows, the TWFs, taught one undergraduate creative writing class of their own each semester. Just the name of the award—*fellowship,* not assistantship—implied approbation and affirmation. The fact that the fellowships provided a few hundred more dollars than the RAs and TAs didn't hurt.

The TWFs in the fiction program also served as the first-pass readers of application manuscripts for the next crop of Workshop students; great experience for that editing job at a big New York City publishing house while you put the finishing touches on your own short story collection or first novel. Each application manuscript was read by at least three of the four TWFs, who rated it either "Outstanding," "Good," "Acceptable but Undistinguished," or "Not Worth Accepting." The readers also were free to write comments like "yes, yes, yes" or "wasn't extremely impressed" or "This writer has a depth of feeling, a sense of his own importance" and so on. After the TWFs gave a manuscript a reading, it went on to the next level for further consideration by Workshop faculty in a process beyond the ken of the first-pass readers.

That system of doling out financial aid and perks no longer exists at the Workshop. In the mid-'90s, the Workshop began providing financial aid to all Workshop students, both to incoming first year students and to current students for their second year.

Certainly an improvement. But the aid amounts are only "nearly" equal, and so young writers, being writers, will have something to resent "Having been a student in the tail end of 'the old days,'" says Samantha Chang (MFA, 1993), the current Workshop director, "I will say that student jobs are not nearly as big a source of discussion as they used to be."

At any rate, by the time our second year began, those of us who didn't get the juiciest plums had had the summer break to sulk and get over it, and then to muster some of that inner strength writers need above all else to get on with our writing, and perhaps even to find it within ourselves to pity—but not too much—the poor bastards who *did* get the juiciest plums because now they'd have the burden of being the chosen, without the freedom to say *screw you* to those with the authority to make arbitrary decisions over another person's career. With the sweet Iowa summer came the leisure to pick oneself up off the mat, having learned one of the writer's most valuable lessons, how to handle rejection.

~

MARVIN BELL: *Handle it*! Don't handle it! *Subsume* it. Write a lot, send out a lot, realize that editorial decisions are not personal, understand that editors are in the business of rejecting submissions and only rarely accepting something, and understand, too, that acceptance doesn't mean what you think it means. If you write long enough, you will come to know what your work is worth and what it is not worth. Of course, by then the knowing won't make any difference.

Rejection is as much a part of a writer's life as snow and cold is to an Eskimo. I think Ted Solotaroff said that first.

DOUG UNGER: Rejection is as much a part of a writer's life as snow and cold is to an Eskimo. I think Ted Solotaroff said that first. We have to get used to rejection and learn how to survive in a world that buries us in all kinds of rejection. Work on the story or novel or essay, and keep working on it. When it's good enough, an editor will accept it and publish it—count on that to happen.

T. C. BOYLE: I kept things circulating. I was not the sort of writer who was discouraged by rejections; I had faith... I made a point that when a story was rejected and came back, that day I'd send it out to another magazine. Keep them circulating. I guess that's one basic principle to being a writer: keep it circulating, don't get discouraged.

GARY IORIO: I do well with rejection. I'm not shaped by it. I'm my own harshest critic, which is why so many of my projects probably don't get finished. In terms of rejection I believe now, as I did in Iowa, that the keepers of the gates (editors, faculty members, et al.) were just regular meatballs like me. Getting into Iowa gave me a certain degree of confidence; the subsequent rejections were minor setbacks.

JOE HALDEMAN: I don't handle rejection well. It generates depressing clouds of self-doubt. Fortunately, I don't get rejected too often.

A key acceptance, a real turning point, was the sale of *Mindbridge* for a hundred thousand dollars. I was still at the Workshop, and Leonard Michaels had just told me it was worthless and I should stop wasting my time on that kind of crap. A valuable lesson.

DOUG UNGER: I read somewhere once that the average number of rejections for a short story sent to literary magazines is thirty-four for every letter of acceptance; and for novels—and I'm only talking about stories and novels that eventually found their way into print—the average is sixteen rejections for every acceptance. These numbers could be way off by now, since I think I read those statistics some time ago. Maybe it's worse now, or maybe it's better. I don't know.

But I like those numbers because they represent what anecdotally I believe to be the case based on twenty-five years of teaching younger or developing writers in creative writing programs. What they mean is this: keep going, keep up the vocation, keep writing, and keep trying with the work you believe is your best. Nobody can ask anything more from you.

ANTHONY BUKOSKI: Whenever I'm rejected, I look for a sign from the rejecter that he or she has found a small thing to credit in a story. The sign might come as a handwritten note saying, "Try us again." Any sign of encouragement helps.

DOUG BORSOM: I sorted my rejections into three categories. I suspect most writers do the same. In descending order of frequency: Form letters; form letters with an added handwritten note, usually along the lines of "Not quite for us," or "Let us see more," and rarely but sometimes a personal letter detailing what the editor liked and didn't.

If all I'd ever received was from smackdowns, I might have given up writing. I have huge respect for writers who go through a long cold stretch and keep at it.

> As I've gotten older, my need for affirmation has lessened. I don't need encouragement to keep me working on my novel. I believe that when it is finished, it will find an audience. Now how delusional is that?

Maybe being slightly delusional is helpful—thinking that chalk dust mixed with water is as nutritious as milk, to borrow an image from Chesterton. So you get a lift out of a form rejection from the *New Yorker* with a hastily scrawled "Let us see more," likely written by a college intern. Or you remind yourself that you did get into the Workshop, after all, so you must have some talent. These things aren't much, but if someone is going to keep writing, they may have to be able to find encouragement that is small and well disguised.

As I've gotten older, my need for affirmation has lessened. I don't need encouragement to keep me working on my novel. I believe that when it is finished, it will find an audience. Now how delusional is that?

CATHERINE GAMMON: I got plenty of rejections from the magazines, but it was okay because I also had some sense of reinforcement or confidence or hope. There are different kinds of rejections, when they don't just give you the standard form, but they say something, sometimes something that's actually helpful and wise or supportive in a way you can tell they really mean it. And sometimes what they say leaves you wondering, why did you say anything if you were going to say that?

Enough stories were accepted that I felt some confidence in what I was doing, that there was an audience. Sometimes, though, it would start to become clear, with a particular story, that nobody was ever going to see whatever merit I thought it might have, and I'd stop seeing merit in it too and stop sending it out. But most pieces would find a place, and with experience, by knowing the magazines, by previous communication with the magazines, by getting a sense of what they liked, I became more skillful in choosing what was the right place for a particular story or novel excerpt, and I started getting fewer rejections.

With the novels, it's a different story. After *Isabel* came out in 1991, *Sorrow* must have been read and rejected by twenty or thirty publishers. With the next novel, I started looking for a new agent, as well as sending it to the few editors I had access to. I got lovely, thoughtful readings and kind rejections. By then it was the mid- and late-'90s, and whether it was true or just convenient, the need for a recognizable niche in the marketplace was a kind of universal theme in those rejections. By 2000 I had decided to stop submitting anything to the market at all.

DOUG UNGER: Still, I must say that I've been terribly lucky. My stories and books have been rejected pretty much according to the statistics I mentioned. But almost every story or book or essay I've written—after taking each piece back, working on it again, grinding it down in the crucible, heating it up and letting it take shape once more—after all that rewriting and revision and rewriting again and again, almost every single story or book I've worked on has eventually seen publication.

And I've got a lot still in process. Some stories are still around that I started ten or even fifteen years ago, and I still pull them out and work on them at times. I've got a long novel about post-traumatic stress disorder, which I believe is the disease of the twenty-first century (like, for all of humanity, stressed to the max as we all are) that I keep returning to, eight years still in the writing.

ANYTHONY BUKOSKI: Whether or not I receive encouragement, I allow myself a few hours, even an evening, to recover from the rejection. A little time passes, I feel better, and I rethink the rejected story. Sometimes I make changes. Other times, without making changes, I send the story to another journal.

Really, there's no mystery: one either finds strength to persist as a writer or one quits. No one cares either way whether you write or don't, so my belief is a person has to make people care. How? By keeping at the writing, by not quitting. My approach isn't logical. This said, I proceed on the assumption that in the end I will succeed at whatever I attempt. There again is the ability always to hope things must get better.

MARVIN BELL: The magazine that meant the most to me was *Poetry*, edited by Henry Rago. In those days, if *Poetry* published you, you could think yourself a poet. But I had been publishing my earliest efforts in numerous "littles." Still, *Poetry* was bigger.

The *New Yorker* was a big deal, but not for aesthetic reasons. If you published in the *New Yorker*, whose poetry editor was Howard Moss, your high school classmates would see it in the dentist's office. And you'd get a significant amount of money for the poem, which made it seem special. But *Poetry* was the place.

On the other hand, one's early successes can work against one's writing. Poets, especially, have a tendency to play for praise and to invest in an image of themselves. Early success can be defining, which is a limitation. Indeed, perhaps writer's block comes from success, real or imagined. As soon as one feels pressure to repeat a success, well, that effectively distorts the future.

DOUG UNGER: When a story or novel is accepted, man, let that be the best feeling—let it be a thrill, a celebration, a time to say, like Pushkin is reputed to have said about himself, you son of a bitch, you did it, you really did it, you pulled it off again! Have a party. Invite your friends. At least call your friends. Celebrate with them. Your real friends will be joyous with you. Let that joy carry you along for as long as it will, and be happy with it—until you get your next rejection letter that grounds you again in this world.

SHERRY KRAMER: One of the scary things about being a playwright is that your greatest rejections, your bad review in the *Times*, or frankly, any bad review, happen at the most public part of your life as a playwright. The bad review hits the day or two after your play opens. That means your play is going to run for a month, and all your friends and family are coming to see it, and if you're in town, you have to go and see those kind people who are coming to your play, and you have to be supportive of the cast, who have to go out there and carry on, no matter how hideous those reviews were, in front of audiences who have all read those horrible reviews, too . . .

The other scary thing is that if a play isn't well reviewed, it dies. Plays only exist, truly, when they're being produced. It takes the collaboration of twenty to a hundred artists and their time and talent to create a play. So the reviews have enormous and enduring impact of a different nature from fiction. My work can be rediscovered, yes, just like a novel, but that rediscovery takes time and money to happen.

> One of the scary things about being a playwright is that your greatest rejections, your bad review in the *Times*, or frankly, any bad review, happen at the most public part of your life as a playwright.

So, how to deal with that? If you work with people you believe in and you make your choices as an artist, the pain of the bad review is bad, but survivable. You've made a work of art together. That's an amazing thing. So my advice on rejection and bad reviews is to work with the right people, to find your collaborators early and stick with them. Make art with people you respect. Then in the middle of the night when the soul eaters arrive to crush you, you'll have a place to go.

SANDRA CISNEROS: When I get a rejection, or applause, I try to remember it's not about me, but acknowledgment for something outside of me, something that traveled through me. It's like fishing: the more you do it, the better you get at it. When you get that applause, it's for the fish; you caught it, but you didn't create the fish. When rejection or success comes, it's not about you. If you're lucky enough to have written a book that nourishes a people at this time in history, you have to stay grounded and not confuse that success with yourself. The way to learn this is by spiritual practice, by learning something that grounds you.

I like the teachings of Pema Chodron and Thich Nhat Hanh. A lot of writers like Hanh because he's a writer, even if they're not Buddhist; he makes a lot of sense. I'd recommend a simple book like *Being Peace*. You don't have to be Buddhist to get something out of it.

JOY HARJO: Keep the faith. There is a larger shape of reason and meaning, much larger than our small human minds. We can hook into this larger shape—we hunger for that connection. That's why we create. Stay in that direction.

The *American Poetry Review* rejected the most famous poems from my book *She Had Some Horses*. Of course, I began to doubt myself. Then I took the manuscript to Norton, to Audre Lorde's editor, John Benedict. I have a carefully written, encouraging rejection letter from him. Thunder's Mouth Press brought the book out and kept it in print until the press folded a few years ago. Norton published the reprint last year! I went to Norton three times before they agreed to publish me. My first book with them was *The Woman Who Fell from the Sky*.

SANDRA CISNEROS: It's important to differentiate the work from yourself. When you get caught up in success as a writer, it can hurt you even more than rejection sometimes. I think the work we do is spiritually divine when we work without ego, with humility, but it takes a lot of work to get to that place. It's important to keep your feet on the ground and remain clear about the work you're doing, to separate the work from the self.

I had the good experience while at Iowa of just concentrating on my writing, and knowing that when writing I sent out got rejected, it wasn't the writing, but that I just hadn't found its right home. So I didn't expend much energy with publishing when I was there until I was practically leaving. Then Alan Kornblum of Toothpaste Press heard me read at a local bookstore and asked me to send him some poems, and so I did and he rejected me. But I didn't take it personally. I figured, well, that's Iowa.

ANTHONY BUKOSKI: I once had a story rejected twenty-seven times. Each time it came back, I made modest changes. Finally, on the twenty-eighth try, the *Laurel Review* took the story and sent me five dollars as payment, and asked whether I would consider sending the money back to buy a subscription.

Another time, I worked for three full years with the University of Illinois Press to try to get a collection of my stories published. This was when they had that wonderful Illinois Short Fiction series. Ann Weir, the senior editor for fiction, kept encouraging me. Their outside evaluators would love some of the stories in my collection but wanted others removed. Then six or eight months later when I did as they recommended, the press had new readers who disliked the stories the first readers liked. As I say, this went on for three years. Then the series cut back from four to two fiction titles a year, and Ann Weir wrote, "Lest you think you are always a bridesmaid and never a bride" that I should keep trying. Despite the cutback, she encouraged me, saying she thought there was a good chance eventually that I'd "find a place on their list."

It was right before Christmas one year, 1991 I believe, that she wrote with the bad news that she and the press could no longer encourage me. I was grateful to her for helping me, and I have told her this over the years, so I am not complaining. It was just one of those things.

CATHERINE GAMMON: One thing I learned at Iowa was that it would be a mistake to quit too soon. Not that this was taught, exactly, but maybe it was clear in the culture. You couldn't have a short-term vision, and I was determined that I would not just write for ten years and then give up. There are gifted people who were writers with me at Iowa and later in Provincetown who in one way or another have stopped, and there are others who have continued, and I just think for some of us it takes a really long time. I had been committed to writing long before I came to Iowa, and I didn't have to let whatever Iowa thought of as "success" determine my sense of continuing. So that was a very helpful state of mind. Even with my other not-so-healthy attitudes, that was a particularly helpful determination, I think.

> One thing I learned at Iowa was that it would be a mistake to quit too soon. Not that this was taught, exactly, but maybe it was clear in the culture. You couldn't have a short-term vision . . .

GERI LIPSCHULTZ: You do get over it. It's interesting for me now that I'm back in school again, seeing how different people respond to my work, and seeing how others respond to criticism, seeing young writers pick and choose what to listen to. I'm thinking particularly of one writer here. I admire the way she handles rejections—she rejects rejection! That's healthy, I think. This is not to say that she rejects all of it, but she weighs it. She doesn't seem to take it to heart. As for me, I find that though I still have the desire to publish, there is something different in the way my expectation functions. Maybe I don't expect as much. It's such a process, or at least it has been for me. I am grateful to be writing now. There's something more, perhaps you would call it "Zenlike" about my process now. I think I'm perhaps more forgiving. I think I can accept the possibility that the writing can have meaning for me even if it doesn't have meaning for others. All I can say, at the moment, is that things are changing for me about this feeling of measurement by others. As a writer, I think you have to let it go and move on to something new.

It's so tricky, but I think how you handle rejection is somehow connected to how seriously deep the urge in you is to write—not necessarily your talent, God help us all, but that urge. And then, of course, is this thing about what the public wants, and if you are going against the grain of the public. If so, then you're up shit creek, so to speak. On the other hand, it's your right to write. It's a freedom. If you keep the urge to write separate from the urge to publish—without kidding yourself, of course—you'll be okay.

MARVIN BELL: One writes up to one's limits: verbal, psychological, emotional, and intellectual. The response of others is a bonus I cherish, but it is a bonus.

If, for me, the form, as discovered, has been used up, if there is no unintentional obscurity, no faking it, no stupidity, neither condescension nor dumbing down, if there is an element of surprise or of the new, if it has a true voice and holds hands with music and dance, then I can't do better by trying to outguess a reader's expectations, demands, reflexes, and prejudices. Let the chips fall where they may. I have already hit the jackpot.

SANDRA CISNEROS: People ask me all the time, how do you handle rejection? I ask if they are writing already. If they never get published and never get famous, and if it means they might not have children, and if it means it might harm their relationships, would they still want to be a writer? I'm interested in the why; why do they want to be writers. I usually ask, "What do you want?" If you don't have expectations of fame or money or relationships or happy unions, if you don't have those expectations and you're doing it already, then you're a writer. You have to have more than talent. You have to have *ganas*. You have to have this desire. Because everyone and his mother are keeping you from writing, and if you don't have the passion, the drive, the *ganas*, you're not going to do it. If you don't have *ganas*, forget it.

JENNIE FIELDS: Rejection? Who wants to dwell on that? Someone once said, the thing that keeps you going when you're writing a novel is your love for your theme, knowing that what you're saying is important, that you have a job to do: state it eloquently, touch someone, make a difference. And if the editor doesn't get it, then you have to believe, in your wretched little heart, that he or she is an idiot for not seeing its importance.

> And if the editor doesn't get it, then you have to believe, in your wretched little heart, that he or she is an idiot for not seeing its importance.

～

There was a qualitative difference between the first and second year, not least because, award decisions having been made, most of us having been denied the big prize, having been *rejected*, we no longer had to please anyone. We weren't competing for anything any longer. Which left us free at last to concentrate on our own work and, having coped with rejection, now and then to cast a sideways glance at a faculty member or two and mutter sotto voce a little *what the hell do they know?*

And to take away from the Workshop what we found helpful and ignore the rest, saving up those useful lessons for future reference. We began to think more critically not only about our own work, but about the way writing was being "taught" to us, or not taught, and what awaited us "out there" in the "real world," until we'd pull back from too much of that sort of thing because it was just too damned depressing to think about. We had free rein, that is, to bitch and moan, and now and then to be thankful, if only a little, because, like Unger says, writers are never satisfied.

～

DON WALLACE: For me, the second year was vastly different for two reasons: one, I'd married Mindy, my fellow Workshop student; and two, I'd received a teaching assistantship and was teaching freshman English, which they called rhetoric. The teaching gig was good inasmuch as it paid the rent and lowered my tuition to instate. But it was a real shock for me at age twenty-four to go into a classroom at eight-twenty in the morning and have to teach basic English to a mixed bag of sorority girls, engineering majors, scholarship athletes, Iowa farm boys, black inner-city kids from

Chicago allowed in via affirmative action, and even one twenty-seven-year-old Chicano slaughterhouse worker, very radicalized, who hated the entire power structure, which was to say, me. He turned out to be my best student, and after I gave a riff to the class about *One Hundred Years of Solitude*, he went and got it and read it and became so emotional talking about it I felt ashamed for my own insufficient reverence.

Before Mindy and I left to get married, in the spring of our first year, we'd been warned by a couple of Workshop faculty that getting married was akin to career suicide. I've since come across a Cyril Connolly line about "the enemies of promise," one of which is "the pram in the hall."

MINDY PENNYBACKER: Older writers not only predicted doom but actively tried to separate us. When John Hawkes, a protégé of my Stanford professor Albert Guerard, came to give a reading and teach a single guest seminar, he remembered me from his visit to Albert's undergraduate writing class in France and decided I had to be his guide through the limbo of nocturnal Iowa City. Don was relegated to chauffeur, and Hawkes, at least twenty years our senior, dubbed him "Old Faithful." It did give me pleasure to hear Hawkes's moans of discomfort stuck in the back of Don's dangerous, bucket-seated Pinto wagon with squealing groupies. We took him to a party at a big old Victorian house, and I remember John Givens dancing and doing some form of pre-rap in homage to Hawkes, and Doug Unger urging me to be nice to Hawkes, and Hawkes kept trying to shoulder Don out of the way until Robin Green magically appeared and, with a stern look like Athena's and a cutting word audible only to Hawkes, suddenly put him in his place.

Don had his own cross to bear. Mary Lee Settle had paid a nocturnal and tipsy visit to our overheated basement apartment to tell Don that he had received a TA thanks to her, this despite his unfortunate connection to me, whom he certainly shouldn't marry, since I'd only be a millstone around his neck!

The only faculty member who gave us his blessing was Jack Leggett, who upon hearing of our engagement lit up and gave me a hug and scratchy kiss.

DON WALLACE: It was wonderful being a married writer. We fell in with our old friends, like the Olsens and the Schaeffers, both married couples, and Sherry Kramer and Bill McCoy and Jeff Abrahams and, well, really everyone. And we made some new, significant ones, including a couple of wise (as we thought of them) women writers who were publishing stories in *Redbook*, *Mademoiselle*, and other magazines that the more auteurish workshop students scorned. Mindy and I, being from the *outre* West, were fascinated. And so we learned of the mystical hierarchy of fiction publishing, the pyramid with the *New Yorker* and the *Atlantic* and *Harper's* at the top, then *Redbook* and *Mademoiselle*—the cream of the women's slicks, as they were called—and then the rest of the Seven Sisters: *Ladies Home Journal, Family Circle*. It was the last gasp of the great short story economy that had fed F. Scott Fitzgerald and other writers, right down to Kurt Vonnegut. The era of $40,000 for a story had long passed, but you could still get $800, or $1,000 or even more, from *Ladies Home Journal*—a rumored $7 grand!—if you could fit the formula. A big if, as it turned out.

So we sat in Stephanie Vaughn's kitchen on snowed-in Saturdays and watched Ohio State football (Stephanie was a serious fan) and she and Pamela Erbe and Sara Vogan swapped notions and tips and, most generously, names of editors. That was the start of professional writing for me: the first stiff letter to a stranger in New York, New York, inquiring if she would be so kind as to take a look at a story, SASE enclosed.

ERIC OLSEN: This was the sort of thing we weren't getting from the faculty, that real-life, practical, professional-writing stuff, the stuff about that SASE enclosed . . . Maybe it was just assumed we'd pick it up along the way. And maybe some of us did. Maybe I just wasn't paying attention, but when I left and got into writing for a living (as if), I was amazed at what a rube I was. I was an Iowa grad, and I didn't know crap about the real world of publishing. . . . We absorbed the occasional dose about the art, but there wasn't much nuts and bolts about the business or the craft.

GORDON MENNENGA: The craft thing? I don't think the topic ever came up, did it? At least not in the workshops I was in. You did your lump and threw it on the table. I was surprised we never picked out an element of "craft" and looked at it, how metaphor was used in a story, for example. We never did exercises of any kind. I suppose it's that way still.

I've looked at programs that have classes where craft is discussed. You take a really interesting example from another's work, such as long passages that are one paragraph, where one paragraph goes on forever, and compare these to a Ray Carver story, where there is one little paragraph after another. We didn't get into why things are done a certain way, or talk about different styles, what styles are tolerated and what aren't . . . why and how.

SANDRA CISNEROS: I thought we got the craft thing at Iowa, but we didn't learn about the *why*, why we write what we write, or for whom. I'm talking about the poetry workshop because I wasn't in the fiction workshop. We never talked about what a writer contributes to society; we never talked about our obligations to community. It was never discussed. There was no discussion of politics, about feminism. No one mentioned sexuality; it was taboo, though it was all around us. And we *never* mentioned class.

I wish there had been some political direction. I never questioned what I was doing until I worked in a school where we couldn't even afford chalk. This made me question whether I should be a writer—is this the best I can do for the planet? I wasn't sure, even when I was writing *Mango* in Provincetown. Maybe, I wondered, I should learn how to administer birth control information and disseminate this to women in poor neighborhoods.

I started teaching in Chicago in an immigrant neighborhood, and I learned so much more in one semester teaching those kids than I did the two years at Iowa. If Iowa had taken us out to the high schools or to the prisons or in the fields, that would have been something to write about. I felt we were too self-centered; we learned the "how," but not the "why." I mean, all the things about craft are important, but they're secondary to who we write for and why.

If Iowa had taken us out to the high schools or to the prisons or in the fields, that would have been something to write about. I felt we were too self-centered; we learned the "how," but not the "why."

I picked up what I needed though; one of the most important things I learned at Iowa was to write as if my worst enemy was going to critique my work. Even now I tell my students, write your first draft as if your best friend is sitting across from you, so you can say anything in any order. You don't get blocked if you're writing in your pajamas; write your first draft in your pajama voice. But when you revise, imagine your enemy is sitting across from you, and revise as if your enemy knows where your weak points are because, believe me, he does.

I got that from Iowa because my worst enemy was there in that classroom.

GORDON MENNENGA: You can take people who are not very good at writing a basic story, and you can help them improve a lot. You can see what their fears are—"Why don't you write much dialogue?" And they say, "Because I'm not good at it." Well, you can do a few exercises and it turns out they're geniuses at it.

I'll separate out the elements with examples—for example, three of the best pages of dialogue. There's a great paragraph in *Love in the Time of Cholera* that condenses the history of mankind into one paragraph. Examples like that.

At the workshop, I felt like we were always being damped, not encouraged to take many risks, because of the "same think" that went on. If you were too wild, if you tried something like a three-page sentence.

Kinsella would put up quite good stories, and people would fall on them with knives because they were too "light" maybe, or too "effusive," and Kinsella would say, "That's okay. I've already published it in Canada."

Sandra fell into that trap, too. If all of her characters had died or thought philosophical stuff, she would have been a star. If you look back at some of the stuff that was praised, it's amazing what was praised. Part of it is youth; most of those there were twenty-four to twenty-eight. No one knew how to act.

JANE SMILEY: Our teachers were writers, not teachers. They knew a lot about writing, but hadn't given a lot of thought to how to communicate what they knew. This is partly my reaction to those hyper-masculine guys because they did praise and criticize and they did alienate the students and they didn't analyze and we weren't given the tools to know what was wrong. We had our instincts, but no tools.

> Our teachers were writers, not teachers. They knew a lot about writing, but hadn't given a lot of thought to how to communicate what they knew.

I decided as a result to give my students tools rather than leave them to rely on their instincts.

T. C. BOYLE: The workshops at Iowa were kind of free-form when I was there. And the teachers, at least the ones I had, didn't seem to know quite how to run a workshop. I think we've become more sophisticated in workshops now.

When I was a student, we didn't know how to handle ourselves. I certainly didn't know what the hell I was doing there. I didn't have the vocabulary for talking about other peoples' work. None of us did. The students now are light-years ahead of where we were then. Some of the teachers are, too.

People who are good artists or writers aren't necessarily the best teachers, of course, or who want to teach or like to teach or have the capacity for it. So it was pretty hit-and-miss.

SANDRA CISNEROS: Everyone was needy there. The teachers were completely fucked up. They seemed to think that free booty was part of their compensation package, and these young women, they look up to these writers and think of them as being gods and don't realize that these are men with no control over their lower chakras.

I always talk to these young women and say be really, really careful here, you're so naive and young and beautiful and you have no concept of your power, but the first person who pays attention to you, you go waaa! And you're completely blinded. And in my case, it went beyond bad. . . .

Too many of the faculty were not leaders in the real sense that teachers ought to be. They may have been great writers, but they weren't great human beings. They were totally dysfunctional. Of course, who isn't? I know some great people who are dysfunctional, but they use that dysfunction in their writing, to process their dysfunction, to make them great human beings. But those weren't the ones at Iowa, and as a result, we had the sick preying on the naive. That's what I saw.

I think what it taught me was there was a complete lack of respect for the students; they didn't look at them as human beings who were young and maybe terrified, whom one should honor. There wasn't that sense of honor that should have been, real integrity. That wasn't there because it hadn't been instilled by the leadership. Well, no one ever wants to hear from the malcontents.

Books by the Bed

SANDRA CISNEROS: I've been reading a lot about Zelda Fitzgerald and about Edie Beale and her mother, Edith Bouvier Beale, cousin and aunt of Jackie Kennedy. They seem like *locas*, but they're women who've been ostracized, who couldn't take care of their money and ended up poor. They're made to look like eccentrics, but I see these fragile old woman as being vulnerable and preyed upon. Hell, I could turn out like this!

JOE HALDEMAN: I don't think I was ever harmed by a workshop, but it's obvious that some people are. Sometimes they're discouraged enough to quit writing. That would be fine if sensitivity to criticism correlated with bad writing, but of course it doesn't. The opposite may be true; I've heard pretty bad writers respond to criticism with a "What the fuck do they know?" attitude.

I wouldn't hesitate to recommend Iowa to any young writer, with these codicils: You won't learn to write there. You will learn a lot about teaching writing. It could be harmful if you're too thin-skinned. You can meet some great people. Also some scoundrels. Iowa City is a wonderful place to live and work (except for the winters). The Workshop is the best credential you can get for teaching writing.

That said, I have to say that at a deep level I have sympathy with Cormac McCarthy, who said that creative writing programs are a scam. Writing is a mysterious process, and saying that you can teach it is uncomfortably like saying you can teach spiritual values. It makes the scam detector ring.

I tell my students that I provide them with a deadline and an audience. Their reaction to those challenges might teach them something.

ANTHONY BUKOSKI: Would I recommend the Workshop to a young writer? Absolutely, I would. As I've said, the Workshop was a great place for me.

Of course, the place isn't for everyone. You have to want to write and to learn to write. A person could merely hang around for two years and get a degree because I don't think the requirements were very stringent. I think my MFA thesis wasn't much over sixty pages. So, as I say, you could probably get by doing very little. Perhaps things have changed. But it was precisely because you weren't expected to take tests or to write term papers or even to take formal, graded classes that the Workshop was so great.

Maturity regarding one's craft, the mature outlook regarding writing, these are essential. If I didn't think a young writer was disciplined, I wouldn't recommend Iowa.

DOUG UNGER: I go back and forth on my opinion about the Iowa Writers' Workshop model for training writers. I think the way we've decided to train our writers should be reexamined. The academy is a little too comfortable right now for a lot of writers, too much of an easy escape. I'm now seeing young writers coming up who intend to make a career of teaching writing rather than being an artist first and foremost—an artist who happens to have a skill set for teaching along with many other skills. That kind of careerism strikes me as too tame, somehow, too safe a path to set out on, its ambitions being to publish enough books to get tenure at a college or university then settle in to the life of being a professor.

> I think the way we've decided to train our writers should be reexamined. The academy is a little too comfortable right now for a lot of writers, too much of an easy escape.

MARVIN BELL: The fiction writer Leonard Michaels used to tell the fiction students, "There is no such thing as prose. There is only poetry." I used to joke that, at parties, the fiction students were in the front room, discussing contracts and advances, while the poets were in the back room, dancing.

It's quite different now, at least in poetry. For one thing, literary theories now have a significant influence. Years ago, we tended to dismiss them except as conversation pieces. For another, the teaching is more organized and intentional, and then there was also the gradual institutionalization of the MFA.

MFA programs sprang up by the dozens, and the Associated Writing Programs was born. It was a small organization that eventually became humongous. It does good work for many people, but has had to change along the way. What began as an organization of writers who teach is now an organization of teachers who write. There is now a lot of "networking" and, in classes, "workshopping." Can you think of a sillier word than "workshopping"? Well, "journaling" is also right up there on my silly list.

DOUG UNGER: Then of course, look at me: a professor for years, who has sacrificed many thousands of hours to teaching and building programs when he could have been making art, and now even, it's worse, God save me—I even became the chair of a very large English department, with all the detail work and annoyance along with the rewards of community building that entails. Still, I'm saying, paradoxically (speaking out here against my own example) that it might be best for the young writer to throw off the traces of the workshop and the university and try something else, at least at first—a profession or an occupation that involves the writer in a world far different from the academy.

BILL MCCOY: I recall that Nicholas Meyer, who'd been an undergrad at Iowa, not in the Workshop, had wanted to come back and give a reading—this was after his big Hollywood success—and the scuttlebutt was they wouldn't let him because he'd gone commercial; there was a certain perverse pride in saying you can't buy us with your money and your seven percent solution, Mr. Hollywood Writer.

Back then, the worst thing you could say about someone's writing was that it was being written with the idea of being turned into a movie. It was a hippie ethos hangover. Now I guess it's okay to want commercial success, but when we were there, it was a badge of shame.

I think back in '75, there was still the belief, though it went against everything logical, that ultimately the academy would take care of you. A look around should have told us otherwise, but we still believed it. If you distinguished yourself, you'd always be able to teach. By the time we graduated in '77, the bottom had fallen out from under the teaching market. There was nothing. Even for people who were good. Everything was changing.

ERIC OLSEN: Everything was changing, but it wasn't something we discussed much in workshops. Of course among ourselves, we were constantly sharing rumors and gossip, and the more detached from reality, the better. But the faculty only rarely shared with us any insights they might have had about the "market" that awaited us, and by market I guess I mean academia and the "market" for creative writing teachers. Who was hiring? Where? Or publishing and the "market" for books. What was selling? What were the trends? But then if you worried about "trends," you were a commercial hack and shame on you.

Could be the faculty were as clueless as we were. They were already established, usually famous, and life was good, so why should they fret about such crass matters as the "market"?

Everything was changing, but it wasn't something we discussed much in workshops. Of course among ourselves, we were constantly sharing rumors and gossip, and the more detached from reality, the better.

But getting back to the idea of a workshop as refuge, it could also be that the faculty assumed such discussions of "the market" weren't something that our tender sensibilities should be burdened with. We were, after all, *artists*.

SANDRA CISNEROS: We bring in agents and editors to meet with students at Macondo, but everyone has access. And we ask among the group who has what skills, or we invite people to give a seminar on a particular topic, the market or the trends, and so on.

I was a poet, and when I got out of Iowa, I learned the business side the wrong way, by signing on the dotted line—and then later on I had to get an agent who helped save me from the big mistakes I'd made as a young writer. Again, it had to do with how naive I was about men. My father was so loving and kind that, when it came to men, I always expected them to love and guide me the way my father did, with usually disastrous results. So the best thing that ever happened to me was to find Susan Bergholz. Susan negotiated back the rights to *Mango Street* and *Woman Hollering Creek* that I'd signed away, and sold *Woman* to Random House and *Mango Street* to Vintage. When I talk to young women, I tell them you don't need a husband, you need an agent.

DOUG UNGER: About agents, well, I don't have a very high opinion of them. All of my book deals, except for foreign rights, I've landed, somehow, on my own. An agent has stepped in to do the contract, and maybe has helped up the amount of money on an advance, or has placed a story here or there, or came in handy when paperback rights were being sold.

Most agents I've known over the years are more destructive to writers and to the creative process than helpful. Mostly, my attitude toward agents these days is let me write what I write, and you go ahead and circulate the manuscript, and collect the percentages, thanks very much. But don't tell me what the so-called market is, and don't advise me about what to write to suit that market because that's an insult. That's obscene consumerism being allowed to take over the artistic process and kill off anything that's original or alive in the writing.

The worst mistake I see younger or developing writers make is to let agents tell them what to write, or how to finish a novel, or what kinds of books to lead with into a publishing house, which most often is advice that works directly against the writer's creative rhythm and artistic process. In nine out of ten cases like this, where the writer sees the big advance check and a limo coming to his or her door instead of his or her artistic vision, the result is a manuscript that never goes anywhere.

> **The worst mistake I see younger or developing writers make is to let agents tell them what to write, or how to finish a novel, or what kinds of books to lead with into a publishing house. . . .**

MICHELLE HUNEVEN: Once I had a manuscript to sell, having an agent was extremely important. Until then—not important at all. I felt extremely close to my first agent and close to my first editor. I trusted them entirely. I rarely asked questions about anything they did. I had very little idea what happened when a book came out, how it came to be reviewed or publicized, if it was selling or not. I lived in a state of blissful ignorance. I had no idea that my first novel actually sold poorly! No idea. Once I did ask my agent how many copies had sold and she said, "Why do you want to know?" I said, "People ask me." She said, "Tell anyone who asks that you sold twenty thousand copies." Well, that wasn't true at all! I like a little more reality— hard as it is to take sometimes—in my professional relationships these days.

The day that agent pronounced my third novel finished and ready to submit, she also said, "Guess what? I'm retiring!" So I had to spend the next three months looking for a new agent. I talked to half a dozen agents and many editors. I went from being at a tiny, handholding boutique agency to being in a much bigger agency—though I'm quite fond of Scott Moyers, whom I mainly work with at Wylie. He's held my hand when needed.

My first editor, Gary Fisketjon, line-edited my first two novels with his famous green pen. I learned a lot. My recent editor, Sarah Crichton, went right to the weakest scenes in the book and asked me to revisit them and hoist them up a bit. Also extremely helpful, if more macro than micro. Also really improved the book.

Mostly, in terms of getting a book to a professionally finished stage, I work very closely with one friend. We swap pages often, know each other's books almost as well as we do our own. Four eyes are better than two. I'm lucky because this person is a superb writer and has really helped bring my writing to a new level.

JOE HALDEMAN: My agents have always been important. They make me more money and allow me to be a writer without the expense of living in New York. I've sold books and movies without agents; that is, I sold them on my own, and then had my agent do the paperwork. But I wouldn't think of trying to make a living at it without an agent. I don't have any special talent in selling myself; rather the opposite. So I hire this guy to tell people how great I am.

ERIC OLSEN: At Iowa, now and then an agent or editor would come to visit, do a little scouting. Access was carefully controlled. On the one hand, I think there was a desire to protect our delicate writerly sensibilities from the crass commercialism of agents. But I also think the powers-that-be didn't want just anyone dumping manuscripts on a visiting agent's lap. Only the Big Dogs got to do that.

Of course, the rest of us would crash the party. Party crashing's a defining skill for a young writer. In fact, that's how Schaeffer and I got our first agent, John Sterling—and thereafter dynamo Esther Newberg—from International Creative Management. We crashed the party and romanced that poor rookie.

GLENN SCHAEFFER: Everyone lined up to meet with ICM agent John Sterling with their coffee tankards and vanilla-foldered manuscripts, but I showed up with *nada*. I believed in exposing my true oeuvre. I waited until the end of the second day and walked in on Sterling, and he looked up at me with dread and moaned, "What do you have?"

"Gumption," I told him.

Then I pitched an idea Olsen and I had for a book that featured pro boxing, as an index of LA lowlife, based on the Olympic Auditorium. We'd cover promoters and fighters and trainers, right down to Romanian loan sharks—*verité*—with a nod to Charles Bukowski. Indeed, we planned for *poète maudit* Bukowski to be a central character. It was assumed that *literature* can't be created through a collaborative process, but why not? Playwrights collaborate. Screenwriters collaborate. Lyricists collaborate. Business is all about collaboration. Why not true-life novelists? Olsen and I bore similar tastes, and we'd double-team a project to generate more and deeper stories. And we both worshipped boxing. Of course, what Olsen and I were sketching out was hardly wan East Coast *literature* of sensibilities. . . . It was to be—that word again—*raunchy* reportage, covering the badlands between facts and truths. We were calling the book *City Business*.

So I sang for Sterling. He responded, "I like boxing. I know a little about boxing. I'd do a boxing book." We took him out for beers. Next thing I knew, we had our agent.

ERIC OLSEN: I had no idea what a big deal it was to have an agent with International Creative Management. I'd never heard of ICM. Nor did I realize that John was Esther Newberg's protégé. I had no idea who Esther was, that she was already big, and due to get bigger.

It was two years after Iowa that Schaeffer and I finally managed to cobble together eighty pages or so of *City Business*. I called to let John know it was in the mail and learned that he'd left the agency to live in a cabin in the woods in Vermont or Maine or some northern stony place to write poetry or plant potatoes or maybe a combo. (Sterling, it turns out, returned to the beat with great future success.)

Our manuscript ended up on the desk of Esther Newberg. A few weeks later, I get a call from Esther. Happens she's in Beverly Hills, staying at the Hotel Bel Aire, negotiating huge movie deals. She's all excited, tells me she thinks the book's *terrific*, it'll be a best seller, there's a movie in it, and I'm going light-headed with excitement, already thinking about my Hollywood move, that Porsche and which color. . . . Then she says, "Now, all you two have to do is finish it." It was not, I suppose, an unreasonable suggestion. . . .

GLENN SCHAEFFER: I guess we both got a little distracted. I was, of a sudden, a young business exec burdened with mortgage and car payments, with a penchant for dressing well. Charles Bukowski wasn't as charming for me as before. Still, Esther dutifully took our calls for a year or two after, until she got a little distracted herself—she had this odd penchant for bankable writers who actually finished stuff.

DOUG UNGER: Let editors guide you—the real editors, the ones who still honor writers and their work, as Ted Solotaroff always did. There are still extremely fine ones out there, and of course I'll name the truly exemplary senior editors here, such as Gary Fisketjon, Terry Karten, Alane Salierno Mason, Morgan Entrekin, Gerald Howard, Judith Gurewich, Jonathan Galassi, John Sterling, and many, many others. Those serious editors are the voices that writers should listen to—and only then when they reach a certain achievement of excellence in their manuscripts.

JAYNE ANNE PHILLIPS: I never really thought about "lit biz" as a young author. I never considered myself a commercial writer, or expected to see my work in anything but literary magazines.

I remember hearing somewhere, probably at Iowa, that if writers published good work in magazines like the *Iowa Review*, agents/editors/prize collections (Pushcart Prize, Best of, etc.) would notice. This was true for me, and I think it's still true. I don't think online publishing has changed this.

I like the online option, but the best online sites (like narrative.com) also publish between covers eventually: a "best of" or annual in-print edition. Many magazines now have an online version of themselves, a website at least, on which they publish teasers of what is in the magazines, or the entire piece, if the author agrees.

> I do think "lit biz" in general is utterly depressing, even to those successful at it, and it's self-defeating, just another way to avoid thinking about the work.

I do think "lit biz" in general is utterly depressing, even to those successful at it, and it's self-defeating, just another way to avoid thinking about the work.

Literary success is like happiness: great to have, but always transitory. Writing is a private enterprise and resembles an enduring spiritual practice far more than it resembles a "career."

MICHELLE HUNEVEN: When my first novel was coming out, Tom Boyle gave me a great heads-up: Everything is a jolt, he said. A good review is a jolt; a bad review is a jolt.

To me, it was amazing how similar the jolts were: While success is preferable to so-called failure, it is no less destabilizing. We spend all this time alone in our woodsheds making stuff up, building whole worlds with spiderwebs, then suddenly people are commenting in very public forums about our efforts. Jolt, jolt, jolt.

Failure and rejection are indeed constant. But there are also victories that nobody can take away from you. Writing an entire novel is a victory, as is writing a beautiful sentence, a finished short story. Those hours spent working? Each one adds to experience, and nobody can erase or obviate them.

There are always going to be groups a writer is not included in: prizes she's not nominated for, major reviews she doesn't get, fellowship committees that turn her down, jobs that go to someone else. There are always going to be other writers who are rewarded, hired, anointed, sometimes for obvious merit, sometimes for no apparent reason. I'm going to sound like a grandmother here, but it is extremely important to count your own blessings. If I look at what other writers "get," I can become envious and morose. If I look at my own career, I feel extremely lucky and grateful—I have the writing life I yearned for.

To me, the main reason to relish success is that it affords the opportunity to keep writing. If I sell a book, I get some time to write another book, hopefully a better one. My goal is to have a shelf of books—I always liked the number twelve. Twelve books. I have three. I have a lot of work to do. Why am I answering these questions? Why am I not working as we speak?

T. C. BOYLE: I try to give my students a little something about the publishing industry each semester, but what I know is antiquated. When I was scrambling to publish, I knew every magazine and every editor, and everything that was going on and all the gossip. Now I don't know about any of that. I tell them what I know, how to get on with an agent. How to send out a manuscript. But I found out. No one ever told me. I found out just by trial and error.

DOUG UNGER: In my own time at Iowa, I didn't think much of the business of writing. I wasn't aware of it, and no one really clued me in. I recognized that a few fellow writers were going to have huge success and were on their way: T. Coraghessan Boyle, Allan Gurganus, Jane Smiley, Richard Bausch. . . .

But I didn't want to think about the "business" of writing. For me, writing is a vocation, it's a way of life, and living a life of letters is the choice I've made: to write, to read, to encourage other writers, and to build on the kind of educational structures that can guide them and support them. That's still the business of writing I'm interested in and was always interested in. I believed that good writing would always rise to the attention of readers, somehow.

Later, just a year or so after Iowa, Ray Carver taught me that by example, and by how he described his own life. Think about it: For eighteen years, he wrote stories and poems that came out almost exclusively in the little or literary magazines and journals, save for two stories, later on, in *Esquire*. Nobody would publish a book of his stories. Then, two years after that, *whammo*—Gordon Lish took a job at McGraw-Hill, which was mainly a textbook publisher at the time, in part to start a fiction line, and he brought Ray's first book of stories, *Would You Please Be Quiet, Please?* with him. That book became a sensation, was a finalist for the National Book Award, and made Ray's first big reputation as a serious writer.

I believed that that is how writers make it—by sticking to making their art, surviving out in the cold, then getting lucky enough that readers find their work.

There's a lot of controversy now about Lish's intrusive editing of Carver's stories. But putting that aside, you've got to give Lish credit that he had the keen eye to see and to recognize the value and potential in the work.

Readers find the good work, the work that lasts, and that's all that matters. The rest is all about a bunch of business people like agents and publishers and marketeers figuring out how to make the most money off of the writer's art so they can . . . what? Buy a bigger house out in the Hamptons? Afford a more exclusive haute cuisine? Or a more private private golf course? Find a more fetching trophy wife?

No self-respecting literary artist hoping to become a great writer should give a shit about any of that. None of that has anything to do with writing well. Writers should work on their stories, novels, poems, essays . . . make them as perfect as possible, make their art. Nothing else matters.

SANDRA CISNEROS: I think it's important for writers to be in workshops, but not the Workshop; there are communities that are alternatives. A workshop should be a disciplined and a caring community, and I didn't have that at Iowa.

Books by the Bed

DOUG UNGER: Mostly these days I read books in manuscript to write comments or blurbs for review. I've just finished blurbing a very fine first book by a writer who won the Iowa Prize, Don Waters, and his truly wonderful, dark book of stories called *Desert Gothic*. And Tony Bukoski's latest book of stories, *North of the Port*. And I've just got the new English translation in manuscript of Horacio Castellanos Moya's *Insensatez*—or *Senselessness*—that I'm reading, hoping to find excerpts that I can use in a project and get Castellanos Moya out to Las Vegas. But published books? That rare pleasure of reading one? Or planning to read one? I have books by my former students, Dan Chaon's *I Am No One You Know*, and Claire Messud's *The Emperor's Children*, and I'm reading Roberto Bolaño's *The Savage Detectives*, and looking forward to the Spanish original arriving in the mail so I can read it in the original. That's just the fiction not connected to a class I'm teaching. For the class, I've got all kinds of critical books surrounding the reading list, which includes Dostoyevsky's *Crime and Punishment*, Paul Auster's *The New York Trilogy,* and a new translation of Roberto Arlt's *The Seven Madmen*, among other books.

DOUG UNGER: Right. I don't believe a hothouse, competitive atmosphere is best for writers at an early stage of development. Like seedling trees, they need a good nurturing start, and they need a supportive literary community. Sure, they need a bit of the hard work of scarifying now and then, to beat back the weeds that will try to choke off their growth. Give them a good start, then they'll be ready to get out there and make art on their own, on their own terms.

So in our program at UNLV, we've decided to support every writer we admit at about equal levels, and to provide that safe place in which they can find their way. I think it's important, to stimulate absolute freedom of artistic expression, to remove the competitive atmosphere. I believe truly fine artists have that sense innately, and they are always trying to outdo themselves, so why put them in a situation in which they feel compelled to engage in such one-upmanship and cocktail party–style derision of one another to succeed socially, as if social success means literary success?

Writing is something that happens on the page. What the world then makes of it, the marketing of that writing, most often should not be left in the hands of the writer. That's for their mentors to help with, and later on, that really is how agents are most useful, and hopefully, after that, it's for the publicity departments at publishing houses. Writers should write. And they should feel they have absolute creative freedom. That's the kind of creative atmosphere I've always tried to foster and nurture in a creative writing program.

ROSALYN DREXLER: Being there is the most important thing in a teacher's arsenal. Opening up, telling stories, asking personal questions, helps; e.g., "I was there when Fred Astaire walked into John Lennon's suite at the St. Regis Hotel..." I remarked casually one afternoon, before critiques began. That got the class's attention.

What is the student's goal? Does the student hear what he/she has written? Understand the shape of a line? Have a visual sense of the writing itself: Should it be fat, thin, composed of walls of words, go on forever without punctuation, be sliced beyond recognition?

And for sure, what is it about? It has to be *about* something. Even a short description of, say, a sunset cannot stand by itself: Who is describing it? Why? Is it an old man about to die? Is it someone who is losing his eyesight? Is it a child who has been given a number of subjects to describe, and does so in his/her own young voice?

Writing is not only torture, it's fun. It's *Let's Pretend*. It's a cheap vacation. It's the way in and out.

One of the books I recommend that students read is *On Being Blue*, by William Gass. This is the book that separates the appreciators (of writing) from the depreciators: an inspiration to anyone who loves literature, who wants to understand what writing well means.

SANDRA CISNEROS: I wrote in the introduction to the tenth edition of *House on Mango Street* that I found my voice for *House* when I discovered my "otherness" at Iowa. It could have gone either way at first; either I would have given up and left (my plan A), and *House* never would have been written, or I would have to get angry to overcome my sense of low self-esteem I felt there. I felt rage, which came after I felt ashamed. How many writers have we never heard of who quit, especially writers of color or women or working-class writers?

If I hadn't had Joy there, and Dennis, I would have left. Fortunately, there was something there that made me strong and angry, and that anger gave me energy. The energy of anger can light a city; unfortunately, most of us turn our anger on ourselves. I asked myself, *Okay, what can I write about now that no one can say I'm wrong?*

> I wrote in the introduction to the tenth edition of *House on Mango Street* that I found my voice for *House* when I discovered my "otherness" at Iowa.

That's how I teach writing now. I tell them about Iowa, and I say, "Okay, tell me ten things that make you different from anyone else in this room. From any writer in your school, from your family, from your church, your ethnicity. Write ten things you remember, ten things you wish you could forget." This gets back to that old adage: Write what you know. But how do you know what you know when you're twenty?

ANTHONY BUKOSKI: I don't recall what I might have learned about grammar and syntax and plot development, those nuts-and-bolts kinds of things. I'm sure I learned something.

One specific lesson I learned from Vance Bourjaily was that to establish an event as having occurred in the past, you had to use the past perfect verb tense only once or twice at the beginning of the scene, and that the reader would then assume, when you shifted to simple past tense, that you were really writing about a time before the past. Whether he was correct grammatically, I don't know, but I have used this advice and tell my students to do so. Honestly, though, this is the only craft tip I recall. I wasn't so much interested in craft.

I learned the valuable lesson I referred to earlier. Partly this was due to my reading Gass's "The Pedersen Kid" in Jane Howard's Form of Fiction class. The story takes place in North Dakota in winter. Characters have names like "Big Hans" and "Pedersen," names that reflect the place where I grew up. I never thought northern Wisconsin could be of any interest to anyone as a literary setting. Gass showed me this was not true. Alas, I wrote only a few Northern stories, still not trusting what I'd learned.

Gradually, I began to set more stories there. They seemed authentic because I knew as well as anyone the place I was explaining in the stories. I also learned to raise the expectations I put on myself as a writer. I tried harder to make stories better before submitting them for my Workshop colleagues' scrutiny. These were the best lessons I could have learned.

SANDRA CISNEROS: I learned what kind of writer I didn't want to be. And I learned how I didn't want to teach. I learned that you have to have balance, so you don't savage people.

There wasn't balance at Iowa. There was no love, but rather me me me, look how wonderful I am. There wasn't a sense of compassion there.

What I learned from Iowa was to ask how to create a community like the ones when I was working in Chicago at the neighborhood community centers, where people really cared about one another and trusted them.

How can we create a community where the teachers have respect for the students and the students have respect for the teachers? And if we don't have a teacher, then a collective, where there's respect for each other. So we create that respectful environment.

T. C. BOYLE: There are different ways of having discourse about a work. You can be belligerent, but that serves no purpose. It has to do with the personality of the person running the class; as the moderator, you need to make sure the discussion stays on the level of investigation and interpretation. And certainly, if the story's not working, it's critical that people can say it's not in a way that's not as hurtful as it might be. And if the author can realize that we're just trying to interpret something, it really takes the personality out of it.

I never took Jack's class. I hear that Frank Conroy often could be very critical of a student's work, but of course he had a huge heart, and I think he had their best interests in mind.

I probably wouldn't offer a critical comment in an overtly negative way. I might question some of the author's choices, and so on, but anything I had to say that would be negative would be leveraged by what is good. Or I might also say something critical privately, not in class.

My interest is more in drawing out the audience—what do they think of it, what does this mean—rather than saying this is wrong because there are no rules. I would never say this is wrong, you should do *this*. I would only offer an opinion, and we have fifteen other opinions, here are the reviews, what other readers said about it, maybe we got it right, maybe we didn't. It's having an instant audience.

JENNIE FIELDS: Having an audience is so critical. We all work in a vacuum. Hearing what others think is valuable to me. I learned to pay attention to every word I wrote and to listen to the music of my writing. When I went to readings of others, I heard how writing had music, and people who did have music in their writing were more readable. We were surrounded by ideas, writing all the time, and pushed by the quality of other's works.

> I learned to pay attention to every word I wrote and to listen to the music of my writing. When I went to readings of others, I heard how writing had music, and people who did have music in their writing were more readable.

I was always aware of every word put on paper, but at Iowa, if you were sloppy in some way, or overwrote, everyone would call you on it.

Iowa made me think more simply about writing, to tear things down to the utter necessity. People would point out sentences, they'd say, "I don't get what you're doing here." And when the dross was removed, then the whole work could breathe and communicate better.

DOUG UNGER: I thought the whole process of being at workshops and watching the way writers talk was very valuable. John Irving, Lenny Michaels, Jack Leggett, whether you agreed with them or not . . . each had something to offer.

Jack would pepper what he said with anecdotes about when he was an editor, and other writers he knew, and what they'd said to him at parties, and so we felt let in on the whole elite New York publishing world where he'd been an editor. Then he would critique stories in the context of the way he thought editors would accept a work, and this was all done with a social polish that was very good, I thought.

Lenny Michaels had a tremendous influence on me, but not so much on my writing as on a manner of teaching: an engaging style in the classroom, and an intensity he brought to his line readings of stories. He was demanding, and expected metaphorical richness in every word, and literary complexity down to the rhythm of each syllable. And he taught by a kind of performance of his explications that was fascinating to observe. I recall him reading Kafka's story, "The Country Doctor," pausing on each line, rephrasing it several times with differing, even cynical intonations, with each enunciation implying an alternate interpretation.

He would explicate our stories in that same manner, as performances, pacing in front of the class, pushing his hand through that 1950s slick black hairstyle he had, his lips curling up at our sentences as if he had just taken a whiff of something distasteful. He was never satisfied, not once, with what we had written. He would read our stories aloud in this way, explaining his reader response to each line, and many times that response was wildly divergent from any reading any of us, much less the writer, could ever have imagined. He would do this until he reached a point at which he believed the story had failed, then he would stop.

Lenny Michaels had a tremendous influence on me, but not so much on my writing as on a manner of teaching: an engaging style in the classroom, and an intensity he brought to his line readings of stories.

We were all incredibly pissed off at him for demeaning us in this way, for, indeed, ridiculing our stories.

"I never read living writers," he would say disparagingly, "because I never know how to judge them. I read Blake, Kafka, and Nietzsche." What a combination!

Still, what he was showing us is how much every word counts, how we must focus on the construction of each sentence with the precision of a composer of music, every note in its place, every period, as Isaac Babel said, placed with the precision of a dagger to the heart.

I was so enthralled with his teaching style that, when I moved to San Francisco the year in between finishing classes at Iowa and graduating (while still finishing my thesis), I took the trouble to sign up for Lenny's class in Wallace Stevens at Berkeley. In between working at Merritt Hospital in Oakland as an admissions clerk and running odd jobs for the St. James Episcopal Church on California Avenue in San Francisco, I'd commute over to Berkeley and sit in on his classes. Michaels put on the most amazing, astonishing one-man performance I have ever witnessed before or since. It was astounding, the way he paced back and forth in front of the class, reciting almost every poem in *The Palm at the End of the Mind*, then he would discourse on it, often articulating wild literary theories about possible meanings in those difficult poems, implications that went way beyond anything Stevens might ever have imagined. It was wonderful.

Michaels made words come alive in ways I've never seen any other teacher do, and I left his class excited about language, and fully meaning, one day, to write a story or novel that would be worthy of his attention.

And, ever since, I've tried to live up to that level of intensity, engagement, and intellectual complexity in my teaching—not that anyone could ever duplicate or imitate what Michaels did; he was such a one-of-a-kind teacher and a truly masterful writer of short stories.

"Slave over your stories," he would say. "Don't settle for less."

He never did, and that's a lesson I hope I've learned, and certainly one I'm committed to teaching.

DENNIS MATHIS: I heard a great story about Gordon Lish (and this is definitely hearsay). It's said that in his guest workshop he tore one girl's story to shreds, drove her to tears. Then came lunch, and he came over with his cafeteria tray to where she was sitting and asked if he could sit down. She was foolish enough to say yes. He says, "I'm sure you felt I was tough on you in there. But I just want to tell you, you have no future as a writer and should look for another career."

Generally for me, the only serious learning at Iowa was in the classroom, mostly Frank Conroy's classes. His famous line-by-line scrutiny. He told us to have a pencil in our hands as we read and mark anyplace we felt a "bump," even if we didn't think there was anything wrong. Then in workshop we went through each story a sentence at a time, and anyplace anyone had felt a bump, we'd stop there and figure out why. The classes went on for hours beyond the allotted time, until they turned out the lights in the building, then we'd go to the Mill and keep the discussion going.

What didn't they teach? How to write a novel. There was just an assumption that if you could do a good short story, you'd figure out how to do a novel by yourself. The emphasis was on short stories, which even then was a commercially dead product.

DOUG UNGER: There were two very bad creative writing teachers I've witnessed over the years, though they were both, in their way, fine writers and fascinating, interesting people to be around. This isn't to say other students didn't find their teaching useful, either.

Stanley Elkin was one. He came to Iowa to do a master's class and mostly ridiculed our writing, reading our lines out in cartoon voices for comic effect.

I remember I'd written this piece, a magical realism thing, from the POV of two Spanish fleas on Francisco Pizarro's boot as he came over to invade the Americas, and Elkin read this in the voice of Jiminy Cricket with a Spanish accent, dropping the pages on the floor as he did so. I was so humiliated, I felt like I could never show my face again. Elkin was such a comedian; he could make anything funny . . .

He transformed our work into material for his own brand of comedy. He got a lot of laughs from the classroom, but still, no developing writer's work should be treated that way, not ever. He was cruel to the student writers, and I believe that was a terribly damaging way to be, to use student writing for his own stand-up act. I'm sure there are a lot of former students of his who love that, but still, I can't stand that kind of disrespect for the courage it takes for a developing writer to put his or her work out there to be judged.

The other bad teacher, also very cruel, was Gordon Lish, though a fine judge of what would sell in New York and what would make a good story in *Esquire*.

I remember once he held up someone's paper by the thumb and finger-tips and said, "This is a piece of shit." He was cynical and mean-spirited, afflicted with a Napoleon complex that made him behave toward student writing as if he had to prove to all who were listening how he could conquer it, that he was better than it was, so small was his own ego.

He claims credit for many of Ray Carver's early stories now, which is a huge crock, and evidentiary of just how pathetic Lish is as a writer himself. Toby Wolff once nailed it exactly right when he said, "Has anyone you know ever come up to you and asked about the latest story by Gordon Lish the way people used to ask about the latest story by Carver?" There it is.

On the other hand, Lish had a sharp editorial eye for a certain kind of story, and did make the careers of certain writers, such as Carver, yes, whose work he introduced to the mainstream in *Esquire*. Also Jim Harrison and Harry Crews and Barry Hannah and other major figures of that period. About how constructively or destructively intrusive his editing was, let's let future readers and scholars decide.

Does a fine editor make a good teacher? Not usually. I don't know why this is, save that perhaps the acquired level of taste that a good editor must develop works against the generosity and patience demanded of a good teacher.

GLENN SCHAEFFER: It certainly wasn't the place to learn to be a novelist. That was too long a hunt. The writers who had success at Iowa tended to write tone poems, or short absurdist stories. There were two ways to be, in my view, what with Jack in charge of the program and Bourjaily doing as little as he could, and there was rivalry between them, yet it was Leggett who controlled the purse strings; Leggett came from that Brahmin school of publishing, where the idea of being a writer was that you stood among the culturally elect, and the *New Yorker* was the highest and best enshrinement a young writer could aspire to. The *Atlantic Monthly*, next up, was Yale to *New Yorker*'s Harvard. To my discredit, I gravitated toward gonzos over at *Esquire*, where skeevy Harry Crews launched fifteen-thousand-word sketches on Pentecostal snake handlers: One more bite, you die. Will

Jesus come through? (Yes, I was drawn to tales of tetched boys without women, or in mortal fear of them.) Anyway, we had the *New Yorker* writers come through here, often as not named Annie, so if you wrote like one of them, or you wrote like Donald Barthelme, then you did well. Everyone could see that Tom Boyle and Allan Gurganus were exceptional talents, who favored the Barthelme side of the equation, and they did well. But they didn't write like that later. Their grown-up novels sound different than their early stories, considerably so, and they've been prizewinners with those. And my friend Jayne Anne Phillips, her limpid prose intact, ditto.

DOUG UNGER: John Irving was my thesis advisor at Iowa. He was also an exemplary teacher in the sense that he let us in on his own creative process, let us read early drafts of his work, such as a false beginning to what later became *The World According to Garp* that contained, toward the end, pages that he later rewrote into the actual beginning of the novel. He allowed us to witness how he wrote around a subject, followed its directions, then, after comprehending what he was truly doing in the book, how he discovered the real story.

The poet John Ashbery wrote an untitled poem that has lines something like "the real story, the one we never knew before, the one that comes to us in bits and pieces, all of them, as it turns out," in that typically Ashbery modernist vein of abstraction without a definite subject. I like to think of this as a process some writers are always going about, and it perhaps best describes Irving's process, at least for that novel, looking for the bits and pieces of the real story in writing the first draft.

Irving was writing as best he could, but at the same time looking for the real story. By example, he showed us that he was confident he would find that story; he would write his way into it. And, as it turns out, all the other bits and pieces of his early draft he would discover were really about that real story. By showing us this process, and by his own often sharp and very opinionated responses to our work—not necessarily always the best responses, as he freely admitted, simply his most honest readings that we could take or leave and make of what we wished—John Irving was exemplary in his teaching.

What he did for me was to read closely, make marginal notes on portions he liked, and very gently, smartly, show me in which direction to take a particular work of fiction. In other words, he found the places in an early, fledgling work that showed off my best writing, then he moved me to follow my own lead. That was a wonderful gift, like helping me to install my own inner compass that could guide my fiction. Not Irving's compass, either, but Unger's compass (for whatever that's worth), and John was very emphatic about my knowing the difference.

I still try to conduct my workshops like John ran his. He'd ask the students to read each story two times; the first time as if we'd picked it up in a magazine or in a book. Read it through, as if it were a published work. Without critiquing it. Then let a little time go by, then read it a second time with pencil in hand, and make comments and edit the story. And at the end of that, write at least a half-page to full-page review, and bring that to workshop. I thought that was tremendously useful. Then the writer would get the story and the reviews back, and you'd end up carrying fourteen edited copies of your story with reviews home, that you could look back through . . . different members of the workshop would find different things. I enjoyed that enormously. I thought then and still think this is a good way to teach.

JOHN IRVING: It might be fun, as an experiment, to teach one course at Iowa again. I would be very plain and up front about it. I would say that I'm going to show you exactly how I construct a book. I'm going to provide you with actual examples. This is what I wrote first in this novel, then I did this, lastly, this. Just lay out the structure, the process because I do follow a structure, and I do have a process. Anyway, I would just spell it out: my method.

I would say only once, "I'm not recommending that you do this; I'm just showing you how I do it." And then, near the end of the course, I would say, "Okay. Now it's your turn. How do you do it?" Because the point is not that they learn my method; the point is they have to come up with their own method, one that will work a little better each time. (That's how you test any method, isn't it? You have to keep refining it, don't you?)

That's what makes criticism such an opposite thing from creating fiction. Criticism is always espousing theory and method—as if there were a right one, and only one! I stick to what Rilke said, "Works of art are of an infinite loneliness and with nothing so little to be reached as with criticism. Only love can grasp and hold and fairly judge them."

Did you read James Wood's *How Fiction Works*? It's a puerile little polemic. I would argue that you can learn more about how fiction works by watching a one-year-old take his diaper off and play with his own shit than by reading that schoolmarmish book of rules.

SANDRA CISNEROS: I got a lot from Bill Matthews and Marvin Bell. They were good teachers for me. They encouraged me to go the way I was heading, writing more narrative poetry.

I started writing a lot of monologues. I was reading *The Burning Plain and Other Stories* by Juan Rulfo. At that time, Rulfo had written only two books. He does things in dialogue, experimental things you can't do in film or radio. We think about the text as being limited, but he took those limitations and twisted them. For example, if you're reading a text, and you have a speaker speaking, Rulfo would have you reading and reading and then you realize someone else is talking, and it happens very suddenly and seamlessly. I did that in *Caramelo*. I learned that from Rulfo. It's a wonderful device; you have to back up and go *Wait a second*. When you're reading to yourself, when it happens, it's magic.

Along with Rulfo and the Boom writers, I was reading a lot of Edward Arlington Robinson. He was out of fashion, but there were all these wonderful monologues, and I realized if I could write monologues and do them in a voice that wasn't mine, it was a way of removing myself from writing about what I was living. So I started doing that. My poems became, sometimes, a kind of narrative, a fusion of prose and poetry . . . I was heading toward *Mango Street*, but in order to write *Mango Street*—because I felt so censored at Iowa in trying to write about myself as a young woman—I took my shame and went back ten years and took a younger voice, a girl's voice, so I could have some distance, someplace that was far from Iowa. That younger voice helped me break the silence. And then I wrote about an older shame. I was ashamed at Iowa, so I wrote about an older shame.

T. C. BOYLE: I had a TWF, so I taught one undergraduate creative writing class each semester, and I was very loose about it. I remember a guy had his story up and he asked if he could bring his buddy, and I said sure, and during the discussion someone said, "You know, the symbolism is so obvious," and this guy's buddy slams his fist down on the table and shouts, "Fuck symbolism!" So that was the end of that.

In my classes at USC now, the writer says nothing. The others in the class, including me, comment on the work, and the writer sits there and takes notes or whatever. Everyone is required to come with written comments, which they give to the writer. I got this from John Irving. This requires the readers to articulate their thoughts, and the writer is not allowed to say anything because it's not relevant. It's a chance for the writer to see how the audience reacts to the work, or more than that, how the audience interprets it.

I give out a schedule at the beginning of the semester: who's first, and so on. And I make them do four pieces a semester, and a midterm and final. It seems to work pretty well.

Also, we look at contemporary writers I admire, analyzing their work in the very same way, structurally, a published story by a famous writer: How does this work? Why start here? What does this mean? So the students get the approach, and it doesn't put the student on edge so much and gives others less opportunity to say, this sucks.

Is there a higher standard now? I suppose. But I don't know how others teach, I don't belong to associations, I don't know the other teachers in my own department and what they do, except what I hear from students. Judging from our students now, there's a much higher level of discourse and awareness about craft and how things are put together and how to talk about it. That doesn't necessarily mean they'll be better writers, but probably the classroom experience is a little more sophisticated than it was back when I was at Iowa, I think just from the accruing of all this experience over all these years.

> Judging from our students now, there's a much higher level of discourse and awareness about craft and how things are put together and how to talk about it. That doesn't necessarily mean they'll be better writers . . .

JANE SMILEY: I started teaching in 1981, at Iowa State in Ames. I had learned while at the Workshop that I didn't want students to write just one or two stories a semester, but draft after draft, so that's how I taught. I wanted the students to get into the habit of writing and also of analyzing each other's writing and watching each other's stories change and progress.

I wanted the students to see the story evolving and to understand that all parts of a story are in play and to not feel committed to any one part of it. One problem with praise is that if you praise something, the student starts protecting that bit. He or she loses the sense of the story as an organic whole, and it becomes harder to learn the process.

I didn't teach my own students at Iowa State in any way similar to how I was taught at Iowa. I had four or five students in a class who produced a draft a week, and we analyzed the work and I absolutely resisted giving praise or criticism. In class discussions, we explored the drafts analytically, trying to figure out how they worked. The student could then decide how to make them work better. When we offered suggestions one week, we could see how they worked out the next week, and sometimes they did not work out at all—this was enlightening to us as readers, and valuable as a means of giving the class members a feeling of common purpose. Nothing like this was done at Iowa.

ALLAN GURGANUS: I required my students to write a story a week. And a few additional exercises. That bypassed anyone's saying, "No, I can't do this." If you don't, you flunk. The teacher uses the pressure of the assignment to relax young writers about risking many things; I wouldn't have asked them to do it if it weren't possible. And if I hadn't first run the course myself.

I realize how much work I got done at Iowa for that reason. Having a very sympathetic reader available around the clock thrilled me. Especially Stanley Elkin. He was a genius critic but resented giving too much time to any single student. He was writing his own fiction there in his office in the EPB. He wrote by longhand in those little blue examination booklets, I guess to give himself a test, an extra sense of going for broke for full credit.

It's poignant to remember that Elkin was already enduring early symptoms of multiple sclerosis; we thought he was just the clumsiest man in the world. He was not a conventionally handsome guy by any means, but he became extremely attractive the more you knew him and, no surprise, he was insanely funny, in the Robin Williams mode of assuming one voice after another when he was truly riffing like the great jazz improviser that he was.

You'd make an appointment with him to discuss your own work and he'd have his office door locked, and the secretary would say, "Oh, he's in there. I saw him go in right after breakfast." You'd be banging on the door: "Stanley, I know you're in there! I hear the pen moving and you chuckling!" And you really could hear him giggling because he was writing something so hilarious he had to respond himself. "Stanley, you're on payroll!" you'd shout. "You're my teacher! I'm not going away!" He had read a third of a new story of mine. I had to know what he thought before I could write the rest of it.

Once he knew he was busted, once he finally unlocked the door, once he dried the tears of mirth still rolling down his cheeks thanks to his own prose, he was focused and great. And his advice was the most expert how-to Rx I ever got from one teacher.

SHERRY KRAMER: Over two years, you had a chance to get what you needed from six or seven different writers when you studied in the Fiction Workshop: Jack and Vance and whoever was visiting that semester. In playwriting you had Okkie Brownstein, and he believed that you can't teach writing, but you can teach rewriting, and so he taught us about the perception shift, which is a way to recognize the structure of a play. Your play, anybody's play. He had a way of focusing our gaze so that we could always see the pattern generated by a play.

The first thing he did was drum it into our heads that we couldn't use a pre-fab model or structural form for looking at a play. Each play is a unique, self-organizing process that generates new states of order spontaneously out of nothing, like a cartoon character drawing herself. We can't talk about a Beckett play using language and expectations engineered to describe drawing-room comedy. A play exists only in terms of itself and it literally creates those terms whole, from the ground up, as it creates itself. The rules that govern a universe are only available to us after that universe is created.

The second thing he did was shake us free of our understanding of where the play occurs. He insisted that the place where a play happens is not on stage, but in the eye and heart and mind of the spectator. In the end, a play happens inside us. In our apprehension, it comes alive and is vital and complete.

This is a more radical thought than it seems—I've seen actors/play-wrights literally shake when we talk about this for the first time in one of my classes because it pulls the rug right out from under them. Playwrights need to understand that the strings they are pulling have their ultimate end effect in the audience, not in what is taking place on stage. Audiences don't come to the theater to see characters change, they come to be changed. They come for insight.

MARVIN BELL: The most significant development in writing programs in the last ten years has been the proliferation of low-residency programs. I teach happily for such a program, based in Oregon at Pacific University.

The students are of another stripe than those in residency programs. The low-residency students are older, bring more life experience to the table, and arrive with a personal commitment to the art form already in place. They usually have jobs and are generally not in the program for a teaching credential. The exchanges we have by e-mail are often more detailed and precise than the exchanges one has in person during residency programs. The low-residency students, being older, tend to be confident about how poetry matters to them.

I have created for these low-residency students a way of being a poet every day, not just during the weekends or summers, or when a deadline approaches. The method is simple. One creates a single document on the desktop. Then, one writes every day by scrolling to the bottom and starting anew. One document only, on which one leaves all the abandoned efforts, the bad starts, the would-be titles, the early versions, etc. It all stays, and one does not constantly look back—especially if one has not yet written something new that day. Date the entries or not. If you miss a day, no big deal, so long as you are a poet every day, and you intend to write something every day. In other words, you don't have to boogie every day as long as you turn on the music.

As you know, one of my teaching rules is, "Teacher has to do the assignment, too." My laptop file, titled "The Dailies," is presently 431 pages long. When an editor requests a poem, I look back. If necessary, I revise. There is always plenty there.

Books by the Bed

MARVIN BELL: Here in this borrowed house in Sag Harbor (where we just got two feet of snow), it's different from in Iowa or Port Townsend. So here is my statement: You have asked me what books are at hand at a time when we are briefly in a borrowed house in Sag Harbor, New York, on the south shore of eastern Long Island. Next to an easy chair in what the owners refer to as "the library," but we call "the TV room," I have the nonfiction book, *Cold,* by Bill Streever; *I Go to the Ruined Place: Contemporary Poems in Defense of Global Human Rights,* edited by Melissa Kwasny and M. L. Smoker; Pushcart Prize volume 34; *Odalisque in Pieces,* poems by Carmen Giménez Smith; and some new issues of magazines: *Ecotone,* the Canadian magazine *Fiddlehead, Third Coast,* and the *Gettysburg Review.* Also, science and "Week in Review" sections from past issues of the *New York Times.*

ANTHONY BUKOSKI: For nineteen years here, I've taught English 350: Advanced Creative Writing, wherein I pick the students I want in the course. I limit class size to ten or eleven students. It is about this type of student, the upper-level English major interested in writing, that I am thinking when I say creativity can be taught.

I encourage these students to avoid hackneyed scenes and plots. I try to show them that they have had moments of surpassing beauty or sadness in their lives. That no matter how inexperienced they are in the business of living, they have done and seen things in a way no one else has. I want to convince them of the value of their experiences, hoping they will write about some odd or beautiful or tragic experience, something that is fresh for readers, not hackneyed.

Is it not creative to look for fresh approaches to old subjects? Have I not taught them creativity?

We discuss technical concerns in class. During one class, I have them write a page of a story that has in it an objective correlative. We puzzle over the term's meaning, read Hemingway's "Cat in the Rain" or perhaps another story with an objective correlative, then set to writing. Isn't this a way to encourage a different view of writing, to give meaning to an object that has no direct relationship to what characters are doing? Isn't this creative? Students are practicing symbolic thinking with the exercise.

We also discuss linguistic questions, such as how to shape a sentence or a paragraph to reflect, through its syntax, a state of mind or a physical experience. Faulkner often does the former, as in the first page of "Barn Burning." Hemingway does the latter in the ski story "Cross-Country Snow." Is this not teaching creativity?

The question of whether creativity can be taught interests me not at all. Let the psychologists and the educationists in their departments of education dispute the matter. I don't care whether creativity can be taught. A student who wants to write and write well will find the way to do that.

JAYNE ANNE PHILLIPS: I teach the way Frank Conroy taught. I was a student in Frank's class in '77, the second year I was at Iowa, which I believe was the first time he taught there. He taught like an editor. We discussed the stories in workshop, and then he began the line-edit and went over every line in the story, everyone with their pencils marking the suggested changes. "Jump in," he would say, and people did.

I teach the way he taught in that I line-edit my student's work, which was a waste with most undergraduates, and a major reason why I wanted to work with grad students and made the move to Rutgers Newark, to be part of building up an excellent MFA program.

SANDRA CISNEROS: If you don't know how to do something, it's good to tap into the genius of your students. At Macondo, if I have a problem, I'll say, "I have this problem, class, what should we do?" They're creative; they come up with brilliant ideas.

That's how we do it; we ask, "Do you like having the workshops from, say, 1:00 to 3:00 PM?" The whole group votes; the board is there, too, and so structural changes come about through the group.

Iowa's been doing the same thing year after year. I think one of the things that wasn't happening there, that I wish we'd had, was a venue for evaluating the structure. They never asked us for our opinion, what works, what doesn't. They never asked us what we thought, so that we're included. There is always a hierarchy.

At Macondo, we try not to have a hierarchy, but rather a collective, a true sense of the collective. More of an indigenous structure, not a hierarchical or patriarchal structure, which is what we had at Iowa, but something more egalitarian. And more circular and more concerned about community, which to me is more a Latino structure, more concerned about the group, the collective, very Latino, very Americano as opposed to Norte Americano, this sharing of power and serving the community.

Iowa fostered a sense of competition, rather than a community with a sense of honoring each other and assisting. At Macondo we drafted a compassionate code of conduct, which was written by the students themselves. It's not perfect, but we're trying. At Iowa, we had no code of conduct; there were violent outbursts in the workshops, and in the social gatherings, where people were drunk and disrespected each other.

At least at Macondo we've been attempting to have a code. We don't want to bring in writers to teach and have them chasing *nalga* instead. You want people who will be honorable and real leaders, and we look for those people who are going to help to guide.

DOUG UNGER: In the creative writing programs I've helped to build and have advised in their building—the MFA at Syracuse University, the MFA in Creative Writing International here at UNLV, as well as putting my two cents in on other programs I won't name, including experiments in South America—I've tried to emphasize this concept of the "person of letters" capable of more than just the work of fiction or the poem or the creative nonfiction piece. I've tried to influence programs to push developing writers to reach broadly into new and different genres and to lay foundations for their art in sound studies of the literature and culture around them.

Here at UNLV, I'll take a lion's share of the credit for the international emphasis. I brought it to the table as a plan when I interviewed for the job of creating an MFA program in the unlikely setting of Las Vegas, as something that would distinguish our program, in that we require residency abroad in a non-English-speaking country, the production of a literary translation, and three years of study, rather than two. Other faculty bought into the idea so immediately and with such enthusiasm that they now claim the international emphasis as their own, and that's okay with me, thinking of that great Eugene O'Neill line, "Let's not concern ourselves with matters of origins." The point is that we're all convinced the international emphasis is working.

Sending writers somewhere else, we hope, can stimulate a view from outside, move new fiction and poetry from the self-centered point of view and bourgeois domestic dullness of the living room, the kitchen, the automobile, the bedroom, the bad marriage—all those stories that have been overdone, it seems to me, and that have become so much a part of the American canon that the writing is as dull as mud.

I believe we should be aspiring to train "persons of letters" capable of many kinds of writing—story, essay, article, poem, eulogy, news feature, interview, arts review, introduction, afterword, and even a wedding toast . . .

The ideal creative writing program even goes beyond this. As the truly great editor and critic and damn fine writer Ted Solotaroff first suggested in his essay "The Literary Campus and the Person of Letters" back in the mid-1980s, I believe we should be aspiring to train "persons of letters" capable of many kinds of writing—story, essay, article, poem, eulogy, news feature, interview, arts review, introduction, afterword, and even a wedding toast—as well as reading, teaching, and more. Able to live their lives as artists and, at the same time, as literary activists, able to influence the world.

JAYNE ANNE PHILLIPS: Rutgers Newark is an entirely different world. It is the most diverse undergraduate campus in the nation, several years running, according to *US News & World Report*, and it's a twenty-minute train ride from NYC. Our motto is "Real Lives, Real Stories," and the hope was to create an excellent MFA program that would be as diverse as the undergrad population and to attract students from all over the country.

Most students attend full-time (only full-time students are eligible for aid), but we have a part-time option, which draws very talented people. Students receive aid in the first year only and are guaranteed the same aid for the second year, provided they remain in good standing as writers and teachers. Those on aid get the aid for their full two years in the program. No one is competing for aid.

A third to a half, in any given year, are students of color. Rutgers Newark is about Newark, a challenging, important city, and the MFA program undertakes major outreach efforts. We work with five high schools in our High School Program, and we work with the Newark Public Library on a Writers at Newark Reading Group for adults, pulling in three generations around the series, with literature as the draw. That group is led by two MFA Reading Group Fellows, a poet and fiction writer chosen for their teaching experience and their enthusiasm for the project.

DOUG UNGER: I think when you listen to others talk about stories in workshops, you come out with certain voices in your mind, and you begin to understand how your fellow writers read works, and you form a complete picture of how the teacher reads the work, and then at the end of that two-year experience of sitting in workshops, I think you leave with about five or six voices from the workshops, teachers or fellow writers, who are complete enough in your head to function as in-house critics of your work. I think that's what happened at Iowa, at least for me.

I think I know how Allan Gurganus would read a work and what he'd say about it . . . I can hear his voice in my head to this day. I can hear Jane Smiley's voice in my head, how she'd read a work. She'd make some whimsical comment that would be very funny, then in the middle of that she'd say something very insightful about the work. She had a way of summing things up in a witty, charming way. And I can hear others: the way John Irving would talk about a work, and Lenny Michaels. . . . They function as in-house critics, like a committee, when I write. When I'm done with a first draft, I ask them what they think.

For example, I'll tend to write very long sentences that are probably grammatically imperfect, and I'll reach for more exotic similes than I should, and I can hear Irving jump on that: *No. This has too long a breath. You can't stand there and read it aloud. You've gotta put a period here.*

> And I can hear others: the way John Irving would talk about a work, and Lenny Michaels. . . . They function as in-house critics, like a committee, when I write. When I'm done with a first draft, I ask them what they think.

I have this guy Robert Pope in my head. I have his voice in my head, pushing for the originality of an idea, and if it's not original, if it seems like it's been done before, his voice is the one that will tell me.

And I have Ray Carver's voice in my head. His is a very strong voice in my head about what it is I should do and how I should work. He was very good at indicating when a work of fiction should shift its time sense, its POV. His advice was always once you have an action or scene started in fiction, you want to stick with it long enough to make sure that it is a complete image in the mind of the reader, so that when you shift away from it—if you flash back or change scenes or if you put a white space in and jump to a consequent action—you'd at least have it established in the reader's mind so the reader would be able to reference it for the rest of the story. He was even good at pacing chapters of novels like that, though he never wrote a novel. He was also very attuned to pointing out words that were probably purple-prose-ish or excessive. He tended to edit toward minimalism. All in all, that's the best thing I got out of the Workshop: that collection of voices in my head.

PART THREE
THOUGHTS ON
SUCCESS AND FAILURE

Chapter 7

HEARTBREAK AND MONO

In his history of creative writing programs and their impact on American letters, *The Elephants Teach*, R. G. Myers tells us that "estimates peg the professional success rate for graduates in creative writing at about one percent (as compared with ninety percent for graduates of medical school)."[33] Kurt Vonnegut was even bleaker in his assessment of a young writer's chances. Vonnegut, who taught at Iowa during the '60s and returned now and then after to give talks or readings or master classes, declared that "virtually everybody's going to fail. If you ran a school of pharmacy like that it would be a scandal."[34]

But if the experiences of our classmates interviewed for this book are any indication, then we'd have to conclude that such declarations of almost certain failure are irrelevant.

Myers doesn't give us any information about who came up with the grim failure rates he quotes, nor does he offer any discussion of what might have been meant by "professional success" in the bleak comparison of the two cohorts. Of course, "professional success" among med school graduates is easy enough to establish: those who pass their boards, get a license, and go on to practice medicine without killing too many patients, thus avoiding an unacceptable number of malpractice suits so they can make a lot of money and join a country club.

But for writers, the definition of *professional* success gets a bit murkier. For that matter, the idea of "success" itself can be rather elusive. Of course, for the commercially oriented writer, professional success is a clear-enough concept. It means a huge seller and an Oprah's pick, with a fat movie deal to top it off. Or at least a modest seller without Oprah's blessing or a movie deal. Or, heck, sales of any sort would be "professional success" for most writers.

There seems to be a never-ending debate in the academy about writing as *art* versus writing as *profession*. One school of thought seems to hold that if one approaches writing as a profession, a way of making a buck, one betrays his or her art. This seemed to be the prevailing view at Iowa when we were there, and often seems to prevail today. The other school of thought holds that anyone who thinks like that is a sap.

"Professional" does entail making money. Pros get paid, and the more they're paid, the more *professional*—which implies *better*—they are deemed to be. This is no doubt the point being made by the stats that Myers provides: If someone pays you to write, you're a success; if they don't, you're a failure, and a *dismal*, abject failure at that, and if you none-

> There seems to be a never-ending debate in the academy about writing as *art* versus writing as *profession*.

theless continue to write, you are (picture a disdainful curl of an upper lip) a mere *amateur*, strictly speaking, someone who does something for the love of it, and only a *schlemiel* would do that.

But the concept of the "professional" originally had nothing to do with making money. The term comes from a Latin word for a "public declaration" and referred specifically to the act of declaring one's religious belief or faith, not ever a big moneymaking endeavor until the TV evangelist with big hair came along. Over time, the term "professional" came to refer to any calling that required intensive and formal training, followed by testing and licensing, all leading up to acceptance into a tight fraternity (early on, women need not apply) of similarly trained, like-minded practitioners, with a fat paycheck a given. The medical degree (or the law degree, or the degree in dentistry or architecture, for that matter) is a necessary part of preparation for entry into the profession. But the degree itself is not sufficient. One needs the degree plus the testing and licensing and formal acceptance into the profession.

All of which might seem to exclude the MFA or PhD in creative writing from consideration as a *professional* degree. Writers hardly need an MFA or any other degree to write, or to write well, or to sell their work and make a living doing so. And if you get caught writing without a degree in writing, so what? You're not going to get fined or sued like someone caught practicing medicine or law without the proper credentials. Write or don't write—who cares?

And yet these days, a young writer does need an MFA or, better yet, a PhD in creative writing in order to land a job teaching creative writing, assuming there's job to land, hardly a safe assumption in this era of budget cuts. And like the MD or JD, these degrees are not *sufficient* for entry into the teaching profession. One almost always needs in addition at least one published book, or conceivably a half-dozen short stories or poems placed in the "right" magazines, to land that teaching gig.

Of course, one might argue that *teaching* creative writing has nothing to do with the *practice* of creative writing. But if a young writer can land that teaching gig, and better yet hang on long enough to get tenure (the coveted job for life), he or she is home free, blessed with plenty of time to write. It's unlikely anyone will expect him or her to spend a lot of time actually teaching once he gets that teaching gig, unless he's unlucky enough to find himself in a college that actually puts a high value on teaching: usually a community or state college with down-to-earth expectations. The more prestige that attaches to an institution of higher learning, it seems, the less value is put on an instructor's setting foot in a classroom. In most elite research establishments, faculty who devote too much time and energy to their students are actually viewed with suspicion and disdain by their colleagues. So maybe it's no coincidence that while the MFA or PhD in creative writing is usually a necessary degree for a teaching job, the programs that confer these degrees rarely if ever offer training in *how* to teach effectively, providing opportunities to gain teaching experience only as a by-product of the system of aid, subsidy, and reward—and as a source of cheap labor, since the tenured profs can be counted on to teach as little as possible.

> Of course, one might argue that *teaching* creative writing has nothing to do with the *practice* of creative writing. But if a young writer can land that teaching gig, and better yet hang on long enough to get tenure ...

Absent other forms of reliable support for writers, absent a marketplace that values writing and rewards writers commensurate with their labor (or at least sufficient to cover basic necessities), a teaching gig is about as good as it gets, until those royalties kick in, anyway. Thus that teaching gig has *everything* to do with writing; it provides steady financial support and enough free time in which to fail, regroup, and recover.

Now what about the negative slice of that "professional success" pie chart Myers describes—the professional failure sector?

In arts such as writing, success can be achieved in a number of ways having nothing to do with filthy lucre. There's such a thing as *artistic success*. How do you measure that? Who does the measuring?

Cultural history is filled with accounts of artists who died unknown and impoverished only to have their genius—Johann Sebastian Bach springs to mind—recognized years later: *et viola!* Artistic success. If too late to do the poor dead bastard any good. These days, when the bottom line seems to rule all, a work's artistic qualities (however they're defined) would seem to be irrelevant, given that the truly big sellers are often by-the-numbers schlock, and better yet, schlock with vampires and zombies. At the same time, much of what does get praised these days by the critics as artistic successes often seems to be the result of an editor looking the other way while the writer cranks out a lot of self-indulgent, overblown prose devoid of anything even remotely resembling a comprehensible plot or clear writing. Indeed, such is the state of criticism today that an accessible story written clearly is often dismissed as *genre fiction*, never literature with a capital *L*.[35]

Some of our classmates got teaching gigs out of Iowa or soon after, and some gained supportive teaching positions only after years of hard work. Almost all of us have published something, in some cases a huge body of work. Many of us have actually made a living off our writing, in some cases a very good living, and without resorting to zombies and vampires to do it.

> ...A work's artistic qualities (however they're defined) would seem to be irrelevant, given that the truly big sellers are by-the-numbers schlock, and better yet, schlock with vampires and zombies.

Some of us found our way into journalism after Iowa, as writers or editors or both, and while some persnickety purists might view journalism as a poor substitute for art, we were lucky, those of us who practiced journalism back in the "good old days," in that we were starting out at a time when the New Journalism was all the rage and journalism was being reinvented, so we were often given freedom by our editors to indulge our urges to use the devices of fiction in our work.

Many of us who didn't teach and who wandered off into journalism or did something totally disconnected with the "po biz" or "prose biz" often drifted into careers where language skills and the ability to shape a narrative were valued and rewarded, and found there considerable professional, financial, and artistic satisfaction. As Schaeffer has noted in chapter one, the skills he learned and refined in the Iowa Workshop served him well in business, surprisingly (or predictably) in the glaring landscape of Las Vegas gaming, hospitality, and entertainment.

Comparisons between creative writing programs and other "professional" programs can be taken only so far. Once a young MD or JD leaves medical or law school, his or her next steps are along a well-defined path of supervised practice, testing, and licensing, all leading (if all goes well) to a long career and lots of money.

When a young writer leaves an MFA or creative writing PhD program, security is far from assured. There are no well-defined steps forward: few teaching jobs, no promise of publication, no certainty of anything other than existential challenge. The graduate of a creative writing program, even one as respected as the Iowa Writers' Workshop, faces a void where he or she is left to draw on whatever stores of determination, fortitude, self-esteem and pure faith he or she might have acquired beyond the classroom. And this could be the most rigorous form of professional training there is.

~

DOUG UNGER: It only makes sense to paraphrase Borges here. The exemplary lives of writers rarely make good examples for young writers because most of them, the vast majority of them, the successful writers, have gone through a long period where they've been marginalized, ignored, and they've had to persevere, before they achieve any success. By success, I mean in purely artistic terms, bringing your story or novel into that form in which it achieves what you as an artist want it to achieve.

Publication is something that happens by a combination of the excellence of the work and luck, and some writers just don't have the luck . . . or not right away. A writer can be writing at a fine level, but the culture won't turn its head until a certain time.

> By success, I mean in purely artistic terms, bringing your story or novel into that form in which it achieves what you as an artist want it to achieve.

Ray Carver was writing wonderful stories from 1959 on, but his breakthrough was two stories in *Esquire* in '72 and '73, I think, and his first mainstream collection came out in 1976, after seventeen years. But he just kept writing—poems and stories—writing when he could because he understood this to be his vocation, what he was supposed to do.

JAYNE ANNE PHILLIPS: Publishing is a process that is very separate from writing. It's important not to publish too soon before the work is ready. And it's important to see writing as independent of publishing.

Writing is the reason. Writing is the process through which writers make sense of the world; it's the creation or apprehension of meaning through language. In that sense, it is our religion, our way in, our connection to consciousness, to elements of divinity within human lives.

JOE HALDEMAN: The details about starting a writing career are so different now—the markets, the mediums, the audiences, the editorial scene—that I'd hesitate to advise a young writer in terms of my own beginning career.

In general terms, I'd say to never accept that writing has to be a life of failure. Your successes tend to be internal, personal. But they have to be thrilling or you're in the wrong line of work.

If you do triumph by some chance, and you do attain a measure of success in conventional terms, the obvious advice is still good: Don't take yourself too seriously. Don't be a son of a bitch with less successful writers. Don't expect it to last. Love it while you have it, but don't despise it when it leaves.

JACK LEGGETT: Of course the need for approval, some kind of approval, lurks out there. I don't mean to rid myself of it since . . . I'm realistic. I mean I *know* the publishing business; I know it's a disaster. Even young writers writing good books find it impossible to publish and that I, at ninety-one, would be a joke in the publishing office. Why are you publishing a ninety-one-year-old guy? He has no future. My old agent told me that. He said they don't publish anybody over fifty now. So I know nobody, other than some crazed editor, who would say we've *got* to do this book. But, still, I think the possibility that that might happen . . .

DOUG UNGER: Almost all the younger writers I've worked with have had to spend five or ten years or longer, after getting an MFA, somehow managing to keep going, to keep writing, before they had enough publications such that they felt they'd achieved what they set out to achieve and had carved out a place for themselves, or reached that point when they feel some comfort in their own shoes. That's very true of my own experience. It was seven years after Iowa before my first novel was accepted, *Leaving the Land*.

MICHELLE HUNEVEN: One of the stories I used to apply to the workshop kept nagging at me. Several people had told me that it wasn't a story, it was really a novel, and for some reason, I became determined to write that novel. I'd start it, go along for fifty or a hundred pages, and stall out. I had some lovely bits and pieces; several agents saw them and expressed interest. But I couldn't get the whole thing down as a piece.

By the time I was fifteen years out of the workshop, I'd published one short story (which ran in *Harper's* and won a GE Younger Writers Award) and some pieces from the alleged novel, but I couldn't seem to finish anything else. I was writing journalism, making an okay living as a restaurant critic and food writer, but I was no closer to my literary goals. At that point, I decided to quit writing fiction. It was too hard. I'd been trying to write fiction for a long time, and it was never easy, not for one minute. I only felt bad about my writing. Never good.

At the same time, I didn't want to write "puff" journalism all my life, either. So I decided to go back to school to become a Unitarian Universalist minister. I thought that the sermon was an elegant and possible literary form for me. I went to seminary in Claremont, California, and had a ball—I loved all the weird arcana and history and philosophy and the diverseness of my fellow seminarians. (Never mind that I didn't believe in God.) One day, during my second year, sitting in my Background of Contemporary Theology class, I had a revelation: I'd been starting my novel in the wrong place! Over and over again, I began it with a big event—which meant, from the get-go, I'd be introducing the three main characters at the same time I was trying to parse how the big event was affecting their relationships to one another. It came to me: Why not start the book where the three people first began their association? I went home that day and wrote seven pages in a whole new voice and thought, if I ever do want to write the damn book, this is where I could start. Then I went back to theology and forgot about it.

Maybe six months later, I got an idea for another novel—a novel about a young woman who wakes up in the middle of the night to find a deer in her house. I finished my second year at seminary and thought I'd start writing that over my summer vacation. But my fiction chops were very rusty and I wanted to warm up. So I thought, let's see if I can do anything with that new opening for the old novel. I started writing it again, and never went back to seminary. Three and a half years later, *Round Rock* was finished. Then I began work on the deer-in-the-house book, which became *Jamesland*.

> One day during my second year, sitting in my Background of Contemporary Theology class, I had a revelation: I'd been starting my novel in the wrong place!

ALLAN GURGANUS: I started selling stories when I was still at Iowa, when I was twenty-five or twenty-six. But I didn't publish my first book, *Oldest Living Confederate Widow Tells All*, until I was forty-two. I had the longest possible apprenticeship.

After I published "Minor Heroism" in the *New Yorker* in 1973 (William Maxwell was my editor, and John Cheever had made all that possible), Maxwell was waiting for more stories. He said, "You've written about a father and a son in a suburban neighborhood. Now tell about a scoutmaster in the same block, then I want you to write about the librarian in the neighborhood, and then the piano teacher. I want you to take every aspect of this boy's life, and hook that life to some local exemplar with the same complex stature that the father has. Then we'll put them all together and you'll have your first book."

It was brilliant advice. Did I follow it? Absolutely not. I ran as far in the other direction as possible. In part, it was the age of Donald Barthelme and Ronald Sukenick, all those guys not being read much anymore. I guess I did it partly from being fearful that the work I'd done in "Minor Heroism" was in some horrible way conventional. To prove my intellectual bona fides, I had to start telling stories from the end instead of the front. I had to divide things into sections and follow the Coover model, instead of the Cheever model, with Maxwell and Cheever telling me: "Baby step number one, then baby step number two..." They were showing me how to make a reputation, à la publishing in 1955. But I wanted the 1973 hipster version.

With the wisdom of being sixty, I realize what good advice they'd given me. I do think my life would have been much easier had I done exactly what they told me, but maybe not as interesting or complicated. But I would also like to read the book I might have written at that time. There is no chance I could compose that sweet book now.

And at first I didn't think I was good enough for a book. I had this exalted vision of what a book had to be, especially a book with my name on it! Not just a gathering of things I'd published; it had to be better than linked stories however good. I couldn't really yet see the interior logic of the stories I'd published, if gathered together. And I guess I'd had enough encouragement and support from teachers and friends and classmates along the way. I was regularly publishing in the *Atlantic* and the *New Yorker*, so there was a kind of validation. Waiting to be good enough, I just went on publishing uncollected stories. Somebody once called me the best-known young writer without a book... I was waiting to grow covers, as a turtle grows a shell.

It was brilliant advice. Did I follow it? Absolutely not. I ran as far in the other direction as possible. In part, it was the age of Donald Barthelme and Ronald Sukenick, all those guys not being read much anymore.

DOUG UNGER: It's frustrating, but you have to make sure that whatever you send out is the best you can do, that it's been ground down in the crucible of your creative process, then remade again, and again, and again, until it's so finished and polished that you can't imagine doing more to the story or book. Only then should you send out the manuscript. Slave over it, as Lenny Michaels used to chant at us, slave over the words, every word, and make sure every one of them is right. And then—and only then—very cautiously, make a submission.

Go to your teachers and fellow writers for advice. Get several readings by them before you send a book out. Look at the book lists or the literary magazines and find editors whose taste you admire, and go for those. Write the editors. And, if necessary, if you have to, try an agent, but make sure you've got your work finished to that point of excellence before you try.

I believe what Ray Carver always said, and something he lived his life by: write well enough, and publication will find your work. That along with some of good old-fashioned luck.

DENNIS MATHIS: I've always been a contrarian, so I'll volunteer to throw a monkey wrench into the accepted wisdom that if a fiction writer (let's stipulate that "writer" means someone with enough competence to graduate from an MFA program) just keeps writing regularly, a little every day, eventually he/she will succeed as an author. I agree with it up to a point, but it's a concept that shouldn't go unexamined.

It's certainly true that if you keep practicing fiction writing and keep studying good examples of the craft (or enlightening bad examples), you'll probably get better at it. If you keep accumulating competent pages day by day, you'll certainly end up with eighty thousand words ending with "the end," which is all publishers really care about anyway. This is a comforting thought to cling to throughout those inevitable miserable days.

But nothing matters once we assume that a good writer will find her audience somehow, someday, despite adversity.

A real writer (meaning a persistent writer) always succeeding in the end, if true, also nicely justifies the peculiar business model of the publishing industry: "Spend a few years making our product on your own time, at your own (or someone else's) expense, and then we'll consider paying you for it."

ANTHONY BUKOSKI: I had my first story taken on October 18, 1974, when I was still in the Workshop. I was so excited that I telephoned Jack Leggett that afternoon. I mean, I flipped out.

On Tuesday in the next week's workshop class, he asked me to tell about the magazine and how I elected to send a story there. I told the class that I had been going through the university library's wonderful collection of literary journals trying to find a journal or quarterly whose work might not be so much better than my own. *Wisconsin Review*, I thought, was a good place. They accepted the story. I was totally thrilled.

My first book of stories, *Twelve Below Zero*, was published twelve years later by New Rivers Press, a small press in the Twin Cities, which enjoys a thriving literary life.

By then, I had a teaching job. After I got my MFA, I stayed on at Iowa to take a PhD with major emphasis in American literature, Colonial to, say, the 1860s. I figured the MFA alone wasn't going to help me land a teaching job.

My heart wasn't often in literary studies though, as I yearned to write stories, not course essays. I hated writing that dissertation and needed an extension of the normal five-year period to finish it. Anyway, I had teaching assistantships at Iowa while my good wife worked various lousy jobs. She got me through the PhD program.

PhD in hand, I got a full-time college teaching position at Northwestern State University of Louisiana in Natchitoches, a beautiful, small, sleepy Southern town on the banks of the Cane River. I loved it there; so did Elaine.

But then fifty-five faculty and staff were let go as a result of the oil economy hitting hard times. We came back to Superior and I was hired at the University of Wisconsin-Superior to be visiting assistant professor and writer-in-residence. A year later, the job became full-time, and I have been here since.

Teaching did interfere with my writing. But I persisted, having work in *New Letters*, *Quarterly West*, the *Literary Review*, *New Orleans Review*, and other good quarterlies. Thank heavens for the great small and university presses. And thank heavens for the fiction imprints of major houses that side with literary fiction. There are plenty of good small presses around, for example, Graywolf and Coffee House in the Twin Cities. Coffee House was started by an Iowa grad. University presses are publishing a little more fiction. The University of Michigan and the University of Wisconsin have taken up a little slack.

A good writer will find a press.

DOUG UNGER: Even the smaller lit magazines can be enough to keep a writer going, going with the sense that it's worth doing, that someone will read what you write. Developing writers need to know that they have readers, or they end up abandoning what they do out of despair.

I had the added advantage, if I wanted to see my name in print, that I'd been writing for newspapers even before I came to the Workshop; I could find a newspaper or a free press to write articles for, and I did that for money. It's not the same as writing fiction, but you can at least feel that your language is doing something in the world.

SANDRA CISNEROS: I was getting published by these small Latino, ethnic, and women's presses while I was still at Iowa. I had a solid relationship with these small presses. While I didn't think my stuff was going to get recognized or "found" in these little magazines, I figured at least people would know where to find me if they were looking. It was one of these small presses that first published *House on Mango Street*. That was in 1984, five years after Iowa.

By the time *Mango Street* was published, I'd been doing all sorts of things to survive while I wrote. Right after Iowa, I got a job at an alternative high school in Chicago. I left Iowa on a Friday and was at work on Monday at the Latino Young Alternative High School. I worked with kids who'd dropped out or been pushed out because they were in gangs or had a baby or a violent history or some kind of record. They were sweet kids, just irresponsible . . .

I became known as the teacher whose kids won writing awards. But it was consuming my life. After about three and a half years, I applied for and got a job as a recruiter and counselor to disadvantaged kids at Loyola University of Chicago, my alma mater. That's where I got some of my stories for *Mango Street*, there and the alternative high school. I worked at Loyola for about a year and a half, and then got my first NEA grant in poetry (I'd win another for fiction in '87) and moved to Provincetown.

DENNIS MATHIS: I was one of the many graduates in my Workshop class who didn't get a teaching job. I went back to Chicago broke, in debt, unemployed, alone (that was the worst part, of course). My first "survival" job was as a street messenger in the financial district. But I was conscientious—my employers were keeping me alive, and I thought I owed it them to make this job my first priority. After the first grueling, bitterly cold winter, I worked myself up to an indoor job on the trading floor of the stock options exchange at the Board of Trade. I was one of those guys in the color-coded jackets you see on the news, staring at monitors over the "pits" and yelling arcane stuff about puts and calls. It was surreal, but also as "real world" as it gets. It was fascinating stuff to a curious type like me, and I actually got paid while I was learning a career. I made friends. I bought Italian shoes. It made fiction writing seem pretty childish.

At night, I'd go home and flop on my mattress on the floor and think about buying groceries, doing laundry, cooking, finding a girlfriend, sex, love, and most of all, sleep. I suppose I managed to do some writing somehow because I got some things published and won an award or two during those three years. I got accepted to the Provincetown Fine Arts Work Center for a six-month residency fellowship.

SANDRA CISNEROS: I'd applied to the Fine Arts Work Center in Provincetown several times, but never got in. There were lots of people from Iowa there, including Michael Cunningham and my friend Dennis Mathis. Dennis needed a summer roommate, and I needed to get away from Chicago so I could concentrate on my writing. My publisher had been after me for more of these little vignettes I was doing, and I said yeah, yeah, they're right here, in my head, and he said, well, when you're ready, when you have them finished, send them and we'll have a book.

I figured if I took my NEA grant and went to live in Provincetown with Dennis, I could finish it.

DENNIS MATHIS: Sandy and I shared a cheap apartment in Provincetown, with Michael Cunningham as the unofficial third roommate. Sandra was writing *House on Mango Street* in the backyard, having me edit the stories each night.

Norris Church, Norman Mailer's wife, rented a painting studio across the parking lot from our apartment, so sometimes we'd fling open the front door and accidentally knock over Mailer walking by in his Bermuda shorts. It was a tiny town where you couldn't spit without hitting some famous writer or artist.

Sand, salt, sunburn . . . it was a memorable summer.

SANDRA CISNEROS: Michael would sneak in through the window to sleep with me. Or I'd climb out the window and go sleep at his house. We had perfect sleeping arrangements. Michael was fun and funny, my summer fling . . .

Before I left for Provincetown, I had bought a one-way ticket to Greece; my departure date was my deadline. But *Mango Street* wasn't done when it came time to head for Greece, so I packed the manuscript, kissed Michael on the cheek and said good-bye, and went to live on the island of Hydra. That was September 1982. I finished *Mango Street* that November on Hydra, went to Athens, and stuck it in an envelope and dropped it in the mail. Then went to France, then Italy, Sarajevo, back to Greece at the end of '83, and then I ran out of money and went back home to Chicago and got a job as a nanny through the fall and winter.

> Michael would sneak in through the window to sleep with me. Or I'd climb out the window and go sleep at his house. We had perfect sleeping arrangements. My summer fling . . .

Then in 1984, I took a job in San Antonio as arts administrator for the lit program of the Guadalupe Cultural Arts Center. I did that for about a year and a half. Anything to survive while I kept the writing going.

JENNIE FIELDS: While I was still at Iowa, I applied for a grant to the Fine Arts Work Center and got in. Iowa ended in May, and Provincetown started in October. When I got there, it looked like the moon: very barren, the only trees were scrub pines, at the very tip of Cape Cod. It was a unique town, to say the least. In the winter, the only people there, except for the people at the work center, were Portuguese fishermen and gay men, and a few were both. The theaters were closed, and only one restaurant was open.

I lived on $100/month there, and I still saved money. I paid $15/week for groceries. I had a small studio with a kitchen.

At the work center, there were a lot of communal readings and art shows. With ten writers and ten artists, it was all very incestuous. I was with some interesting people, though. We'd have long talks and wait through blizzards together. I had my heart broken when my boyfriend went off with another girl, and then another guy said he was in love with me, and then I had a roaring case of mono for six weeks and . . . well, you get the idea. Soap opera in the dunes.

I loved it there on the Cape, and I still go back to P-town and rent a place on the water for two weeks just to write. There was something about being at the end of the earth that made it a great place to write. I wrote a lot during my year there, though I didn't do much with what I wrote. I was working on a novel that didn't amount to anything. But it was an important part of my learning how to be a writer. It made writing important.

CATHERINE GAMMON: After Iowa I went back to Berkeley and worked freelance typing and teaching writing to a few people in an informal way, patching it together while I started another, a novel. Doug Unger and Amy were in San Francisco, and there was a writers' scene they were part of, but in my life that was more where the party was, not the writing, and I had a kind of fear of falling back into some completely anonymous, welfare-mother existence.

And then in the same week my first story acceptance came in the mail, I was offered the fellowship to Provincetown. At the end of summer, my daughter and I got off that little airplane and got a ride through the sand and the scrub pines and I felt like I was home. When the fellowship year was up, we stayed in Provincetown, and I worked for the local newspaper, first as a typesetter, then writing about the summer arts scene. I also worked as a chambermaid in resort season and took minutes for local government boards, and I continued to write. In the off-season, it didn't cost a lot to live there.

In 1979 I suddenly found myself with a teaching job in Fredonia, New York. It was a last-minute thing, too late for them to advertise; someone I had just met the month before knew I was available. During the year I taught there, I was given an NEA grant, so in spring of '80, I went back to Provincetown.

That year Dennis Mathis arrived as a fellow, and there were many others who had been at Iowa a little before or after me. There were wonderful readers in Provincetown, Roger Skillings was one, and Dennis especially. It was like the Workshop, but more so. I was getting a kind of editorial input that was—instead of "you can't do this" or "don't do that" or "who cares" or whatever, you know, dismissive, which is what we got a little of at Iowa, and that I dished out myself—this was more like "if you want to do this, this is a way of doing what you want to do," or "this would enhance what you're doing." A nourishing kind of editorial relationship, more intimate than a just "this sucks" kind. But it was still very sharp, really sharp. These are really sharp, good readers. There was a quality and character there that I thrived on.

DENNIS MATHIS: After my six-month residency was up, Michael Cunningham and I rented a rickety beach house in Provincetown and stayed on for the summer. Michael waited tables, and I got a job, through Cathy Gammon, at the local newspaper, eventually became production manager there for a few years. (I hired Michael as a typesetter, so I suppose the paper can now say it had a Pulitzer Prize winner on its staff.)

Then a few blurry years . . . Yaddo, an NEA grant, a second FAWC fellowship. Boston, New York City, a Connecticut teaching gig for a summer . . .

FAWC hired me as chairman of the Writing Committee ($9,000 a year), and for two years, I got to schmooze with Grace Paley, Alan Dugan, Ray Carver, and (sigh) so many others who are now gone . . . and got to call up people and tell them they'd been accepted, the best part of the job.

But I got burned out on the whole literary scene. I didn't fit in. I didn't have a book to my credit, so I was the perpetual "who is this guy?" character at cocktail parties. And I didn't like New York.

My father died suddenly, and my mother needed me, so I moved back to Illinois and threw my sorry novel in the dumpster and gave up writing permanently. Got work as a typesetter, eventually got a job in the corporate communications department of Amoco, the big oil company in Chicago, where I worked for seven years.

I was happy as a clam not being in the creative writing field (except for reading Sandra's drafts).

DOUG BORSOM: Writing is a wonderful thing, but it's not the only thing. If you aren't also good at something else, you may be missing out. Nabokov had his butterflies, and Conrad his Master Mariner's certificate. Mailer, Capote, and others have proven that nonfiction can be art. Tracy Kidder and John McPhee have demonstrated a different kind of nonfiction art. Fiction best-seller lists are loaded with formulaic junk that doesn't begin to rise to the level of creativity and style of these writers.

A downside to programs like Iowa's is that they may create the perception that a life in academia is the one true path for a creative writer. One size doesn't fit all. Eliot spent eight years working for a bank. Wallace Stevens was a lawyer and later an officer in an insurance company. He turned down a position at Harvard because he didn't want to leave the insurance job.

Books by the Bed

DOUG BORSOM: Currently on my bedside table reading pile are the three most recent *New Yorkers*, a collection of stories by Damon Runyan, *Silas Marner*, and *Knowledge and Wonder* by the late physicist Victor Weisskopf.

GARY IORIO: After Iowa I came home and applied for a job at Kingsborough Community College. I had an interview, showed them my resume. They said, "We pay $3,000 a year, and at the end of the year, you don't come back." And you know what happened? I didn't get that lousy job!

So I'm looking down the barrel of supporting myself as a writer . . . I wanted to get married and have a family. I wanted to live in the metro New York area. I got various jobs; I worked for the government for three years, the Social Security Administration, drinking at my desk like most of my coworkers. Then to law school, the path of least resistance. I went into real estate law. I've been doing it ever since. I like it a lot. I like my clients. No emergencies. No one dies.

I didn't write for the better part of thirty years. Iowa gave me an excellent opportunity. My problem was making the transition from being a student of writing to being a writer. The problem wasn't anything that happened at Iowa, but something I brought to the game. I was easily distracted, but unlike many of my Iowa classmates, these distractions were not the demands of living and paying the bills while I tried to write. I created my own diversions. I spent five years where the racetrack was "my life." That type of shit.

> I didn't write for the better part of thirty years. Iowa gave me an excellent opportunity. My problem was making the transition from being a student of writing to being a writer. The problem wasn't anything that happened at Iowa, but something I brought to the game . . .

Now, I feel a wonderful passion to write again. This is an awakening. It's a great feeling.

JEFFREY ABRAHAMS: I had a moment of sheer, incandescent panic at the end of my time in the Workshop. I'd finished my thesis, turned it in, and suddenly it dawned on me: I couldn't do anything out there in the world, other than maybe to teach. Not that I could have gotten a teaching job. There was a glut of MFAs then. I assumed only the brightest of the brightest at Iowa were going to get what few teaching jobs there were; all the programs created in the first boom were staffed up. Besides, I'd taught freshman comp at Miami University before coming to Iowa and I hated it. What could I do?

BILL MCCOY: I taught college for a year and a half after Iowa. It was kind of a fluke that I got the job. I was pulling in $9,000 a year and did it for a year and a half. They wouldn't hire me for a fourth semester because then they would have had to put me on tenure track. They would much rather have found someone else to hire for nine grand a year, and then keep doing that year after year. Cheap labor.

But after a year and a half there, I was eligible for unemployment. So I went back to State College, Pennsylvania, my hometown, planning to write, but after three months, I hated not working. I couldn't write anything, I felt useless.

I ended up taking a job at a local paper, which actually paid me less than unemployment. I had no experience, but they thought I could write, and they liked the idea of having a local boy.

ALLAN GURGANUS: Teaching's a wonderful way of not making a living. What's odd, we're so susceptible to other people, and so starved for praise, that you take a job at Burger King thinking you'll free up your mind for early morning writing. And soon you're promoted to manager, and then to the national level, because you're smart and work hard and pay attention and come on time, so there's a danger that you become so involved in whatever else you're doing short-term, there's no juice left over for the fiction.

It would be better if your parents had some money. Or if you sold drugs. . . . But that corporate ladder is more dangerous than most, I guess.

JANE SMILEY: I had a PhD, so after Iowa, I got a job as an assistant professor at Iowa State. I had a child, and the world of Ames was wonderful for me, convenient in every way, with great day care, and nothing going on, so I had plenty of time to write. I also met other writers in Ames, my colleagues, and I shared a lot with them. We had good students in our grad program (though when we called them to admit them, we had to be sure that they knew we were Iowa State, not the U of I).

Teaching helped my writing, especially doing the draft method, because I often found that analyzing the knots in my students' stories gave me ways to analyze the knots in my own stories.

Iowa State was a much more idio-syncratic and in some ways distinct world than the University of Iowa. I remember standing in the middle of the quad and looking at the buildings, thinking, "So this is the university that the legislature prefers." I found Iowa State inspiring—both *A Thousand Acres* and *Moo* grew out of what I learned at Iowa State.

Teaching helped my writing, especially doing the draft method, because I often found that analyzing the knots in my students' stories gave me ways to analyze the knots in my own stories. And teaching is good because you are talking about what you are thinking about. And living and working with people who love literature is also great. But the academic environment is a little stultifying and time consuming.

My only other job has been child rearing, and for that, you need some kind of trustworthy day care and the will to use it. At the same time, children are endlessly inspiring, both as your children and as sample humans.

JOE HALDEMAN: Joining a writing faculty can be deadly. I managed it, but then I'd been a writer for some time before taking the plunge. (After I'd taught at MIT for ten years, I considered quitting, but then looked at my bibliography and found that I'd written the same number of books in those ten years as in the ten previous.)

If you don't do the teaching route (and can't find a spouse with a job), I think the best bet is to look for something part-time that involves dealing with a variety of people. Counseling would be an obvious choice, though I'm not sure that good writers necessarily make good counselors! ("Tell the bastard to take his job and shove it!" "Tell him you'd rather dig septic tanks than put up with his shit." "I'd murder the bitch and then chop her bones up with a shovel.")

If you have a religious leaning, I think that being a preacher or priest in charge of a small congregation could be ideal. Write one short sermon a week, and stories under a nom de plume. Preferably hot gay S and M.

I think that newspaper or magazine writing won't work for most people. I spent a couple of months working for *Astronomy* magazine after Iowa, and it was great fun, but I didn't write two paragraphs of fiction during that period. You get burned out cranking out pedestrian prose all day long.

ERIC OLSEN: While it's true that it's tough to write fiction after cranking out pedestrian prose, I have to admit I rather enjoyed cranking out pedestrian prose, especially when my editors happened to be old chums from Iowa. Even better when the check cleared. . . . I did the occasional piece for Bill McCoy for years after he became a magazine editor, and the occasional piece for Don Wallace when he was a magazine editor.

MICHELLE HUNEVEN: All the time I was in seminary, and when I was writing *Round Rock* and *Jamesland*, I worked as a restaurant critic. It is, in many ways, the ideal job for a writer. Restaurant reviews are not like a magazine feature: you don't have to do a full immersion into the material; you eat a few meals, think about them, maybe do a tiny bit of research, and then write 750 words. There is a lot of room for creativity, and also for developing one's own voice. In writing about food, really, you can write about any and everything: people, customs, money, agriculture, the culture, etc. Also, restaurant reviewing is good if you're a writer because it keeps you fed. It gets you out of the house. It forces you to have a social life. And, of course, it provides a steady base income, which can be augmented by taking on the occasional feature assignment and/or teaching gigs. I reviewed restaurants from 1987 to 2003. (Of course, now I rarely eat out. What a treat to cook, to make what I actually want to eat!)

Once I really started writing fiction—i.e., when I finally got hold of my first novel and was writing daily, in the early 1990s—my journalism did not interfere. In fact, it was a big help. It supported me and also, while working on a long project, it was a pleasure to finish something on a weekly basis.

> . . . and when I was writing *Round Rock* and *Jamesland,* I worked as a restaurant critic. It is, in many ways, the ideal job for a writer.

Only once did journalism seriously disrupt my novel writing. For three months in 1994, my editor went on maternity leave and brought me in to help edit the food section. (Before doing this, she'd had me edit some pieces—and was struck by what I did with them. "Where did you learn how to edit like that?" she asked. "Writing fiction," I said.) Showing up at a nine-to-five job, editing and writing food pieces and restaurant reviews left *no* time for fiction writing. But I had a wonderful time. Working with other writers and editors and a test kitchen was great fun, especially after working alone for all those years.

BILL MCCOY: When I left Iowa, I felt like a failure. I think one of the reasons I felt bad about my writing when I got out, I was still trying to write something that would make my former classmates change their minds about me.

But at the newspaper, I had to churn out copy every morning and then had the opportunity to see it printed, out in the world, the same afternoon. I got some encouragement from people I respected and started feeling better about my writing. I was writing a lot and making sort of a living at it, and I was writing for people who liked what I was doing and who wanted me to succeed.

While I was at the paper, the city editor told me I belonged in New York. She had some connections there and got me an interview with a friend of hers at a travel magazine. It was called *Signature*, a Diners Club magazine about travel and the good life. It was sold in the mid-'80s to Condé Nast, which shut it down and used the subscriber list to start *Condé Nast Travel*.

From there, I went to various magazines, and eventually became the only male editor at *Parents* magazine. When my daughter was born, I wrote a few essays about being a father and sent them to an agent, who was a new father himself. The essays resonated with him, I guess, because he helped me sell it to a real publisher: Times Books, at the time part of Random House. The book was *Father's Day: Notes from a Dad in the Real World*. It was a snapshot of a period, an important time in my life, and it will always mean a lot to our family and especially my daughter, I hope. The book also resonated with the times, I suppose, as a lot of guys my age were becoming fathers then and trying to be more involved than their own dads had been. To paraphrase something Calvin Trillin said, when you're writing, suddenly changing diapers becomes an attractive alternative.

> When I left Iowa, I felt like a failure. I think one of the reasons I felt bad about my writing when I got out, I was still trying to write something that would make my former classmates change their minds about me.

JEFFREY ABRAHAMS: After the panic subsided, I realized that I could do something that I'd been doing for many years: advertising copywriting. While in high school in Dayton, Ohio, I started writing for a small ad agency. In college I worked in radio a bit. I knew how to write print ads and radio commercials. I also wrote some ad copy for small businesses in Iowa City to make a little cash for living expenses. A week after I graduated from the Workshop, I found a job at a local 80-watt AM radio station called KCJJ that played the same ten songs every hour all summer long. It was just outside of Iowa City in the middle of a cornfield. I wrote commercials, hosted a Sunday talk show program, did a little sales work, and I think I got paid about $200 a month.

After three months of working in Iowa City through one of the hottest summers anyone could remember—happily indoors in an air-conditioned building—I was invited by a college buddy to work as the staff writer for an all-jazz station in Denver. I left Iowa City in the fall after playing a lot of softball and saying good-bye to a lot of people, many who would become lifelong friends.

For the next two years, I lived in the world of jazz, wrote for *Downbeat Magazine* and local newspapers, interviewed the greats like Dizzy Gillespie . . . I even had a nightly poetry reading segment I called "Poetry 'Round Midnight." Every day, I'd record a poem, and the DJ at night would play it at midnight. I was receiving books from publishers, so I still had my hand in poetry. Had a pretty big audience, too, bigger than I ever had for my own poetry.

And I was building a portfolio. So when I had a chance to interview for an advertising job in San Francisco, I had something I could actually show that had more impact on potential employers than a degree from the prestigious Iowa Writers' Workshop. Once I started working in advertising in San Francisco, it seemed that a life in academia was receding faster and faster in the rearview mirror.

Books by the Bed

JEFFREY ABRAHAMS—I have a bedroom filled with books. And stashes all around me. I happen to have open right now *The Gathering Storm* by Winston Churchill, on the early history of WWII. It's impossible to read without hearing Churchill's voice. I'm also reading about wine, fishing, and photography on a regular basis. And jazz. Only a dash of fiction right now. And always a book of Billy Collins poems by my side, presently *Ballistics*. Also by the bed: back issues of the *New Yorker*; *Digital Photographer's Handbook*, Tom Ang; *The Tango Singer*, Tomas Martinez; *Monk's Music*, Gabriel Solis; *A Hedonist in the Cellar*, Jay McInerney; *Body & Soul*, Frank Conroy; *Complete Stories*, Dorothy Parker; *Travelers' Tales, Spain*, Lucy McCauley; *Death, Taxes, and Leaky Waders*, John Gierach; and *The Raw and the Cooked*, Jim Harrison.

JENNIE FIELDS: I decided in the end that I didn't want to be a grantsman—living off arts grants—the rest of my life. Some people were cyclical grantsmen, and I thought that's not real. I wanted to do something real.

When I was still in Iowa, Vance told us about someone who had just shot a commercial on his farm. He had some of the man's business cards and said if any of us was interested in advertising, we should give the guy a call, so I took one and carried it around in my purse for a year while I was in Provincetown. Then at the end of my time there, I pulled it out (all dirty and mutilated from sitting on the bottom of my purse for a year) and called the man. He sent me a creative test to take, part of which was inventing three products that had marketing potential and creating an ad campaign for them. I got hired.

When I took the job, I thought I would work for a year, save money, and then write full-time. When I started my career, women were the exception. It really was like *Mad Men*. Sometimes my clients were more interested in the slit in my skirt than the campaign I was showing them. (The experience taught me not to wear skirts with slits.) I never thought I'd be in advertising as long as I was, thirty-two years. Insane longevity. You're supposed to be killed off at forty.

Advertising was great when I started, and I had a lot of fun. I'd get to produce the music, choose a director, direct famous actors to do voice-overs. I'd get to travel all over the world.

Around the time I started living with my first husband, my writing took a backseat. I somehow thought that I had to give up what mattered to me when I committed to a relationship. Of course, it was a subconscious thing and terribly destructive. When my daughter was about three, however, I began to feel a sense of loss and thought I had to reclaim myself. So I started writing again. That was eighteen years ago.

And then my husband and I separated, and we got divorced, and the company I was working for at the time was taken over by a crazy lady who fired half the staff, and so there I was with a small child, divorced with no income and I was terrified.

But it was a wonderful thing to face my worst fears and survive them. In the end, I got five months of severance, and I had a new job in three weeks; and shortly after, I published my first novel, *Lily Beach*. It was 1993. I was forty years old. It took me far too long. But I'm glad I got there.

CATHERINE GAMMON: While I was in Provincetown, I wrote a story that I felt was a world beyond anything I'd done before. I could feel it, you know, one of those things where you just really know you did something you never did before. And that's not to minimize any of the work I'd done before, but it was like I had jumped a step in some deep and visible way, and I sent it out into the world, and it was published in *The Missouri Review*. And I think that was the story that got me an agent. It was called "Night Vision."

That was a successful story in the literary marketplace, and it started a series of stories that were individual stories, somewhat experimental, that could be published as individual stories, but which I was actually constructing as chapters of a novel. There was something strategic in that approach. That's something that comes out of Iowa perhaps, to be strategic. I was writing chapters as short stories that could go into the marketplace because I was looking at that marketplace.

Along with *Missouri Review, Fiction International* and *Agni* each published one of these story/chapters, but the novel remained homeless. That was *China Blue*. It's my Provincetown novel, and I still kind of love it.

JENNIE FIELDS: My first novel was published by Athenaeum. My editor there, Lee Goerner, was the perfect first editor for me because he understood what I was trying to do. He was kind, thoughtful, encouraging. He died, at the age of forty-eight, before I completed my second book. I was devastated!

Some editors I've had since have been great, some horrible. I got orphaned at one place. The editor there was excited about my second book, *Crossing Brooklyn Ferry*, but she left and I became the foster child of another editor who really didn't love my book at all. She wanted a complete rewrite, but it was all picky subjective stuff. She didn't understand the music or poetry of what I was trying to do. We fought tooth and nail.

> I love a hands-on editor who can say, "When I read this, I think it might be better as . . ." I love an editor with the insight to say, "This character isn't developed" or "I don't understand the motivation" or . . .

I love a hands-on editor who can say, "When I read this, I think it might be better as . . ." I love an editor with the insight to say, "This character isn't developed" or "I don't understand the motivation" or "This person's dialogue sounds like that person's." Writers need feedback they can sink their teeth into.

DENNIS MATHIS: Turns out I had a knack for computer programming, graphics software, databases, publishing technology.

One day at Amoco, I came across this new thing called the World Wide Web. Only a few tech-heads like me knew about it. I spent two years passionately lobbying the top executives of Amoco to get them to realize this was important, and finally they committed $475,000 and put me in charge of developing the company's first website. When that was a big success, I was picked to do an intranet for the entire forty-thousand-employee organization. But I was restless, so I put my resume on the Internet (a wildly new idea at that time, when Yahoo! had indexed a whopping twelve-thousand pages).

A California company near Malibu hired me, paid to move my wife, my cat, and me from Chicago, doubled my salary, and gave me thousands of stock options at $20 a share. The company went public my first full day on the job, opening at $80 a share.

So I rode the tech bubble at several such start-ups, became a millionaire (on paper) several times. And then along came Dubya, and soon the dot-com bubble (puffed up by deregulation) imploded. My employer went belly-up, laid us all off, I turned fifty, and 9/11 happened—all in one month. That left me competing with a zillion teenagers making websites for the cost of a Slurpee.

But all those years I'd been in corporations, Sandra had relied on me as her unofficial editor. When some stranger sent her a manuscript Sandra thought was promising but needed a lot of work, she talked the author into hiring me to edit it. That book was a success, so now I'm scrambling around as a freelance book editor.

Editing other people's manuscripts has made me realize I'm still reasonably good at fiction, at least at seeing how to improve someone else's work. Writing my own stuff is still agonizing for me.

DOUG BORSOM: Nothing I learned at Iowa helped me get a job after graduation. But I got a teaching position because I had an MFA from the Iowa Writers' Workshop. Back then, the cachet in academic circles that went with attending Iowa surprised me. It seems even more powerful today, when attorneys, dentists, and the like all seem to know about the program.

After I graduated, I got married. I had no job. I sent out résumés, looked for any kind of work. I was getting desperate, looking at retail sales, anything. Then Southwest Missouri State University called. They needed someone in a hurry.

I spent three years teaching at Missouri. I enjoyed the students and teaching, but there were the to-be-expected department politics. And I wasn't comfortable with the idea of a life teaching lit and creative writing while also trying to write. Many have done this and done it wonderfully. But for me, it would have been too claustrophobic.

I liked the idea of doing something orthogonal to writing. So I went back to school at the University of Wisconsin studying physics first, then mathematics. I'd started my undergraduate career in the sciences and had never lost my interest, so it wasn't as odd as it might seem. After that, going into the computer industry was a natural. It was the early 1980s, the field was exploding, and there were lots of choices.

Over the years I did a lot of different things, including software and hardware testing, and multimedia development. The single biggest chunk of my career involved developing secure versions of operating systems, like UNIX, and demonstrating to an independent panel that the software met standards set by the National Security Agency. Trips to the restroom at a secure site always included an escort who waited discreetly outside while I conducted my business.

I never thought of myself as having stopped writing through all of this. But when I worked in the computer industry, sometimes months would go by without my writing anything. These periods usually coincided with the push to get a new product out, which could mean a couple months of sixty- to seventy-hour weeks. Once, I didn't write for maybe half a year. I didn't like that, but it didn't kill me.

DENNIS MATHIS: I remember when Vonnegut came back to do a guest workshop/reading at Iowa. He said he'd pay for a plaque dedicated to the 90 percent of Workshop graduates who don't go on to become writers. He said, "Can you imagine if 90 percent of the graduates of the Harvard Law School didn't become lawyers?"

ERIC OLSEN: I remember that, how bummed I was. Here I was, trying to "be a writer," living on a pittance, and he's telling us all how hopeless it was to try to be a writer. Like I needed him to tell me that? I loved his stuff; I'd come of age reading it. He was my hero, ferkrissakes, my role model, and I'm listening to him go on about how we should quit? Worse, here's a guy who'd made it! And now he's telling us we can't, like he's special and we're not? I didn't realize at the time he made his real money as a Saab dealer . . .

Not only was I bummed, I was pissed. He was getting paid by the university to come to read, do a master class, impart a bit of his wisdom, go to a party afterward with students, and get drunk and be an asshole like so many of the other visiting writers we admired so much, so where did he get off, famous writer that he was, giving us nothing but a lot of whiney crap and trying to discourage us? And he wasn't the only one; again and again, big-shot writers would come through and spew the same rot. Of course, I think they thought they had our best interests in mind. Maybe they thought telling us to give up was wisdom. Probably it was.

But as much as anyone, these big-shot writers must have understood that writers can't help themselves sometimes; writing's not a choice.

DENNIS MATHIS: Yeah, but what I also remember was Vonnegut saying that if it weren't for the 90 percent of Workshop grads (and their students, children, friends . . .) who didn't become professional writers, there wouldn't be any worthy readers for those who did. That was the point of the plaque.

It actually gave me hope. No matter what becomes of my own career, maybe there's honor just in being a dedicated consumer of literature. Maybe that's also success. I still live by that faith.

By the way, here's another hearsay story. Apparently, at the party at Leggett's house after Vonnegut's reading (a riot, a circus, a blast, like no other reading I'd been to in two years at Iowa), Vonnegut installed himself in Jack's bedroom where he thought he'd be out of the way. Naturally, he found himself surrounded by twittering coeds: "Can I get you another drink, Kurt? Some hors d'oeuvres? Is there anything you want?"

"You know what I wish?" Vonnegut (reportedly) said.

"No, Kurt. What do you wish?" they twittered.

"I wish I was dead."

I suspect future generations will consider Kurt Vonnegut the definitive American realist.

ALLAN GURGANUS: I'd received a Stegner right after I finished the Workshop. At the time, the Stegner was one year; now it's two. I stayed on at Stanford for a second year to teach as a Jones Lecturer. That was supposed to be a two-year appointment, but I didn't stay for two years. I really didn't feel at ease or at home in California. The light was like a spilled white latex paint splashed daily on everything.

I was writing and publishing all along. Always stories, in okay magazines. But my community per se, my writing circle, was dispersed; I didn't have a true network of readers. It's true, I had Workshop friends who still read my work, and I theirs, but this was back before FedEx and e-mail. Anytime you mailed something, it was a two-, two-and-a-half-week wait before you heard anything; it was like the fucking Pony Express, so all that immediacy that I was used to at Iowa was lost, and I had to fall back on my own resources. I was very much on my own with my work.

It was a very isolated time and, in a way, a very dark time, but I kept working through the depression. I was as flat on my back as I've ever been, but you learn to live with it, to work around it, to take the portion of the day that's the most hopeful and promising and use it to work, and then just coast into the shadows of the rest of it. Eventually, publication cured me like a tailor-made psychotropic drug.

GORDON MENNENGA: Ted Solotaroff wrote a great essay, "Writing in the Cold," about this. Once you get out into the real world, you don't have anyone to talk to about writing; you have your wife or husband and maybe a friend or two, but none of the camaraderie you had in a workshop, none of the things that encouraged you to write and be more creative in the first place. You work on a novel for two or three or four years and send it out and no one wants to read it; agents don't care about it; people tell you things like "it's not timely," and you want to kill yourself. You really end up facing your naked ambition, and for me, at least for a year or two, I wasn't seeing what I wanted to see.

ERIC OLSEN: I think it's especially important for young writers just out of a writing program to try to remain part of some sort of community of writers like they'd had in school, a few people whose opinion they can trust, people who'll read their new story or poem or chapter. For that matter, community is just as important for not-so-young writers long out of school. The Internet and e-mail are a big help in this, as Allan notes, because the immediacy of e-mail recreates some of the immediacy we all enjoyed in a workshop.

It's especially helpful to have others waiting for that next poem or story; the thought of disappointing one's "fans" can be a useful motivation, especially if one is given to periods of ennui and self-doubt. In a way, being part of a community of writers is a little like being in a twelve-step program; the fear of letting others down is probably a more powerful motivation than the fear of letting oneself down.

SANDRA CISNEROS: The low point for me came in '87. After San Antonio, I got a job teaching at Cal State, Chico, and thought, Shit, I hate academia. I was in such a funk, at a real low point. I couldn't make any money. All I could do was teach, and I didn't feel like I belonged there. I nosedived into depression, I had this low self-esteem, and I had these terrible students, and I thought it was my fault. I stopped writing. I had no one to confide in. I just felt like nothing . . . a failure. I even started plotting my suicide, how I was going to do it in my car, close the windows, do it on the weekend so no one would find me. I was thirty-three years old. I found out later from a spiritual person that everyone has their year of the cross, and it happens around age thirty-three.

But I was lucky. I went home, and Dennis made an appointment for me with his Jungian analyst in Chicago. I was filled with such shame about my inability to take care of myself.

My advice to young writers? Make sure you have friends keeping you alive during the dark nights of the soul. And make sure you have a therapist if you are clinically depressed, and make sure you recognize depression as a disease. Don't be ashamed of being depressed.

And then it all turned around for me. First, I got a second NEA grant, which reminded me that I'm a writer. And then I got a great agent, Susan Bergholz.

ALLAN GURGANUS: During those years I was eking out a living with grants and publishing stories and taking seven years to write my first novel, I had a famous agent, now dead, Mario Puzo's agent for *The Godfather*. She bought a stone mansion with her 10 percent of Puzo. She discovered Thomas Pynchon. She had an extraordinary stable. She took me on because of Cheever. Only later did I realize that she always thought of me as this slender little thing that John found in Iowa City; she never really took my measure as a writer.

There are no shortcuts. It was her young assistant, Eric Ashworth, who saw what I was trying to do. I later learned that he was sending out my work on his own, after hours. He was an early victim of HIV in New York, and for me and many other young writers he helped, he will always be a hero.

JENNIE FIELDS: How do you find an agent? I tell people to first figure out who writes like you do. Who do you relate to in your own writing? Call the publisher, tell them you want to write an article about the writer, and ask them, "Who's their agent?" Then send a query to the agent.

But I found my agent, Lisa Bankoff, through a friend. She was my friend's agent, and my friend recommended her. Lisa was one of five agents I sent queries to, and out of those five, two said they were interested in seeing my book. I sent it to both. Both said they were interested, but then Lisa asked, "Do you like Edith Wharton?" I said yes, and she said, "Your writing reminds me of her..." Edith Wharton is my favorite writer, so I was thrilled. I had named *Lily Beach* as a homage to Lily Bart in *House of Mirth*. And without my saying a thing, Lisa got me. I was sold.

You want an agent who understands your book, understands what you're trying to do. I've been with Lisa since 1990. She's represented all of my books. She's a go-getter and tough. Sometimes an agent can be terse with you if they're tough, but you don't need a mother; you need someone to give advice. You need a shark, someone to get that best offer...

It helps to have an agent with a big agency. Lisa's at ICM. The larger agencies have agents dedicated to selling foreign rights, and you're assigned a movie agent out in LA. I sold the movie option for *Crossing Brooklyn Ferry* three times through my agency. And foreign rights as well.

I'm probably Lisa's least-known client. I guess I hope that will change with my new book! I guess every writer has to believe that recognition is always around the corner.

DOUG UNGER: Of course, no matter what success you have, it'll never be enough. Your work will never be good enough, and no matter how it's received, it'll never be good enough, and you'll always be dissatisfied with your work and with your life. That's just the nature of being an artist, and if you understand that at the outset, and can live with the discontent and frustration of it, and can find a way to make a life within that discontent and frustration, which is natural as an artist, then you can persevere long enough so your work is worth reading.

I was in Chicago, in the spring of '89, and I had lunch in a group with Saul Bellow. The subject of book reviews came up, and of Bellow's book *A Theft*, and of other books, including *The Dean's December*. Bellow was very unhappy about mixed reviews. And it suddenly struck me: what else could he have wanted? He had won the Nobel Prize. His books had earned three National Book Awards. How much more critical acclaim could he wish for? But he was still stung by critics who took aim at his latest book, and I understood that here was a man who would never be content with what he was doing and never really happy about the way the world received him because writers never are.

I don't think successful writers are ever happy with whatever they're doing. It's those who can't deal with the dissatisfaction and unhappiness and frustration with the kind of life we lead who walk away and do something else.

GORDON MENNENGA: I think when we were in the Workshop, we all assumed we'd send a story to the *New Yorker* and it would get published and we'd be on our way. When you find out that isn't true, then you take a deep breath and wonder, now what do I do?

To make a living, I started teaching at the University of Wisconsin, LaCrosse. I taught eight classes of comp a year, twenty-five in each class.

Minimal benefits, bull-pen office shared with three other instructors. It killed my writing.

I lasted two years and left to take a job teaching fiction writing at DePauw University in Indiana. It took me a couple years to recover and start writing again. Then I wrote some stories and sent them out and got a number of encouraging rejection notices, including a number from Daniel Menaker at the *New Yorker*. He sent back a two-hundred-word rejection letter that kept me going for many months. And one of those rejected stories got me a job with Garrison Keillor.

I answered an ad in the *New Yorker* that said "A Prairie Home Companion" was looking for a writer. I submitted two of the rejected stories and was hired to write monologue material. I wrote a piece about Buddy Holly that made it into Keillor's Twentieth Anniversary Collection. An agent called me and offered me television work, but at the time, television was pretty bad, so I turned it down. And of course I still kick myself for that. Is there such a thing as writer's regret?

I used a lot of my story ideas for Keillor. I worked for him from 1987 to 1990. If I hadn't gotten a teaching job right out of Iowa, I might have written more and taken myself more seriously. But I had a baby and a wife, and it looked like teaching was the way to go.

DOUG UNGER: It was the tail end of that time when one could get a teaching job right out of Iowa, but I did get a job at a community college teaching Spanish as a substitute teacher for someone who was ill. Later, I also taught English composition at the Lummi College of Aquaculture, run by the Lummi Indian tribe. These were just pickup teaching jobs that didn't pay enough to live on.

Amy and I had moved to San Francisco after Iowa. The first job I landed was at Merritt Hospital in Oakland, in admissions. It was tough. I had to dress in a white uniform. I used my abilities to speak Spanish—in those days, they didn't have many Spanish-speaking admissions people—and when they needed medical interpreting, I'd interpret. I also had a second job in San Francisco working at the St. James Episcopal Church, running little old ladies around and picking up heavy objects for the church bazaar, and in general, working as the minister's assistant. In exchange for that, we got reduced rent on a nice flat in San Francisco, on California Avenue.

After San Francisco, we tried New York City, and we totally failed in New York. I managed both the Eastside and Westside bookstores, two bookstores, and Amy worked in one of them, even as she was trying to do theater at night and I was trying to write. But it wasn't long before that life crashed because of the financial exigencies of living in New York.

Then Amy had a chance at getting a job at Whatcom Community College, in Bellingham, Washington State, near where her dying aunt owned some land. So we moved to Washington, and I started to do journalism for the Gannett paper there, the *Bellingham Herald*, mainly writing theater reviews and art features, and that got me into writing again.

I also picked up some teaching jobs and cut firewood and gill-netted at night. Often, I would sit on the boat and write after I set the gill nets because that's usually a laid-back kind of fishing. On a good night, I could set the gill nets with the tide and relax. I had an old manual typewriter on the boat, and I would work on the novel; and then a few hours later, I'd haul in and pick the net and have a hundred or two hundred bucks' worth of salmon. And then I'd set the net out again and go to sleep, then pick up before dawn and I'd have another fifty bucks worth of salmon. Then I'd sell the salmon and head off to teach.

That's the kind of life we lived for some years after Iowa, trying to make a living in any way we could, my wife and stepdaughter and I, while I kept writing.

CATHERINE GAMMON: I lived in Provincetown on the NEA grant, and then was given a second-year fellowship at FAWC, and when all that fellowship time ran out, I moved to New York. I worked at a photo agency for a while and then I got a job at the *New York Review of Books*, mostly typesetting and copyediting and on my own time writing, and at long last getting sober.

I was finishing *China Blue*. One of the later chapters has two women characters who meet. One of the women is the mother of a teenage girl who's disappeared, and the other is a figure based on an iconic woman I used to see in the morning streets of Provincetown, kind of draped in her bedspread like a dramatically beautiful drunk. The mother's looking for the daughter and this woman knows where she is. And they have this conversation—and I'm still a drunk myself when this conversation's being written—and this beautiful iconic drunk is saying things to the mother who doesn't get it, but what she's saying was really about me and my own drinking, really telling me that *I'm* a drunk. I recognized this only later, after my drinking had stopped. Then I could see how clearly the writing was trying to tell me to look at myself and how writing that novel had started to bring out some of the things that were hidden from me in my own life, dramatized in these characters in ways that I wasn't consciously doing.

I was almost done with the work on it when sobriety hit me. It was January 1984. When I started in recovery, I heard people say that if anything in your life was more important than sobriety you would lose the sobriety and everything else. I was afraid someone was going to tell me I had to give up writing; I was afraid they would say it was another addiction.

That didn't happen, but after I'd been sober a year or so, I did stop writing for a while. I had always argued that it was a mistake to use our writing to fulfill our own psychological needs, but suddenly I saw the ways in which I had really been doing that, the ways I had come to use being a writer to feel okay about being in the world, which had never been what I thought I was doing. I thought my writing had to be free of that, and that I needed to be able to just walk around in the world being a human being, and a drunk in recovery, whether I wrote again or not. So that's what I did, and then one day I was writing again. The writing I started at that time became *Isabel Out of the Rain*, my only published novel. And I'm still sober.

JAYNE ANNE PHILLIPS: I was lucky in that *Black Tickets* happened to be published in an era in which the American short story thrived. Numerous wonderful collections were published in that five- to seven-year period.

It was accepted for publication in the summer of 1978, just after I left Iowa. Sam Lawrence, who was to be my publisher for the next twenty years, saw a copy of *Sweethearts* at the St. Lawrence Writers Conference, and asked me to send him my manuscript of stories. I was there as a Houghton Mifflin fellow, and he was there to try to recruit Peggy Atwood to his imprint. The title of the book I sent him was *The Heavenly Animal*, but he suggested calling it *Black Tickets*. Morgan Entrekin (now head of Atlantic Monthly Press) was working for Sam then, and we worked together on the order of the stories, including some of the one-page fictions first published in *Sweethearts*. *Black Tickets* came out in fall '79.

That same year I got a teaching job—I was so impressed that I could get a real teaching job, and in California, by the Pacific—assistant professor at Humboldt State in Arcata, California. I lived in a little cement-block house with a concrete floor in Trinidad, above the bay. It was cold; I had a woodstove for heat. I split my own wood that winter and wrote "Bluegill" in that house, looking at the bay in the cold. My teaching load was 3/3 (three classes for both semesters), and I soon realized that I wasn't able to teach that much and do my own writing.

I had turned down a Fellowship at the Fine Arts Work Center in Provincetown to take the teaching job, and so I applied again, and was accepted. I went back east to FAWC, where I began working on *Machine Dreams*, and continued work on it the next year, as a Fellow at the Bunting Institute of Radcliff College, at which point I moved to Cambridge, and then to Jamaica Plain.

ALLAN GURGANUS: I left Stanford when I won an NEA grant. Reynolds Price, my mentor at the time, invited me to teach undergrads at Duke, not a tenure-track position at that point; I hadn't published a book yet. So I gave up the Stanford job to come back to North Carolina to teach.

The NEA was then like $7,000, which seemed a fortune to me. And the pay at Duke was around $3,000. My rent was $150 a month; this was decades ago. (My rent at Iowa had been $60 a month.) So I came back to my home state.

I bought a house in Chapel Hill with the NEA money. The house cost only $25,000, and the payments were $132 a month. There were many months when I was going through the couch looking for that last fifteen cents; they'd roll their eyes when I'd come into the bank, like I was someone buying penny candy. I taught there for two years.

Then Grace Paley, who'd been my mentor at Sarah Lawrence, asked if I'd come back and teach there. So I rented out the little house I'd bought and moved to New York, to a lower-middle-income housing project at Ninetieth and lower Amsterdam, a one-bedroom with a balcony in a sleek building. I lived there my whole time in New York City. Sarah Lawrence was a thirty-minute train ride out of the city. Eventually I got tenure at Sarah Lawrence.

During that whole time, I had been writing *Widow*. When it found good reviews and sales, I gave up teaching. Yes, I gave up a tenured teaching position thirty minutes from Manhattan! I moved south.

CATHERINE GAMMON: *Isabel* was published in 1991 by Mercury House, a small independent press. It sold maybe twelve or fourteen hundred copies. It got a few minor friendly reviews, but it was ignored in the major places. I was really pleased when I found out that there was a little group of young women artists in Soho reading it. They had an Isabel reading club or something. The book found readers, and I was always amazed when somebody would know about it.

After *Isabel,* I got a wonderful teaching job. The book came out in '91, and in '92 I started at the University Pittsburgh, which was the perfect place for me, partly because they wanted someone who could do critical theory, which I was engaged with even though I hadn't studied it in a formal way. It was exhilarating reading Derrida and Foucault and Kristevsa and Blanchot. My background in philosophy at Pomona helped me read these difficult things, and I could love them and didn't have to master them or prove anything or write in their language. I could just read them with playfulness and delight.

At Pittsburgh, the writing students were required to take critical theory. A lot of them resisted it, so I was a real addition for the writing program because I could encourage the people who liked theory, give them a way to play with it by using it in workshop in a way that made it more accessible than it seemed in the lit classes. It helped get people more engaged with it. So I was a perfect fit for the department, and the department was a perfect fit for me, and I was really happy there and very productive. I got tenure, and then, after nearly ten years, I left to move back to California and enter full-time formal Zen training.

ALLAN GURGANUS: After *Widow* had come out, I was traveling all the time, and New York had become a very . . . it's a weird paradox, the very thing you think you want, to be invited to every party in the universe, when it finally happens, it turns out to be very dull and unpleasant. And I even got asked to be a spokesman for Paul Stuart clothes, to pose wearing a turtleneck in a GAP ad, all of which I turned down. Mr. Integrity. I just didn't want to do any of it. I felt it would be whoring.

At the time I didn't know who my real friends were. Even my closest friends became extremely angry and jealous, even though they all knew how long and hard I'd been working. They stopped speaking to me. . . . The day the novel was reviewed on page one of the *Times Book Review*, my closest friend left a brown paper bag outside my apartment door containing every piece of jewelry, every toy and treasure I had ever given her. New York made itself so easy to leave.

Plus there was HIV. While all of this was going on, I'd been nursing and looking after and eulogizing an ex-lover and many friends. In a way, my community was dead already. I just determined I needed to get out of there.

I still love the city as you love a person; I love being there, but you don't have to live in Manhattan to enjoy the hell out of it.

Now I wanted to live in a village and be part of it, part of the sum and substance of the place. There's part of me that thinks this is just a dodge from being at the desk, but another sector knows that this is rich, aerating, privileged . . . I have a lawyer friend (this is the county seat) who's a brilliant guy, anti-death penalty, a very generous, open-hearted guy, always taking indigent cases, a lot of drug stuff. He has to visit these sketchy fellows, the suspects, and check out the crime scenes. But in some parts of my village, a single white guy can't go walking around unaccompanied. But if there are two white guys in one car, they look like FBI or revenuers, so my friend would be safe with another white guy. So sometimes

> And I'm thinking here I am talking to a crackhead about an ancient Persian poet! I suspect Rumi had exacerbated some underlying paranoia that demanded, what else, a flare gun.

he'll come and pick me up and take me to these crack houses . . . I'm the second white guy.

Not long ago, he took me along with him when he went to see this very handsome light-skinned black guy. The fellow had a poetry-reading circle where they also just happened to smoke crack. Some deranged white kid arrived to hear poetry while having a bipolar episode. He came in and fired a flare gun into the house and set the place on fire. Trying to be agreeable, I asked the owner of the place to tell me about the poetry readings. What were you reading the night of the fire?

He said at once, "Rumi."

I said, "He's great—isn't he always better than you remember?"

He nodded, "Yeah, man. I read Rumi in the morning to know what kind of day I'm going to have. Everything's there waiting for you in Rumi."

And I'm thinking here I am talking to a crackhead about an ancient Persian poet! I suspect Rumi had exacerbated some underlying paranoia that demanded, what else, a flare gun.

But this is village life for me.

CATHERINE GAMMON: From the beginning, meditation in one form or another was an important part of my recovery from alcoholism, and it pretty quickly took on a Zen flavor. I had first met Zen in the '60s in Berkeley, reading Alan Watts and listening to him on the radio, but those were drug times. At the *New York Review*, mountains of review copies of mostly unreviewed books would pile up on an old gray steel desk, and the staff could take whatever we wanted. I collected obscure European novels and books on Puritans and witchcraft and Zen, and I started practicing some very self-taught zazen. I visited a Zen center in Greenwich Village once and did a daylong workshop or two, but mostly I was on my own.

By the time I moved to Pittsburgh, I was in a long-term relationship and, you know, very busy, and had not been sitting regularly for a number of years. I had a clear sense that my spiritual task for that year was to become a good teacher, but I continued to feel the loss of the regular meditation I had done before. In 1997, I finally started looking for a group to practice with, and I found a little Zen group and went and did some sitting with them.

Shortly after that, I was in the Santa Cruz mountains, at Djerassi Resident Artists Program, and several of the artists there at that time also practiced zazen. One of them knew Green Gulch, in Marin County. So one Sunday, four of us got in a van and drove up here together to sit zazen and hear a Dharma talk. It knocked me out, to sit in this huge former barn with maybe two hundred people and then to hear this talk, which flowed out as if it was addressed directly to me. I was struggling with some amends I needed to make to somebody that I was clueless about how to do without getting all involved in the story of it, and then listening to this talk I saw immediately the simple action to take. By the time we left, I was totally blissed-out. When I went back to Pittsburgh a few weeks later, I devoted myself to that little Zen group.

From then on, the more I practiced, the more I wanted to practice, and the more I practiced, the more clearly I saw I needed a teacher. Over the next few years, I came back to California for retreats and developed a relationship with my teacher, and before long, I started asking how to make this practice my whole life.

Throughout that time I was holding open the question, a kind of either-or, about Zen versus writing, doing both until I would see how things would unfold. Then in 2000, I devoted a sabbatical year to residential practice, with my teacher and others, as a way of discerning which path to take. When I got back to Pittsburgh, I was ready to choose full-time Zen training. I wrote my letter of resignation on my fifty-fifth birthday.

I knew that entering Zen training meant setting writing aside. It felt sort of like setting writing aside had before, but with a difference. When I set it aside in early sobriety, it wasn't that I was never going to pick it up again; it was just that I didn't know. I had set it aside to just be willing to walk on the planet without being a writer. This time, setting it aside in order to do this training, the not knowing was a lot bigger, because I had this either-or idea and because what I was going to do was going to take all of my attention, and I didn't know if the two practices would ever live together in me again.

DON WALLACE: We drove away from Iowa City on the heels of a tornado, which I blithely followed up the road because it lacked the traditional funnel shape.

This was a time of testing and survival. I'm sure that leaving Iowa, for all of us, was the moment of truth. A few, the anointed, had publishing jobs waiting in the East, others accepted the yoke of teaching five freshman English classes on the promise that they would get a writing class in the future. A true unruly Westerner, I thought we wanted more. But Mindy also had a surprise in store: she'd applied to law school. "I'm tired of men having all the power," she said.

At the University of California at Davis, in the vast rural Central Valley of California, we found ourselves in a very Iowa City landscape, complete with silage smells and a lack of employment outside of the university. I couldn't catch on at the lumber mill, the hardware store, or the mysterious factory down by the river that turned out counterfeit Muppets. Thus, while Mindy went to law classes (immediately hating every minute of it), I became a temp for the U, which was an ag school, with all that implies in terms of male chauvinism. (Several male professors pointedly wore cowboy boots and cowboy hats.) As the first male office temp—they checked that my wife was, indeed, enrolled in the law school before hiring me—I felt like a narc making an undercover estrogen buy. Spurred by the snickers of the beehived gender, I dethroned the queen of the typing pool with my first timed test: 96 wpm, no errors. At $3.96 an hour, all that practice writing fiction was already paying off.

ERIC OLSEN: My wife and I moved to San Francisco after Iowa. We didn't have a clue what came next, and we both scrambled to find work to pay the bills: I found a job writing PR copy for a heavy machinery company. This was back in that long-gone era when things like heavy machinery were still made in this country. Cheryl got a job as a secretary in an ad agency, looking to climb higher. We sent out resumes for jobs as editors and staff writers—this was back in that also long-gone era when publishers still hired editors and staff writers. We both nibbled at our writing, cranking out the occasional short story, collecting rejection slips.

I didn't try to get a teaching gig. There weren't any. At least not in California, not for a guy who'd published all of six short stories so far.

Don Wallace was responsible for my first published fiction. I'd put up a couple short pieces in a workshop that were received well enough, and later Don suggested I send them to a friend of his who edited a literary magazine out of UC Santa Cruz called *Quarry West*. There were five stories in all, connected by the same anonymous narrator, a kid growing up in Turlock, a little farming town in California's Central Valley. They were meant as chapters for a novel-in-progress, though there wasn't much in the way of narrative motion after the first five.

> **I didn't try to get a teaching gig. There weren't any. At least not in California, not for a guy who'd published all of six short stories so far.**

Don's friend took the stories. I got five copies of the issue for payment. The stories were set in California's delta country. They had those short sentences like everyone seemed to be writing back then—unless they were magical realists or wrote metafiction—one simple sentence piled on another, like I was imparting the most profound insights: "The delta was always changing. What was land became water. Water became land. Roads went nowhere." That sort of thing. But that same year, I published another short story in *Carolina Quarterly*, "My Father's Son," the first sentence of which was 210 words. Good-bye minimalism.

We rented a little studio apartment in San Francisco that had a big walk-in closet, which came in handy when Glenn Schaeffer moved in with us. The closet became his study and he slept in our dining nook while he trained to become a stockbroker.

The place was in the Richmond District, the Russian neighborhood, just a block or two from the big Russian church with the onion dome, near the Russian Tea Room. We're talking pierogies and black tea with strawberry jam out of glasses instead of cups (my grandmother was from Russia, so I knew from jam and tea in glasses and felt right at home). Our landlord lived in the same building, a cranky old Russian who viewed us with dark suspicion, especially after he first caught sight of Glenn done up in a suit and tie, carrying a briefcase and leaving our apartment one weekday dawn to go to stockbroker school. The landlord probably took him for KGB. I mean, Glenn did look pretty snorked up, as Cheryl's people would say, presumably on a mission. I lied to the landlord, telling him that Glenn was my cousin visiting from LA and he'd be there only a couple of weeks . . . it was a ball to have the opportunity to spend a little time with family again, and I was so *grateful* that the landlord was, well, so accommodating. . . . Glenn used our closet for an office for nearly five months.

Books by the Bed

ERIC OLSEN: *The War of the World*, Niall Ferguson; *Berlin Noir*, Philip Kerr; a biography of Albert Einstein by Walter Isaacson; *Name of the Rose*, Umberto Eco; *Cider House Rules*, John Irving; *Polonaise* and *North of the Port*, both by Anthony Bukoski; *Bangkok 8*, John Burdett; and *Army at Dawn*, Rick Atkinson, the first volume in a three-volume account of the campaign in North Africa and Italy. I also keep a collection of essays by Isaiah Berlin handy, *The Proper Study of Mankind*. Of an evening, I'll usually start with some Berlin because it's good for the soul. But I can handle that for about five minutes at that hour, so then I turn to a stale issue of the *New Yorker* or *Atlantic* and try to finish one of the several articles I started weeks ago but never quite got through because I'd always fall asleep. And then I'll fall asleep. . . .

GLENN SCHAEFFER: So what'd I get out of the Workshop? A divorce, for one, which was a rather profitable thing. I kept trying to make the marriage work. I couldn't let it go. But without my ex-wife, I would never have been what I became. My ex-wife's the reason I walked into a Beverly Hills brokerage office and applied for a job with upside, instead of finishing my PhD in ten years or doing a Stegner on offer, with shades of Ken Kesey and Robert Stone. So it could have gone far worse; I might have become a writer.

When I was still waiting tables at the Ironman Inn out in Coralville, one of the waiters there was an MBA student, a kid from Libya named Ahmed. We were taking a break at the water station and he said, "What's this shit about you being a writer? What are you, *nuts*? You're a smart guy. You should be in business."

"Like what in business?" I asked. I didn't have a clue.

A few days later, I'm sitting in with Ahmed during his financial accounting class, watching a prof spinning formulae on the board. That's when I first got the idea. That wasn't nuclear engineering up there ... it was plain ol' math, mere algebra at most, one of my aptitudes. Plus, I wanted to do something where advancing age and experience would work in my favor. One of the things I'd noticed while at Iowa was that writers didn't necessarily prosper with age. In business, you tend to become more valuable with age. But in the arts and entertainment, the bright young thing is preferred over the more mature artist, names of the new, as Proust once described the seasons of culture. That's why older writers take on pseudonyms. Getting old in the arts is like being blacklisted. Not in business, though. At forty, you're more valuable than you were at thirty. At fifty, more than forty. To a point.

When Olsen and I left Iowa together in my balky Falcon with an ice chest full of fermenting vegetables and fruit, I had already made the decision that I was not going to be a writer. I was disconsolate over my doomed marriage, and Olsen said, "You need to leave that shit behind, all that negativity."

"I need to be successful," I said. This was someplace in South Dakota, between the Corn Palace and Wall Drugs, where we admired row upon row of Bowie knives arrayed in long glass counters. "And that's harder to do by subtraction."

And Olsen said, "Don't worry, at thirty you're going to be as successful as you want to be." It was validating to me, this fugitive workshop.

Problem was, I had an MFA, not an MBA. I thought you had to have an MBA to go into business, unless you wanted to sell something. I knew a few career salesmen with a little dash; they didn't have MBAs. The father of one of my friends sold carpets out of a mill. The father of another friend sold pharmaceuticals, and one of my best friends from college was selling medical devices in Portland, Oregon, and at the ripe age of twenty-four was making more than either Jack Leggett or Vance Bourjaily. So I figured that I'd sell something, but what? Axminster carpets? Tranquilizers? I don't think so. ... The father of another friend was a stockbroker. I wasn't even sure what a stockbroker did, other than my glimpses of Nick Carraway in *Gatsby*;

but I knew that in addition to his home in Pomona, this stockbroker had a weekend place in Laguna Beach.

So that's how I ended up walking into the Dean Witter office in Beverly Hills. Why Beverly Hills? It was full of rich people, and ingenuous as I might have been at the time, I understood that if you were going to sell something and make a pecunious living off commissions, you'd better sell big-ticket stuff to rich people.

ERIC OLSEN: During those months Schaeffer was learning how to be a stockbroker and operating from our closet, dodging our prying landlord as best he could, while he and I were scribbling away on *City Business*, now and then after work we'd go to Newman's Gym on Eddy at Leavenworth, in San Francisco's Tenderloin, an old-fashioned boxing gym, straight out of an A. J. Liebling article with fat guys sitting on the top rows of the bleachers chewing stubby dime-store cigars and pretending to make deals and goofy ex-fighters hanging around because they had nowhere else to go to stay warm. But some good young pro prospects also trained there. The gym's long gone, but it had a storied history in California's sweet science. Anyone was welcome, just drop your three-dollar gym fee—cash only—on Mr. Newman's desk on your way in. We'd work the heavy bags and try to look halfway competent on the speed bags, and then after the real boxers were through for the evening and one or another of the rings would be empty, Glenn and I would spar. Occasionally, we'd spar with other interlopers, and Glenn once sparred with a pro seeking some target practice and got himself softened up a little.

Actually, the feel of the place was rather like that of the Workshop: performers bound for a tough business, hopeful, but with the nagging sense that only a few would make it big, everyone sizing up everyone else, with the business guys lurking around ready to pick off the best of the best, like the agents who'd come through Iowa now and then. But Newman's had a buzzer that went off at three-minute and one-minute intervals, marking off the rounds and rests. Time was a looser concept at Iowa. Plus writers drank more than boxers; boxers are monks for violence, generally sober.

> The gym's long gone, but it had a storied history in California's sweet science. Anyone was welcome, just drop your three-dollar gym fee—cash only—on Mr. Newman's desk on your way in.

GLENN SCHAEFFER: We'd been working out regularly at Newman's and we considered ourselves as passably tough, so one night after a session I told Olsen that I could shut him down. I invited him to pick his own time of trial, any time.

"Right now?" Olsen inquired.

"Well, whenever you're ready. I don't want any of your belly-aching about it later."

"Deal," Olsen said, and we finished toweling off.

A couple weeks go by and I've sort of forgotten about the Challenge, and one night Olsen and his wife cook up this sumptuous dinner of chicken fricassee and mashed potatoes and I planned to handle my financial market homework in the closet as usual, figuring a couple helpings of fricassee wouldn't hurt that cause, and I didn't notice that Olsen was just nibbling at the food on his plate. And then Olsen announced, "Now."

"Now what?"

"Newman's."

"Criminy, you can't be serious. We just ate."

"You said any time," Olsen said, pouting a little.

"Pick your poison, sissy," I said, trying to bluff him.

Olsen called me.

And thus we ended up at Newman's in the ring and Olsen is dancing around with that fancy jab of his—striking me at will—and I'm like a fairytale wolf with stones in his belly, lurching, trying to load up my right hand, when Olsen shoots me one in the stomach and, whoo boy, here's a froth of fricassee spouting from my nose.

ERIC OLSEN: Sun Tzu or von Clausewitz or one of those guys said a battle is won or lost before it's ever fought. So I suppose the chicken fricassee was my finest ring triumph. Glenn got his revenge, though. He suggested I write an article about Newman's Gym and try to sell it to a magazine. This was way back in those heady days when magazines were still a viable business proposition. This was 1978, just at the start of the so-called "fitness boom," when all sorts of magazines were starting up devoted activities such as jogging and tennis in which no one much tries to punch you in the nose. These weren't the sorts of magazines that would do an article about a boxing gym, but I wrote one anyway, a funny (I hoped) little piece about hanging out at Newman's waiting for a genuine heavyweight contender, Stan Ward, to show up to spar. Eventually he did and was a delightful interview—an MA from Sacramento State who rose to number six before Mike Weaver, Glenn's teammate from high school football in Pomona, clocked him. I sent it to *CitySports Magazine,* a San Francisco throwaway, and they bought it and sent me a check for $50 and asked me if I'd like to do another piece for them for another $50 and I said, gosh, *would I ever!* Imagine! Someone paying me

$50 to write a story! I couldn't believe my good fortune. So I quit my day job and decided I was a—quote—professional—end quote—writer.

It got worse from there. Soon enough I was pegged as a sportswriter. Too bad I didn't write my first magazine article about, say, a trip to the south of France; maybe I'd have become a travel writer. Or about the early days of the hi-tech scene in what would become Silicon Valley; I might have gotten in on some lucrative start-ups, with stock options. But no, it had to be sports. Meanwhile, I kept trying to make progress on *City Business* and various short stories, but I was finding it tough to write fiction after spending all day trying to meet a deadline. In truth, I found nonfiction as satisfying as fiction. This was back when the New Journalism was still in vogue, so I found I could do things in magazine articles that I aspired to in fiction; the timing was right, anyway. Editors seemed to like my stuff and I started getting more and more assignments. Except for McCoy and Wallace though, none of the editors I wrote for had ever heard of the Workshop, or if they had, they didn't give a damn. They just wanted the copy on time and long enough to fill the empty spaces between the ads.

DON WALLACE: Our friends, for the most part, were too far away and, in that time without the Internet and the web, easy to lose touch with. But Eric and Cheryl Olsen had moved to San Francisco and so, just as in Iowa City, provided a haven for us on our desperate visits to the city. At Davis we found a writing professor, Alice Adams, whose stories we'd been reading in the *New Yorker*. She was generous and wise, and allowed us both to audit her classes.

After reading our first stories, Alice took Mindy and me aside and read us the riot act: If we wanted to break into the slicks, we had to write by the rules: twenty-five lines per page, double-spaced; no more than fifteen pages, max; no cross-outs, no handwritten corrections; and every story had to follow the Five-Step Formula: (1) open *in medias res*, middle of a scene; (2) pull back in third paragraph to fill in conflict and characters; (3) scenes building up history of conflict and finally returning to story's opening scene; (4) showdown, conflict, climax; (5) and resolution in one paragraph. (If writing for the *New Yorker*, cut number five and substitute random enigmatic thought, comment by passerby, or sign glimpsed in shop window. Oh, and no stories set on Christmas, Easter, the Fourth of July, or Thanksgiving—unless we were writing specifically for the Seven Sisters, in which case every story had to be set during a holiday.

Around about this time, Mindy decided her soul was in mortal peril and began to write fiction late at night instead of studying law. We also started up a law school paper just to see our names in print and ran a concert series in the cafeteria, booking Devo and Talking Heads for $800 apiece.

This ambivalence, too, was what a lot of our Iowa mates were going through. The world was saying, *Get a job, go to grad school, wise up*. Most did. And yet for some of us it just didn't take, no matter how we tried.

Fortunately, Mindy won the NEA for the story she'd written while convinced her soul was dying. She elected to finish her law degree, having finished the second year, so we banked the money. In her third year, thanks to a freelance article Olsen had landed for me in a free paper called *City Sports*, I had a job as sole sportswriter for the *Woodland-Davis Daily Democrat*. It was eight stories and a photo every day six days a week, but there was the Central Valley to cover and all the great Mexican and Basque restaurants to go with it.

GLENN SCHAEFFER: I detested making cold calls as a stockbroker, so I started looking around. At Dean Witter, because I was the rookie broker, I had to field stray calls, and I kept getting calls from this PR exec, asking me questions about stocks that seemed elementary, and so I asked him what he did, and he said "financial PR," and I'm thinking this guy doesn't know balls about finance. So one day I asked him where exactly his office was. Turns out it was just around the corner in Brentwood and I went right over.

I had actually heard about PR as a profession while still at Iowa, when Bill McCoy told me about his job offer working for Burger King in New York wearing a fireman's costume and talking to grade-school kids about fire safety. So it had been in the back of my mind as a long-shot possibility, provided I didn't have to deck myself in fireman's duds. Better a suit and briefcase.

I delved into financial PR and asked my new pal who the big players were, and next thing I knew, I'd talked my way into a job as an account executive with Hill & Knowlton, the biggest corporate PR firm in the world.

I was there a couple years and started getting known around town, and then one day, I got a call from a woman who owned her own corporate PR firm. She wanted to take a young partner into her business. So I walk into her office in Century City and who's there but Robin Green, holding down the receptionist's desk.

She goes, *"Glenn?"*

And I go, "*Robin?*"

I'd been talking up the prestige of an Iowa MFA, and now how's it going to look if I come in to interview for a *partnership* at this corporate PR firm and one of my classmates, a TWF no less, is temping on the telephone? "Don't dare tell anyone about *your* MFA," I pleaded with Robin. "Let's keep up institutional appearances, for everyone's sake."

Robin thought that was pretty funny.

Books by the Bed

ROBIN GREEN: I can't say what books are by my night nightstand; there's a stack. It's a big mistake for me to buy books in a pile. I need to buy them one by one and then read them. But right now we're working so hard on producing a pilot that I don't have time to read. I'm not kidding. But it doesn't last very long, a couple of intense months, and then it's a writer's life again.

ROBIN GREEN: At Iowa, I was awarded a TWF, but I should point out that I got it because another student who'd gotten it first didn't return, so I was upgraded from rhetoric teacher to TWF in her place.

I don't know if I was a good teacher or not, but truthfully I didn't have much tolerance for or patience with student efforts. I only liked the talented ones, and in two semesters, there were only two or three. One of them was Mitchell Burgess; he was the best. A rhetoric teacher had read a piece of his writing and told him he was a writer and sent him to my class. He was the best writer I read in Iowa, better than the Workshop people even, a writer with a distinct voice. After the semester was over and he had his A, he and I got together as a couple. At least we waited until the term was over, right? We are still together, of course, married and also writing and producing partners in TV.

We left Iowa in a $200 car with $1,300 in our pockets and went to LA. We supported ourselves as temp workers here and there. I got a full-time job or two (PR mostly, at the Music Center and also business firms) but meantime got back into journalism—wrote for the *LA Weekly* and for *California Magazine* where Harold Hayes was then editor, and what a guy he was. My friend Ruth Reichl, who was food editor at the *Los Angeles Times*, gave me a job as an occasional second-string restaurant reporter.

One of those reviews (it was funny and had a definite voice) caught the eye of Josh Brand, who was John Falsey's TV-writing partner. John had been one of my classmates at Iowa. They'd already created *St. Elsewhere*, and now they had a new show. John told Josh about my short stories at the Workshop and that I'd be right for this new show, *A Year in the Life*, with Richard Kiley and Sarah Jessica Parker when she was, like, seventeen.

John was a handsome boy and a wonderful writer. He was an old-fashioned short story writer. There were some avant-garde types and one pukey teacher at Iowa who really gave him a bad time in class, but I loved his stuff and defended him. He was the only one in my two years in the Workshop to get something in the *New Yorker* (hah!), and it's this published story that got him an agent in Hollywood and got him started there.

John asked me to write a script for the new show. I failed the first attempt, but he and Josh told me to read the stories of John Updike, that was the tone they wanted. I tried again and was hired. My script was episode one of the first season, and that was a thrill, believe me. I loved writing the show—it was writing from the heart, not so much from the head like journalism. I loved it. Love it still.

GLENN SCHAEFFER: While I was still at Hill & Knowlton, one of my clients was Caesars World. This was when gaming companies were just starting to go public and needed to tell their stories to Wall Street. I thrived on that account. I was writing annual reports, dealing with traders on Wall Street, serving as interface between the company and its bankers and institutional shareholders, presenting the company's story. It took Caesars a spell to figure out that they could hire me on staff doing the same thing for a fraction of my billings. By the time they did figure it out, I was at Ramada. And then Circus Circus made me an offer and I moved to Las Vegas. That was in 1983, and I became their CFO at thirty. I've been in gaming ever since.

DON WALLACE: After Mindy took the bar exam, we headed to Europe. In our backpacks we had a copy of *Ulysses*, a portable typewriter, and a ream of paper. Europe was the promised land.

But the London and Paris we found bore only the most tired resemblance to the fabled clichés of Fitzgerald and Hemingway. In fact, we rattled around with a vague sense of embarrassment.

On our flight back to the States in the spring, Mindy called her old friend and first writing teacher at Stanford, who told her she'd won a Stegner Fellowship for the '81–'82 academic year. So we settled in at Stanford for the year, with me working for a publisher in the same building where Gordon Lish first met Ray Carver and began screwing with his short stories. It was good to be in a community of writers again, and a lot of work flowed. But all anyone aimed for was the *New Yorker*, which produced a certain demographic sensibility (good clothes, good schools, eccentric aristocratic occupations, petit emotions) in the work.

DOUG UNGER: The *McSweeney's* crowd is where it's at now, and the *Tin House* crowd, and I'm sensing a new neo-romantic movement in American letters among the young writers: surrealism, romance, exaggeration, long sentences, a self-conscious effort to imitate the postmodern form, to cut up the story and not tell it straight, like the metafiction movement of the '60s. Less like what Carver, Wolff, Ford, and Beattie were doing. But I'm not an authority on what's new these days. I should be, but I'm not. Mainly I'm not because I'm so distracted by reading manuscripts, thousands of pages of manuscripts, admissions manuscripts and the MFA and PhD theses that are all book length, anywhere from 150 to 500 pages long, plus all the book manuscripts I'm getting from the presses, and the manuscripts by former students and friends.

I am seeing a few trends in all of this. Many young American writers are still stuck in relationship stories. I'm starting to see the relationship story as ultimately boring. The love relationship, over and over and over, in its many variations. I think it's a terrain that's been overdeveloped.

> **I am seeing a few trends in all of this. Many young American writers are still stuck in relationship stories. I'm starting to see the relationship story as ultimately boring. The love relationship, over and over and over, in its many variations.**

This is just not very interesting to me. What interests me—which is why I left a tenured job at Syracuse, arguably one of the best even then, to come here to UNLV to found the international program—are the writers who go somewhere else and experience the culture shock of being out of America and away from the bedroom and the backyard, away from the kind of sticky restrictions of the bourgeois marriage or dating game, the sort of problems that arise out of the privileged American not being able to get his/her love life straightened out.

The American writer is as insulated as the American voter, and most of what I read just isn't dealing with the rest of the world at all. It should. International writers are dealing with it; they're all over the map, moving from country to country.

JENNIE FIELDS: Women in book groups seem to be a major audience for trade paperbacks these days, or so my agent tells me. They look for books that bridge a gap: books that are both accessible and literary. You'll notice "book group discussion guides" in the backs of so many novels these days. That's why.

In the '70s, male fiction was king. Those "oh what a funny bad boy I am" books sold well. Now, you see a lot less of them. The great male writers still sell. Writers like the Richards: Russo, Ford, and Price; they're out there and they're writing and they do well.

You definitely have to be special to stand out. There's no time or money to nurture new talent these days. This is a tough time in all businesses and certainly in the business of fiction.

ANTHONY BUKOSKI: When we were at Iowa, it seemed that America had a more vibrant literary culture. Now the major publishers are going for blockbusters. The trend at the big places is, for the most part, to get away from publishing literary fiction. More and more big publishers publish books that a sensitive, educated, discerning reader will find despicable. If you don't hit it big fast, at least with the big houses, you'll end up forgotten, remaindered in six weeks to the discount-book bin at Walmart.

DOUG UNGER: We're now in the age of the debut novel, and it skews the culture in a wrong direction, in my opinion, part of the "false market-place" that's been created around fiction. If the market is so skewed that the debut novel is everything, and a writer's career depends on it, then we've basically lost the genre of fiction, which may be happening anyway, because the marketing for nonfiction is so much easier, and so publishers shy away from fiction.

JAYNE ANNE PHILLIPS: There are more good small presses that are compensating for the abandonment by the big conglomerate publishers of a lot of good literary fiction these days. The five big megapublishers—Bertels-mans, Pearson-Lehman, HarperCollins, SonyViacom, and TimeWarner—are going more for nonfiction, pop-culture dreadfuls, and a very few very fine novels to round out their lists. They follow the fads . . . a few years ago, it was pink covers, now it seems to be the "debut" novel, that first novel they are going to gamble will break through into best-sellerdom, mainly because they know how to promote the "new" face, the "new" style. They'll pay big money for that. It's hard to imagine, these days, how a writer of the dark literary talents of a Cormac McCarthy could survive in such a marketplace, an author who wrote five books before *Blood Meridian* broke through and established his serious reputation. Or Richard Ford, who wrote three very fine books—*A Piece of My Heart*, *The Ultimate Good Luck*, and *Rock Springs*, his book of stories—before he had enough sales with *The Sportswriter*, in

> There are more good small presses that are compensating for the abandonment by the big conglomerate publishers of a lot of good literary fiction these days..

> **Well, we're lucky there are the smaller presses to compensate. I believe in them. I do all I can to help them out. And that's where I feel the great new writer will emerge on the American literary landscape . . .**

a Vintage Contemporary paperback original series, that a larger marketplace found him.

The point is that it seems publishers were patient enough to support, nurture, and stay with a writer through the early stages of refining and honing a native talent. I don't believe that's so now. Agents and editors want to rush the young writer's first book into a make-it-or-break-it sales situation, gambling the young writer's career on a book that may not be anything as fine as what that writer might, in time, finally write. A very few lucky and talented writers may break through this way. But what happens to the others?

Well, we're lucky there are the smaller presses to compensate. I believe in them. I do all I can to help them out. And that's where I feel the great new writer will emerge on the American literary landscape, if given enough time. It will happen. Readers will find that writer.

T. C. BOYLE: It used to be, you're a young writer, you get some experience, learn more, and we'll market you after five books. They just threw us out there. I didn't know my publisher had a marketing division until 1987, with *World's End.*

Now they're bringing out writers, a lot of them getting books with a first run of five hundred thousand copies. It's just like the record industry. This may be great for a few authors, but I wonder if they'll have sustained careers or not. Or are their expectations up too high after one success, which was orchestrated by the publisher? Will the publisher sustain you? Or you have one or two books and you're gone?

I think it's going to be tough for writers in general; for the few who get the blockbuster, great. It's going to be tough on publishers too because their bread and butter is the backlist, and if you have one-hit or two-hit wonders, where's the backlist?

I've been lucky; my publisher keeps my books in print and on the shelves in the bookstores. That's ideal for a publisher, and if publishing is going to continue, they'll have to realize that, unless they go the route of downloadable books or something. But who wants to read a book on a screen? A book is a beautiful actual thing. Like record albums. Remember how we'd stare at them and look at the pictures and read the liner notes . . . a work of art, and that can't be transmitted through a screen.

JAYNE ANNE PHILLIPS: Just as in music, there's a lot more literature out there for free. This is surely a good thing, though I don't like reading literature or poetry on a computer screen. I want to hold the book in my hands, lie in my bed, etc. People can find out what's out there fast, then buy what they want, remaindered, used, or whatever.

As for royalties, royalties for literary books seem to pretty much disappear in "costs" to publishers, or returns, or who knows. The Internet is a means to an end: a way of getting information, making reservations, ordering groceries. There is no "death" of the author. The author lives. Cyberspace throbs. Art has never been about the money. Entertainment and schlock are about money.

DENNIS MATHIS: In Provincetown in the '80s, Cathy Gammon and I would have these late-night philosophical discussions (well, philosophical for her part, just goofy at my end). I was obsessively programming FAWC's first office PC at the time, and I remember telling her that I really, really wanted to see networked, interactive fiction someday. The Fiction Collective, Sukenick and those cats, had already noodled around with group authorship, but that was just a lark. What I envisioned were vast novels of branching stories, serious stuff generated by sincere authors, which a reader could wander around in endlessly.

I also wanted a little typewriter that would fit in a briefcase.

About that same time, I started writing a set-in-the-future story that begins with a shocking event: the main character receives an invitation printed on paper. It's delivered by helicopter. He's whisked off to some Yaddo-like retreat where there are rooms lined with actual books.

At that point, my concept—that paper and ink would someday be an inconceivable luxury—gave out. I realized there would always be plenty of books. They might stop being printed (and it would be a glorious thing to stop pulping trees), but the human race isn't going to throw away all the books that already exist; we're hoarders by nature, like crows. And new artisans will spring up to make beautiful new books, even if they have to excavate landfills for paper.

I'm absolutely confident about the future of literature, even in its most traditional forms, and absolutely despairing in equal measures. I see a great, liberated, kaleidoscopic future for publishing, in whatever forms it takes.

What worries me is social media, reading groups, instant messaging, criticism based on polling—constant connectedness. I fear that young people already consider solitude, being cut off even for a minute, a symptom of disease. Will there still be a place for loners like me, or will we be euthanized?

I don't believe any book is ever created by only one person; that's an evil myth. But reading should always be a blissfully solitary state of mind.

SHERRY KRAMER: I think the times demand better art: better plays, fiction, poetry. We've come out of a time when emotional sloppiness was rewarded and out of a huge time of moral relativism in the arts. In times like these when we're at war, when we're in the center of an economic catastrophe, people need their art—especially in a (for now) nonfundamentalist nation—to provide organizing principles, to create ways to celebrate value, to understand what matters and how we belong to each other, to keep us alive to our higher selves.

DOUG UNGER: Young writers need to avoid buying into the notion that writing is undervalued because the market doesn't value it. I think literature is more valuable now than it ever was, and let's put the emphasis on value as a humane concept, completely detached from marketplace values. We live in a culture that, to paraphrase Oscar Wilde, puts a price on everything but values little else.

In literature, human beings find a sanctuary from that obscene consumerism produced by an economy that is killing us all, as Barry López and others have been warning us for years. Literature preserves, protects, and defends the imagination; it transports the mind and spirit to some "other" place removed from the pitch and buzz of daily life. Of course literature is valued, letters are valued, by those who comprehend value as a humane ideal worth pursuing.

Young writers need to avoid buying into the notion that writing is undervalued because the market doesn't value it. I think literature is more valuable now than it ever was ...

Literature is what will survive us, what will last, what will sum our count and make our old excuse. Future generations, I must believe, will sit with the great books our culture produces, and with other fine art it produces, and judge our time on earth by its measure.

Does literature have a value? Of course! Is it practical? Is it economically viable within today's marketplace ideologies? I don't know. Literature is a high-powered verbal object—talk is cheap, literature is not; still, we love words in all shapes and forms, and significations . . . and haven't we always?

MARVIN BELL: The future? For poets, it may mean small independent presses, pamphlets, broadsides, and a specialized audience—a future, that is, like the past. And, of course, the Internet. For prose writers, it may require a career of constant self-promotion, which we pretty much already have, what with social networking, mindless twittering, TV guest spots to hustle books and films, etc. Our current version of capitalism spreads the wealth by thinning it out.

For me, the writing of poetry has to do with new forms of thought and with what used to be called "the meaning of life." It has to do with philosophy as much as emotion. It is a survival skill. It is a vehicle for expressing what one didn't know one knew, for using words to go beyond words. But I'm a dinosaur.

> The future? For poets, it may mean small independent presses, pamphlets, broadsides, and a specialized audience—a future, that is, like the past. And, of course, the Internet.

Some of the poetry being studied now is about finding out what one doesn't know and can't know, and much of the rest is, as always, the skillful expression of a petty first person. Fortunately, many of those poets who are categorized as "ethnic" aren't having any of it. In literature, as in national politics, our minorities may reinvigorate us.

SANDRA CISNEROS: One thing I became aware of, as an author, is the big New York houses view a writer's work as a product; it's not what you want to write, but what sells. So you get pushed to thinking more about a novel, as opposed to the short story, or as opposed to the memoir, which has kind of had it. The publishing world doesn't want to look at memoirs now. Now they get all bushy-tailed when you say novel because that's what sells.

JOE HALDEMAN: I don't think fiction is dead or dying, but it's easy to see a future where the "serious" fiction industry is shaped like the poetry industry is today: Very few people buy poetry books unless they also write poetry, or at least teach it. I can see that happening to the novel, with the significant difference that fiction provides scaffolding for movies and television, and so enters everyday life more often than poetry.

JAYNE ANNE PHILLIPS: I don't think writing fiction is a dying art, nor do I believe the desire out there to read good literary fiction is dying. What I'm coming to believe is that it is an acquired taste, the way appreciating any art is an acquired taste, and that, perhaps, mass culture, popular culture, is turning away from stories and novels, and especially the short story as a form.

Still, I don't think much has changed, and this feels like an old complaint.

GORDON MENNENGA: These days, editors no longer edit. Or they can't. Young talent is no longer nurtured. Sixty percent of editors are under thirty because they're cheaper than more experienced editors.

I've been mentoring fiction and nonfiction writers for ten years. I essentially do what editors used to do: suggest, rearrange, fix, hint, and encourage. I've worked with writers who have been through three editors on the same novel. Each one suggested different changes. Most editors are in a like/don't like mode. They don't have good reasons, just vague hunches.

> These days, editors no longer edit. Or they can't. Young talent is no longer nurtured. Sixty percent of editors are under thirty because they're cheaper than more experienced editors.

DON WALLACE: At this point in time, with the newspaper and magazine worlds in steep decline and the publishing world teetering on the brink, it would seem that most tactical advice is useless. There is no sinecure out there, no easy tenured teaching gig. Unlike the flush days of the memoir after the success of Frank McCourt's *Angela's Ashes*, there is no surefire genre—except vampires and zombies, of course. The writing level of these is, as one former student of mine recently e-mailed me, "remedial." (That doesn't mean we shouldn't all try our hand at one.)

Similarly, the old refuge of Hollywood, for writers who were so lucky as to catch such a break, is just about played out. Several of my classmates made lucrative careers out of television—my old basketball partner John Falsey with *St. Elsewhere* and *Northern Exposure*, my classmate Robin Green writing and producing *The Sopranos*, for the scripts of which she hired my first Iowa teacher, Henry Bromell.

But the expense of the long-form scripted television show has led to hour after hour of cheap reality programming. The genie is out of the bottle in film, too, as indie production companies drop like flies after a cold snap. I worked on a treatment last year that seemed to be heading to a quick sale when (thanks, Lehman Brothers!) the financing for everything dried up.

Yet even though money is tight and it's hard to find much optimism out there right now, some good has come of this global gut check. Something called BookScan has given the publishing houses a tool that nails your sales figures to the door in full view: a lot of precious writing, trendy stuff, was revealed to be deeply irrelevant, propped up by academic back scratchers. Also, in the full flush of subprime times, it often seemed as though books were published and reviewed in lock-step for their slavish faithfulness to the tenets of postmodernism and, later, K-Mart Realism (or as the French say, *le raycarverisme*). As an outsider, maybe a bit of a nihilist, certainly a true believer when it comes to art and literature, I didn't mind seeing that well dry up.

If I were starting out today, my advice would be ... but, wait, I *am* starting out today. Tomorrow morning I can guarantee that most of us wracking our brains for the right word, hunched over our laptop or legal pads, trying to ignore the jiggling leg of the guy at the other end of the table or the girl chair-dancing to whatever her iPod's playing. Most of us will be searching for the moment when all distraction drops away, when all worries about where and whether and how much will cease to matter . . . because the story has just kicked in and it's taking us places we've never been before.

DOUG UNGER: As for changing as a writer . . . really, I feel like a different writer every time I approach a new work. Part of the struggle in writing a novel is not to change too much every time I work on it, so as to be able to maintain a consistent style and tone. Still, every book is different; every story is new, at least to me. Though my work might read as written by the same, unchanged writer, that's not the way I perceive the writing process. And I wouldn't know how to describe the changes since Iowa, unless it be by looking at how the work has changed. It has definitely changed. I'm more careful now.

And, though my early work, the work closest to the Iowa experience, is the best known, I believe I'm writing better than I did then. All in all, though, the quality of the struggle is the same, which means it's always difficult, at least for me. I'm less sure now how good the work really is when it's finished, and I'm more able to take a step back from it and see its faults and, by seeing them, to try to do better next time. I write less now, though.

Teaching writers and doing all the work of administering academic programs allows me less time to write now than I had back then. Sometimes I think back to Iowa and the sessions at the typewriter—remember those? I wrote on a Smith Corona electric in those days—I think back to that typewriter and realize I could spend ten and twelve hours at a stretch just writing. I seldom can do that now, though I feel great when I can. I don't waste as much time now, though, nor as much paper. Still, even on a very good day, four to five hours of concentrated writing time is about all I can manage to sustain. That's a change.

ALLAN GURGANUS: I really feel that, at age sixty, I'm just getting started. It sounds like something you say in interviews, but it really is true. Maybe because I published my first book when I was already forty-two. I still have this sense of excitement, of beginning. I'm still overawed by the notion of what a book can be. That can be intimidating, but it's also served me. Enough has gotten through my intense filtering system; enough that seems acceptable.

You know, I'll read Proust or the first one hundred pages of *Great Expectations* or Henry James or *The Beast in the Jungle* or *To the Lighthouse*, or *Emma*, *Robinson Crusoe*, early Evelyn Waugh, *The Importance of Being Ernest*, or *Life on the Mississippi* and I'm still like a fourteen-year-old kid: Gee willikers, someday I'll be able to do this! Having that kind of excitement and enthusiasm is the thing that keeps me clambering back up on the horse, starting over each day.

DON WALLACE: At the end of our year in Stanford, I put my foot down. "We're going to New York," I said.

Here at last was the literary center of America, and we were there, if somewhat belatedly. Times were hard, we had little money, and the cockroaches were big; but there was also a tidal surge of writers and artists sloshing back and forth, from readings to publication parties (free cheese and crackers!) to blowouts in dirty downtown lofts—everything pre-gentrification, pre–*Sex and the City*, AIDS appearing as a mystery killer of our gay neighbors, muggers a fact of life, dinner a one-dollar slice of pizza.

Many were the paths to success or anonymity. After six months temping (again), I got an editing job at a boating magazine. Why boats? Because my college thesis had been on Melville. Instead of teaching five units of Rhetoric 101 to a bunch of bored freshmen, I found myself interviewing Colombian cocaine smugglers, round-the-world solo sailors, blue-blood relics from the yacht clubs who'd raced JFK at Hyannis, and adventurers such as Richard Branson, then just a brash record company president with a pronounced death wish. An encounter with a case of murder involving professional bass fishermen led to my writing a comic novel about that world. In 1991, Soho Press published *Hot Water*.

I thought it would be easy after that. It wasn't. Each novel is, at least for me, an experience in starting over again from square one.

CATHERINE GAMMON: I used to always have a way to write something down as soon as it occurred to me, always like a pen and paper in my bag. It wasn't necessarily a notebook, but there were paper and pen available in my bag somewhere when some thought would come because these words do come. And the more I was writing, the more these interesting suggestions for writing would come.

When I basically stopped being a writer in order to be a Zen student, when I'd go on walks, I wouldn't have paper and pen with me, and many times I'd notice a thought, and then I'd think, "Oh, a writer has a pen and paper. I'm not a writer because I'm not carrying a pen and paper anymore."

Often a story would start with just a sentence or a phrase or two sentences or something. You have no idea where it's going, but it would be a start, and if you go with it, something might develop. So now when I'd be out there walking without a pen and paper, I would just have the sentence and I would memorize the sentence and see if I could come back with the sentence. So maybe I was still a writer after all, and in fact now I'm writing again.

When I started again, knowing I wanted to write with intention again, after some time I sent some things out. This was a little more than a year ago, and nothing was accepted. So then I could think, "Well, maybe it's a mistake after all." But two of the places I sent stories to (one that I was published in previously) gave me encouragement. And that can be enough to keep you going.

It's a different question for me now, though. At the beginning of my life in writing, it was "I'm not going to give up too soon," and now I'm sort of, "Am I really going back into this or not?" It's a different kind of starting point.

ALLAN GURGANUS: Check in with me in forty years, if you can, but I really do have a feeling that I'm just getting the outboard motor cranked and purring at last. I mean, I have six unpublished books that I think are better than anything I've put out there yet.... They're looking for that last revision, or that permission I give myself when you suddenly say it's done. My agent threatens to come in with a gun and get them out of the house. But it suits me . . . I'll know when they're done.

Sixty's the new forty, baby. That's what everyone over sixty says. I do think people are living longer and taking better care of themselves. I think that's the thing that keeps you going. I mean, Cheever was sixty-five when we were at Iowa. And even he, after all those cigarettes and those rivers of Scotch, lasted quite a while after Iowa, didn't he? And he got some wonderful critical attention at the end.

Good things can come to those willing to work and wait.

SHERRY KRAMER: I don't know if we improve with time, but I think we become the writer we were meant to be. It's not a change, but becoming who we are. And I think you learn to read your own work better.

In the theater, they say that playwriting is a young man's game, that there are no second acts in American theater. This has been mostly true: the theater treated Williams abysmally, Albee too, and cut playwrights like Durang off at the knees when they were just coming into their own. I think novelists have better luck at growing and blossoming later.

I just finished a new play. I'm fifty-four years old, and I think I finally got it right. It's not that I didn't make mistakes in this play, but it's a play where I was finally able to take my own advice. I was writing and writing and having a great time, but didn't know where I was going. I got halfway through and thought, Okay, *now what?* I'm not positive about what's happening, so I said, *Okay, let's go back to the beginning, and it'll tell you what you need to know.* A play generates these things we call "pointers"—it generates them spontaneously, they just happen, so if I look carefully, they'll show me what I need to know.

This is something I've said to younger writers for like twenty years . . . but finding them in your own work is of course so much harder. So for the first time, I went back and looked—and everything I needed was there.

Some people think a play writes itself, and some don't. I'm in the middle. I believe that a play arrives whole and complete, and you stay true to it and try to write it down. The theater is a metaphoric art form, so story is sometimes the enabler of that, and sometimes the story is the metaphor, and sometimes? Sometimes a play just redefines what story and metaphor are.

JANE SMILEY: The stories I wrote at Iowa make no sense to me now. I think I was built to be a novelist, and a realist at that, so the tempering fire for my aesthetic was writing by myself in Iceland and then in Ames. But Iowa gave me the sense that I was on the escalator, if only at the bottom, and that progress was likely, if not inevitable.

GARY IORIO: My second wife, Kristine, got me back to writing. I started again in March 2009. She was reading a novel, *Easter Parade* by Richard Yates (I loved that book; I love his work), and one of the characters goes to Iowa. It's the late '50s, and they're having classes out in the Quonset huts, and my wife asks, "Didn't you go there?"

"Yeah," I said.

And she said, "Why aren't you writing?"

She likes novels, not short stories, and the thicker the better so she gets her money's worth. So she gave me a little challenge: to write something we can share. So I'll write a few pages, show it to her, and go from there. She encourages me to finish things. It's one more thing we can share, so it's not like I'm writing in a vacuum.

I started sending short pieces to some online magazines. I was looking for some type of writing community, so then my wife got me into this writers' group through the Internet. It's some sort of "meet up" thing, like groups for people looking for sex, but this one was for writers. There's one for sculptors, too, and one for landscape painters and so on. I went to the first meeting, and it was surprisingly good.

I was drastically rewriting a short story that was in my thesis, revising and bringing it up to the times. Kristine was reading it and liked it, but she was too close, so she got me into this group. A writing workshop.

We put the maximum number in the group at six, so it'd be small enough that we can go over everyone's stories. Five people signed up for the first meeting, but two couldn't make it, so it was me, another guy, and a woman. We e-mailed our stories to one another in advance; the others took a blue pencil to mine, and then we went over it in the meeting. When I got it back, it took me thirty minutes to rewrite it, and it was better.

We met at a franchise coffee place; I think it's called Panera. It was like meeting in the Cleveland bus station, but the others wanted to meet on neutral ground. The woman in the group, Kim Luisi, wrote a short story about an artist, a young kid in Brooklyn. It was like something Flannery O'Connor wrote; beautiful, but it needed an ending. I was impressed by her talent. The other guy was writing a Star Trek novel. It wasn't like the Iowa workshop at all, as there are a lot of fantasy writers in the group; everyone wants to rewrite *The Stand* by Steven King.

ERIC OLSEN: While I wrote articles for magazines and a few nonfiction books, I was always working on a novel or two, but I'd always get distracted by another assignment and leave it off, sometimes for months at a time. And all along, Schaeffer and I continued to collaborate on various projects. After *City Business*, we worked together on a book about the gaming industry, but we got distracted. Then when poker was hot, we worked together on a novel about poker and got distracted.

Then in 1995, I got a job as an editor at a Time Inc. company, and once I got a taste of editing, I swore I'd never go back. It was a revelation! Editors had all the power, after all, and the work was much, much less emotionally draining. No sitting staring at a blank page all day, no tearing out your hair, desperate for a good idea. No, let some poor schlub of a writer do that! And then you could savage what he'd slaved over with your blue pencil! The sense of power was heady, wonderful, intoxicating!

ROBIN GREEN: Before I started writing scripts for John Falsey, I was an editor at *California Magazine*, and I remember when I first got that job, that first taste of editing, I swore I'd never be a sniveling writer again. I was so brilliant and smart.

DON WALLACE: At the same time my editing career paid the bills, with the immediate gratification of monthly publication but the implied oblivion that comes with the territory: Hearst, Condé Nast, the *New York Times*, Time Inc. I focused on being a consummate editor instead of a staff writer, nurturing others while reserving my writing juice for my own stuff. Though I had more bad luck with my third novel, I began placing memoirs with *Harper's* and signed up to write a serialized novel for *Naval History* magazine.

In December 2000, I spotted a newspaper item: my high school football team, ranked number one in the country in preseason polls, was scheduled to play the number two ranked team, which hadn't lost a game in eleven years. Ten months in advance of the game, I took a chance, left my job, went back home to SoCal, and immersed myself in the culture of the two schools, their communities, the kids and the coaches, all against the backdrop of a increasingly commercialized high school sports scene. *One Great Game* came out in 2003 and did pretty well for a football book (if you're going to get rich, write about golf or baseball). Last December the *Los Angeles Times* even did a retrospective on that game and the book, calling it a classic and a "game-changer" in high school athletics. Best of all, for me, was how it brought my father joy and connection to his town and school, at a time when we all knew he was dying of cancer. When my *Naval History* novel won an author-of-the-year prize and my dad, a Naval Academy grad, traveled with me and my son to Annapolis to pick up the plaque and address the Joint Chiefs of Staff, I also received something I'd unconsciously given up on ever getting: parental approval.

GLENN SCHAEFFER: One reason I'm so fond of Iowa and have this relationship with the Workshop is that, early on, it was an affirmation of my self-image as a creative thinker. They let me in! And Connie Brothers—she doesn't know the wonder she did, speaking up for me when that *Des Moines Register* reporter, mentioned before, came nosing around—but she's the reason I reconnected years later, along with the superlative director at the time, Frank Conroy. I hadn't concerned myself with the Workshop for quite a long time.

Later, when I donated money to the Workshop so they could build a library-and-archives annex to the Dey House, I quipped that my writing checks was probably the best writing I could do. But I was haunted by the fact my MFA thesis was stinking up the archives. No good could come of that, I thought. And now I'm back at it, rewriting my thesis, *Holy Shaker*.

Maybe I'll put it up for a workshop. Certainly I'll have Olsen savage it with his blue pencil. He still likes to stick me with *that* jab. And my once and future novella, "Kicks," is well along in rewrite, already sold to a publisher.

The process of writing now is different. For the first time, a story's actually speaking to me, telling me what it wants to be, writing itself. This time around, writing's fun. Who'd have thought?

DOUG UNGER: I've got another third-draft novel, which I keep thinking of as a comic novel about an actor's life that no reader I've ever shown it to thinks is very funny. Still, I find it such a scream that I've finished it three times through, completed a third draft four years ago. But I still feel it needs more work. It's stewing there, in one of my file drawers. Or call it still in hibernation inside one of my hard drives. One of these days, I'll get back to that one, too, and take it through another draft to see if my sense of humor can, somehow, communicate to readers.

I'm grateful to be alive. I'm grateful to be alive and still writing. More than this, I'm grateful for my writer friends, and to my students for keeping me up to date and always thinking new thoughts, seeing the world renewed through their young eyes.

And I'm very, very grateful—more than I can say—and indebted to the Iowa Writers' Workshop for taking a chance on me when I was young. I hope that I've lived up to the faith and encouragement, the good teaching and financial support, those wonderful writers and administrators there provided me.

The life after Iowa has not been easy. It's never been easy. I don't know any writer who has it easy. Still . . . what more could I ask for? What more could any writer ask? Isn't where I am and what I'm doing right now what I always wanted to do? And what I was taught at Iowa to do?

One last thing, and I think I speak for us all, I want to say thank you. Thank you to everybody who helped us along the way. Thank you. *Gracias. Merci beaucoup.* Thank you. *Les agradesco de corazón.* Thank you. Thank you. Thank you.

—END—

ABOUT THE CONTRIBUTORS

JEFFREY ABRAHAMS

Jeffrey was born and grew up in Ohio, where he graduated from Miami University, Oxford. He earned an MFA in poetry from the Iowa Writers' Workshop in 1977.

He has worked as a journalist (staff writer for the *Los Angeles Times* and *Oakland Tribune*) and freelance writer, and currently serves as a consultant and copywriter in communications, marketing, and advertising in San Francisco. In addition to publishing poems, short stories, magazine articles, and newspaper columns, he is the author of *The Mission Statement Book: 301 Corporate Mission Statements from America's Top Companies* (Ten Speed Press, 1995, now in its third edition). Jeffrey is also an enthusiastic salsa dancer and photographer.

MARVIN BELL

Marvin was born in New York City and grew up in Center Moriches on eastern Long Island. He attended Alfred University in western New York. He later received an MA in literature from the University of Chicago and an MFA in poetry from the University of Iowa. Following two years in the Army, he served forty years on the faculty of the Iowa Writers' Workshop. He lives with his wife, Dorothy, in both Iowa City and Port Townsend, Washington, and at times in Sag Harbor, New York. He teaches now for the brief-residency MFA program at Pacific University. He has collaborated with musicians, composers, dancers, and photographers, frequently performs with the bassist Glen Moore of the jazz group, Oregon, and is the creator of a poetic form known as the "Dead Man" poem.

Honors include awards from the American Academy of Arts and Letters, the Academy of American Poets, and the *American Poetry Review;* fellowships from the Guggenheim Foundation and the National Endowment for the Arts; and Senior Fulbright appointments to Yugoslavia and Australia. He was the first Poet Laureate of Iowa.

Poetry by Marvin Bell

Vertigo: The Living Dead Man Poems (Copper Canyon Press, 2011)

Whiteout: Dead Man Poems by Marvin Bell in Response to Photographs by Nathan Lyons (Lodima Press, 2011)

A Primer about the Flag, children's picture book illustrated by Chris Raschka (Candlewick Press, forthcoming 2011)

Mars Being Red (Copper Canyon Press, 2007)

Rampant (Copper Canyon Press, 2004)

Nightworks: Poems, 1962–2000 (Copper Canyon Press, 2000)

Wednesday: Selected Poems 1966–1997 (Salmon Publishing, Ireland, 1998)

Poetry for a Midsummer's Night (Seventy Fourth Street Productions, 1998)

Ardor: The Book of the Dead Man, Vol. 2 (poems) (Copper Canyon Press, 1997)

A Marvin Bell Reader (selected prose and poetry) (Middlebury College Press / University Press of New England, 1994)

The Book of the Dead Man (poems) (Copper Canyon Press, 1994)

Iris of Creation (Copper Canyon Press, 1990)

New and Selected Poems (Athenaeum, 1987)

Drawn by Stones, by Earth, by Things That Have Been in the Fire (poems) (Athenaeum, 1984)

These Green-Going-to-Yellow (Athenaeum, 1981)

Stars Which See, Stars Which Do Not See (Athenaeum, 1977) [Reissued, Carnegie Mellon Classic Contemporary Series, 1992]

Residue of Song (Athenaeum, 1974)

The Escape into You (Athenaeum, 1971) [Reissued, Carnegie Mellon Classic Contemporary Series, 1994]

A Probable Volume of Dreams (Athenaeum, 1969)

Things We Dreamt We Died For (Stone Wall Press, 1966)

Other

7 Poets, 4 Days, 1 Book, coauthored with Istvan Laszlo Geher, Ksenia Golubovich, Simone Inguanez, Christopher Merrill, Tomaz Salamun, and Dean Young (Trinity University Press, 2009)

Segues: A Correspondence in Poetry [coauthored with William Stafford] (David R. Godine, Publisher, 1983)

Old Snow Just Melting: Essays and Interviews (University of Michigan Press, 1983)

DOUGLAS BORSOM

Doug grew up in Hinsdale, Illinois. He studied physics at Case Western Reserve University in Cleveland, but transferred to Knox College in Galesburg, Illinois, to study literature and discovered creative writing classes. He had started writing at age twelve because he thought books were powerful, so writing conferred power. He completed his MFA in fiction from the Iowa Writers' Workshop in 1975. "I don't think of myself as a writer," he says. "It's just something I do." After Iowa, he taught creative writing for three years at Southwest Missouri State before returning to school to study mathematics at the University of Wisconsin. For twenty years, his day job was in the computer industry. Doug lives in Pasadena and is writing a novel.

T. C. BOYLE

T. C. grew up in a working-class home in Peekskill, New York. While his parents encouraged him to do well in school, T.C . had other ideas and set out to make music his career. At the age of seventeen, he changed his middle name to Coraghessan (pronounced "kuh-rag-issun") from John, in homage to his Irish ancestry. On his graduation from Lakeland High School, he went to the State University of New York (SUNY) at Potsdam, intending to major in music. His audition on the saxophone for the music program did not go as well as planned, however, and when a play he wrote for one of his classes got a few laughs, he began to rethink his priorities.

T. C. graduated from SUNY in 1968 in English and history, played in a rock band, and "drifted" a bit. Then he became a high school teacher at his alma mater.

His first published short story, "The OD and Hepatitis Railroad," appeared in the *North American Review* and helped him get into the Iowa Writers' Workshop. He received an MFA in fiction writing in 1974 and then stayed on to get a PhD. He also served as fiction editor of the *Iowa Review*.

T. C. joined the faculty of the University of Southern California in 1978 as an assistant professor of creative writing. His first collection of short stories, *Descent of Man*, was published a year later, followed by his first novel, *Water Music*, in 1981. His third novel, *World's End*, 1987, earned the PEN/Faulkner Award for best novel of the year. By then he was a full professor of creative writing at USC. In the years since, he has published many more novels and short stories and won numerous other awards including an O. Henry Award and the PEN/Malamud Award for the short story.

His work has been translated into more than two dozen languages. His stories have appeared in most of the major American magazines, including the *New Yorker, Harper's, Esquire,* the *Atlantic Monthly, Playboy,* the *Paris Review, GQ, Antaeus, Granta,* and *McSweeney's.*

He and his wife, whom he married in 1974, currently live near Santa Barbara. They have three children. His daughter Kerrie followed her father's lead and attended the Iowa Writers' Workshop. T. C. still wears red Converse high-tops.

Books

When the Killing's Done (Viking, 2011)
Wild Child and Other Stories (Viking, 2010)
The Women (Viking, 2009)
Talk Talk (Viking, 2006)
The Human Fly and Other Stories (Viking, 2005)
Tooth and Claw (Viking, 2005)
The Inner Circle (Viking, 2004)
Drop City (Viking, 2003)
Doubletakes: Contemporary Short Stories, ed. (Wadsworth, 2003)
After the Plague (Viking, 2001)
A Friend of the Earth (Viking, 2000)
Riven Rock (Viking, 1998)
T. C. Boyle Stories (Viking, 1998)
The Tortilla Curtain (Viking, 1995)
Without a Hero (Viking, 1994)
The Road to Wellville (Viking, 1993)
East Is East (Viking, 1990)
If the River Was Whiskey (Viking, 1989)
World's End (Viking, 1987)
Greasy Lake and Other Stories (Viking, 1985)
Budding Prospects: A Pastoral (Viking, 1984)
Water Music (Little, Brown, 1981)
Descent of Man (Little, Brown, 1979)

ANTHONY BUKOSKI

Anthony was born in the East End of Superior, Wisconsin, attended St. Adalbert's Grade School, and began his undergraduate work at Wisconsin State University Superior. He left after a year, joined the Marines in the summer of 1964, and went to Vietnam. He returned three years later and finished school. Next it was on to Brown University for an MA in English, then to Iowa for an MFA in fiction from the Writers' Workshop in 1976, and a PhD in English in 1984. Anthony teaches English at his alma mater. His father, an accordion player and laborer in a flour mill, had once been a merchant seaman on the Great Lakes and ocean. His influence is evident in many of the younger Bukoski's Polish American stories. (The accordion, a Scandalli Imperio VII, now reposes in the Accordion Hall of Fame in Superior.) Anthony's awards include the R. V. Cassill Fellowship in Fiction from the Christopher Isherwood Foundation, a Booklist "Editor's Choice" for *Time Between Trains*, and the first literary prize presented by the Polish Institute of Houston.

Short Story Collections
North of the Port (Southern Methodist University Press, 2008)
Time Between Trains (Southern Methodist University Press, 2003)
Polonaise (Southern Methodist University Press, 1998)
Children of Strangers (Southern Methodist University Press, 1993)
Twelve Below Zero (Holy Cow! Press, 1986, 2008)

SANDRA CISNEROS
Sandra was born in Chicago, where she earned a BA in English from Loyola University. Her MFA in fiction from the Iowa Writers' Workshop came in 1978. Her father, who was from Mexico, worked as an upholsterer; her mother was Mexican American. Sandra is the middle child and only girl among six siblings. She has worked as a teacher and counselor to high school dropouts, as an artist in the schools, a college recruiter, an arts administrator, and as a visiting writer at a number of universities including the University of California, Berkeley, and the University of Michigan, Ann Arbor. She lives in San Antonio, Texas. Awards include two National Endowment for the Arts fellowships in fiction and poetry; American Book Award; Paisano Dobie fellowship; Segundo Concurso Nacional del Cuento Chicano (University of Arizona); Lannan Foundation Literary Award; H.D.L., State University of New York at Purchase; and a MacArthur fellowship. Sandra is at work on several new books, including a collection of essays, *Writing in My Pajamas*; *Bravo, Bruno*, a children's book; *Have You Seen, Marie?* a picture book for adults; a screenplay of *House on Mango Street*; and several collaborative works including art projects. She is the founder of two foundations, the Alfredo Cisneros Del Moral Foundation and the Macondo Foundation, which serve creative writers.

Books
Vintage Cisneros (Vintage, 2004)
Caramelo (Knopf Spanish edition, Vintage Español, 2002, 2003)
Caramelo (Knopf, Vintage, 2002, 2003)
El Arroyo de la Llorona (Vintage Español, 1996)

Hairs/Pelitos (Knopf Children's Books, 1994)
Loose Woman (Knopf, 1994; Vintage, 1995)
La Casa en Mango Street (Vintage Español, 1992, Vintage Español 25th anniversary, 2009)
Woman Hollering Creek and Other Stories (Random House, 1991; Vintage, 1992)
My Wicked Wicked Ways (Third Woman, 1987; Random House, 1992)
The House on Mango Street (Arte Publico Press, 1984; Vintage, 1991; Knopf, 10th anniversary, 1994; Vintage, 25th anniversary, 2009)
Bad Boys (Mango Press, 1980)

ROSALYN DREXLER
A novelist, playwright, and painter, Rosalyn lives in the Ironbound section of Newark, NJ. She painted and exhibited among pop artists such as Andy Warhol and Roy Lichtenstein in the 1960s. Warhol featured her in his 1962 prints *Album of a Mat Queen*, which depicted her as "Rosa Carlo, the Mexican Spitfire," who would become the heroine of one of her novels a decade later. Her visual art is among the collections of museums such as the Whitney Museum of American Art, the Hirshhorn Museum and Sculpture Garden, the Wadsworth Athenaeum, and the Walker Art Center.

She has won three Obie Awards for Off-Broadway productions, an Emmy for writing excellence for the TV special *The Lily Show: A Lily Tomlin Special*, and four Rockefeller Grants for playwriting. She has also received a Guggenheim Fellowship, two Pollock-Krasner awards in painting, and a grant in painting from the Bunting Fellowship Program at Harvard/Radcliffe. The holder of an Honorary Doctorate in Visual Arts from the University of the Arts in Philadelphia, Rosalyn has also earned Yaddo and MacDowell fellowships.

Ros is currently working on an edition of prints and paintings. She has also just finished a book titled *Tree Man: A Tough Situation*, which she says is "possibly unpublishable."

Partial List of Publications
Vulgar Lives (Chiasmus, 2007)
Dear: A New Play (Applause Books, 1997, 2000)
Art Does (Not!) Exist (Fiction Collective 2, 1996)
Transients Welcome: Three One-Act Plays (Broadway Play Publishing Inc., 1984)
Bad Guy (Dutton, 1982)
Starburn: The Story of Jennie Love (Simon & Schuster, 1979)
Rocky [novelization under Julia Sorel] (Ballentine Books, 1976)

The Cosmopolitan Girl (M. Evans & Company, Inc., 1974)
To Smithereens (Signet Books, 1972)
One or Another (Dell, 1971)
The Line of Least Existence and Other Plays (Random House, 1967)
I Am the Beautiful Stranger: Paintings of the '60s (Grossman Publishers, 1965)

JENNIE FIELDS
Jennie was born in Chicago and raised in Highland Park, Illinois. She received her BFA in creative writing from the University of Illinois and an MFA in fiction in 1976 from the Iowa Writers' Workshop, which helped to toughen her up for her next career: advertising. After thirty-two years of writing McDonald's jingles and dreaming up green moths to help sell sleeping pills, all the while writing novels, she decided to finally take the plunge to write fiction full-time, leaving New York to live with her husband in Nashville, Tennessee. Her next book, *The Age of Ecstasy*, will be published by Viking in 2012. She has a twenty-four-year-old daughter, two grown step-children and, missing the patter of little feet, has adopted a little black dog named Violet, who thinks everything Jennie writes is delicious.

Books
The Age of Ecstasy (forthcoming, Viking, 2012)
The Middle Ages (William Morrow & Co., 2002)
Crossing Brooklyn Ferry (William Morrow & Co., 1997)
Lily Beach (Maxwell MacMillan International, 1993) Her books are also published in Germany, Great Britain, Australia, and New Zealand.

CATHERINE GAMMON
Catherine was born in Los Angeles, California. She earned a BA in philosophy at Pomona College and an MFA in fiction from the Iowa Writers' Workshop in 1976. Catherine was a fellow of the Fine Arts Work Center in Provincetown in 1977 and 1981 and worked for many years in the type production department of the *New York Review of Books*. In 1991, her novel *Isabel Out of the Rain* was published by Mercury House, and in 1992, she joined the faculty of the MFA program at the University of Pittsburgh. Her fiction has appeared in *Ploughshares*, the *North American Review, Kenyon Review, Manoa, Central Park, Fiction International, Other Voices*, and other journals. She served as fiction editor for *Cape Discovery*, an anthology of fiction and poetry by Fine Arts Work Center fellows. Catherine has received NEA and New York Foundation for the Arts grants for her fiction, as well as a creative research fellowship from the American Antiquarian Society

for work in the Esther Forbes Papers and the Cotton Mather collection in preparation for a novel about the Salem witchcraft trials. In 2001, she left both the academy and the literary marketplace to begin residential training at San Francisco Zen Center. In 2005, she was ordained a Soto Zen priest by Tenshin Reb Anderson and in 2010 served as Shuso, or head monk, for the spring practice period at Green Dragon Temple/Green Gulch Farm. In January 2011, she returned to Pitt's MFA program as a visiting professor and hopes to continue reweaving her life in writing into her life in Zen.

Books
Isabel Out of the Rain (Mercury House, 1991)
Cape Discovery: The Provincetown Fine Arts Work Center Anthology [editor]
    (Sheep Meadow Press, 1994)

ROBIN GREEN
Robin was born in Rhode Island. She earned a BA in American literature from Brown University in 1967, where she took a few fiction classes from John Hawkes. After graduating, she worked as a secretary for Stan Lee, editor in chief of Marvel Comics. She then became a freelance journalist, writing for *Rolling Stone* in the heady days of the New Journalism. Then, wanting to get back to her fiction, she applied to the Iowa Writers' Workshop, where she earned an MFA in 1977.

She met her husband, Mitch Burgess, her writing/producing partner, at Iowa. (He was an undergrad in a fiction class she taught; they didn't date until the semester was over, she's quick to point out.) After Iowa, she went to LA and worked as an editor at *California Magazine*. After a few years, John Falsey, a classmate from Iowa, asked her to write a script for a show he'd created with Joshua Brand, *A Year in the Life*. From there, she went on to write for a number of critically acclaimed TV series, including *Northern Exposure* and *The Sopranos*.

Awards
Robin won an Emmy Award and two Golden Globe Awards for her work on the CBS series *Northern Exposure*. She was awarded the 2001 and 2003 Emmys for Best Writing of a Drama Series for episodes of *The Sopranos* and in 2004 for Outstanding Drama Series. In 2007, she shared with Mitch Burgess a Writers Guild of America award for best Dramatic Series, *The Sopranos*. In addition, she also has won two Peabody Awards and a Golden Globe for that show.

Television Work
Blue Bloods (2010–present)
The Sopranos (22 episodes, 1999–2006)
- "Live Free or Die" (2006) TV episode (written by)
- "All Due Respect" (2004) TV episode (written by)
- "Cold Cuts" (2004) TV episode (written by)
- "Irregular Around the Margins" (2004) TV episode (written by)
- "Whitecaps" (2002) TV episode (written by) (17 more)
Party of Five (4 episodes, 1997–1998)
- "Free and Clear" (1998) TV episode (written by)
- "Of Human Bonding" (1998) TV episode (written by)
- "Adjustments" (1997) TV episode (written by)
- "Zap" (1997) TV episode (written by)
Mr. & Mrs. Smith (1996) TV series (unknown episodes)
American Gothic (1 episode, 1995)
- "Dead to the World" (1995) TV episode (writer)
Northern Exposure (25 episodes, 1991–1995)
- "Tranquility Base" (1995) TV episode (written by)
- "Buss Stop" (1995) TV episode (written by)
- "The Mommy's Curse" (1995) TV episode (written by)
- "Mi Casa, Su Casa" (1995) TV episode (written by)
- "Full Upright Position" (1994) TV episode (written by) (20 more)
Capital News (1 episode, 1990)
- "Tapes of Wrath" (1990) TV episode (writer)
Almost Grown (1 episode, 1988)
- "If That Diamond Ring Don't Shine" (1988) TV episode (writer)
A Year in the Life (2 episodes, 1988)
- "Peter Creek Road" (1988) TV episode (writer)
- "The Little Disturbance of Man" (1988) TV episode (writer)

ALLAN GURGANUS
Allan was born the son of a schoolteacher and a businessman in Rocky Mount, North Carolina. He first trained as a painter, studying at the University of Pennsylvania and the Pennsylvania Academy of Fine Arts; he has illustrated three limited editions of his fiction. During a three-year stint onboard the USS *Yorktown* during the Vietnam War, he turned to writing. He earned a BA from Sarah Lawrence where he worked with Grace Paley. In 1975, he received an MFA in fiction from the Iowa Writers' Workshop where his mentors were John Cheever and Stanley Elkin. Allan's stories and essays have appeared in the *New Yorker*, *Harper's*, the *Atlantic Monthly*, the *Paris Review*, the *New York Times*, and other publications. He has been

awarded a Guggenheim Fellowship, and his short fiction has been honored by the *O'Henry Prize Stories*, *Best American Stories*, *The Norton Anthology of Short Fiction*, and *Best New Stories of the South*. His fiction has been translated into sixteen languages. Adaptations have appeared on Broadway and won four Emmy awards. He has taught writing and literature at Stanford, Duke, and Sarah Lawrence and has returned to teach at the Iowa Writers' Workshop in 1989 and 2010.

Books
The Practical Heart: Four Novellas (Knopf, 2001), Lambda Literary Award
Plays Well with Others (Knopf, 1997)
White People (Knopf, 1990), Los Angeles Times Book Prize, Pen-Faulkner
    finalist
Oldest Living Confederate Widow Tells All (Knopf, 1989), American
    Academy of Arts and Letters Sue Kaufman Prize for Best Work of First
    Fiction

JOE HALDEMAN
Joe was born in Oklahoma City. He grew up in Puerto Rico, New Orleans, Washington, D. C., and Alaska. Drafted in 1967, he fought in the Central Highlands of Vietnam as a combat engineer and received the Purple Heart. He earned a BS in physics and astronomy at the University of Maryland, followed by graduate work in math and computer science, but he dropped out to write, eventually completing his MFA in fiction at the University of Iowa Writers' Workshop in 1975.

Joe lives in Gainesville, Florida, and Cambridge, Massachusetts, with his wife of forty-four years, Gay. He has been a part-time professor at the Massachusetts Institute of Technology since 1983 and has taught writing workshops at Michigan State (Clarion), Clarion West Seattle, SUNY Buffalo, Princeton, University of North Dakota, Kent State, and the University of North Florida. He has also worked as a statistician's assistant, librarian, computer programmer, musician, laborer, occasional platform speaker, and consultant.

Books
Starbound (Ace Books, 2010)
Marsbound (Ace Books, 2008)
The Accidental Time Machine (Ace Books, 2007)
A Separate War [short story collection] (Ace Books, 2006)

War Stories (Nightshade Press, 2005), collection of *War Year, 1968* and
   shorter pieces
Old Twentieth (Ace Books, 2005)
Camouflage (Ace Books, 2004)
Guardian (Ace Books, 2002)
The Coming (Ace Books, 2000)
Forever Free [sequel to *The Forever War*] (Ace Books, 1999)
Forever Peace (Berkley, 1997), Hugo, John Campbell Award, and Nebula
   Award
Saul's Death [poetry collection] (Anamnesis Press, 1997)
None So Blind [short story collection] (AvoNova Books, 1996)
1968 [novel] (Hodder & Stoughton, UK, 1994; William Morrow, Inc.,
   1995)
Vietnam and Other Alien Worlds [essays, fiction, poetry] (NESFA Press,
   1993)
Worlds Enough and Time [novel] (Morrow, 1992)
The Hemingway Hoax [short novel] Morrow, 1990)
Buying Time [novel] (Morrow, 1989)
Tool of the Trade [novel] (Morrow, 1987)
Dealing in Futures [short story collection] (Viking, 1985)
Nebula Awards 17 [anthology] (Holt, 1983)
Worlds Apart [novel] (Viking, 1983)
Worlds [novel] (Viking, 1981)
World Without End [Star Trek novel] (Bantam, 1979)
Infinite Dreams [short story collection] (St. Martin's Press, 1978)
Study War No More [anthology] (St. Martin's Press, 1977)
All My Sins Remembered [novel] (St. Martin's Press, 1977)
Planet of Judgment [Star Trek novel] (Bantam, 1977)
Mindbridge [novel] (St. Martin's Press, 1976)
The Forever War [novel, master's thesis] (St. Martin's Press, 1975; reissue
   in an Author's Approved Edition, Avon 1997; reissue, Thomas Dunne
   Books/St. Martins Press, 2009)
Cosmic Laughter [anthology] (Holt, 1974)
War Year [short novel] (Holt, 1972)

Some titles have been published in as many as twenty languages.
Dozens of Joe's short stories, novelettes, and novellas have appeared in
various science fiction magazines, along with a few appearances in mainstream magazines such as *Playboy*. He has also published songs and poetry,
primarily in smaller magazines, but also in *Harper's* and *Omni*. Several of
his books have been made into movies or adapted for the stage. Joe has

been awarded his genre's highest honors multiple times, including the Hugo, Nebula, Ditmar, Rhysling, World Fantasy, and John W. Campbell awards.

JOY HARJO

Joy was born in Tulsa, Oklahoma, and is a member of the Mvskoke Nation. Her poetry has garnered many awards, including the New Mexico Governor's Award for Excellence in the Arts, the Lifetime Achievement Award from the Native Writers Circle of the Americas; and the William Carlos Williams Award from the Poetry Society of America. She has released four award-winning CDs of original music and performances including her most recent, *Winding Through the Milky Way*, for which she won a Nammy (Native American Music Award) for Best Female Artist of the Year. She received Rasmuson: US Artists Fellowships for 2009 and 2011. She performs internationally with the Arrow Dynamics Band. Her one-woman show, *Wings of Night Sky, Wings of Morning Light*, premiered at the Wells Fargo Theater in 2009. She is a founding board member of the Native Arts and Cultures Foundation. Joy writes a column "Comings and Goings" for her tribal newspaper, the *Muscogee Nation News*. She lives in Albuquerque, New Mexico.

Books

For a Girl Becoming [young adult/children's book] (University of Arizona Press, 2009)

How We Became Human, New and Selected Poems (W. W. Norton, 2003)

A Map to the Next World (W. W. Norton, 2000)

The Good Luck Cat (Harcourt, 2000)

Reinventing the Enemy's Language, Contemporary Native Women's Writing of North America (W. W. Norton, 1997)

The Spiral of Memory [interviews, coedited with Laura Coltelli] (University of Michigan Press, 1996)

The Woman Who Fell from the Sky (W. W. Norton, 1994)

Fishing [fine press chapbook] (Oxhead Press, 1991)

In Mad Love and War (Wesleyan University Press, 1990)

Secrets from the Center of the World [poetic prose with Stephen Strom's photographs] (University of Arizona Press, 1989)

She Had Some Horses (Thunder's Mouth Press 1984, through three editions, W. W. Norton, 2008)

What Moon Drove Me to This? (I. Reed Books, 1979, out of print)

The Last Song [poetry chapbook] (Puerto del Sol Press, 1975, out of print)

Music CDs

Red Dreams, a Trail Beyond Tears (Mekko Productions, Inc., 2010)

Winding Through the Milky Way [music/songs] (Joy Harjo, Fast Horse Recordings, 2008; Mekko Productions, Inc., 2009)

She Had Some Horses [spoken word with a few music bonus tracks] (Mekko Productions, Inc., 2006)

Native Joy for Real [music with poetry/songs] (Joy Harjo, Mekko Productions, Inc., 2004)

Letter from the End of the Twentieth Century [with Poetic Justice, reggae/dub style music with spoken poetry] (Mekko Productions Inc., 2002; Silverwave Records, 1997; Red Horses Records, 1995)

MICHELLE HUNEVEN

Michelle was in the Iowa Writers' Workshop Class of '77. She spent the next twenty years writing fiction while working in food service (waitressing, cooking, restaurant reviewing, food writing). Her first novel, *Round Rock*, was published in 1997, followed by *Jamesland* in 2003 and *Blame* in 2009, a National Book Critics Circle finalist. She lives in the town where she grew up, Altadena, California, with her husband, Jim Potter, her terrier, black cat, and African grey parrot.

GARY IORIO

Gary was born in Brooklyn and moved to Massapequa, New York, at the age of eleven. He earned a BA in English from Hofstra University, followed by an MFA in fiction from the Iowa Writers' Workshop in 1976, and a JD from St. John's University School of Law in 1984. His fiction has appeared in the *Mississippi Review*, *Pig Iron*, *Wisconsin Review*, the *Penny Dreadful*, and other literary magazines and newspapers. He is married to Kristine Romani and has a daughter from his first marriage. He is currently a real estate attorney and resides in Islip and Montauk, NY.

JOHN IRVING

John was born and raised in Exeter, New Hampshire, where he attended Phillips Exeter Academy, the setting of several of his books and short stories. It is also where he learned to wrestle and became assistant coach in the sport that figures prominently in his life and to which he credits much of his success as a writer. He earned a BA from the University of New Hampshire in 1965, after a year at the University of Pittsburgh, where he also wrestled, and another year at the University of Vienna and the Institute of European Studies, followed by an MFA in fiction from the Iowa Writers' Workshop in 1967. He has been a writer in residence at Bread Loaf Writers' Conference as well as the Iowa Writers' Workshop; he has also taught at Mount Holyoke College and Brandeis University in Massachusetts and has coached wrestling at various New England prep schools. Awards include National Endowment for the Arts and Guggenheim Foundation fellowships, a Rockefeller Foundation grant, a National Book Award, and an Oscar for Best Adapted Screenplay. Since the international success of *The World According to Garp*, all of his books have been best sellers.

John lives with his second wife and three children in Vermont, Toronto, and northern Ontario.

Books
Last Night in Twisted River (Random House, 2009)
A Sound Like Someone Trying Not to Make a Sound [children's book] (2004)
Until I Find You (Random House, 2005)
The Fourth Hand (Random House, 2001)
My Movie Business: A Memoir (Random House, 1999)
A Widow for One Year (Random House, 1998)
The Imaginary Girlfriend: A Memoir (Ballantine Books, 2002)
A Son of the Circus (Random House, 1994)
Trying to Save Piggy Sneed [shorter pieces] (Arcade Publishing, 1996)
A Prayer for Owen Meany (William Morrow, 1989)
The Cider House Rules (William Morrow, 1985), 2000 Oscar for Best
    Adapted   Screenplay
The Hotel New Hampshire (E. P. Dutton, 1981)
The World According to Garp (E. P. Dutton, 1978), National Book Award
    winner
The 158-Pound Marriage (Random House, 1974)
The Water Method Man (Random House, 1972)
Setting Free the Bears (Random House, 1968)

SHERRY KRAMER
Sherry was born in Springfield, Missouri. She holds a BA in English from Wellesley College and received her MFA in fiction from the Iowa Writer's Workshop in 1977 and her MFA in playwriting from the University of Iowa Playwrights Workshop in 1978. She is a recipient of a National Endowment for the Arts Fellowship, a New York Foundation for the Arts Fellowship, a McKnight National Fellowship, a commission from the Audrey Skirball-Kenis Foundation, and was the first national member of New Dramatists. She has taught playwriting at Northwestern University and the MFA programs of Carnegie Mellon University and Catholic University and teaches regularly at both the Michener Center for Writers, University of Texas,

Austin, and the Iowa Playwrights Workshop, where she was head of the workshop. She lives in New York City and Vermont and currently teaches playwriting at Bennington College, Bennington, Vermont.

Plays

When Something Wonderful Ends [first produced Actors Theatre of Louisville Humana Festival, 2007] (Playscripts, Inc. *Humana Anthology*, 2007; *The Complete Plays*, 2008, Broadway Play Publishing, 2008, 2009)

A Permanent Signal [first produced Attica Stage Productions, Edinburgh Fringe Festival, 2004] (Broadway Play Publishing *Facing Forward*, 1995)

Things That Break [first produced Theatre of the First Amendment, Fairfax, VA, 1997] (Broadway Play Publishing *Plays by Sherry Kramer*, 2001)

Partial Objects [first produced Mill Mountain Theatre, 1993] (Broadway Play Publishing, 2010)

David's RedHaired Death [first produced Woolly Mammoth Theatre, Washington, DC, 1991] (Theatre Communication Group *Plays in Process*, 1992; Vintage Books *Plays for Actresses*, 1997; Broadway Play Publishing *Plays by Sherry Kramer*, 2001, 2006), Jane Chambers Playwriting Award, 1992

The World at Absolute Zero [first produced Ensemble Studio Theatre MARATHON, New York, New York, 1991] (Broadway Play Publishing, 1993)

What a Man Weighs [first produced Second Stage Theatre, New York, 1990] (Broadway Play Publishing, 1993, 2010), Arnold Weissberger Playwriting Award, 1990; NBC New Voices Award, 1990; New York Drama League Award, 1990; Marvin Taylor Playwriting Award, 1993

The Wall of Water [first produced Yale Repertory Theatre, New Haven, 1988] (Broadway Play Publishing, 1989; *Plays by Sherry Kramer*, 2001, 2008), LA Women in Theatre New Play Award

The Release of a Live Performance [first produced Brass Tacks Theatre, Minneapolis, 1982] (Broadway Play Publishing, 2010)

About Spontaneous Combustion [first produced Brass Tacks Theatre, Minneapolis, 1982] (Broadway Play Publishing, 2010)

JOHN "JACK" LEGGETT

Jack was born in New York, NY. He attended Andover and graduated from Yale University in 1942, after which he served as a lieutenant in the US Naval Reserve until 1945. He was married to Mary Lee Fahnestock, with whom he had three children, from 1948 to 1986. He now lives in Napa, California, where he has long directed the Napa Valley Writers' Conference.

He lives with his second wife, Edwina Bennington, of San Francisco, in a house designed by one of his sons.

Jack was an editor and publicity director for Houghton Mifflin in Boston throughout the '50s, then an editor at Harper & Row Publishing in New York for seven years. In 1969, he became a professor of English and the director of the Iowa Writers' Workshop, serving in those capacities for nearly twenty years. In 2008, he presented his extensive research files for his biography of William Saroyan to the University Libraries as an addendum to papers given earlier.

Books

A Daring Young Man: A Biography of William Saroyan (Knopf, 2002), [his research files and drafts for it constitute the 2003 Addendum]

Making Believe (Houghton Mifflin, 1986)

Gulliver House (Houghton Mifflin, 1979)

Ross and Tom: Two American Tragedies (Simon & Schuster, 1974)

Who Took the Gold Away (Random House, 1969)

The Gloucester Branch (Harper & Row, 1964)

Wilder Stone (Harper & Brothers, 1960)

GERI LIPSCHULTZ

Geri is a Jersey girl raised in a town (Park Ridge) known for the Roches, of whom she is a fan, and Nixon, of whom she was not. And not to mention James Gandolfini of *The Sopranos*, who was but a young'n when Geri was in high school. She graduated from UMass (Amherst) with a BA in elementary education, followed by an MFA in fiction from the Iowa Writers' Workshop in 1976. Her writing has appeared in the *New York Times, Kalliope, Black Warrior Review, North Atlantic Review, College English*, and other publications. She performed in her one-woman show, *Once Upon the Present Time*, produced in New York City by Woodie King, Jr. Her production, *Rising Above the Shadow—Women's Artistic Responses to September 11th*, featured the work of fifty women artists—painters, musicians, dancers, writers. She was awarded a CAPS grant from New York State for one of her novels. Her fiction was nominated for the Foley Award, and she was a Heekin semifinalist. Having spent more than a score and seven years trying and failing to both publish her novels and find a full-time teaching position, she decided to go back to school. She divides her time between Athens, Ohio, where she's a doctoral candidate in the English department at Ohio University, and Huntington Station, New York, where she lives with her husband, Erwin Wong. Their two children, both aspiring violinists, are David (twenty-four), who's gone electric, and Eliza (thirteen), who, at the moment, seems to prefer the classical tradition.

BILL MANHIRE

Bill was born in Invercargill, New Zealand—called by Rudyard Kipling "the last lamppost in the world"—and educated at the University of Otago and University College London. Back then, he was an Old Norse scholar; he can still pronounce "Eyjafjallajökull." In 1975, he founded New Zealand's first creative writing course at Victoria University of Wellington, where he is now professor of English and creative writing and director of the International Institute of Modern Letters. He was appointed New Zealand's inaugural Poet Laureate, is an Arts Foundation Laureate, and has won the New Zealand Poetry Award five times. Other honors include the Katherine Mansfield Fellowship to Menton, France, and the Prime Minister's Award. He is a Companion of the New Zealand Order of Merit.

His many publications include a *Collected Poems* (published in 2001 by Victoria University Press and Carcanet) and, since that volume, the prize-winning *Lifted* and *The Victims of Lightning*. Recent poems have appeared in the *London Review of Books*, the *New Yorker*, *Poetry London*, *Sport*, and the *Times Literary Supplement*. He is known for his collaborative work: in science with the physicist Paul Callaghan (the *Are Angels OK?* sci-art project), in the visual arts with the notable Maori painter Ralph Hotere (the *Song Cycle* and MALADY series), and in music with the jazz musician Norman Meehan (the CD *Buddhist Rain*).

He is also the author of several short story collections (including *South Pacific* and *Songs of My Life*) and the editor of best-selling anthologies (including *100 New Zealand Poems* and *Some Other Country: New Zealand's Best Short Stories*). He is probably a little too proud of his groundbreaking anthology of Antarctic poetry and fiction, *The Wide White Page*, but he has in fact visited Antarctica and once spent forty-five semi-heroic minutes at the South Pole.

DENNIS MATHIS

Dennis grew up in Peoria, Illinois, and graduated from Bradley University there, where he studied creative writing under George Chambers and double-majored in English and studio art. He moved to Chicago in 1974 before earning his MFA in fiction from the Iowa Writers' Workshop in 1978. His fiction has been honored with a grant from the National Endowment for the Arts, a residency at Yaddo, and two fellowships to the Fine Arts Work Center in Provincetown, Massachusetts, where he joined the staff as chairman of FAWC's Writing Committee, which at the time included Grace Paley and Alan Dugan. A fascination with computer technology in the '80s led him into the publishing industry in NYC and Boston and then into a twenty-year career in corporate communications during the infancy of the Internet. Dennis currently works as a consulting editor with a special interest in helping debut novelists and memoirists. He lives in Thousand Oaks, California, with his wife, Barbara. He is still working on his first book.

BILL McCOY

Bill grew up in State College, Pennsylvania. At Penn State (where he supported himself by playing bass in a funk band), he started out wanting to be a filmmaker but switched to English in time to get his BA. From there, he was off to Iowa, receiving an MFA in fiction from the Writers' Workshop in 1977. After a couple of decades working in the world of magazines—he has been on staff at *Arthur Frommer's Budget Travel*, *Parents*, and other lesser-known publications—he stumbled into marketing. He is now an editor and writer at Merrill Lynch. His articles have appeared in a number of publications, including *Travel & Leisure*, *Parenting*, *Utne Reader*, the *Los Angeles Times Book Review*, and *Chief Executive*. His book of essays, *Father's Day: Notes from a New Dad in the Real World*, was published by Times Books / Random House in 1995. He lives in Ivyland, Pennsylvania, with his wife, Sharon, and their two teenage children.

GORDON MENNENGA

Gordon was born and grew up in Reinbeck, Iowa, and attended the University of Northern Iowa for his degree in English education. Next came an MFA in fiction from the Iowa Writers' Workshop in 1977. He has taught creative writing and literature at DePauw University and Oregon State University. He has given readings and workshops in Tennessee, Oregon, Indiana, and Iowa. His fiction has appeared in the *North American Review*, *Northwest Magazine*, *Seems*, *Folio*, and other publications. He has written for NPR's *Good Evening* and Garrison Keillor's *A Prairie Home Companion*, and one of the monologues he wrote for the show provided the basis for the film *Everyday*, released in 1999/2000. He was a 1995 recipient of the *Chicago Tribune's* Nelson Algren Award for Short Fiction. Gordon lives in Iowa City with his wife, Lynn. They have two children—Kate and Andy. He currently teaches creative writing and film studies at Coe College in Cedar Rapids, Iowa.

ERIC OLSEN

Eric was born and raised in Oakland—*go As!*—California and started college as a pre-med student at UC Berkeley, like all ambitious young freshmen at the time. His interest in medicine lasted about halfway through his first quiz in "orgo." He finished college many years and false starts later with a BA in comparative literature (Classical Greek, a long story and we won't get into that here). He got his MFA in fiction in 1977. With Glenn Schaeffer, he cofounded in 2000 and then directed the International Institute of Modern Letters, a literary think tank that helped writers who were victims of censorship and persecution. Eric also helped establish the first American City of Asylum, in Las Vegas, an Institute program. The Institute also ran programs to support emerging writers in this country and abroad. Before that, Eric was executive editor of custom publishing at Time Inc. Health, a Time Warner company. He left Time Warner after that company's disastrous merger with AOL—in other words, too late. And before that, he was a freelance journalist. He has published hundreds of magazine articles, a few short stories, and six nonfiction books, including this one. He was a Teaching/Writing Fellow at Iowa (1976–77), and after leaving the Workshop, he received a James A. Michener Fellowship for fiction. Most recently, his writing has delved into art and design. He continues, despite common sense and the advice of family and friends, to work on a novel and screenplay. Eric does sometimes wish he'd toughed it out in orgo.

Books

Concrete at Home: Innovative Forms and Finishes: Countertops, Floors, Walls, and Fireplaces, with Fu-Tung Cheng (Taunton Press, 2005)

Concrete Countertops: Design, Forms, and Finishes for the New Kitchen and Bath, with Fu-Tung Cheng (Taunton Press, 2002)

LifeFit: An Effective Exercise Program for Optimal Health and a Longer Life, with Ralph Paffenbarger, MD, PhD (Human Kinetics Publications, 1996)

Forming a Moral Community (Bioethics Consultation Group, Berkeley, California, 1995)

On the Right Track (Bobbs Merrill, New York, 1984)

Articles

More than he cares to remember.

Fiction

"In Turlock," five short chapters from a novel in progress (and never finished), in *Quarry West*, 1977, reprinted in *Valley Light*, edited by Jane Watts (Poet & Printer Press, 1978)

"My Father's Son," short story in *Carolina Quarterly*, winter 1977

MINDY PENNYBACKER

An environmental journalist by trade, Mindy is the author of *Do One Green Thing: Saving the Earth Through Simple, Everyday Choices* (St. Martin's Press, 2010). She's editor and founder of the green lifestyle website and blog www.GreenerPenny.com and a columnist for Martha Stewart's *Body + Soul Magazine.*

Mindy is married to Iowa classmate Don Wallace, a fellow 1977 graduate of the Writers' Workshop with an MFA in fiction. She was born and raised in Honolulu, Hawaii, by her mother and her grandparents, who owned Halm's Kimchee, the islands' premium Korean food manufacturer. When she wasn't studying hard or working in the kimchi shop, she surfed her brains out. She graduated from Punahou School, the elite academy founded by missionaries and Hawaiian royalty that is also President Barack Obama's alma mater. Mindy also holds a BA in English literature from Stanford, where she later returned as a Stegner Fellow in Fiction, and a JD from U.C. Davis. She and Don have recently relocated to Honolulu after twenty-seven years in Manhattan. Their son, Rory Donald Wallace, studied history at Stanford and works at a hedge fund in New York City.

Mindy's fiction and journalism have appeared in the *Atlantic Monthly, Fiction Magazine, Bamboo Ridge,* the *New York Times,* the *Nation, Sierra, Worldwatch, Natural Home, E. Magazine, TheDailyGreen.com,* and elsewhere.

JAYNE ANNE PHILLIPS

Jayne Anne was born in Buckhannon, West Virginia. She majored in English at West Virginia University before getting her MFA in fiction from the Iowa Writers' Workshop in 1978. Her writing has been translated and published in twelve languages. She is the recipient of a Guggenheim Fellowship, two National Endowment for the Arts Fellowships, a Bunting Fellowship from the Bunting Institute of Radcliffe College, a Howard Foundation Fellowship, and she was a 2009 National Book Award finalist. Jayne Anne has held teaching positions at several colleges and universities, including Harvard, Williams, Boston University, and Brandeis. She is currently professor of English and director of the MFA program in creative writing at Rutgers Newark, the State University of New Jersey (www.mfa.newark.rutgers.edu). She and her husband have two sons.

Books

Lark and Termite [novel] (Knopf, 2009), National Book Award finalist, National Book Critic's Circle Award finalist

MotherKind [novel] (Knopf, 2000), Massachusetts Book Award, Orange Prize (UK) nominee

Shelter [novel] (Delta, 1995), Academy Award in Literature by the American Academy and Institute of Arts and Letters; one of "Publishers Weekly's" Best Books of the Year

Fast Lanes [short story collection] (Vintage, 1987, 2000)

Machine Dreams [novel] (Vintage, 1984, 1999), National Book Critics Circle Award nominee, *The New York Times* "Best Books of the Year"

Black Tickets (Delacorte/Seymour Lawrence, 1979; Delta, 1989), Sue Kaufman Prize for First Fiction

Counting [short story collection] (Vehicle Editions, 1978), St. Lawrence Award

Sweethearts [short story collection] (Truck Press, 1976), Pushcart Prize, Coordinating Council of Literary Magazines Fels Award

GLENN SCHAEFFER

Glenn received his BA and MA in literature at the University of California, Irvine. He graduated with an MFA from the Iowa Writers' Workshop in 1977.

During his thirty-year career in the gaming industry, he served for nearly twenty years as president and chief financial officer of Mandalay Resort Group. He is cofounder and CEO of Perpetual Gaming, a slot machine company based in Las Vegas.

Glenn has been the subject of numerous articles and several books covering the rise of modern Las Vegas, including *Super Casino* by Pete Earley and *High Stakes* by Gary Provost. *Las Vegas Magazine* listed him as one of the five inventors of modern Las Vegas, and *Institutional Investor* has profiled him as one of America's top ten corporate financiers. From 1999 to 2005, he was the world's leading site promoter for championship boxing.

Although he took a different route from most of his peers after leaving the Workshop, Glenn has had a lifelong involvement with literature. He counts scores of well-known writers, essayists, playwrights, and poets among his friends. In support of the literary arts, in 2000, he founded, with Eric Olsen, a think tank for public intellectuals, the International Institute of Modern Letters at the University of Nevada Las Vegas (since incorporated into the Black Mountain Institute at UNLV). Its mission was to "identify and financially support writers from around the world whose voices are muffled by persecution or censorship." Glenn is also principal owner of Intellectual Property Group, a Hollywood literary agency with an author list that includes Don DeLillo, Joyce Carol Oates, James Ellroy, Dennis Lehane, Richard Russo, and Sting, plus the literary estates of James M. Cain, John O'Hara, and Frank McCourt. IPG also serves as executive producer of movies such as *Hollywoodland* and television series.

Along the way, he also became an art collector and was included among the "Big Dippers" in *Vanity Fair's* art issue (December '06)—one of the biggest of the big-dog art collectors, with the likes of Paul Allen, Steven Wynn, Si Newhouse, and David Rockefeller.

All That Glitters, and his first novel, *Holy Shaker*, begun at Iowa thirty years ago, are in the works.

Glenn also played himself on NBC's televised series *Las Vegas*.

JANE SMILEY

Jane was born in Los Angeles but moved to the suburbs of St. Louis, Missouri, soon afterward, where she lived until she left for Vassar College. From New York, she went to Europe for a year, then headed for Iowa and an MFA in fiction from the Writers' Workshop in 1976. An interest in dead languages (including classes in Old Norse, Old and Middle English, Old Irish, Gothic, and Old High German) led her to Iceland on a Fulbright for a year to learn Modern Icelandic and devise a dissertation topic involving Old Norse, but this was never completed—she turned in a creative dissertation for her PhD. While in Iceland, she heard about the Medieval Norse colony on the southern tip of Greenland, and the eventual result was her novel *The Greenlanders*.

After Iowa, she taught at Iowa State University in Ames until 1996, when she quit to write full-time. Thrice married, she is the mother of two daughters and a son and lives in northern California, where she owns too many horses; but she has inserted them as characters in many of her novels, so they have proved useful in more ways than one.

Jane has received numerous literary awards and honors, including an O. Henry Award for her short story "Lily" in 1985, a Pulitzer and a National Book Critic's Circle Award in 1992 for *A Thousand Acres*, and induction into the American Academy of Arts and Letters in 2001. *Horse Heaven* was shortlisted for the Orange Prize in 2001.

Jane's essays and articles have appeared in anthologies, *Harper's Magazine*, *Salon*, *Redbook*, *Vogue*, the *New Yorker*, *Mirabella*, *Allure*, the *Nation*, and many others.

Books
True Blue (Knopf Books for Young Readers, 2011)
The Man Who Invented the Computer (Doubleday, 2010)
A Good Horse (Knopf Books for Young Readers, 2010)
Private Life (Knopf, 2010)
The Georges and the Jewels (Knopf Books for Young Readers, 2010)
Ten Days in the Hills (Knopf, 2007)
Thirteen Ways of Looking at the Novel (Knopf, 2005)

A Year at the Races: Reflections on Horses, Humans, Love, Money and Luck
    (Knopf, 2004)
Good Faith (Knopf, 2003)
Charles Dickens (Viking, 2003)
Horse Heaven (Knopf, 2000)
The All-True Travels and Adventures of Lidie Newton (Knopf, 1998)
Moo (Knopf, 1995)
A Thousand Acres (Knopf, 1991) (won Pulitzer Prize in 1992)
Ordinary Love and Good Will [two novellas] (Knopf, 1989)
The Greenlanders (Knopf, 1988)
The Age of Grief: A Novella and Stories (Knopf, 1987)
Duplicate Keys (Knopf, 1984)
At Paradise Gate (Free Press, 1981)
Barn Blind (Harper & Row, 1980)

DOUGLAS UNGER

Born in Moscow, Idaho, Doug studied abroad in Argentina and Germany and received his undergraduate degree in general studies in the humanities from the University of Chicago in 1973. He earned his MFA in fiction from the Iowa Writers' Workshop in 1977. He has worked as a photographer for a weekly newspaper chain then briefly for UPI, as an arts journalist and theatre critic for the *Bellingham Herald*, and as a screenwriter and story consultant, earning Writers' Guild membership. He was managing editor of the *Chicago Review*, an editorial assistant at the *Iowa Review*, an essayist for the *MacNeil/Lehrer News Hour*, and currently serves on the Executive Boards of *Words Without Borders*, *Point of Contact/Punto de Contacto*, and as an advisory editor for *The Americas Literary Initiative* (TALI) at The University of Wisconsin Press, now at Texas Tech University Press. He has taught at universities in Argentina, Chile, and Uruguay on a Fulbright Comparative Literature Fellowship and has guest-lectured or taught at more than thirty universities or arts institutes in the Spanish-speaking world. Doug taught literature and creative writing at Syracuse University for eight years before joining the faculty of the University of Nevada, Las Vegas, in 1991, where he cofounded the MFA in Creative Writing International Program, serving as its founding director then again as director for a four-year term; and from 2007 to 2009, he served as chair of the Department of English at UNLV. He was inducted into the Nevada Writers Hall of Fame in 2007.

Awards include the Nevada Writers Hall of Fame, Nevada Board of Regents Creative Activities Award, the Nevada Silver Pen Award, a State of Washington Governor's Writer Award, the Society of Midland Authors Award for Fiction, a Hemingway Foundation/PEN Special Citation, a Fulbright Comparative Literature Fellowship, and the John Simon Guggenheim Memorial Foundation Fellowship. His short story "Leslie and Sam" was short-listed for the 2002 O. Henry Award and named a distinguished story in *Best American Short Stories 2002*. His first novel, *Leaving the Land*, was a finalist for the Pulitzer Prize for Fiction, and his fourth novel, *Voices From Silence*, was a year's end selection of *The Washington Post Book World* and was republished in France with a new closing chapter in 2008 with the title *Mes frères de sang* by Daniel Arsand / Editions Phebus. He currently is at work completing two novels in progress and the revisions on two screenplays. A bookstore clerk once introduced him at a reading by saying, "Doug Unger may be a minor writer, but he's one of the most major minor writers in America." Doug's first instinct was to call an old friend in Vegas and send a leg-breaker after the guy. Then after thinking about it for a while, he ended up profoundly grateful the clerk had said anything at all. His conclusion: "It's freer and better to be known as writing from the margins than in any mainstream."

Books
Looking for War and Other Stories (Ontario Review Press / Persea / W. W. Norton, 2004)
Voices from Silence (A Wyatt book for St. Martin's Press, 1995; Daniel Arsand / Editions Phebus, Paris, 2008 as *Mes frères de sang*)
The Turkey War (Harper & Row, 1988; Ballantine Books, 1991)
El Yanqui (Harper & Row, 1986; Ballantine Books, 1988)
Leaving the Land (Harper & Row, 1984; Ballantine Books, 1985; Bison Books, University of Nebraska Press, 1995), finalist for the 1985 Pulitzer Prize for Fiction and Robert F. Kennedy Award

DON WALLACE
Don was born in Long Beach, California. He wrote his way through UC Santa Cruz, then it was on to Iowa for an MFA in fiction in 1978 and marriage to fellow workshopper Mindy Pennybacker—to whom he was first introduced by Eric Olsen. He worked for twenty-six years in Manhattan as a magazine editor at Hearst, Condé Nast, Time Inc, and The New York Times Magazine Group, becoming a specialist in start-ups, sports, and leisure (*Yachting, Motorboating & Sailing, Golf Digest Woman*), business (*Fast Company, Success*), women's (*Self, Parents*), and other publications. During the same period, he wrote fiction and reviewed over one hundred novels, mostly debuts, in *Kirkus Reviews*, and taught fiction and creative nonfiction at the New School for Social Research and journalism at the graduate publishing program at Pace University. His essays, op-eds, columns, reviews,

and articles have appeared in *Harper's*, the *New York Times*, *Kirkus Reviews*, MediaLifeMagazine.com, the *Green Guide*, *Fast Company*, *Naval History*, *Islands*, *Wine Spectator*, *Diversion*, *Robb Report*, and others. An essay on Baja California won the 1985 Pluma de Plata Mexicana for reporting on Mexico; a short story, "The Injunction," was a 2006 selection for *Next Stop Hollywood* (St. Martins). His greatest/strangest writing-related moment came on the occasion of receiving an author-of-the-year award from the US Naval Institute. He found himself addressing the Joint Chiefs of Staff of the US Armed Forces, twenty-five foreign military attachés and several hundred naval and marine officers in 2002, at the US Naval Academy, hours before the invasion of Baghdad. He and Mindy now live in Honolulu, while their son, Rory, has taken up the baton in Manhattan. He recently completed the script for a documentary about the fifty-year search for the last remaining singers and composers of the ancient Hawaiian music, *Those Who Came Before*, directed by Eddie Kamae, founder of the Sons of Hawaii, and Myrna Kamae.

Books
One Great Game: Two Teams, Two Dreams, in the First Ever National Championship High School Football Game [nonfiction] (Atria Books, 2003)
A Tide in Time: The Log of Matthew Roving [serialized novel] (Naval History, 2000–03)
Hot Water [novel] (Soho Press, 1991)
WaterSports Basics (Prentice-Hall, 1985)

ENDNOTES

[1] Solotaroff, T, "Writing in the Cold: The First Ten Years." *A Few Good Voices in My Head*. New York: Harper & Row, 1987; pg 54.

[2] Dick, Philip, *Eye in the Sky*. New York: Ace Books, 1957.

[3] McGrath, Charles, "The Ponzi Workshop." *The New York Times*, April 19, 2009.

[4] McGurl, M., *The Program Era: Postwar Fiction and the Rise of Creative Writing*. Cambridge, MA: Harvard University Press, 2009; pg 281.

[5] Letter to John Gerber, February 2, 1968; University of Iowa Archives.

[6] Myers, D.G., *The Elephants Teach*. Chicago: The University of Chicago Press, 1996; pg 127.

[7] Wilbers, S., *The Iowa Writers' Workshop*. Iowa City: The University of Iowa Press, 1980; pg 3.

[8] Wilbers, pg 19.

[9] Myers, D.G., "The Lessons of Creative Writing's History." *AWP Chronicle 26*, February 1994.

[10] Sim, Stuart, ed., *Derrida and the End of History*. New York: Totem Books, 1999; pg 31.

[11] Wilbers, pg 112.

[12] Menand, Louis, "Show or Tell." *The New Yorker*, June 8, 2009.

[13] Howard, Maureen, "Can Writing be Taught in Iowa?" *The New York Times*, May 25, 1986.

[14] Macondo, founded in 1995 by Sandra Cisneros; a once-a-year workshop in San Antonio, named after the town in Marquez's *One Hundred Years of Solitude*.

[15] Ghiselin, Brewster, *The Creative Process*. Berkeley: The University of California Press, 1952; pg 4.

[16] Grimes, Tom., ed. *The Workshop: Seven Decades of the Iowa Writers' Workshop*. New York: Hyperion, 1999; pg 3.

[17] Csikszentmihalyi, Mihaly, *Creativity: Flow and the Psychology of Discovery and Invention*. New York: Harper Perennial, 1996.

[18] Kuhn, Thomas, *The Structure of Scientific Revolutions,* 3rd edition. Chicago: University of Chicago Press, 1996.

[19] Flaherty, Alice, W. *The Midnight Disease*. New York: Houghton Mifflin, 2004; pg 63.

[20] May, Rollo, *The Courage to Create*. New York: Norton, 1975. See also: Keyes, Ralph, *The Courage to Write*. New York: Henry Holt and Company, 1995.

[21] Since the interview, Jennie retired to work on the novel, *The Age of Ecstasy,* published by Viking, 2012.

[22] Oates, Joyce Carol, *Faith of a Writer*. New York: Ecco, 2003; pg xii.

[23] Kenner, Hugh, *The Mechanic Muse*. New York: Oxford University Press, 1987.

[24] Krippner, Stanley, *Dreams Stimulate Creativity (Paper)*. 2008; pg 5.

[25] Krippner, S., 2008, pg 6.

[26] Oates, 2003; pg 79.

[27] Lehrer, Jonah, "The Eureka Hunt." *The New Yorker*, July 28, 2008; pg 43.

[28] Lehrer, J., July 28, 2008; pg 43.

[29] Olsen, Eric, "Pumping Irony." *The Runner*, February 1986.

[30] Wind, Edgar, *Art and Anarchy*. New York: Vintage Books, 1969; pg 1.

[31] Sukenick, Ron, *The Death of the Novel and Other Stories*. New York: Dial, 1969.

[32] Kinsella, W.P., "Pretend Dinners." *The Pushcart Prize of Short Stories: The Best From a Quarter Century of Winning Stories*. Pushcart Press, 2002.

[33] Myers, D.G., *The Elephants Teach. Chicago*: The University of Chicago Press, 1996; pg 2.

[34] Leopold, Wendy, "Homecoming: Iowa Writers' Workshop Celebrates 50 Years." *Los Angeles Times*, May 28, 1986.

[35] Myers, B.R. *A Reader's Manifesto*. Hoboken, NJ: Melville House, 2002; pg 3.

INDEX

"The Workshop was the best teaching-writing job I ever had." —John Irving

We Wanted to be Writers is a rollicking and insightful blend of original interviews, commentary, advice, gossip, anecdotes, analyses, history, and asides with nearly thirty graduates and teachers at the now legendary Iowa Writers' Workshop between 1974 and 1978. Among the talents that emerged in those years—writing, criticizing, drinking, and debating in the classrooms and barrooms of Iowa City—were the younger versions of writers who became John Irving, Jane Smiley, T. C. Boyle, Michelle Huneven, Allan Gurganus, Sandra Cisneros, Jayne Anne Phillips, Jennie Fields, Joy Harjo, Joe Haldeman, and many others. It is chock full of insights and a treasure trove of inspiration for all writers, readers, history lovers, and anyone who ever "wanted to be a writer."

JANE SMILEY ON THE IOWA WRITERS' WORKSHOP:

"In that period, the teachers tended to be men of a certain age, with the idea that competition was somehow the key—the Norman Mailer period. The story was that if you disagreed with Norman, or gave him a bad review, he'd punch you in the nose. You were supposed to get in fights in restaurants."

T.C. BOYLE ON HIS SHORT STORY "DROWNING":

"I got $25 for it, which was wonderful . . . You know, getting $25 for the product of your own brain? You could buy a lot of beer in Iowa City back then for that."

ERIC OLSEN is a journalist and graduate of the Iowa Writers' Workshop. Olsen directed the U.S. branch of the International Institute of Modern Letters and created the first American City of Asylum, which provided a safe haven for persecuted writers. He was also an executive editor at Time Inc. Health, a Time Warner company. This is his sixth book.

GLENN SCHAEFFER was, for twenty years, president of Mandalay Resort Group in Las Vegas. In 2009, *Liberty Media* rated him as the gaming industry's most influential executive, after Steve Wynn. Schaeffer is a graduate of the Iowa Writers' Workshop, and he's finally finishing a novel he started there thirty years ago, *Holy Shaker*.

WWW.WEWANTEDTOBEWRITERS.COM • TWITTER.COM/2BWRITERS

Skyhorse Publishing, Inc.
New York, New York
www.skyhorsepublishing.com

Cover design by Adam Bozarth
Printed in Canada

ISBN-10: 1-60239-735-X
ISBN-13: 978-1-60239-735-4

51695

9 781602 397354

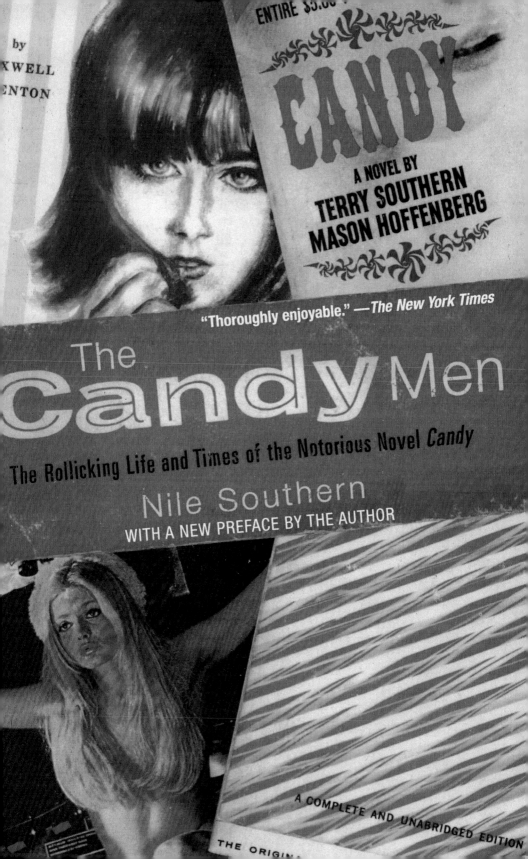

ENTIRE $5.00

CANDY

A NOVEL BY
TERRY SOUTHERN
MASON HOFFENBERG

by
XWELL
ENTON

"Thoroughly enjoyable." —*The New York Times*

The Candy Men

The Rollicking Life and Times of the Notorious Novel *Candy*

Nile Southern

WITH A NEW PREFACE BY THE AUTHOR

A COMPLETE AND UNABRIDGED EDITION

THE ORIGINA